THE RISE OF SPANISH AMERICAN POETRY 1500–1700
LITERARY AND CULTURAL TRANSMISSION IN THE NEW WORLD

LEGENDA

LEGENDA is the Modern Humanities Research Association's book imprint for new research in the Humanities. Founded in 1995 by Malcolm Bowie and others within the University of Oxford, Legenda has always been a collaborative publishing enterprise, directly governed by scholars. The Modern Humanities Research Association (MHRA) joined this collaboration in 1998, became half-owner in 2004, in partnership with Maney Publishing and then Routledge, and has since 2016 been sole owner. Titles range from medieval texts to contemporary cinema and form a widely comparative view of the modern humanities, including works on Arabic, Catalan, English, French, German, Greek, Italian, Portuguese, Russian, Spanish, and Yiddish literature. Editorial boards and committees of more than 60 leading academic specialists work in collaboration with bodies such as the Society for French Studies, the British Comparative Literature Association and the Association of Hispanists of Great Britain & Ireland.

The MHRA encourages and promotes advanced study and research in the field of the modern humanities, especially modern European languages and literature, including English, and also cinema. It aims to break down the barriers between scholars working in different disciplines and to maintain the unity of humanistic scholarship. The Association fulfils this purpose through the publication of journals, bibliographies, monographs, critical editions, and the MHRA Style Guide, and by making grants in support of research. Membership is open to all who work in the Humanities, whether independent or in a University post, and the participation of younger colleagues entering the field is especially welcomed.

ALSO PUBLISHED BY THE ASSOCIATION

Critical Texts
Tudor and Stuart Translations • *New Translations* • *European Translations*
MHRA Library of Medieval Welsh Literature

MHRA Bibliographies
Publications of the Modern Humanities Research Association

The Annual Bibliography of English Language & Literature
Austrian Studies
Modern Language Review
Portuguese Studies
The Slavonic and East European Review
Working Papers in the Humanities
The Yearbook of English Studies

www.mhra.org.uk
www.legendabooks.com

STUDIES IN HISPANIC AND LUSOPHONE CULTURES

Studies in Hispanic and Lusophone Cultures are selected and edited by the Association of Hispanists of Great Britain & Ireland. The series seeks to publish the best new research in all areas of the literature, thought, history, culture, film, and languages of Spain, Spanish America, and the Portuguese-speaking world.

The Association of Hispanists of Great Britain & Ireland is a professional association which represents a very diverse discipline, in terms of both geographical coverage and objects of study. Its website showcases new work by members, and publicises jobs, conferences and grants in the field.

www.legendabooks.com/series/shlc

STUDIES IN HISPANIC AND LUSOPHONE CULTURES

The Rise of Spanish American Poetry
1500–1700

Literary and Cultural Transmission in the New World

EDITED BY
RODRIGO CACHO CASAL AND IMOGEN CHOI

LEGENDA

Studies in Hispanic and Lusophone Cultures 22
Modern Humanities Research Association
2019

Published by Legenda
an imprint of the Modern Humanities Research Association
Salisbury House, Station Road, Cambridge CB1 2LA

ISBN 978-1-78188-706-6

First published 2019

Copy-Editor: Richard Correll

CONTENTS

NOTES ON THE CONTRIBUTORS

Rolena Adorno is the Sterling Professor of Spanish at Yale University. Her books include *Colonial Latin American Literature: A Very Short Introduction*, *De Guancane a Macondo: Estudios de literatura latinoamericana*, *The Polemics of Possession in Spanish American Narrative*, and *Guaman Poma: Writing and Resistance in Colonial Peru*. She is the co-author of *Álvar Núñez Cabeza de Vaca: His Account, His Life, and the Expedition of Pánfilo de Narváez*, and the co-editor of print and digital editions of Felipe Guaman Poma de Ayala's *Nueva corónica y buen gobierno*. Her books have received awards from the Modern Language Association, the American Historical Association, the Western Historical Association, and the New England Council of Latin American Studies. Her most recent book, co-authored with Roberto González Echevarría, is *Breve historia de la literatura latinoamericana colonial y moderna*. Adorno is an Honorary Professor at the Pontificia Universidad Católica del Perú, an Honorary Associate of the Hispanic Society of America, and a Fellow of the American Academy of Arts and Sciences. Appointed in 2009 by President Barack Obama, Adorno serves on the National Council on the Humanities. She is the seventh recipient (2015) of the Modern Language Association's Award for Lifetime Scholarly Achievement.

Raquel Barragán Aroche is a full-time Definitive Associate Researcher Level C at the Instituto de Investigaciones Filológicas of the Universidad Nacional Autónoma de México. Some of her publications include 'Lo poético burlesco como recurso teatral en *No hay burlas con el amor*', *Anuario Calderoniano*, 6 (2013), 15–30; 'Letras del crítico Alfonso Reyes: la mirada del poeta en la obra de Góngora', *Revista Mexicana de Literatura Contemporánea*, 47 (2010), 41–49; 'El uso de las burlas desde el concepto de "eutropelia" en las *Novelas ejemplares*', in *Las 'Novelas ejemplares': texto y contexto (1613–2013)*, ed. by Aurelio González and Nieves Rodríguez Valle (El colegio de México, 2014), pp. 61–74; 'El modelo del vejamen en el Viaje del Parnaso', in *Viaje del Parnaso: texto y contexto (1614–2014)*, ed. by Aurelio González y Nieves Rodríguez Valle (El Colegio de México, 2017); 'La presencia de la lengua epigramática de Marcial dentro de la práctica burlesca de las academias del Siglo de Oro', *Nova Tellus*, 33 (2015), 119–33; *Espacios y tiempos en diálogo: lecturas y reescrituras mitológicas en el Siglo de Oro Español*, Raquel Barragán (ed.), *Supplementum Nova Tellus* (UNAM, México, 2018).

Alice Brooke is Lecturer in Spanish and Director of Studies in Modern Languages at Merton College, Oxford. She has previously held posts as Queen Sofía Fellow and Tutor in Spanish at Exeter College, Oxford, as Assistant Professor of Latin American Literature at the University of Warwick, and as a British Research

Council Fellow at the John W. Kluge Center at the Library of Congress. Her research focuses on Spanish Golden Age and colonial literature, with particular interest in women's writing, religious culture, and the works of Sor Juana Inés de la Cruz. She has also published on the Golden Age comedia. Her monograph, *The autos sacramentales of Sor Juana Inés de la Cruz: Natural Philosophy and Sacramental Theology* was published by Oxford University Press in 2018.

Rodrigo Cacho Casal is Reader in Spanish Golden Age and Colonial Studies at the University of Cambridge. His publications have been concerned with literary genres such as burlesque and epic poetry, and the works of Francisco de Quevedo. They also treat aspects related to the transmission of culture in Early Modern Europe and Latin America, including interdisciplinary approaches such as theory of painting and the art of memory. These last are studied particularly in his monograph *La esfera del ingenio: las silvas de Quevedo y la tradición europea* (Madrid: Biblioteca Nueva, 2012). He also works on colonial literature, especially on the emergence of a new American poetics with authors such as Bernardo de Balbuena and Pedro de Oña, and is currently preparing a monograph on Spanish American colonial poetry. He has been the recipient of the Standard Research Grant by the Social Sciences and Humanities Research Council of Canada, the British Academy Mid-Career Fellowship and the Philip Leverhulme Prize.

Raquel Chang-Rodríguez is Distinguished Professor of Spanish American literature and culture at The Graduate Center and The City College of the City University of New York (CUNY). Among her publications are the annotated and modernized editions of Oré's *Relación de los mártires de La Florida* (PUCP, 2014) and of the poetry by Clarinda and Amarilis, two anonymous authors of colonial Peru (PUCP, 2009), *Cartografía garcilasista* (Universidad de Alicante, 2013), *'Aquí, ninfas del sur, venid ligeras': voces poéticas virreinales* (Iberoamericana/Vervuert, 2008). She was the guest editor of *Imaginarios poéticos virreinales*, special issue of *Calíope, Journal of the Society for Renaissance and Baroque Hispanic Poetry* 16.1 (Fall 2010). Chang-Rodríguez is the founding editor of the interdisciplinary journal *Colonial Latin American Review* and was the recipient of a National Endowment for the Humanities Fellowship (NEH). She is 'Profesora Honoraria' of the Universidad Nacional Mayor de San Marcos, Miembro Correspondiente of the Peruvian Academy of the Spanish Language, and Doctor Honoris Causa from the National Hellenic University of Athens, Greece.

Imogen Choi is Associate Professor of Golden Age Spanish at Exeter College, University of Oxford. She completed her PhD thesis on 'Conflict Ethics and Political Community in Early Peruvian Epic' at the University of Cambridge in 2017. This work, awarded the Annual Publication Prize of the Association of Hispanists of Great Britain & Ireland, is due to appear as an expanded monograph with Tamesis. It connects the 'new wars' of the sixteenth and seventeenth centuries to political thought in the connected communities of Hispanic Europe and the Americas. Her next project, 'Epic Testaments: Textual Communities and Judaeo-Christian Identities in the Hispanic World, 1580–1680', sets out a new approach to sacred epic written in Spanish. She has published on epic poetry, on the comedia in early modern Spain, and on the reception of Italian thinking on Hispanic literature.

Paul Firbas is Associate Professor in the Dept of Hispanic Languages and Literature at Stony Brook University, NY. He specializes in colonial Spanish American texts, particularly on epic poetry, historiography, textual criticism and the colonial geography of transatlantic South America. He has published diverse articles on Andean colonial culture, a study and critical edition of the poem *Armas antárticas* by Juan de Miramontes Zuázola (2006) and edited the collective volume *Épica y colonia* (2008). In 2016 he co-edited *La biblioteca del Inca Garcilaso de la Vega* (Biblioteca Nacional de España) and, in the following year, he published, with José A. Rodríguez Garrido, a study and edition of what is considered the first periodical news-sheets of the Americas: *Diario de noticias sobresalientes en Lima y Noticias de Europa* (1700–11).

Andrew Laird moved in 2016 from Warwick University in the United Kingdom to Brown University, Rhode Island, where he is John Rowe Workman Distinguished Professor of Classics and Humanities. His publications on classical literature, humanism and history of scholarship in Europe and the Americas include: *Powers of Expression, Expressions of Power* (Oxford University Press, 1999), *Ancient Literary Criticism* (OUP, 2006), *The Epic of America* (Duckworth, 2006), *Italy and the Classical Tradition: Language, Thought and Poetry, 1300–1600* (Duckworth, 2009), *Antiquities and Classical Traditions in Latin America* (Wiley, 2018) and the first comprehensive surveys of Latin writing from colonial Spanish America and Brazil for *Brill's Encyclopaedia of the Neo-Latin World* (Brill 2014) and for the *Oxford Handbook of Neo-Latin* (OUP, 2015). His most recent work examines the role of Renaissance humanism in mediating indigenous Nahua legacies in sixteenth-century Mexico.

Raúl Marrero-Fente is Professor of Spanish and Law at the University of Minnesota and Correspondent Member of the North American Academy of the Spanish Language. His work focuses on colonial Latin America and Global Colonial Studies in the Hispanic World. He is the author of *Poesía épica colonial del siglo XVI: historia, teoría y práctica* (2017), *Trayectorias globales: estudios coloniales en el mundo hispánico* (2013), *Bodies, Texts, and Ghosts: Writing on Literature and Law in Colonial Latin America* (2010), *Epic, Empire and Community in the Atlantic World: Silvestre de Balboa's 'Espejo de Paciencia'* (2008), *Playas del árbol: una visión trasatlántica de las literaturas hispánicas* (2002), *La poética de la ley en las Capitulaciones de Santa Fe* (2000), and *Al margen de la tradición: relaciones entre la literatura colonial y peninsular de los siglos XV, XVI, y XVII* (1999). He is also editor of *Espejo de paciencia* (2010), *Poéticas de la restitución: literatura y cultura en Hispanoamérica colonial* (2005), and *Perspectivas transatlánticas: estudios coloniales hispanoamericanos* (2004); and co-editor of *Gertrudis Gómez de Avellaneda: Gender and the Politics of Literature* (2017), *Coloniality, Religion and the Law in the Early Iberian World* (2014), and *Human Rights in Latin American and Iberian Cultures* (2009).

Miguel Martínez is Associate Professor of Spanish at the University of Chicago. He writes and teaches on the cultural and literary histories of early modern Iberia and its colonial worlds. He is the author of articles and book chapters on topics such as war writing, book history, epic poetry, and popular culture. His book *Front Lines: Soldiers' Writing in the Early Modern Hispanic World* (Philadelphia: University of Pennsylvania Press, 2016) documents the literary practices of imperial Spain's common soldiers. He is currently working on two book projects, the first one on popular culture in early modern Iberia, and the second on the literary history of colonial Manila.

Arantza Mayo is Senior Lecturer in Hispanic Studies at Royal Holloway, University of London. She specializes in Golden Age literature and culture in Spain and colonial America, particularly religious poetry, its devotional background and the relationship between literature and the visual arts. She also has an active interest in twentieth-century Bolivian poetry. Her publications include *La lírica sacra de Lope de Vega y José de Valdivielso* (Real Academia Española's 'Conde de Cartagena' prize, Iberoamericana/Vervuert, 2007), essays on Hernando Domínguez Camargo, Spanish Golden Age poetry, book ownership in seventeenth-century Spain, the translation and the reception of Cervantes's work in Britain and the poetic works of the Bolivian author Pedro Shimose.

Luis Fernando Restrepo is a Professor of Spanish and the Director of the graduate programme in Comparative Literature and Cultural Studies at the University of Arkansas, Fayetteville. His areas of specialization are colonial Latin America and Literature and Human Rights. He has published *Un nuevo reino imaginado, antología crítica de Juan de Castellanos*, and *El Estado impostor* (awarded the Premio Roggiano in Latin American Literary criticism) as well as nearly fifty publications including editions, articles, chapters, and reviews. He has been a visiting scholar at the Universidad Javeriana, Bogotá, with a Fulbright scholarship, and he has also taught at the Universidad de Antioquia, Universidad EAFIT, and the Universidad de Buenos Aires. He serves in the editorial boards of *Confluencia* (Colorado), *Revista Estudios de Literatura Colombiana* (Universidad de Antioquia), and *Perífrasis* (Universidad de los Andes), *Cuadernos de Literatura* (Javeriana) and *Co-herencia* (EAFIT). His current research project focuses on early modern humanitarianism.

Lorena Uribe Bracho holds a PhD in Latin American, Iberian, and Latino Cultures from The Graduate Center, City University of New York (2018). Her research offers an interdisciplinary approach to poetic and musical cultures of early modern Spain and colonial Latin America, with a focus on lyric theory and early modern affect. Her dissertation, which she is now in the process of turning into a book (*Orphans of Orpheus: Poetry and Music in Early Modern Spanish Culture*, 2018) addresses how music shapes the discourse and self-image of poetry, and seeks to understand why music and poetry turn to each other when they strive to be the most effective. She has published on the power of music in Golden Age poetry, on music in the work of Miguel de Cervantes, and on Quevedo's moral and love poetry.

INTRODUCTION

Locating Early Modern
Spanish American Poetry

Rodrigo Cacho Casal

Beyond Dualism: Regarding Method and Critical Approaches

De la conquista a la independencia [From Conquest to Independence], a seminal book first published in 1944 by the Venezuelan scholar and diplomat Mariano Picón-Salas, is one of the first attempts to articulate a synthesis of the various historical interpretations of the political and cultural consequences brought about by the colonization of America.[1] This very influential work, later demolished by modern historiography, offers a discussion of a number of questions that have played a fundamental role in the ideological construction of a Latin American identity over the centuries.[2] One of the earliest manifestations of this intellectual discourse is, according to Picón-Salas, the clash between two irreconcilable points of view:

> La disputa [...] ha dividido, preferentemente desde el siglo XIX, las dos corrientes políticas del pensamiento histórico hispanoamericano: una corriente colonialista y tradicionalista, que ponía todo su énfasis en el predominio de las formas españolas de nuestra cultura; y otra liberal y revolucionaria, que proclamaba en forma agresiva su ruptura con España.

> [This dispute [...] has, particularly since the nineteenth century, kept at odds two political currents of Spanish American historical thought: the colonial and traditionalist, emphasizing the predominance of Spanish elements in our culture, and the liberal and revolutionary, vehemently proclaiming its complete break with Spain.][3]

Scholarship on the literature and culture of early modern Spanish America has grown considerably in the last decades both thanks to and in spite of such binaries. First developed in nineteenth-century Latin America, colonial studies fostered the rediscovery of texts that allegedly embodied the spirit of the newly constituted countries. Research concentrated on single authors as well as on more general approaches that tried to seize the essence of what José Lezama Lima called in 1957 'The American Expression'.[4] This was to find its roots in the development of the American Baroque or *Barroco de Indias*, which he defined as a 'counter-conquest artistic movement', a polemical response to the cultural and political dominion of Spain. The concept *Barroco de Indias* was first employed by Picón-Salas, and lacked the political urgency ascribed to it by Lezama Lima.[5] It was, however, the thesis of the latter that took root and was further developed in literary studies concerned with early modern Spanish American authors, looking for signs that indicated the growth of a creole identity leading up to the nineteenth-century independentist movements.[6]

Spanish American colonial studies have proven to be a particularly fruitful area of study in the US academia, where identitarian readings have been buttressed by the development of postcolonialism, ethnic and subaltern studies.[7] On the other hand, more traditional European methodologies, such as those fostered by Hispanic philology, have had the tendency to appropriate texts written in the New World while ignoring the American substrate of their political discourse and focusing on their formal aspects.[8] This view is concerned with an aesthetic of continuity that often characterizes colonial texts as derivative or strongly indebted to the Peninsular tradition. However, by denying creole readings, such scholarship is also silently projecting an identitarian interpretation of the Spanish American corpus, presenting it as a mere extension of European literature. The polemics of possession, as Rolena Adorno has called it, are thus very much alive in the discourse concerning the New World and its cultural production.[9] But if it is extremely reductive to close our eyes to the individuality of early modern Spanish American poetry, it is also anachronistic to frame this corpus exclusively within the field of Latin American studies, which is a cultural and political concept that developed only after independence. Hence certain readings of *criollismo* in literary studies have often fallen within the category of 'mythology of doctrines', which, according to Quentin Skinner, manifests itself when we artificially reconstruct the origin of a given modern theory or thesis, for which 'the writers of the past are simply praised or blamed according to how far they seem to have aspired to the condition of being ourselves'.[10]

Spanish American colonial studies should, and indeed often do, stimulate dialogue and scholarly interaction between Iberian and Latin American studies. Its privileged vantage point can also provide critical alternatives to teleological readings that offer a retrospective interpretation of this corpus as a series of steps leading to independence, or belated post-imperialistic analyses that claim that these texts are satellites of Spanish literature. The conquest of the New World brought desolation and destruction, but simultaneously established a new hybrid culture that deserves to be studied in its historical context, paying attention to its contradictions and limitations as well as to its artistic achievements. It seems to me that the main problem is that analyses of these texts have often adopted critical angles that are principally committed to our modern understanding of politics. We do not always ask the right questions and, when we do, we do not use the right tools to do so.[11] This is particularly problematic when it comes to poetry.

Because of the preponderance of *Barroco de Indias* as a critical concept, seventeenth-century Spanish American poetry has overshadowed the literary works of the sixteenth century, which have, accordingly, often been considered as not creole enough, derivative or, quite simply, poor. This tendency has also been encouraged by the leading role of Sor Juana Inés de la Cruz in the history and cultural imagination of the New World, whose unique artistic voice has detracted interest from earlier writers, save for some notable exceptions such as Bernardo de Balbuena. There is still a significant number of authors requiring more scholarly attention. Moreover, our knowledge of early modern Spanish American poetry is largely fragmentary and clouded by substantial gaps. Further research needs to be carried out in libraries and archives in order to establish a more reliable account of the poetic production in the viceroyalties of New Spain and Peru.

This is not only the case for untraced, lost and unknown works; it applies also to some of the well-established sources of the Spanish American canon. A good example of this is the manuscript poetic anthology *Flores de varia poesía* [Flowers of Various Poems].[12] As stated on the front page, the volume was composed in Mexico, 'Recopilose en la Ciudad de México', in 1577. The manuscript, originally divided into five books — only two of which are extant — contains works by Peninsular authors as well as a smaller group of others who were born or who settled in America, including Martín Cortés (son of Hernán Cortés), Fernán González de Eslava and Francisco de Terrazas. The first book contains religious poems and the second love lyric. Yet, while the former is a rather short collection (pp. 2–33), the latter contains an extensive number of texts (pp. 34–400). This is the reason why *Flores* has been usually framed within the tradition of Petrarchan poetry and its dissemination in the New World. As such, the love lyric included in the anthology has been interpreted as a manifestation of the imposition of views and discourses of the colonizer over the colonized, authorizing 'a first-person understanding of the stresses and contradictions of early colonial experience in New Spain, albeit from a colonial rather than a *criollo* or mestizo perspective', as it has been argued by Roland Greene.[13]

The truth is that we do not possess the manuscript in the original format that it was likely to have taken in 1577, and that the gaps and silences of *Flores* are significant enough to make it very difficult to come to definitive conclusions on the nature of the anthology. The index placed at the beginning of the volume indicates that the third book was also devoted to love lyric, the fourth to burlesque works ('lo de burlas') and the fifth to a variety of genres that did not fit within any of the previous labels ('cosas indiferentes que no pudieron aplicarse a ninguno de los demás'). Did the third book showcase more works by creole authors? Did the fourth challenge the colonial discourse allegedly put forward by Petrarchan poems? Lastly, did the fifth include texts where Mexican society was more clearly represented and addressed through occasional poems, eulogies and panegyrics? The geographical, semiotic and ideological variety of *Flores* may well have been wider than we assume. Was it compiled by a creole resident or by a Spaniard who only spent a limited amount of time in New Spain? All these questions address issues of readership, identity and cultural colonialism that are at the core of early modern Spanish American poetry.

What texts such as *Flores* tell us is that the Atlantic was not a one-way avenue and that cultural transmission between America and the metropolis was also significant. Thanks to a handwritten note appended on the third page, we can place *Flores* in

Spain in the early years of the seventeenth century: 'Es de Andrés Fajardo en Sevilla 1612 años' [This belongs to Andrés Fajardo in Seville, year 1612]. Individual readers would have travelled back to Europe with poetic manuscript texts, allowing for the dissemination of Spanish American works in the Iberian Peninsula. It is perhaps through a copy of *Flores* or a similar source that Cervantes became acquainted with several authors based in the New World mentioned in 'Canto de Calíope' [Calliope's Song], a poem in praise of contemporary Spanish poets included in his pastoral novel *La Galatea* (1585). Particularly noteworthy is Cervantes's awareness of authors whose works would not be published during his lifetime. One name stands out, Francisco de Terrazas, who is mentioned in the first place in the list of American writers: 'Terrazas, tiene | el nombre acá y allá tan conocido' [Terrazas, whose name is well known both here and there].[14] Son of a *conquistador*, Terrazas was born in Mexico and authored love poems (some of which feature in *Flores*) and the epic text *Nuevo mundo y conquista*, only a few fragments of which are extant. In spite of Cervantes's praise, very few of Terrazas's works have reached us. This is not an isolated case and suggests that many sources and information have been lost, or are yet to be recovered, and that one should tread carefully when trying to establish the nature and the quantity of poetry produced in early modern Spanish America and to what extent this was disseminated in Europe.

Recent scholarship on the subject has moved its focus to a more fluid and nuanced understanding of sixteenth- and seventeenth-century practices of cultural transmission concerning the New World, trying to leave behind the great intellectual divide outlined by Picón-Salas. Locating Spanish American poetry requires a deeper historical contextualization of life in the viceroyalties of New Spain and Peru, as well as a wider consideration of the cultural and political role of literature in early modern Europe and in the New World. Poetry was hardwired in society in ways that escape our modern understanding, since this has become nowadays a literary genre for private consumption addressed to a rather select group of readers. Poetry was an omnipresent voice in social gatherings such as royal coronations, birthdays and funerals, religious celebrations and anniversaries of important institutions such as churches and universities. The new developing American capital cities, Mexico City and Lima, employed poetic compositions to give voice to their self-proclaimed greatness, which, more often than not, was tacitly set up to challenge the supremacy of Madrid and other Spanish and European urban centres. At the same time, poetry played a crucial and vexed role in the conversion and assimilation of natives, translating Christian codes and liturgy to languages such as Quechua and Nahuatl. Poetry provided also a flexible tool able to recount (and often reinvent) the history of the colonization, promoting imperial ideology while also allowing perception of some of the problems and contradictions of the developing American society. This critique was even more obvious in anonymous satires and libels which were pasted to the walls of public buildings or circulated via manuscript copies.

These are only a few of the possible manifestations of poetry in the New World, where it possessed a strong cultural capital associated with its ability to mediate between quite a complex set of ideological discourses: the assimilation of pre-

Columbian civilizations, the construction of new political identities, the interaction between urban centres within America and also between these and the rest of the world. Modes of production, readership and audience, urban life; these critical avenues allow for more articulate interpretations of Spanish American poetry in the sixteenth and seventeenth centuries. From this point of view, the composition of Petrarchan poetry in New Spain in 1577 is not a mere reproduction of European models, even if the language and the metaphors employed share common patterns. Collecting poems such as those of *Flores de varia poesía* indicating in the front page that the manuscript has been compiled in Mexico City is a clear statement of intentions, the sign of a poetic community in the making set against the backdrop of a society that was negotiating its own identity in an ever-developing globalized world. I am not suggesting that new critical methodologies should entirely replace other well-established theoretical or philological readings, but rather that a non-polarized dialogue among various hermeneutical traditions could be extremely beneficial. In the last decades, colonial literature is on the road to being de-essentialized and released from the straitjacket of being defined in terms of agreement (imperialism) or rejection (revolution) with regards to Spain. Besides being quite reductive, both approaches presuppose a uniformity of voices in early modern Latin America that does not resist historical scrutiny.

Revising the American Corpus

It follows from what has been outlined so far that a re-consideration of the poetic corpus of the New World is necessary. Let us provide some examples of the work that still lies ahead. Among the various texts that could be mentioned here, it is worth recalling the manuscript volume *Relación historiada de las solennes fiestas que se hicieron en la muy noble y leal ciudad de México al glorioso padre y esclarecido patriarca san Pedro Nolasco* [Historical account of the solemn festival celebrated in the most noble and loyal City of Mexico in honour of the glorious patriarch Saint Peter Nolasco], composed in 1633 by the Mercedarian Fray Juan de Alavés. The volume, which contains a series of poems celebrating Saint Peter Nolasco, was first brought to critical attention by Dorothy Schons as one of the earliest examples of the influence of Góngora in New Spain; a suggestion that was later explored with a detailed formal analysis of the poems and their links with the *poesía culta* by Martha Lilia Tenorio.[15] *Relación*, however, does not only showcase the development of Gongorism in America; it is also an eloquent example of the fundamental role played by poetry in early Mexican society. The material composition of the manuscript as well as the introduction and commentaries, written in a lively and captivating prose by Fray Alavés, are extremely revealing. According to José Mariano Beristáin, he was born in Mexico and soon acquired an impressive humanistic knowledge.[16] Beristáin indicates also that Alavés died at the age of 52 on 17 December 1642,

> dejando dispuesto para la prensa el siguiente manuscrito, que con las licencias para su impresión existe en la biblioteca de los padres mercedarios del convento principal de México, y he leído: *Relación historiada* [...]

[leaving ready for the press the following manuscript, which, containing its publication licences, is held at the library of the Mercedarian friars in the main convent of Mexico City, and I have read it: *Relación historiada* [...].

This is the earliest known reference to *Relación historiada*, and stresses the fact that the manuscript was ready to be released to the press. The front page of the manuscript indicates that the volume was to be published 'en la imprenta de Francisco Salvago' [in the printing house of Francisco Salvago] (fol. III), and in the preliminary pages we also find the approbation by Fray Bartolomé Ladrón de Guevara signed on 9 October 1633.[17] As far as we know, the book never made it to the press and has been largely ignored by modern scholarship, save for the few exceptions that I have mentioned earlier. The volume is organized in two books: in the first one Alavés describes the celebrations in honour of the canonization of Nolasco held in Mexico City in 1633 ('Libro primero de las fiestas de nuestro glorioso padre san Pedro Nolasco, en que se trata de las prevenciones y adorno de el convento y de los nueve días de su celebración'), and in the second there is an account of the poetic contest organized by Alavés for the Mercedarian saint ('Libro segundo de las fiestas de nuestro glorioso padre san Pedro Nolasco, en que se trata de la distribución de los premios que se prometieron a los poetas mexicanos'). Most of the critical interest shown for this manuscript to date has focused on the second book, which contains an anthology of poems, though the first is an invaluable source of information on the cultural life of Mexico City and the role played by poetry within this context.

The relevance of this festival is even more remarkable if one takes into account the natural catastrophe that had hit the city only a few years earlier. On 21 September 1629, after forty hours of constant rain, Mexico City experienced a massive flooding that left it on its knees:

Este año de 1629, el día de san Mateo, sobrevino la inundación general que universalmente anegó toda la ciudad, sin reservar della cosa alguna; cuyo cuerpo de agua fue tan grande y violento en las plazas, calles, conventos y casas desta ciudad que llegó a tener dos varas de alto el agua por donde menos; trajinándose en canoas y barcos, rompiendo las calzadas, albarrada de San Lázaro, presa de Oculma y las demás que se habían hecho, sin que ninguna hiciese resistencia.[18]

[This year, 1629, on the day of Saint Matthew, there was a general flooding that inundated the whole city, sparing nothing; the volume of water was so large and violent in squares, streets, convents and houses of the city that the water reached the height of two *varas* where it was lowest; people had to travel in canoes and boats while the water shattered roads, San Lázaro's cistern, Oculma dam and the other ones that had been built, since none of these was able to contain the flooding.]

Many inhabitants fled the city, and those who remained were faced with the problem of coexisting with the structural and economic problems caused by the water. The years that followed saw growing conflict and divergence of opinions between various local authorities, including the archbishop, which resulted in stagnation of the flood control program. Raised sidewalks (*calzadillas*) were built in several parts of the city, and its residents were often forced to use canoes. Heavy rains during the summer of 1630 made things worse and the city remained flooded until 1634.[19]

Alavés's *Relación historiada* is set against the backdrop of this natural disaster. There are a number of references to the flooding, especially when the author accounts for the lack of certain public events that would have been otherwise expected in a festival of this nature. This is particularly the case for the *sortija* games, which could not take place due to the shortage of horses in the city: 'Hubiérala si pudiera hacerse en caballos marinos, que el día de hoy tienen más campo, en que corren dentro de México, que los caballos terrestres' [We could have carried this out if only it were possible to do so with seahorses, which nowadays have more space to run through Mexico City than land horses] (I, fol. 95).[20] Alavés's irony is echoed by other, more serious, allusions to the damage caused by water. These are found in the poems included in the volume, such as the *liras* by Diego Ramírez de Villegas ('Si alguna vez al cielo') where the poet addresses Saint Peter Nolasco while describing a struggling Mexico City after the flooding: 'México a vuestras plantas, | hecha mar de agua y piélago de penas' [Mexico at your feet, | turned into a sea of water and a deep of sorrows] (II, fol. 27[v]).[21] This reference is fitting and goes back to one of the miracles attributed to the saint; according to popular belief, Nolasco crossed the sea by transforming his cape into a sail and his cane into an oar. The Saint is here celebrated because of his leading role in the Mercedarian Order, as well as for his watery nature. Thanks to his thaumaturgical power, Nolasco could offer a spiritual and symbolic bridge to the Mexican citizens through which they could overcome the crisis that they were facing. The compositions written in his honour and the festival celebrated in Mexico City described in *Relación historiada* account for the crucial role that culture and poetry had at the time, acting for Mexican society as a response and a defence mechanism against natural catastrophe. Through these texts, the local lettered community was reclaiming the self-proclaimed identity of the city as the American urban capital of knowledge and intellectual sophistication.[22] The production of poetry within the context of the Nolasco festival manifests the will of the city to leave the flooding behind and re-establish its hegemonic role in the New World and beyond. Alavés's jovial reference to seahorses in the face of natural adversity is there to remind the reader that in Mexico City it was business as usual.

The information provided in *Relación historiada* gives us a clear timeline of how the festival came to be, despite various delays. Saint Peter Nolasco was canonized by Urban VIII on 30 September 1628. This information did not reach Mexico City until June 1630, a year after the great flooding. Due to the obvious difficulties faced by the Mercedarians in celebrating the canonization of their Saint and claiming the prestige that this brought to the Order, the festival in honour of Nolasco had to be postponed until February 1633. The poetic contest for Nolasco, thus, came almost five years late, delayed by the flooding and the physical distance between Europe and the New World, to which news would often arrive years after events had taken place. In spite of the various practical obstacles faced, Mexico City put forward a sumptuous commemoration where poetry occupied a central role. There are several cases such as this in early modern Spanish America (particularly in tributes to deceased monarchs), in which we often perceive a mechanism of compensation where belatedness is counterbalanced by accounts that emphasize the spectacular and luxurious nature of a given cultural celebration, almost as if to imply that being last could be an advantage: the New World had the ultimate task of culminating and reinterpreting political, ideological or aesthetic discourses originated in Europe, often re-signifying them in a new fashion.[23] A manifest sign of such practices is the care devoted to the publication of the poster 'en dos pliegos de marca mayor, con estudio y cuidado' [in two large sheets format, with care and attention to detail] (I, fol. 17^v) proclaiming the poetic contest in honour of Peter Nolasco.[24] According to Alavés, this expense was perceived by many as excessive and unusual:

> No faltó algún curioso y discreto que juzgase esta impresión por escusada, y engañose, porque no alcanzó este motivo que fue poderoso con los hombres cuerdos a esta discreta resolución, porque, siendo México centro de Nueva España, debía comunicar sus placeres a toda su circumferencia, lo cual se hizo suavemente por el camino breve y seguro de la impresión. (I, fols 17^v–18)

> [There was more than one among the solicitous and studious who considered this publication unnecessary, and they were wrong, since they did not understand the powerful reason for which this decision was supported by wise men: because Mexico is the centre of New Spain it had to share its pleasures to the whole of its circumference, something which was easily achieved through the expeditious and safe vehicle of printing.]

There is a copy of the poster designed by Alavés attached to the manuscript of *Relación historiada*, which is a unique and rather wonderful witness of Mexican poetic culture (Fig. I.1).[25] The text, crowned by an image of Nolasco and addressed to 'los ingeniosos y eruditos poetas de esta muy noble y leal ciudad de México' [the ingenious and learned poets of this most noble and loyal City of Mexico], was published by Pedro Quiñones in the printing house of Bernardo Calderón.[26] Quiñones was the typographer charged with the publication of Salvago's books, who, according to the front page of *Relación historiada*, was also the publisher chosen by Alavés to publish this manuscript. The work is dedicated to the viceroy don Lope Díaz de Almendáriz, who took up his post on 16 September 1635. This means that, despite the fact that *Relación historiada* was completed by 9 October 1633 (date of the approbation by Ladrón de Guevara), its publication was delayed for at least two years and eventually dropped. In spite of this failed attempt, both the poster of the poetic contest and the manuscript of *Relación historiada* are an eloquent example

FIG. I.1 (right). Poster for the *Certamen poético* in honour of Saint Peter Nolasco organized in Mexico City in 1633. The poster was published in Mexico City by Pedro Quiñones in the printing house of Bernardo Calderón in January 1633 (the poster bears no date but indicates that the texts written for the poetic contest should be handed in 'a veinte de este mes de enero'[on the 20th of the current month of January]). The only extant copy of the poster is attached to the manuscript of Fray Juan de Alavés, *Relación historiada de las solennes fiestas que se hicieron en la muy noble y leal ciudad de México al glorioso padre y esclarecido patriarca san Pedro Nolasco, fundador y primer religioso de la Real y Militar Orden de Nuestra Señora de la Merced, Redempción de Captivos.* Biblioteca Nacional de México, Ms. 1799. Courtesy of the Biblioteca Nacional de Mexico (Mexico City).

CERTAMEN POETICO

QVE PROPONE A LOS INGENIOSOS

y eruditos Poetas de esta muy noble, y leal Ciudad de Mexico, cabeça coronada del insigne Imperio Mexicano, el Religiosissimo Conuento de el Real, y militar Orden de Nra. Señora de la Merced, Redempcion de captiuos, que en ella esta fundado, en la solemne fiesta, que celebra a su illustrisimo Padre, y santisimo Patriarcha san Pedro Nolasco, gloriosissimo Martyr, Virgen, y Confessor, piedra primera de su Real edificio.

LOS curiosos Astrologos, que sin auer subido al Cielo, ni passeado los espaciosos circulos de sus esfericos globos, tratan de sus distancias, y medidas, como si vuieran baxado de sus retirados alcaçares, ó le vuieran sustentado en sus ombros, á fuer de el Mauritano Atlante, señalan siete cielos inferiores al primer mobil, que impelidos de su rapto mouimiento, influyen por ocultas conductos [illegible] en las criaturas inferiores, ser, vida, operacion, y sentimiento. En el primero colocaron la Luna, que sentada sobre el fuego, con imperioso cetro le domina, cuya superficie conuexa es abraçada de la comunia de Mercurio, a quien con harmonico concierto, y seruazon uniforme, se siguen el cielo de Venus, de el Sol, de Marte, Iupiter, y Saturno. En cada esfera de estas, el palacio, el alcaçar, y Real assiento de su Planeta. Entre los quales, el Sol en belleza, y resplandores solo, ocupa el quarto aposento, en artificiosas columnas leuantado, amuradas las paredes de Oro, de roxos pyropos, y relumbrantes perlas guarnecido (que assi nos le pinto el pinzel de Ouidio) Como Rey de todas ellas, reside en medio, para que con ygualdad reparta con los vezinos Planetas sus influxos, franquee sus tesoros, y comunique sus riquezas. De donde el choro bien concertado de los Poetas le llamó Principe de Planetas, como dixo Virgilio; por q todos ellos reconocen al Sol por su Rey, y con reuerencial acato le llaman Presidente de la luz, en cuya aduana se registran sus luzes, y se acrisolan sus virtudes. Y aun enseña Ptolomeo [illegible], y Albumazar de Iudicijs stellarū (a quien siguen los demas Astrologos a velas llenas de aprobacion, y aplauso) que los influxos de los demas Planetas no fueran prouechosos a los sublunares cuerpos, si primeramente no se reciuieran en el Sol, que los modifica, y perficiona en el crisol de sus lumbres, para obrar con todos ellos. De aqui se origino, el llamarle Homero, Gigante de cien manos: por la celeridad, y presteza de su actiuidad, conque presuroso acude a todas las generaciones sublunares, sin que aya alguna que se escuse de su calor, y fomento, cuyo vehiculo es la luz, que derrama desterradora de caliginosas sombras. A este veneró la antiguedad con nobre de Apolo, hijo de Iupiter, y Latona, y hermano mellizo de la hermosa Diana: El nombre illustre, el titulo honroso, y lleno de zumbido, de Apolo, muy de lleno quadra, y entalla a nuestro glorioso Padre, e inclyto Patriarcha, Patron, y Fundador de la Real, y militar Religion de nuestra Señora de la Merced, San Pedro Nolasco, descendiente de los Reales Casas de Aragon, Castilla, y Francia, y Duques de Bretaña, y de Florencia, pimpollo, y renueuo illustre de estas ramas generosas, cuyos gloriosos hechos, e inmortales hazañas pretende elogiar su sagrada Religion, en estos dias. Por que, si Apolo, antes de subir al cielo, derribo los Cyclopes atrecados, que con trisulcos sulfureos rayos, forjados en su herrería desconcertada, quitaron el vital aliento a su hijo Esculapio: Nolasco, estampando sus vencedoras plantas en Berberia, degollador [illegible] de Christianos, [illegible] dia, y decreo[illegible] a los Principes Sarracenos, Gigantes de vn ojo, por faltarles el de la Fé, que desde muy lexos columbra, y diuisa sus retirados mysterios. Si Apolo se ocupo en el exercicio pastoril, guardando tal vez los ganados de el Rey Admeto: á nuestro glorioso Patriarcha encomendó Dios (ó illustre encomienda) como a cuydadoso ganadero, las ouejas de su candido rebaño, para que las repastasse con su diuina enseñança, en los [illegible] prados, y fertiles dehesas de su Iglesia. Si aquel ostentaua por armas, y diuisa, vna bien templada lyra, vn azerado escudo refulgente, y vnas penetrantes saetas: nuestro mystico Apolo no le es inferior en los blasones, pues gozó de la lyra, con que en sus enfermedades, y congoxosos aprietos, le solazauan, y consolauan los ministriles de la capilla Real de la Gloria: del vistoso escudo, conque adornó su pecho el Serenissimo Rey don Iayme el Conquistador, en que sus Reales armas brillan, y campean, bermejeando lo dorado de su campo, con el fino bermellon, y escarlata de la sangre de sus Reales Progenitores, y de las saetas bellicas, conque peleo en Seuilla, ayudando esforçadamente, en la conquista de aquella grandiosa Ciudad, al santo Rey don Fernando, a cuyo lado Real entro triunfando por sus calles, lonjas, y plaças: theatro, y coliseo de tan esperada victoria. Y finalmente se llamó como Apolo, Liber Pater, Padre de la libertad: pues el fin de su sagrado Instituto es, restaurar gloriosamente, la que pierden los fieles en la Morisma. Siendo pues nuestro glorioso Capitan, y caudillo, vna viua imagen, y retrato verdadero del fabuloso Apolo: facilmente se deduce, que los demas Planetas, que adornan este cielo material, y visible, le reconozcan por Rey, por superior, y Presidente suyo, y como a Deidad eminente le presten la obediencia, y paguen el deuido vassallaje. En este dia pues (en que su Religion sagrada con festiua pompa, y magestuoso aparato celebra sus vitorias, y aclama sus triunfos) conuoca alegre, y placentera a los siete Planetas, gouernadores de las siete mouibles esferas, para que, solicitados de sus ebúrneos thronos, y solios de safir, a gozar de este festejo, celebren los merecimientos raros, y portentosas hazañas de el vencedor diuino, que como Candidato Romano, viene vestido de blanca toga, y argentado velo, en que se significa la candidez de su alma: leuantando bandera en publico theatro, a cuya sombra se recojan los elegantes, facundos, y fecundos Poetas, que cria, y alimenta esta muy noble, y leal Ciudad Mexicana, que agradecida a los amorosos afectos de los hijos de Nolasco, deue celebrar su gloria, a banderas desplegadas. En la siniestra trae vnos grillos, ó cadenas, conque prende los coraçones, y aficiona dulcemente las voluntades de sus deuotos, y piadosos ciudadanos, cuyos coraçones se encrespan de gozo en su triunfo, en que brillan los regozijos de la tierra.

Epigrama

I. CERTAMEN.

LA LVNA, Presidente de el primer Cielo abrasada en fuego de amor casto de nuestro glorioso Santo, vencida de sus llamas: aunque vencedora de el material, que encarcela, y aprisiona en su esfera capacissima, como madre del rocio (assi la llamó S. Ambrosio: Mater roris) de cuyas menudas gotas forman sus indu[illegible] abejas sus melifluos panales. PIDE vn ingenioso, y agudo Epigrama, que no passe la raya de quatro dillisticos compendiosos, en que con elegante poesia se pondere aquel sucesso milagroso, quando, estando nuestro Santo en la cuna, en su mano derecha formaron las abejas vn panal, significacion prognostico de la dulçura, y suauidad de este diuino Aristeo. ¶ Al Primero se le dara en premio vna Taça de plata grande. ¶ Al Segundo vn Cucharon de plata grande. ¶ Al Tercero, vna Caxa de plata redonda.

Decimas.

II. CERTAMEN.

AL Discreto, y eloquente Mercurio, que domina en el segundo Cielo, le atribuyeron los Gentiles el verde ramo de la frondosa oliua, para oria de su Caduceo, como aquel conciliaua la paz entre los animos discordes, quando exercia sus embaxadas. PIDE, que en seys Decimas, se celebre aquella marauillosa vision en que San Pedro Nolasco, estando durmiendo vio vna oliua hermosa, coronada de verdes esmeraldas, que le mostrauan dos ancianos venerables (que segū se pienso, fueron San Pedro, y San Pablo sus Tutelares, y Patrones) para q la defendiera contra vnos Ethyopes feos, y denegridos, que pretendian talarla, la qual entregauan al cuydado de Nolasco, para que la asegurara de sus enemigos, que la acometiessen. ¶ Al Primero se le dara en premio vna Xarrilla de plata. ¶ Al Segundo, vn Cucharon de plata. ¶ Al Tercero, vn Plato de plata.

Soneto.

III. CERTAMEN.

VENVS [illegible] Seraphino Dios del amor, QVIERE, que en vn compendioso Soneto, con elegantes palabras, y comprehensiuos conceptos, se realçen, y sublimen los extraordinarios fauores, que la Virgen Santissima Maria (a quien llamó el Espiritu Santo: Mater pulchræ dilectionis) hizo a nuestro bendito Padre, quando con pasos de verdadera Atalanta baxó del Cielo, al hilo de media noche, siruiendole las ayres, y plateando las nubes, y assistio por si, presidiendo en los maytines en el choro dichoso de su Conuento de Barcelona. Al que mejor echare el contrapunto al canto llano de la celestial Maestra, y Ministriles de su capilla, que son los Angeles, le prometen dos premios. ¶ Al Primero sera vna Papelina de plata. ¶ El Segundo dos Escudillas de plata grauadas. ¶ El Tercero, quatro Cucharas de plata.

Octauas.

IIII CERTAMEN.

EL SOL material, gozoso, de auer seruido de prototypo, y exemplar a nuestro glorioso Patriarcha, por quanto le significaron los antiguos Egypcios, en figura de vn hombre sentado, gouernando vn nauio, ó galera machinosa, QVIERE, que en seys Octauas Castellanas, se realçe aquel milagroso, y estupendo, obrado por Nolasco, quando a vista de la Morisma echado por los Moros de Argel, en vn barco viejo, roto, sin vela, ni remo, sin bastimento, ni vitualla, haziendo mastil de su cuerpo, y vela de su blanca capa, se engolfó en el tormentoso mar, y mal enojado elemento, y le passó con seguridad, hasta desembarcar sin detrimento alguno en la playa de Valencia, en menos de dos horas, dando las circunstancias preguntado: Quis est iste, qui venit, et mare obediunt? ¶ Al Primero se dara vn Xarro de plata de pico. ¶ Al Segundo, vna Bebedera. ¶ Al Tercero, vn pomo de plata.

Canciones

V. CERTAMEN.

MARTE, presidente del quinto Cielo, Capitan general de las sangrientas batallas, y porfiadas lides, que entre furiosas campos se traban, acudiendo a su condicion natural, de ver sangre derramada con que los verdes campos se matizan, y hermosean, DEMANDA vna gran Cancion Real de seis estancias Castellanas, con su remate en que con delicada pluma, y primoroso pinzel los ingeniosos Poetas Mexicanos, en cuyas venas de oro rebosan los cristales de Hipocrene [illegible] el cerco, y toma de la populosa Ciudad de Seuilla, en q se hallo presente S. Pedro Nolasco cō toda la Caualleria primitiua de su Orden, y entro triunfando al lado del S. Rey D. Fernando, y fundo el Conuento magnifico, q alli tiene esta sagrada Religion. ¶ Al Primero se dara vn Cubilete de plata grauado. ¶ Al Segundo, vna Xarrilla de plata. ¶ Al Tercero vna Caxa de plata para Rosario.

Lyras.

VI. CERTAMEN.

IVPITER, que se precia de fauorecer a los mortales en sus trabajos, y fatigas, como lo significa bien la etymologia de su nombre: Iuuans pater, PROPONE que en diez Lyras sonoras, y bien templadas, se le pida a nuestro glorioso P. san Pedro Nolasco, recebido en los alcaçares del cielo, y amphitheatro de la gloria, que mire con ojos piadosos, y compassiuos, a esta nobilissima, y fidelissima ciudad de Mexico, afligida con la presente inundacion, y pida feruorosamente, a que las cielo, que retire, y recoja las aguas licenciosas, que la cercan, al profundo centro de el abismo, de donde parece que se acrecientan, defienda celosa y [illegible] de la beldad, y hermosura de esta Ciudad florentissima, y se de escuella entre las demas de Europa. ¶ Al primero se le dara vna Bebedera de plata grande. ¶ Al Segundo seys Agujetas de plata. ¶ Al Tercero, 4. Cucharas de plata.

Glosa.

VII. CERTAMEN.

DE SATVRNO dizen los Astrologos, que fue hijo de Celo, el que en su falsa imaginacion crió el mundo y le sacó a luz de el tenebroso abismo de la nada. PIDE vna glossa Española, en que se trate de la milagrosa fundacion de la Orden de Nuestra Señora de la Merced Redēcion de captiuos, cuya leuantada fabrica puso Dios en los ombros de Nolasco, como de verdadero Atlante, para que la sustentasse contra los vaiuenes, y variedades de el tiempo, y de la fortuna. Letra.

Nolasco Santo, pues vos / Decis, que con lo que haueys,
La Merced fundays, podeys / Hazer mercedes a Dios.

¶ El Primer premio sera vn Vernegal de plata grande. ¶ El Segundo, vna Xarrilla de plata acanalada, con su plato de lo mismo. ¶ El Tercero, vna Caxita de plata grauada para Rosario.

Dancas.

VIII. CERTAMEN.

NOSOLO quisieron, que en esta ocasion de vniuersal regozijo, saliessen solos los Poetas laureados, y assi, para ordenar el vltimo Certamen, se juntaron los siete Planetas en conclaue, y atentos al concertado mouimiento de sus volubles esferas, con que, segun Pythagoras, hazen consonancias, y musica, decretaron, que se propongan premios a las dançes, que con mejores bayles, y mas artificiosas dançes, festejaren las tardes de los nueue dias, en que se ha de celebrar la fiesta de nuestro inclyto Patriarcha, en que imitaran los regulares mouimientos de los cielos. Y se les asegura, que los premios de sus pies, no se les vayan por pies. ¶ Al Primero se le dara en premio vna Taça de plata, que vale treinta pesos. ¶ Al Segundo, vna Xarrilla de plata, que vale veinte pesos. ¶ Al Tercero vn Cubilete de plata, que vale quinze pesos.

Vltimo Certamen

PORQVE la festiuidad acompañada de materias altas, y [illegible] los, no se fatigue al auditorio, establecieron, que se den otros tres Premios a los Poetas, que con mas [illegible] vena, y donaire pluma compusieren vn Soneto, a la fiesta [illegible] del santo, y de su Religion sagrada, en que se glosen los [illegible] que aqui van señalados.
¶ Nolasco. Marte. [illegible] Redencion. ¶ Frasco. Orejas. Castañetas. Damasco. ¶ Celada. Vasijas. Luz. ¶ Espada. Baratija. Capa.
¶ Al Primero, se le dara vn Cubilete de plata grande. ¶ Al Segundo, vn Tenedor de plata. ¶ Al Tercero, quatro Cucharas de plata.

Soneto faceto.

¶ Las leyes de este Certamen seran las ordinarias en semejantes justas: Iustas, Iouiales, pocas, y bien guardadas.

Los Iuezes, que con toda equidad, y Iusticia inuiolable, juzgaran las composiciones, y premiaran las mejores, seran Nuestro muy Reuerendo P. P. Maestro. Fr. Iuan de Arriaga, Prouincial de esta Prouincia de la Nueua España, del Orden de Nuestra Señora de la Merced, y M. Fr. Iuan de Herrera, Comendador de el Conuento de esta Ciudad de Mexico.

Las composiciones se entregaran al P. M. Fr. Iuan de Alb[illegible], secretario de este Certamen, [illegible] Han de estar duplicadas: vna de ellas escrita en papel blanco, Visible, y firmada con el nombre de la autor, y otra en vna tarja, para la [illegible], y llamada con varios lettras. Y no viniendo de la suerte dicha, no podran entrar [illegible].

[illegible]

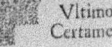

of the networks shared by literary authors and publishers, as well as the significance granted to the printing press as a vehicle able to establish an image of cultural supremacy associated with Mexico City and its 'ingenious' poets. These, touch-stones of the capital city of New Spain, are the true protagonists of Alavés's account:

> Asistieron también muchos dotores de la Real Universidad, graduados en diversas facultades, muchos caballeros de la ciudad, muchos religiosos graves, doctos y letrados de los conventos, y un copioso número de estudiantes, a quienes principalmente se echaba el guante y se encaminaba el desafío presente. (I, fol. 17^v)

> [Among the people who came there were many doctors of the Royal University, graduates of a number of disciplines, many knights of the city, many solemn religious men, cultivated and learned men from the convents, and a copious number of students, to whom, in the first instance, the gauntlet was thrown down and this contest was addressed.]

This social catalogue offers a veritable account of the Mexican privileged and educated classes signalled out as the main practitioners of poetry, especially students. This was the principal audience addressed by the poetic festival, which was organized on the basis of a 'curioso discurso astrológico' [ingenious astrological topic] arranged over seven sections. Each of these was inspired in one of the seven classical planets (Moon, Mercury, Venus, Sun, Mars, Jupiter and Saturn) (I, fol. 17^v). Authors had to make reference in their poems to episodes of Nolasco's life within this astrological framework using different kinds of metrical forms. There was a further eighth contest that differed quite radically in tone with the previous seven, since it awarded three prizes to the best burlesque sonnet ('soneto a lo faceto') based on the following rhymes: 'Nolasco. Abejas. Ovejas. Peñasco. Frasco. Orejas. Cañahejas. Damasco. Celada. Valija. Loa. Espada. Baratija. Canoa' [Nolasco. Bees. Sheep. Rock. Jar. Ears. Giant fennels. Damask. Ambush. Bag. Praise. Sword. Trinket. Canoe].[27] The cacophonic ending in –*asco* is combined with a series of pedestrian terms (*frasco*, *orejas*) which constitute a random and hence rather difficult exercise when it comes to composing a meaningful text using all of these words. The nuances, variety of registers, metres and tones, and, more generally, the overall sophistication of the *certamen* is matched by the enthusiastic endorsement of the Mexican lettered community:

> Luego se fijó el cartel del certamen en un dosel de damasco carmesí que estaba colgado en un lienzo del claustro de la Real Universidad, donde estuvo pendiente tres días. Allí llegaban enjambres de poetas, como de moscas a la miel, a trasladar los temas del certamen. [...] No durmieron noche entera asaltados de este repentino cuidado, y hubo hombre que le cogían las tres de la mañana trasnochado, con la péndola en la mano, hechos cohetes buscapiés; tanto puede con un poeta la viva imaginación, la pretensión eficaz de verse rico. Es gente que gana de comer con la pluma, y no falta quien diga que *calamita* viene de *calamus*, que en el latino idioma significa la pluma con que se escribe. (I, fols 18–18^v)

> [Afterwards the poster of the poetic contest was pasted over a crimson damask canopy which was hanging from a linen string in the cloister of the Royal

University, where it was left for three days. Swarms of poets gathered here in order to copy the topics of the contest, as if they were flies attracted by honey. [...] They did not manage to sleep at night obsessed, as they were, by this sudden urge; and there were men who found themselves awake at three in the morning holding the quill in their hands, behaving as if they were firecrackers; such is the power that imagination holds over poets, as well as the aspiration of making themselves rich. These are people who make a living with their quills, and many are of the opinion that the word magnet [*calamita*] derives from *calamus*, which in Latin means the quill used to write.]

Alavés's prose is witty and highly entertaining, capturing with humorous tone the excitement produced among the poets when the contest was advertised. Authors are portrayed as obsessive in their creative endeavours, dominated by the frenzy of poetry, here metaphorically represented by their quills taking the shape of magnets to which they are irresistibly attracted. Alavés does not fail to mention also the economic reasons behind such anxiety, pointing out the role that *certámenes* such as this could have in promoting a literary career, not the mention the actual prizes awarded to the winners. Despite the poetic flurry in Mexico City highlighted in *Relación historiada*, it is not always possible to estimate the number of people who would have taken part in these festivals. Alavés indicates that there were almost fifty — 'casi cincuenta' (II, fols 30, 34) — contestants for the seventh and the eighth competitions.[28] This may be considered a limited number taking into account the population of Mexico City in the early seventeenth century.

According to the report submitted by Pedro de Vega in 1595, the Spanish (hence, 'white') population of the capital of New Spain consisted of approximately 5000 registered families, for a total of 40,000 people (accounting for the average number of eight members per family). On top of this figure, there were more than 2000 friars and nuns, 400 priests and 800 students registered at the University and religious *colegios*.[29] These numbers, which are approximate and were certainly higher in the late 1620s and early 1630s, give a good measure of the distribution of Spanish citizens in Mexico City, where religious men and students were a significant part of the adult population; they were, however, also a clear minority. It is around this select group (including the educated 'caballeros' mentioned by Alavés) that Nolasco's *certamen* revolves in the first instance, though the porous nature of poetry within the social context of seventeenth-century Mexico City allows for these learned texts to be disseminated more widely than one could have anticipated. Alavés accounts for the great interest aroused by the compositions written for the festival, to such an extent that people would steal copies of these texts that had been placed in the Mercedarian convent for public display: 'Algunas de ellas se perdieron o las perdieron algunas personas curiosas que gustaron de leerlas en su casa, sentados y más de espacio' [Some of them disappeared or rather they were disappeared by solicitous individuals who preferred to read them at home, sitting down and at their leisure] (I, fols 34^v–35).

This act of appropriation, making private what was meant to be public, underscores the fluid nature of poetic works in early modern America, able to move at ease between a variety of social spheres and discourses. Nolasco's festival was produced by the lettered community, but its audience went beyond this group. As we saw, copies of the poems were placed in the Mercedarian convent and, more generally, literature, music and the arts informed the various days of celebrations dedicated to the Spanish saint. Alavés describes the triumphal arch erected in his honour, the processions that were carried out, the plays that were represented as well as the bullfighting events that took place. Poetry was located in spaces that attracted a variety of social groups, bringing forth the local pride of Mexican society manifested by the quality of its authors: 'los buenos y lucidos ingenios de esta nobilísima ciudad de México, que son águilas en la velocidad de su vuelo y perspicacia de su vista intelectual' [the skilled and accomplished authors of this most noble City of Mexico, who are like eagles because of the swiftness of their flight and the discernment of their intellectual sight] (II, fol. 4^v). Among these eagles of wit, and despite the overwhelming male presence, there were also remarkable female authors. Doña María Estrada de Medinilla, who was likely a member of the *criollo* elite, participated in the poetic festival for Nolasco earning a prize for her *décimas* 'Nolasco con paz fingida' (II, fols 8^v–9^v).[30] She was one of the earliest and more accomplished imitators of Góngora in New Spain and some of her works, present in several Mexican poetic festivals, made it to the printing press. The quality of her poetry and her relevance as a woman in the Mexican *clase letrada* would deserve more scholarly attention than that which she has received so far.

Relación historiada offers an invaluable example of the ways in which poetry permeated early modern society, interlacing spheres that ranged across a wide spectrum within society, culture and gender. What Alavés's account fails to show, however, is the satirical and polemical voices that poetry could embody in the New World. The public use of literature can lead towards panegyrics and the celebration of local authorities and institutions, but it can also precipitate towards the bathetic and personal insult. In 1618 Mexican silversmiths organized a series of lavish celebrations and a poetic festival in honour of the Virgin Mary as a result of the decree issued by Pope Paul V a year earlier where he had prohibited speaking or writing against the Immaculate Conception. This was not to become a dogma of the Catholic Church until 1854 and, hence, incited a quarrel between various religious orders. The Franciscans supported the Pope's resolution, while the Dominicans upheld the *anti-concepcionista* opinion. The latter responded to the *certamen* organized by the silversmiths and the sermons in defence of the Immaculate Conception that were read during the celebrations with a series of satirical poems, which were later reported to the local Inquisition in February 1619.[31]

This is but another chapter in the long history of conflicts between religious orders concerned with issues of political and economic hegemony in the New World. The seeds of this controversy are four sonnets allegedly composed by a Dominican friar; these were glossed and also gave rise to a series of acrimonious responses that spread quickly across the capital of New Spain and surrounding areas. The various individuals who came forward and declared what they knew to the Holy Office described the circulation of these texts among men and women belonging to multiple social groups: friars, students, innkeepers, tailors, wax chandlers, merchants, doormen, shopkeepers and actors read or heard, copied, shared and imitated these poems. Each of the *respuestas* [answers] to the sonnets bears witness of the power of semiotic proliferation embedded in early modern poetry. These compositions are sources of new discourses shared by an ever-expanding number of readers, some of whom decide to write back becoming themselves authors in this many-layered 'multitext'. The insults are often quite explicit, including sexual references, accusations of ignorance and heresy. One of the Inquisition's sources in their investigation was the Dominican friar Hernando de Luna, who had copies of various satirical sonnets. Among these, there is one in response to the first sonnet ('Anduvo el dominico recatado') that originated this satirical chain reaction back in 1618. Rather than taking sides, Luna's text names and shames the various religious orders present in Mexico City:

> Que el dominico huya y diga poco,
> que el franciscano arguya a lo grosero,
> que el agustino valga solo un cero
> y el mercedario se arronje como loco,
>   que el carmelita diga: 'en lo que toco
> tengo a Mahoma por fiel y verdadero',
> que anduviese el teatino novelero
> fingiendo santos a quien yo no invoco,
>   que Cagayán no diga más que nada
> no importa, pues que ya los conocemos.
> Mas, vive Dios, que a mí quien más me enfada
>   es el de Serna, porque no le vemos
> sino en meter en pleitos su manada
> sin que alcance victoria aun en lo menos.[32]

> [If the Dominican gets away with saying very little,
> if the Franciscan argues with ignorance,
> if the Augustinian is only worth a zero
> and the Mercedarian dares to speak as a madman,
>   and the Carmelite says: 'My argument claims
> that Muhammad was trustworthy and truthful',
> if the Jesuit has spoken inane words
> pretending that there are saints who I do not believe in,
>   if Cagayan says little more than nothing
> it does not matter, since we already know who these are.
> But, for God's sake, he who really makes me mad
>   is Serna, because he is always seen
> getting his flock into trouble,
> without ever earning the slightest victory.]

The sonnet is an opportunity to attack various individuals and the religious orders they represented. The *dominico* was Fray Bartolomé Gómez, the *franciscano* Fray Juan de Salas, the *teatino* Father Pedro Díaz and *Serna* was Juan Pérez de la Serna, Archbishop of Mexico. *Cagayán* is a not too veiled allusion to the Bishop of New Segovia (Philippines), since Cagayan is a province of the Luzon Island in the Philippines. This name provides also an opportunity to introduce a scatological reference based on a paronomasia with *cagar* [to shit]. The text is found at the end of the satirical trail originated in 1618, and its initial ideological purpose has been lost. This no longer represents an ideological clash between two opposing views and the religious orders that stood behind them: the quarrel over the Immaculate Conception is now but a mere pretext to spread accusations against members of the Mexican clergy described as a cohesive gang of ignorant and morally dubious characters. The language of satire spirals out of control infesting the convents, *colegios*, shops and squares of Mexico City.

What seems to be absent in early modern Spanish American poetry is the voice of the socially marginalized groups, mainly the natives and black slaves. While there is increasing evidence that indigenous people and *mestizos* had more access to literacy than has been assumed so far, their contribution to Spanish poetry has proven difficult to assess and quantify.[33] Indians, black slaves and mulattoes are often represented in accounts of public events and processions, more or less integrated into colonial society. For instance, Diego Cano Gutiérrez, graduate in Theology and *colegial* of the Colegio Real Mayor de San Felipe y San Marcos, wrote a thorough description of the celebrations organized in 1619 by the University of Lima in honour of the Immaculate Conception of the Virgin. The book was published in the same year and, very much like *Relación historiada*, contains a poetic anthology of members of the Peruvian lettered community. Among the various procession carts described by Cano there are also those of the black and the Indian populations, with the former portrayed according to the stereotype of the uncivilized savage, 'sus galas eran desnudarse y, en cueros, con aljabas a la espalda, arcos y flechas en las manos, representar naturalmente su nación' [their elegant attire consisted of taking off their clothes, and, once naked, carrying a quiver and arrows in their hands in order to represent their nation accurately]. The natives are described in a similarly reductive fashion:

> Salieron veinte caciques, los más nobles de su antigüedad y memoria, gober-nadores que fueron de las mayores provincias, vestidos con propriedad y riqueza, pues por no faltar a aquella usaron mantas y camisetas de cumbe, y por no ser inferiores a nadie en esta, las juntaron entrambas, llenando las vestiduras de muchas joyas, las más groseras que hallaban, como tejuelos, cadenas, barretoncillos de oro y metales brutos, como los crían las minas.[34]

> [Twenty caciques paraded the streets. These were among the noblest ones because of their antiquity and history, former governors of the most important provinces, and they were dressed with propriety and lavishness. In order to maintain the former, they wore cloths and *cumbe* vests, and, so that they would not be inferior to anybody with regards to the latter, they combined both by filling their garments with many jewels. These were the roughest they could find, such as small gold ingots, chains, little bars made of gold and other raw metals such as are found in the mines.]

Blacks and Indians perform an act of reversed mimicry, imitating the traditional image that the white Spanish population had of them. They are required to highlight their otherness in order to please the European imagination revamping myths of imperialism and colonization. Not surprisingly, the caciques wear garments that are linked with the extraction of silver and gold in the New World exploiting native labour ('como los crían las minas'). While the black population is devoid of any external marker of civilization ('en cueros'), the Indians carry symbols of the wealth found in America of which they have been dispossessed. They no longer govern their provinces and the rough and untreated precious metals they carry are not processed as the Spaniards would do; their raw nature is also a reflection of the perceived lack of technological development within the native community.

A similarly reductive representation of racial minorities is also found in Rodrigo de Carvajal's account of the celebrations organized in Lima for the birth of Prince Baltasar Carlos (1629), son of Philip IV. The book, published in 1632, contains a poem organized in sixteen *silvas* where the spectacular nature of Peruvian society is underscored. Throughout Carvajal's lines we find a catalogue of the various strata of society and their contribution to the festivities in honour of the young prince. The appearance of the black citizens on scene is signalled by switching to a bathetic style and content, where the lavishness of the other processions clashes with a burlesque description of the ugly features ('tan feos') of the blacks and their meagre attempt to finance their procession by stealing chickens and rabbits ('saqueados gallineros', 'taladradas conejeras'). This comical interlude is followed by Silva IX, which is devoted to the mulattoes. Racial *mestizaje* is here described as a disharmonious mixture that produces grotesque outcomes. Once again, when ethnic groups other than the white are mentioned in these texts they are often undermined, if not scorned. They are, nevertheless, recognized as visible and distinct communities that were essential to the configuration of early modern colonial societies:

> A esta fiesta siguió la de la gente
> en quien naturaleza
> de mezcla se vistió más que de gala;
> por lo que se señala
> en variar la próspera riqueza
> de su virtud potente,
> aunque lo vario sea
> de una especie hermosa y otra fea,
> como en esta se vido.[35]

> [To this celebration followed that of those people
> for whom Nature
> wore mixed garments rather than elegant ones;
> since in her noteworthy
> ability to change lies the abundant richness
> of her powerful strength,
> even if the mixture pertains
> partly to a beautiful species and partly to an ugly one,
> as it is apparent here.]

Serafino Aquilano's famous dictum, 'per tal variar natura é bella' [nature is beautiful because it is varied], is turned on its head. American hybridity is perceived in these texts as a silent threat to Spanish supremacy, and it has thus to be belittled in order to be tamed. Indians, blacks and mulattoes are figures devoid of agency: their literary essence is that of being passive objects of representation, rather than having a voice of their own.[36] Echoes of urban *mestizaje* are to be found again within the confines of burlesque and satirical poetry. A number of poems, generally attributed to Mateo Rosas de Oquendo, describe the life and idiolect of Indians and mixed-race living in Mexico City. Though they offer invaluable information on the life of colonial New Spain, their tone is clearly parodic and they are hardly to be taken as real-life documents. In the 'Romance en lengua de indio mexicano medio ladino' [Ballad in the language of an Indian who has some proficiency in Spanish] an Indian gives an account of his modest life, protesting against those 'pillacas' [crooked men] who have stolen his three 'callos' [mispronunciation of 'gallos', roosters]. His protestation is quite hyperbolic, not leaving much room for compassion. The protagonist of the text and the language in which he speaks are indeed figures of ridicule, and so too is the speaker in the ballad '¡Ay, señora Juana!', a 'mestiso pobre' [poor mestizo] who proclaims his love for a certain Juana.[37] His name, revealed at the end of the text, is Juan de Diego, and he embodies the stereotype of the 'valentón' [*miles gloriosus*], a proud 'coyote' [mixed-race] who does not hide his sexual appetite, represented euphemistically through a series of Nahua terms associated with food:

> el que con tamales
> y solos elotes
> pasa como un puto
> este mar de amores;
> el que en la laguna
> no deja xolote,
> rana ni juil
> que no se lo come.[38]

> [he who with tamales
> and corn alone
> crosses like a faggot
> this sea of love;
> he who does not leave any *xolote*,
> frog or *juil*
> uneaten.]

Sexual metaphors disguised under references to food were rather common in burlesque texts of the sixteenth and seventeenth centuries, going back to the Italian tradition of Francesco Berni and his imitators. Diego Hurtado de Mendoza, one of his earliest Spanish followers, wrote texts in this vein such as his comic praise 'A la zanahoria' [To the Carrot], which has a clear phallic meaning.[39] I believe that several of the food references included in this Mexican ballad are of similar nature, since these items share an elongated shape: tamales, elotes [corn], xolote and juil [types of fish]. The expression 'como un puto' creates a sense of sexual ambiguity that permeates the last lines of the poem, where local Nahua words are merged with the bernesque code, creating an American version of a very popular European genre. Despite their significance, the ballads of the Indian 'medio ladino' and the mestizo have not been edited and studied as they deserve. Most of their dirty jokes have been left unexplored, and their true semantic range kept on a leash. A mere picturesque reading of these works does not account for the ambitious intertextual exercise behind them. Here there is a manifest intention of experimenting with some of the most irreverent poetic forms of the Renaissance, placing them within a new cultural and linguistic context. It is not only the protagonist of the poem who is a 'coyote': the whole ballad embodies a new mestizo poetics.

A further gap in the configuration of an early modern poetic corpus in the New World springs from the fact that it is often the literary production of great cities such as Mexico City and Lima that has capitalized scholarly attention. Poetry was a general phenomenon, cultivated also in other cities and in more peripheral regions, which brought these smaller communities together, circulating both locally and transatlantically. An early example is found in the ballad traditionally attributed to Luis de Miranda, likely composed not long after 1536 (date of the first foundation of the city of Buenos Aires). This text made it to Europe in the 1560s, included in a document sent to the Council of the Indies by Francisco Ortiz de Zárate making the case for the establishment of an autonomous government in the region of the Río de la Plata. Ortiz states that the ballad had been requested by the President of the Council, Juan de Ovando, 'el romance que vuestra señoría ilustrísima me pidió y mandó que le diese' [the ballad that your most illustrious excellency requested and asked me to deliver].[40] It follows that the poem was already known in Spain, probably because of its polemical content regarding the tumultuous events that surrounded the foundation and administration of Buenos Aires. The tensions aired in the ballad exemplify the use of poetry as a vehicle for political debate within a colonial context, as well as the way in which these discourses could transcend their American confines. The *Romance* represents a community divided by social disorder and the lack of a worthy leader. This is achieved by describing the unfair execution of the *maestre de campo* Juan Osorio, a member in the army of Pedro de Mendoza. After this ominous event, Mendoza's men arrived at the mouth of La Plata River where they founded the city of Santa María de los Buenos Aires under bad omens. What follows is a series of violent encounters with the native population and semi-starvation, leading the Spanish troops to commit such atrocities as 'la carne de hombre también | la comieron' [they even ate human flesh].[41]

Miranda's ballad represents the body politic divided into factions on the more remote frontiers of the New World. Poetry was employed to voice these conflicts as well as to establish the distinctiveness of newly formed lettered communities. Even smaller and peripheral urban centres would take pride in reinforcing their cultural identity through literary production. Such is the case of Juan de Castellanos' *Elegías de varones ilustres de Indias* [Elegies of Illustrious Men from the Indies], the first part of which was published in Madrid in 1589. Castellanos, formerly a soldier who had come to America looking for fortune, was *beneficiado* of Tunja, in the Kingdom of New Granada. His enormous epic poem, consisting of more than 113,000 lines, describes the deeds of the conquistadors who forged the myths of colonial America, such as Columbus and Lope de Aguirre. Despite its focus on such important figures, *Elegías* pays considerable attention also to the exploration of New Granada, establishing bonds between its geopolitical configuration and its developing lettered community. Castellanos includes in the paratexts a xylography of his portrait, holding a copy of *Elegías* with his right hand (Fig. I.2), which is preceded by a series of poems written by members of the local intellectual elite. By praising Castellanos these authors are also disseminating their own names via the printing press in a book that was going to circulate both in Europe and in the New World, allowing for their reputation to flourish beyond the confines of provincial Tunja. One of them, Gaspar de Villarroel y Coruña, who wrote a sonnet in honour of Castellanos in *Elegías* ('Dichoso en vida y muerte a quien destina'), was to present a dedicatory sonnet in Pedro de Oña's *Arauco domado* [Arauco Tamed], published in Lima in 1596. The text, he claims, is written on behalf of the 'Academia Antártica' [Antarctic Academy], formed by a group of writers who associated themselves with the viceroyalty of Peru.[42] Both sonnets, addressed respectively to Castellanos and Oña, exemplify the constitution of lettered communities in American cities as well as the cultural exchanges developed between them.

The Rise of Spanish American Poetry

Locating Spanish American poetry is a work in progress, one that will require further research in archives and libraries in order to expand its current corpus. This work will have to go hand in hand with a critical reassessment of the current canon. Some of its most important texts will require a new and more complete revision, moving beyond dualist readings that have not allowed us to appreciate their complexity in full. I have previously discussed the example of *Flores de varia poesía*. Also, some lesser-known sources, such as *Relación historiada*, will have to be rediscovered and analysed against their social and cultural backdrop. Early modern poetry inhabits a number of spheres that often escape our modern taste and understanding. These are private spaces as well as public, where literary compositions are usually at the centre of the stage, articulating dialogues between different classes, voicing social conflicts both through panegyrics (because of what they fail to say) and satires (because of what they do say). *The Rise of Spanish American Poetry* is the first book in English that collectively sets out to explore and study the complexities of early modern Spanish poetry in the New World. The essays have been written by scholars from the UK, the US and Latin America, allowing for an open dialogue between different methodological approaches. They cover a wide chronological and geographical spectrum, including texts composed in Central and South America as well as the Caribbean. The volume is organized in four sections.

I. The Spaces of Poetry: Civic Spectacle and Religious Proselytism

The first section frames two of the main discursive spaces of early modern poetry in America: civic spectacle and evangelization of the native population. By doing this, it addresses one of the issues that is central to the conquest and colonization of the New World: the problematic encounter between different civilizations. Spain imposed a political, cultural and religious system on the indigenous

FIG. I.2. Juan de Castellanos, *Primera parte de las elegías de varones ilustres de Indias* (Madrid: En casa de la viuda de Alonso Gómez, 1589), portrait of the author. Courtesy of the Hispanic Society of America (New York).

population. This process, however, was extremely complex and left an indelible impression both in the conquered and in the conquerors. The westernization of Indian societies, and the semiotic reshaping of their collective imagination, led to the constitution of hybrid societies that are often described placing particular emphasis on critical concepts such as heterogeneity and *mestizaje*, which in the last decades have contributed a great deal to our understanding of early modern Spanish American political and cultural life.[43] The conquerors too saw their own horizon of expectations affected and changed by the imperialistic enterprise, a shift studied in the various chapters included in this volume. The first two chapters in particular offer a gateway into the intricacies of cultural *mestizaje*. This process became the basis for globalization as transatlantic and transpacific ties grew stronger and became more complex. The two chapters contained in this section analyse a series of key questions that frame the volume as a whole, addressing paradigmatic discursive spaces that early modern Spanish American poetry inhabited and shaped: cultural hybridization, evangelization, warfare, orality, written tradition, visual culture, public performance. Such spaces will be interrogated, reimagined and indeed remapped by the authors and texts explored in later sections.

In the first chapter, Rolena Adorno focuses on Carlos de Sigüenza y Góngora's *Teatro de virtudes políticas* (1680), written to commemorate the installation of the viceroy of New Spain, Don Tomás de la Cerda, analysing also the panegyric in honour of the viceroy composed by the Mexican polymath and the contrapuntal dialogue that Sor Juana establishes with it in her sonnet 'Dulce, canoro cisne mexicano'. In *Teatro*, Sigüenza y Góngora gives a thorough description of the triumphal arch that he designed combining references to classical sources with an iconographic representation of twelve Aztec rulers. The arch is an eloquent example of cultural syncretism between the Old and the New World as well as between the visual arts and literature. Amerindian iconography is incorporated into the Spanish archive, producing an intertext that does not simply tame and Hispanicize Mexica symbols. *Teatro* empowers indigenous culture adopting it as one of the motivations upon which American identity rests, displaying arguments that were at the core of creole vindications, increasingly prominent between the seventeenth and the eighteenth centuries. While Adorno's study of Sigüenza y Góngora moves away from the military and spiritual conquest of the sixteenth century toward allegorized cultural *mestizaje*, Raquel Chang-Rodríguez shifts our focus back to that earlier period, in the Andean context, in her study of the incipient hybridity of Luis Jerónimo de Oré's *Símbolo católico indiano* (1598). Here the Franciscan friar includes a number of religious compositions written in Quechua devised as aid in the evangelization of the native population of Peru. Chang-Rodríguez contextualizes this work, which was published in a critical period when the church in America was in a time of transition, eager to attract and evangelize peoples of diverse cultures. The seven hymns ('cánticos') place Quechua on the same level with Latin and Spanish, producing complex devotional texts while negotiating a more inclusive and hybrid approach to the spreading of Christian doctrine among the Indian population. Amerindian oral traditions are re-framed within a Hispanic context where voice and written text meet in a problematic as well as creative fashion.

II. Satire, Balladry and Burlesque Poetry

Orality, artistic hybridization and ideological conflict are seminal concepts found also in the second section of the book. Here genres that have often been left at the margins of the research devoted to colonial poetry are considered from a number of complementary perspectives: satire, burlesque texts and ballads. These texts offer a contrapuntal approach to those studied in the previous two chapters, analysing authors whose reflections on the meeting of Amerindian and European civilizations were not always in line with the official discourse put forward by the imperialistic apparatus, but were instead polemical in nature. A good example is Fray Cristóbal Cabrera, active in New Spain in the early sixteenth century, whose works are studied by Andrew Laird. His Latin composition 'Dicolon icastichon' is of paramount importance since it was the first poem to be published in the Indies (Mexico City, 1540). This and other Latin texts that he composed in New Spain are imbued with classical and humanist references set within an American context, and often display an acrimonious tone against the Spaniards for their conduct in the New World. Cabrera stands in a liminal position between orthodoxy and social dissent, using the classical canon as a weapon against the moral corruption produced by the material conquest of the Indies. Standing on the opposite end of this ideal literary scale, Miguel Martínez draws our attention towards the 'other' poets of the New World, those whose works were crafted within an oral context. These ephemeral texts, composed by soldiers and conquistadors, were born as a consequence of warfare and social conflict. Historic figures such as Pizarro, Cortés and Lope de Aguirre were scorned in ballads where this medieval poetic form was adapted in order to articulate satire in the Indies. Martínez's corpus shows the other side of satire moving away from written classical sources and its predominating tone of indignation that generally referred to society as a whole. These satires *ad personam* have clear individual targets and were produced by a number of authors who were alien to the lettered community described by Rama or, at least, who did not participate fully in its codes and practices, establishing parallel ones instead. Rather different is the case of Agustín de Salazar y Torres, active in the second half of the seventeenth century, whose ambitious editorial practices placed him in a privileged position within the Hispanic literary canon. Raquel Barragán Aroche's chapter studies his production of burlesque poetry, where the main goal is no longer the production of eloquent and politicized satires, but rather linguistic experimentation and the proliferation of conceptist wit. Like the texts studied in the previous chapters, although with a very different goal in mind, mockery, laughter and the practice of intertextuality are at the core of Salazar y Torres's works. The author spent his life between Europe and New Spain, producing a large quantity of burlesque poems where he engages with models such as Góngora, Quevedo, Lope de Vega and Polo de Medina. Detailed readings of his rhetorical devices reveal a complex imitative exercise that underscores some of the most important traits of the uses of Baroque *ingenio* across both sides of the Atlantic, demonstrating that there was a fluid communication between the two continents.

III. Religious Culture, villancicos and Music

The third part of this edited collection links back to Raquel Chang-Rodríguez's essay on the uses of poetry as a tool for evangelization and the propagation of Christian ideology. The denunciatory and irreverent qualities of the previous section are contrasted by the didactic and devotional drives of the texts studied here. As we have argued above, such discursive spaces are far from irreconcilable, since they moved fluidly between the private and the public spheres, often interlacing with each other. The chapters here included are devoted to religious poetry and its practical and theoretical connection with political thought and music. Arantza Mayo studies Diego de Hojeda's epic poem *La Christiada* (1611), which is an adaptation of Marco Girolamo Vida's neo-Latin text *Christias* (1535) to the Spanish and, particularly, to the Peruvian context. This work describes the sufferings of Christ during his passion, drawing parallels between these and the arduous responsibilities of kings and rulers. As with the case of Fray Cristóbal Cabrera, we see the adaptation of prestigious Latin and neo-Latin models in an American context, though Hojeda preferred to write his text in the Spanish vernacular, widening the target audience of his poem. As a matter of fact, the intendent recipients of *La Christiada* are multiple: this is a didactic mirror of princes that, in the first instance, addresses the viceroy of Peru, the Marquis of Montesclaros, while also directing its message to the New World society broadly. Hojeda takes full advantage of the porous nature of the heroic genre, which will be explored further in Section IV. By using the far-reaching narrative structure of epic poetry, the author encompasses a moral, religious and ideological message that echoes some of the tensions and contradictions of colonialism as he experienced it in the viceroyalty of Peru. Alice Brooke's essay takes us back to New Spain, looking at more popular manifestations of religious poetry, namely the *villancicos*, and how these were used by Sor Juana Inés de la Cruz, who we had already encountered in Adorno's piece. Sor Juana is one of the ultimate expressions of the hybrid and multifaceted culture of the New World, drawing from a multitude of classical, indigenous and early modern sources. The *villancicos* written for the Feast of the Assumption in 1676 are among her first published poetic works and display the author's originality in the way in which she portrays the Virgin Mary. The Mother of Christ is characterized as a professor of theology, as a heavenly choir mistress, as a knight errant, and as a teacher of rhetoric. These attributes and imagery, grounded in scriptural and literary tradition, showcase some of the qualities that Sor Juana recognized in herself as an independent thinker and writer, thus offering a representation of the Virgin that is also a declaration of the intellectual intentions of the author. Poetic genres such as *villancicos* are strongly rooted in music and performance. Lorena Uribe Bracho sets out to analyse the relationship between musical theory and poetic imagery in early modern thought. Her essay opens up a dialogical relationship with Martínez's chapter on balladry, though her work focuses less on the analysis of musical genres and songs as a public and political performance than as a part of an intellectual discipline. Uribe Bracho analyses music as this was used to theorize on its role as a vehicle capable of stimulating a variety of social practices, which ranged from spiritual uplifting to collective disorder. The spaces of music, shared by the liturgy and public celebrations, also staged more controversial performances that emphasized the role of the body, namely through dancing. Focusing on musical treatises and philosophic ideas such as the theory of the harmony of celestial spheres, this multidisciplinary essay showcases links and intertwined conventions between Spain and America.

IV. Epic Poetry and the New Frontier

The final section of the book focuses on epic poetry and its uses in the conceptualization of new geographic spaces, especially in those territories that were removed from great urban centres such as Lima or Mexico City. The chapters here included underscore the capacity of the heroic genre to take full advantage of its versatility and encyclopaedic content, a capacity also explored in Mayo's chapter devoted to Hojeda's *Christiada*. Recent scholarship on Hispanic epics has shown how these texts were some of the most popular poetic forms when it came to representing the conquest of the New World. The extensive and comprehensive nature of these poems allowed their authors to represent warfare, the process of evangelization and the conflicts that ensued from the imposition of a European political system onto indigenous civilizations.[44] This is often shown through a symbolic identification of specific areas of the American geography and the alleged traits of the native population that inhabited them. Epic, as shown by Ricardo Padrón, was one of the most productive means for literary mappings in early modern Latin America.[45] Stemming from this theoretical framework, Paul Firbas analyses the uses of territorial transgression in Alonso de Ercilla's *La Araucana* (1569–89), comparing its lexical and ideological expressions with those of other colonial epic works. One of Ercilla's key-terms is *término* [boundary, frontier], which possesses a variety of meanings that go beyond the mere territorial reference, encompassing moral and ethical issues that are paramount to the military campaigns in America. Luis Fernando Restrepo applies the theories of Carl Schmitt on political imperialism over land and sea to the works of Juan de Castellanos (*Elegías de varones ilustres de Indias* and *Discurso del capitán Francisco Draque*) in order to showcase the complex geopolitical implications of the colonialist rhetoric used by the Spanish author. In spite of the substantial presence of sea journeys and piracy in his poems, Castellanos shows a mentality that is still land-centred, grounded on a feudal understanding of wealth and political control. The sea has a significant presence in Castellanos, though it is mostly perceived as a perilous space, the ultimate frontier where the unknown lies. Imogen Choi reads the epic motif of the sea journey in Juan de Miramontes Zuázola's *Armas antárticas* (c. 1608–09) in relation to one of its most important literary models, Luis de Camões's *Os Lusíadas*, published in 1572. In particular, the essay considers the role played by erotic interludes in both texts. Love and lust act as counterpoint to the desire implicit in imperial warfare. The drive to take on new territories often adopts in these poems the metaphorical shape of romantic conquest, displaying some of the most productive dualisms (love and war) of the epic tradition. The last work included in the volume looks at *Espejo de paciencia* (1608) by Silvestre de

Balboa, which was composed to celebrate the liberation of the Bishop of Cuba, Fray Juan de las Cabezas Altamirano, who had been captured by French pirates. Raúl Marrero-Fente pays special attention to the final section of the poem's first canto, where there is a lavish description of a cornucopia of tropical goods offered to the Bishop. This section, which acts as a shorter epic fragment (or *epyllion*) in *Espejo de paciencia*, is framed within the bucolic tradition, particularly the *locus amoenus* topos. In spite of the obvious links with classical sources, Balboa displays a fascination for the local natural world, fostering a mythical reading of the Cuban fauna and flora.

The Rise of Spanish American Poetry explores the extent to which early modern poetry contributed to shaping the societies of the New World in connection with the development of literary practices imported from Europe, which quite soon had to adapt and change to a new geographic and cultural set of realities. The various chapters consist of a series of key studies that focus on a number of significant issues, such as genres, modes of transmission, political and ideological discourses, the ties between different artistic disciplines (visual culture, literature, music), and the dialectic encounter of chorography and poetry. Rather than trying to impose a false sense of homogeneity, this variety offers a valuable glimpse into the complexity of New World poetic tradition, which is often as fragmented and contradictory as the societies that produced it. Consequently, the essays here included can also be read geographically, across space, as a series of insights on the various ties and conflicts within the viceroyalties of Peru and New Spain, as well as between them and Europe. By studying specific examples, these chapters also promote a wider discussion that takes into account some of the most influential and current debates surrounding colonial studies, approaching *mestizaje* in a broad sense that encompasses race, culture, politics and faith. Ultimately, the volume has been crafted with the hope that it will stimulate further research, contributing to the rising scholarship on early modern Spanish American poetry.

The majority of essays included here originated in an international conference held at Clare College, Cambridge, 19–20 November 2015, 'Poets of the New World: Literary and Cultural Transmission in Early Modern Spanish America'. The keynote speakers were Rolena Adorno (Norman MacColl Lecturer) and Raquel Chang-Rodríguez. We would like to thank the various funding bodies that allowed us to run the conference and supported the publication of this book: the Department of Spanish and Portuguese and the Centre of Latin American Studies at the University of Cambridge, and, most importantly, the British Academy, whose support through the award of a 'Mid-Career Fellowship' has been invaluable. We would also like to express our gratitude to the editorial team of Legenda, in particular, to Trevor Dadson and Graham Nelson for their enthusiastic support, and also to the anonymous external reader for their very valuable comments and corrections. Translations into English of the chapters by Raquel Barragán Aroche, Paul Firbas and Raúl Marrero-Fente are by Imogen Choi. The spelling and punctuation of old Spanish texts have been modernized throughout.

Notes to the Introduction

1. In the words of Henríquez Ureña, 'es uno de los primeros intentos de síntesis de las nuevas maneras de considerar los tres siglos coloniales' [it is one of the first attempts to summarize the new critical approaches to the three colonial centuries]; Pedro Henríquez Ureña, 'Nota', in Mariano Picón-Salas, *De la conquista a la independencia: tres siglos de historia cultural hispanoamericana* (Mexico City: Fondo de Cultura Económica, 1985), pp. 9–14 (p. 12).
2. Lockhart and Schwartz consider Picón-Salas's work 'extraordinarily out of touch with the social, economic, and ethnic history of early Spanish America'; James Lockhart and Stuart B. Schwartz, *Early Latin America: A History of Colonial Spanish America and Brazil* (Cambridge: Cambridge University Press, 1983), p. 431.
3. Picón-Salas, *De la conquista*, pp. 51–52. The English translation is drawn from *A Cultural History of Spanish America: From Conquest to Independence*, trans. by Irving A. Leonard (Berkeley and Los Angeles: University of California Press, 1962), pp. 26–27.
4. José Lezama Lima, *La expresión americana* (La Habana: Instituto Nacional de Cultura, 1957).
5. Picón-Salas, *De la conquista*, pp. 121–46. Picón-Salas was likely inspired by Pedro Henríquez Ureña's 1940 article, 'Barroco de América', in *Ensayos*, ed. by José Luis Abellán and Ana María Barrenechea (Madrid: ALLCA XX/Universidad de Costa Rica, 1998), pp. 353–57. See also Leonardo Acosta, 'El Barroco de Indias y la ideología colonialista', in *Ensayos escogidos* (La Habana: Editorial Letras Cubanas, 2009), pp. 219–69.
6. For instance, see Georgina Sabat de Rivers, *Estudios de literatura hispanoamericana: sor Juana Inés de la Cruz y otros poetas barrocos de la colonia* (Barcelona: PPU, 1992), pp. 17–48; Daniel Torres, *El palimpsesto del calco aparente: una poética del Barroco de Indias* (New York: Peter Lang, 1993); Mabel Moraña, *Viaje al silencio: exploraciones del discurso barroco* (Mexico City: Universidad Nacional Autónoma de México, 1998).
7. Rolena Adorno, *Colonial Latin American Literature: A Very Short Introduction* (Oxford and New York: Oxford University Press, 2011), pp. 3–6.
8. According to Martha Lilia Tenorio, 'el concepto "literatura colonial" entendido como una categoría diferente de "literatura hispánica" es totalmente incorrecto. [...] En realidad, la literatura del virreinato no es otra que la literatura española de los Siglos de Oro' [the concept of 'colonial literature' understood as a different category than 'Hispanic literature' is totally inaccurate. [...] As a matter of fact, the literature of the viceroyalty is no other than the Spanish literature of the Golden Age]; Martha Lilia Tenorio (ed.), *Poesía novohispana. Antología*, 2 vols (Mexico City: El Colegio de México/Fundación para las Letras Mexicanas, 2010), I, 17. See the state of the question outlined by Ángel Estévez Molinero, 'Señas de identidad de la poesía hispanoamericana en el siglo XVII', in *Tras el canon: la poesía del Barroco tardío*, ed. by Ignacio García Aguilar (Vigo: Academia del Hispanismo, 2009), pp. 127–42.
9. Rolena Adorno, *The Polemics of Possession in Spanish American Narrative* (New Haven, CT, and London: Yale University Press, 2007).
10. Quentin Skinner, *Visions of Politics, I: Regarding Method* (Cambridge: Cambridge University Press, 2002), p. 63.
11. J. Jorge Klor de Alva, 'Colonialism and Postcolonialism as (Latin) American Mirages', *Colonial Latin American Review*, 1.1–2 (1992), 3–23; Rolena Adorno, 'Reconsidering Colonial Discourse for Sixteenth- and Seventeenth-Century Spanish America', *Latin American Review*, 28.3 (1993), 135–45.
12. Margarita Peña (ed.), *Flores de baria poesía: cancionero novohispano del siglo XVI* (Mexico City: Fondo de Cultura Económica, 2003). The original manuscript is held at the Biblioteca Nacional de España (Madrid), Ms. 2973. See also María José Rodríguez Mosquera, '*Flores de baria poesía* (México, 1577): estudio y análisis del manuscrito' (PhD dissertation, Universitat de Barcelona, 2013).
13. Roland Greene, *Unrequited Conquests: Love and Empire in the Colonial Americas* (Chicago, IL: University of Chicago Press, 1999), p. 166.
14. Miguel de Cervantes, 'Canto de Calíope', in *La Galatea*, ed. by Francisco López Estrada and María Teresa García-Berdoy (Madrid: Cátedra, 1999), pp. 563–89 (stanza 67).

15. The manuscript of *Relación historiada* is held at the Biblioteca Nacional de México (Mexico City), Ms. 1799. See Dorothy Schons, 'The Influence of Góngora on Mexican literature during the Seventeenth Century', *Hispanic Review*, 7 (1939), 22–34 (p. 25); and Martha Lilia Tenorio, *El gongorismo en Nueva España: ensayo de restitución* (Mexico City: El Colegio de México, 2013), pp. 47–55. Tenorio publishes a selection of poems from *Relación historiada* in her anthology, *Poesía novohispana*, I, 359–69.

16. José Mariano Beristáin de Souza, *Biblioteca hispano-americana septentrional*, 3 vols (Mexico City: Oficina de don Alejandro Valdés, 1816–21), I, p. 39.

17. Francisco Salvago started his own printing business in the late 1620s and carried it out until 1638. Between 1633 and 1634 he brought Pedro de Quiñones to work with him, who was apparently charged with the printing job proper, while Salvago focused his attention on running the book shop; José Toribio Medina, *La imprenta en México (1539–1821)*, 8 vols (Santiago de Chile: Impreso en casa del autor, 1907–11), I, p. cxxvii.

18. Fernando de Cepeda and Fernando Alfonso Carrillo, *Relación universal legítima y verdadera del sitio en que está fundada la muy noble, insigne y muy leal Ciudad de México* (Mexico City: Francisco Salvago, 1637), II, fol. 27. The *vara* was a measurement used in early modern Spain equal to approximately 84 cms.

19. Louisa Hoberman, 'Bureaucracy and Disaster: Mexico City and the Flood of 1629', *Journal of Latin American Studies*, 6.2 (1974), 211–30.

20. *Sortija* games consisted of a jousting practice in which knights had to thread their lance through a small ring (*sortija*) while riding their horse.

21. See the modern edition by Tenorio (ed.), *Poesía novohispana*, I, 368.

22. For the concept of *clase letrada* within this context, see the seminal work by Ángel Rama, *La ciudad letrada* (Hanover: Ediciones del Norte, 1984).

23. On the spectacular nature of social and cultural life in early modern Mexico City, see Stephanie Merrim, *The Spectacular City, Mexico, and Colonial Hispanic Literary Culture* (Austin: University of Texas Press, 2010).

24. *Marca mayor* is paper roughly twice the size of a typical sheet, and it is also thicker. I wish to thank Dr Ken Ward for his assistance on this point.

25. I would like to thank my colleagues at the Instituto de Investigaciones Bibliográficas in Mexico City, Pablo Tadeo Stein and César Manrique Figueroa. The former drew my attention to the *Relación historiada* and the poster of the poetic contest; the latter sent me the image of the poster and obtained the permission to publish it in this volume.

26. On Calderón, active in Mexico City between 1631 and 1641, see Medina, *La imprenta en México*, I, p. cxxviii. Quiñones worked for him between 1631 and 1633.

27. The printed poster of the poetic festival also makes reference to an eighth *certamen* which should have combined the seven planets, followed by a ninth and final contest ('Último certamen') devoted to burlesque sonnets. There is, however, no reference to this eighth contest including the seven planets in the account included in *Relación historiada*; the slot for the eighth and final contest is, instead, reserved to the composition of burlesque sonnets.

28. Balbuena claims that in a late sixteenth-century poetic festival in which he took part in Mexico City there were 300 contestants; Bernardo de Balbuena, *Grandeza mexicana*, ed. by Asima F. X. Saad Maura (Madrid: Cátedra, 2011), p. 136. The number appears to be rather inflated.

29. Archivo Histórico Nacional (Madrid), Inquisición, L.1049, fol. 54. Pedro de la Vega was *contador* and notary of the Mexican Inquisition. He also accounts for 2000 *mestizos*, 10,000 black and mulatto slaves, 1500 free blacks and mulattoes and 3000 foreigners. He does not account for the large native population of Mexico City, which constituted a clear majority.

30. On Estrada de Medinilla, see Josefina Muriel, *Cultura femenina novohispana* (Mexico City: Universidad Nacional Autónoma de México, 1994), pp. 124–43; Tenorio (ed.), *Poesía novohispana*, I, 49–50; Tenorio, *El gongorismo en Nueva España*, pp. 58–65.

31. The documents containing these texts are held at the Archivo General de la Nación (Mexico City), Inquisición, Vol. 485, Exp. 1.

32. I quote from the thoroughly annotated edition by Andrés Íñigo Silva, 'Los sonetos derivados de las predicaciones que en 1618 acompañaron la fiesta de la Inmaculada Concepción y sus

respuestas: propuesta de edición crítica' (Tesis de Licenciatura, Universidad Nacional Autónoma de México, 2012), p. 108. I have modified slightly Íñigo Silva's punctuation of the sonnet. See also the selection of texts from the *certamen* in Tenorio (ed.), *Poesía novohispana*, I, 319–37.

33. Joanne Rappaport and Tom Cummins, *Beyond the Lettered City: Indigenous Literacies in the Andes* (Durham, NC, and London: Duke University Press, 2012).

34. Diego Cano Gutiérrez, *Relación de las fiestas triunfales que la insigne Universidad de Lima hizo a la Inmaculada Concepción de nuestra Señora* (Lima: Francisco Lasso, 1619), fols 41, 42–42ᵛ. *Cumbe* (also spelled *cunbe, cunpi, qumbi, cunpi, qunpi* and *qumpi*) is the Quechua word for 'fine cloth'.

35. Rodrigo de Carvajal y Robles, *Fiestas que celebró la Ciudad de los Reyes del Pirú al nacimiento del serenísimo príncipe don Baltasar Carlos de Austria nuestro señor* (Lima: Gerónimo de Contreras, 1632), fols 43ᵛ, 45ᵛ.

36. The ultimate threat is represented by the rebellious Araucanians or the estranged 'negros cimarrones' [slaves that have escaped] found in epic poems such as Pedro de Oña's *Arauco domado* (1596) and Juan de Miramontes Zuázola, *Armas antárticas* (c. 1608–09), both written in Lima.

37. Both poems are included in Ms. 19387, held at the Biblioteca Nacional de España (Madrid), in folios 82–82ᵛ, 199–199ᵛ. A modern transcription of both texts is found in Alfonso Reyes, 'Rosas de Oquendo en América', in *Capítulos de literatura española (Primera serie)* (Mexico City: La Casa de España en México, 1939), pp. 21–71 (pp. 47–50, 60–61). For a linguistic analysis of the 'Romance en lengua de indio mexicano medio ladino', see Mirta A. González, 'Primeras parodias del español hablado por indios y africanos en la Nueva España', in *Actas del XXIX Congreso del Instituto Internacional de Literatura Iberoamericana*, ed. by Joaquín Marco, 3 vols (Barcelona: PPU, 1994), I, pp. 381–87 (pp. 381–84).

38. Reyes, 'Rosas de Oquendo en América', p. 61. I have slightly modified Reyes's punctuation.

39. Rodrigo Cacho Casal, 'Zanahorias y otras picardías: Hurtado de Mendoza ante la tradición bernesca', *Calíope*, 12.2 (2006), 13–32.

40. In Luis de Miranda, *Romance*, ed. by Silvia Tieffemberg (Madrid and Frankfurt: Iberoamericana/Vervuert, 2014), p. 177.

41. Miranda, *Romance*, ll. 83–84.

42. In Pedro de Oña, *Arauco domado*, ed. by J. T. Medina (Santiago de Chile: Imprenta Universitaria, 1917), p. 22.

43. See, among others, the seminal works of Néstor García Canclini, *Culturas híbridas: estrategias para entrar y salir de la modernidad* (Mexico City: Grijalbo, 1990); Antonio Cornejo Polar, *Escribir en el aire: ensayo sobre la heterogeneidad socio-cultural en las literaturas andinas* (Lima: Centro de Estudios Literarios "Antonio Cornejo Polar"/Latinoamericana Editores, 2003); Serge Gruzinski, *La Colonisation de l'imaginaire: sociétés indigènes et occidentalisation dans le Mexique espagnol, XVIᵉ–XVIIᵉ siècle* (Paris: Gallimard, 1988), and his *La Pensée métisse* (Paris: Fayard, 1999).

44. Juan Bautista de Avalle-Arce, *La épica colonial* (Pamplona: EUNSA, 2000); Paul Firbas (ed.), *Épica y colonia: ensayos sobre el género épico en Iberoamérica (siglos XVI y XVII)* (Lima: Universidad Nacional Mayor de San Marcos, 2008); Imogen Choi, 'Conflict Ethics and Political Community in Early Peruvian Epic' (unpublished PhD dissertation, University of Cambridge, 2016); Raúl Marrero-Fente, *Poesía épica colonial del siglo XVI: historia, teoría y práctica* (Madrid and Frankfurt: Iberoamericana/Vervuert, 2017).

45. Ricardo Padrón, *The Spacious Word: Cartography, Literature, and Empire in Early Modern Spain* (Chicago, IL, and London: University of Chicago Press, 2004).

PART I

The Spaces of Poetry: Civic Spectacle and Religious Proselytism

CHAPTER 1

Poetry's Place in Civic Spectacle: The 'Baroque Contredanse' of Carlos de Sigüenza y Góngora and Sor Juana Inés de la Cruz

Rolena Adorno

> The poem is the cry of its occasion,
> Part of the res itself and not about it
>   (Wallace Stevens, 'An Ordinary Evening
>   in New Haven', 1950)[1]

Imagine a young Nahua woman, dressed in traditional native Mexican garb, allegorically representing the capital of New Spain and standing atop a triumphal arch to welcome, in verse, the new viceroy of New Spain. She recites a long praise poem — a panegyric — in his honour and, as she concludes it, a trumpet sounds to evoke the strains of the cithara played by eternal Fame. Thus concludes the memoir, *Teatro de virtudes políticas que constituyen a un príncipe, advertidas en los monarcas antiguos del mexicano imperio* [A display of the civic virtues that comprise an exemplary prince, notice of which is given by the ancient monarchs of the Mexican Empire] (1680), that the Mexican creole polymath Carlos de Sigüenza y Góngora (1645–1700) wrote to commemorate the installation on 30 November 1680 of the new viceroy, Don Tomás de la Cerda, Conde de Paredes, Marqués de la Laguna.[2]

Poetry was an essential element of such public festivities (Wallace Stevens' 'Part of the res itself and not about it'). In Baroque times the recitation of poetry was never absent from the ritualization of current events or the representation of history in public commemorations and allegory, created by visual and verbal means, played a large role. Octavio Paz has argued that such ceremonies constituted an 'etiquette'.[3] This etiquette was a system of symbolic representation of social relations that was neither explicit nor literal, but rather a figurative language of verbal and visual art whose symbolic artistic expressions were 'disfraces transparentes' [transparent disguises]: transparent to those who understood them, opaque, that is, 'disguised', to those who did not.[4]

In such circumstances, poetry was part of a more complex configuration. Separately, poem and performer offered sound and sight, words recited aloud in an animated tableau. The live performance was a theatrical display (*teatro*, the site of games and spectacles in its Baroque sense) that, after the event, lived on in the ekphrastic memoirs and *relaciones* that described them (in the English tradition, these were known as festival books). The Renaissance-style emblems that enlivened the ceremonial, ephemeral Baroque portal or arch became even more 'animate' in print where, as if unfurling the mottos' banners, their short, versified expressions condensing deeper meanings were explained. Surface and substance: the surface of the public spectacle for the general audience, its substance for the contemplative learned one. The public forum and the private study: the performed event and its written record.

The public site of such commemorations was the triumphal arch, whose origins are found in imperial Rome. Invigorated in the Renaissance, the triumphal arch constructed of stone and mortar was augmented by new temporary ones made of lath and plaster. Arches with multiple portals, adorned with sculptures and paintings, populated the ceremonial landscape. Whether permanent or ephemeral, the triumphal arch was a monument brought to life by the performances that marked its inauguration. Actors and dancers performed, poetry was recited, prophecies were proclaimed, and admonitions given, all before a public audience that included all the castes and classes of society.

Sor Juana Inés de la Cruz (1648–1695), too, had been commissioned to create a triumphal arch for the new viceroy's installation, and we have its memoir, *Neptuno alegórico* [Allegorical Neptune] (1680), in her *Inundación castálida* [The Muses's overflowing fountain] (1689).[5] For both Sigüenza and Sor Juana, the public festival required what Paz has described as 'una geometría que encarna una visión del mundo' [a geometry that incarnates a vision of the world], which reflected three levels of reality: the divine, political and natural orders in which the kingdoms of nature (animal, vegetable and mineral) were seen as copies or images of divine order, and the royal court, as a copy of the celestial kingdom. In public festivals, the task was to represent in symbolic form the political relationship that presumed to unite the lord with his subjects: the loyalty of the vassals to the lord, the love of the prince for his subjects.[6]

Sor Juana and Sigüenza were each other's most important interlocutor regarding their parallel commemorative commissions.[7] The immediacy of their interactions can be seen in Sigüenza's panegyric and the sonnet that Sor Juana penned in response to it, which were published together in a pamphlet, as well as in Sigüenza's *Teatro* arguments about the signification of the figure of Neptune, which was the result of his familiarity with *Neptuno alegórico*.[8] The complexity of their interactions can be explored through the figures from history and myth that they celebrated (Huitzilopochtli and Neptune, respectively), the methods of exegesis and interpretation they employed, and the play between the solemnity of the poetry they produced for the formal occasion and the light-hearted ways they engaged poetry among themselves. I make the argument here that Sigüenza's and Sor Juana's respective artistic efforts were ultimately 'in step' with one another (not at odds, as is often thought), and that they were engaged in what I call a 'Baroque contredanse' of creative symbolic thinking. To advance my arguments, I have divided this essay into seven sections: (1) Sigüenza's *Teatro*; (2) The Viceregal Couple, The Mexica Lords; (3) Huitzilopochtli, Mexican Moses; (4) The Mexica Lords' Zodiacal Light; (5) Mexico Personified and Her Panegyric; (6) Sor Juana's 'Sweet, sonorous Mexican swans'; and (7) Neptune, Figural Foreshadower.

Sigüenza's *Teatro*

In *Teatro* Sigüenza employed ekphrasis to describe the features of the triumphal arch (or civic portal) that he had designed; he included the poems he had written for recitation on the inaugural occasion and explained in detail the allegorical meanings of the iconography he employed. To provide the rationale for the conception and execution of all these elements he drew on a remarkable repertory of ancient classical and modern Renaissance and Baroque sources; for the arch's iconography in particular, he relied extensively on native Mexican codices and artefacts. A brief, extremely dense work, Sigüenza's *Teatro* has had a long life; along with Sor Juana's *Neptuno alegórico*, it is without a doubt one of the most famous 'festival books' of Spain's viceroyalties in the Americas.

Pertinent to Sigüenza's *Teatro* project is the unusual author's mark that he created; it graced as well the frontispiece of *Panegírico* and his other few books that appeared in print.[9] Consisting of the traditional configuration of a pictorial image, a motto and an epigram or brief discussion of the emblem's topic, often but not always in verse, Sigüenza chose as the pictorial image the winged Pegasus. The motto 'Sic itur ad astra' that appears beneath the unfurled banner explains the meaning of his emblem as the strivings of man, with his soul focused on the sublime, for the benefit of the *patria* [homeland]; commonly translated as 'Such is the path to the stars' or 'Thus one journeys to the stars', Sigüenza's source was Virgil's *Aeneid*. On this point Sigüenza (p. 124) cites *De simulacro reipublicae sive De imaginibus politicae et oeconomicae virtutis* [On the portrait of the republic, or on the images of political and economic virtue] (1593) of the Belgian-born jurist and philologist Enrico Farnese (*c.* 1550–1616), whose works he much admired ('cuyos estudios venero') and whose views on devoted service to the homeland he took as his own. Sigüenza's ceremonial arch and its *Teatro* fulfilled that patriotic purpose, but not in the way that might have been expected.

The *Teatro de virtudes políticas* presented its author with a compositional problem and, therefore, a rhetorical one. *Teatro* was designed to be a memoir of the event, providing both the retrospective narration of its occurrence and a self-contained, present-time and independent explanation of it to the reader (Émile Benveniste's distinction between the verbal systems of 'history' and 'discourse' is apt).[10] Sigüenza (pp. 62–63) anticipated the confusion between his account of the past event and his current effort to describe it, writing that he would proceed not according to the arrangement of the triumphal arch's painted panels that featured representations of the Mexica rulers 'that all had seen', but rather that he would follow the 'chronology of the Mexican Empire'.[11] Still, today's reader must thread through the exposition carefully to discern the presence of the two registers; this is one of the tasks I have set myself here.

As with many Baroque works, *Teatro*'s organization must be disentangled from the array of its constituent parts: the author presented prefatory materials in three separate 'preludios' [preludes]. The Spanish lexicographer Sebastián de Covarrubias defined 'preludio' as the reasons or arguments presented by an author to prepare the auditor or viewer for the subsequent oration or public act, and he colourfully attributed its use to games of chance, that is, he asserted that the preludio was the 'warm-up' of gamblers as they flexed their arms and practised rolling the dice before the start of the game.[12] One might say the same of Sigüenza's preludios, because in *Teatro*, as in the performed event that it memorialized, Sigüenza took a number of chances (his celebration of the pagan Mexica rulers as models of princely Christian conduct) and along the way readjusted his gaming strategy by creating Preludio III in response to Sor Juana's *Neptuno*, as we will see, below, in 'Neptune, Figural Foreshadower'.

In dedicating *Teatro* to the viceroy, Sigüenza (pp. 3–4) asked rhetorically, given the Marquis's noble rank, how he could have chosen as his topic any other than that of kings, since the royal line of the Marquis's house was embellished with the French fleur-de-lis and adorned with the lions of Castile and the eagles of the Germanic (Holy Roman) Empire. Why not then also, Sigüenza suggests, the Mexican monarchs, 'Phoenixes of the West' [Fenices del Occidente]? And on what better occasion, Sigüenza continued, than the present one, when the Mexica lords could be looked upon with favour by the Marquis and immortalized by allegorical Fame?

Sigüenza thus inserted into his symbolic program the celebration of the princely members of the Mexica lineage, and he made the bolder move of creating a genealogy of twelve rulers. To the nine canonical Mexica emperors from Acamapichtli to Motecuhzoma Xocoyotzin (Motecuhzoma II), he added three more: the legendary Huitzilopochtli, whom Sigüenza credits for inspiring and leading the migration from Aztlán to Anáhuac (Mexico's Central Valley), and Motecuhzoma II's two post-Spanish-conquest successors, Cuitláhuac and Cuauhtémoc.[13] Although Spanish historians had given accounts of Cuitláhuac and Cuauhtémoc, they did not present them as legitimate dynastic Mexica rulers. And no one in post-conquest times had made the Mexica god Huitzilopochtli into the human leader of the migration from Aztlán to Anáhuac or assigned him a role as leader and prophet of a twelve-member dynasty.[14]

Sigüenza (p. 50) announced that he would take up the challenge through 'el medio suave' [the gentle medium] of painting, which he judged to be the most efficacious means of persuasion for its subtlety as well as its power. Citing Isidore of Seville to the effect that meritorious subjects gained brilliance and lustre not because of wealth, beauty, or power, but rather through the exercise of virtue, Sigüenza (p. 49) credited Basil of Seleucia with the notion that, contemplating the images of kings and being overpowered by the richness of the spectacle, the viewer would in the moment of his astonished absorption comprehend the virtues of the honoured personage that the image represented. Sigüenza's task, he wrote (pp. 46–47), was to determine how best to represent heroic princely virtues that could serve the new viceroy as examples to follow in his own governorship. His solution was to feature 'el ardiente espíritu' [the ardent spirit] of the 'Mexican emperors', and he commissioned this lineage to be painted in costumes adorned with coloured feathers as part of their vestments. He added that this particularity was anticipated by 'el hijo primogénito de Apolo y pariente mío' [the first-born son of Apollo and my relative] Don Luis de Góngora, when he wrote: 'Al de plumas vestido mexicano' [To the Mexican with feathers adorned].[15]

How would Sigüenza present the Mexica kings in a manner consistent with the Baroque artistic practice of his day that favoured literary emblems and enigmas?[16] He resolved the conundrum by relying on the rulers' personal name glyphs that appeared in the Mexican codices he knew and collected.[17] This was a stroke of genius. However fancifully the artists whom Sigüenza commissioned, José Rodríguez Carnero and Antonio de Alvarado, might have rendered the painted effigies of the vanished Mexica lords, Sigüenza (p. 53) instructed them to employ the traditional name glyphs. In this way he assured that there would be some measure of visual historical accuracy at the same time as he honoured current, highly interpretive Baroque literary practice with its passion for symbolic representation.

This was not a self-evident solution, and Sigüenza took pains to justify his actions. He (p. 49) explained that if the merit that deserved to be immortalized in painting was the incomparable grandeur of one's princely actions, as Pliny [the Elder] had declared, and if the emblem or hieroglyphic chosen to represent it was extracted either from the most notable actions of that personage's life, the name of the respective Emperor, or *the means by which the ancient Mexicans signified them in their paintings*, then he, Sigüenza — having read the authorities on the subject of emblems, from Alciato to Kircher, and being aware of the strict laws governing their generic structure — would attend more to the subtle explanation of the hieroglyphs' meanings than to the rules for structuring them.[18] Taking up their works on the role of emblematic signification, Sigüenza cited the opinions of Farnese as well as Kircher. Although, Sigüenza (pp. 50–51) insisted, he could have pursued more elaborate forms of signification, he judged it best 'not to abandon' emblems and hieroglyphs, remembering Farnese's dictum in *De simulacro reipublicae*: 'Just as rivers empty into the sea, hieroglyphics by their artfulness open out onto wisdom, with virtue and knowledge being their purpose'.[19]

Sigüenza's bold move was to present images of the Mexica lords where the Habsburg kings might have appeared, and Sigüenza's early Jesuit training undoubtedly gave him confidence on this point. Paz remarked that the Jesuits offered Mexican creoles like Sigüenza a syncretism whose spiritual and intellectual core was an openness to the discovery of universal and supernatural truths and that the Jesuits' experimental pursuit of worldwide unification, combined with nascent creole patriotism in New Spain, not only modified traditional attitudes toward pre-Columbian Amerindian civilizations but also stimulated the resurrection of their respective pasts.[20] Sigüenza would have been schooled in that trend and later practised it independently, after he was expelled from the Society of Jesus.[21]

What, specifically, were the 'tools' from the Jesuit 'tool kit', that is, the *Ratio atque institutio studiorum Societatis Jesu* [Method and System of the Studies of the Society of Jesus] of 1599, that Sigüenza brought to life in his triumphal arch? The *Ratio*'s 'Rules of the Teacher of Rhetoric' as well as the instructions for teachers of the humanities and advanced work in Greek and Latin are pertinent. The technique called 'prelection' was the preferred method of teaching. The prelection was an intense, ten-to-fifteen minute oral presentation by a teacher during which his students were to concentrate on the lesson given, following the exposition closely without taking notes. Demanding close collaboration between teacher and student, it was a method that aimed to 'create the mental situation and stimulate the imminent activity of the student' as well as to train the teacher to present the lesson effectively, whether or not he was pedagogically inspired.[22] When used for teaching advanced Greek and Latin, the prelection concentrated on perfecting the students' vocabulary and syntax; when employed for the subjects of rhetoric and humanities, it focused on the students' development of ideas and their expression.[23] The classes on rhetoric in particular were devoted to teaching the refinement of style and the use of erudition, which was based on the study of historical events, ethnological descriptions, authoritative views of earlier scholars, and general sources of knowledge, all of which were to be employed sparingly, in accordance with the capacity of the students.[24] For Tomás de la Cerda's 1680 installation as viceroy, Sigüenza utilized historical and ethnological materials, as unexpected as these particular ones might have been; if for the inaugural occasion the painted display of Mexica rulers and live performance by allegorical Mexico sufficed, in *Teatro* Sigüenza provided lengthy, learned explanations (justifications) of his controversial choices.

The *Ratio* also stressed the importance of composing prose and verse at every stage of a Jesuit's education, and it encouraged especially the students' creation of emblems and enigmas by periodically posting the best of the students' work so that their peers could admire and learn from them.[25] The composition of poems was part of the curriculum from the earliest to the most advanced stages of study, and the analysis of poetry included the task of creating a versified text and recasting it in different poetic genres.[26] This was a lesson Sigüenza seems to have learned well. He worked in a variety of poetic forms and, although small in number, their configurations into various thematic patterns suggest that they were chosen with purposeful intent.

Alongside (and beyond) Jesuit principles of the interpretation of human history and its universalism, Sigüenza's academic disciplines were mathematics and astronomy. He was the second chaired professor (catedrático) of mathematics and astrology/astronomy to be appointed at the viceregal capital's Real y Pontificia Universidad de México.[27] In my view, his professional labours in mathematics and astronomy were central to his investigations in ancient Mexican history. In concert, the disciplinary tools of astronomy, Mexican calendar calculations, and chronology enabled him to conceive the ancient Mexican past as historical, as measured in chronological time, not mythical in the sense of the fabulous. This was his strongest suit; with his deep reliance on chronology and sequence, he privileged history over myth, historiography over mythology. His contribution to Mexica history was credible and, even a century after his death, his studies were acknowledged to be essential to further progress in the field.[28]

The relationship between history and mythology in the Baroque period, however, was not dichotomous. We will see that figural interpretation built a significant bridge between them. As Erich Auerbach observed in his imperishable essay 'Figura' (1944), the basic view was that the Old Testament, 'both as a whole and in its most important details', was a concrete historical prefiguration of the Gospel that became a firmly rooted tradition from the fourth century on, thanks to the influence of Saint Augustine who 'favoured a living, figural interpretation, for his thinking was far too concrete and historical to content itself with pure abstract allegory'.[29] As we will see in 'Neptune, Figural Foreshadower', Sigüenza and Sor Juana followed Renaissance mythographers who applied figural relationships not only to Scripture but also to classical mythology.

If mathematics and astronomy constituted Sigüenza's academic vocation (and his creation of yearly almanacs was its commissioned but not relished adjunct), poetry was his lifelong avocation. Writing poetry, the practice of which was no doubt fomented by his Jesuit training, was his most enduring humanistic effort, starting with his sacred-historical poem [poema sacro-histórico] *Primavera indiana* [Indian Spring] (1668) on the miracle of the appearance of the Virgin of Tepeyac (the Virgin of Guadalupe). Composed at the age of seventeen or eighteen, when he was studying at the Jesuit novitiate house in Tepotzotlán, the poem's seventy-nine octavas reales marked the beginning of his poetic avocation that was concluded with his *Oriental planeta evangélico: Epopeya sacro panegírica al apóstol grande de las Indias san Francisco Javier* [Oriental Evangelical Planet: Sacred Epic Panegyric to the Great Apostol of the Indies Saint Francis Xavier] (1700). Recognizing Sigüenza's early Jesuit training and his lifelong devotion to poetry, we are better prepared to appreciate the seriousness with which he approached its composition for the viceroy's inauguration in 1680 and also the role that he hoped those poems would have in it.

The Viceregal Couple, The Mexica Lords

To turn briefly to the performative event at hand: Sigüenza features the vicereine, Dona María Luisa Manrique de Lara y Gonzaga, Condesa de Paredes, Marquesa de la Laguna, as well as the viceroy, referring repeatedly to the two of them together as 'los dos excelentíssimos consortes', 'los excelentíssimos señores virreyes', 'siendo luminares grandes nuestros excelentíssimos príncipes' [the two most excellent consorts; the most excellent lord and lady, viceroy and vicereine; being great luminaries, our excellent prince and princess] (pp. 55–57, 59). As the viceroy and vicereine faced the northern façade of Sigüenza's arch, they would have seen medallion portraits of themselves, painted from life ('retratos al vivo'), being held by the figures of Mercury and Venus, who were depicted as flying among the clouds, painted 'as antiquity had described them'. Calling Góngora 'el Píndaro andaluz' [the Andalusian Pindar], Sigüenza (p. 59) quotes his kinsman's verses to honour the vicereine under the emblem of love.[30]

The Marqueses de la Laguna also would have seen, perched atop the arch, the already-mentioned 'Ciudad de México representada en una india' [City of Mexico represented by a young Indian woman] (p. 55). Such use of live actors was not unusual, as the painting by the creole artist and architect Melchor Pérez Holguín (c. 1660–after 1724), 'Entrada del arzobispo virrey Morcillo en Potosí' (The Entrance of the Archbishop Viceroy Morcillo in Potosí) (1716), suggests.[31] Below Mexico's perch the viceregal couple also would have noticed the Latin inscription that appeared on a large shield over the central archway, welcoming Don Tomás de la Cerda as 'padre de la patria' [father of the homeland] and anticipating the worthiness of his impending governorship by citing the citizenry's expectation that he would consult with them, honourably and generously, on each and every matter (pp. 51–52). The inscription announces that the arch is illustrated with the portraits of the emperors of the ancient Mexican nation, and that it is offered, as time and effort have allowed, by the city of Mexico on the thirtieth day of November, on the three hundred and fifty-third year since the (Mexica) founding of Mexico (Sigüenza here has in mind the year 1327; he was remarkably close to the date of 1325, commonly cited today).

To turn again to the explanatory text of *Teatro*: having made arguments earlier to justify the pictorial representation of the Mexica lords (see 'Sigüenza's *Teatro*', above), he now argues for honouring them with poetry, including references to Scripture. First, he declares, if offering poems of praise was acceptable among the ancients, why not for him? Had not some of the ancient Sophists, as Tertullian (today often called the 'father of Latin Christianity') pointed out, sipped from the fountain of the prophets? Second, knowing all that Tertullian wrote, why would it not be proper for Sigüenza to dignify human letters with the divine? Third, since hieroglyphics, emblems and symbols were, as both Kircher and Beyerlinck had observed, 'artefactos animados' [animated artefacts] whose material bodies were the paintings to which their epigraphs gave life, why should Sigüenza not also inform or adorn his emblems with 'el espíritu de sagrados hemistichios' [the spirit of sacred hemistiches] (pp. 59–61), as so many learned authors had done?

Fourth and finally, it was his goal to provide the Marquis with a display of political virtues that could serve as his ethical guide. Plutarch had advised his readers, as if in a mirror, to compare and adorn their own lives by contemplating the virtues of others. Did this not include those subjects who lacked the true light of divine knowledge, but who nevertheless cultivated virtue and created writings whose 'floridas voces' [virtue-filled voices], much improved by Holy Scripture, instructed later generations? All the books of Holy Scripture could be called 'flores' [flowers], because they encouraged their readers to flourish like flowers, that is, with virtue.[32] So, concludes Sigüenza (pp. 61–62), just like a bee, he has chosen from this cultivated field the essential judgments and declarations from which he has formed a 'panal de perfecciones' [a honeycomb of perfections]. If, he adds in warning, it is an error to follow this practice, he would rather err with the lessons that the great masters have taught him through his readings than confirm the assertions that vicious and ill-informed critics ('zoilos') in their fantasies claimed to be true.[33] Citing one of the canons of Pope Hadrian VI, declaring that anyone who defames another without proof should be flogged, this direct, defiant warning suggests that Preludio II was to have been Sigüenza's concluding prefatory statement.

As Sigüenza (pp. 122–23) informed his readers, all his poems had as their purpose the explanation of the pictorial rendering and principal meanings of moral and political virtue with which he interpreted them. Aware that the Mexica name glyphs he featured would be as unintelligible to the ordinary viewer as to the learned reader, he created short poems to connect the glyphs to his desired meaning for the event's spectators and now, for *Teatro*'s readers, he buttressed the poems with assemblages of quotations from ancient and modern classical and Christian authorities. He began with the rulers' personal name glyphs, and on the basis of his knowledge of the chronology and sequence of each ruler's historical reign, selected a moral (and political) virtue to serve as the glyph's signification (the three exceptions to Sigüenza's use of onomastic Mexica glyphs are the symbols for Huitzilopochtli, Cuitláhuac and Cuauhtémoc, because they were outside the traditional Mexica pantheon). Sigüenza's extraordinary achievement was to articulate Mexican iconography and history with Castilian prosody and Western learning, drawing together Mexican pictorial images (the Mexica glyphs), their traditional signification (within Mexica history), poetic epigrams of his own composition, classical mottos, and Scriptural passages with their respective iconographies, all for the purpose of producing new configurations of meaning.

To synthesize the pertinent information about the emblems in Sigüenza's multi-dimensional, ekphrastic *Teatro*, I have created a Table ('Sigüenza's Baroque Display of the Mexica Dynasty') that takes account of the complex articulation of pictorial (Mexica or Western) images, poetic tributes in Castilian meter, and prose discussions of the virtues represented:[34]

To wed the Mexica icon and the Greek or Roman marker with the abstract classical virtue, Sigüenza created an epigram (in its generic meaning of brief explanation) for each of his twelve Mexica lords, and to do so in verse, he employed three poetic forms: the epigrama, the octava real and the décima.[35] He created epigramas for four key figures in his pantheon: the prophet and guide Huitzilopochtli, the fifth Aztec prince (the first Motecuhzoma, Motecuhzoma Ilhuicamina), and the two post-conquest rulers, Cuitláhuac and Cuauhtémoc. To each portrait he attributes a decidedly spiritual dimension: we discover that the epigrama signals actions that Sigüenza characterized as being founded on trust in supernatural powers (Huitzilopochtli), religious piety (Motecuhzoma Ilhuicamina), and a transcendent belief in the unbreakable human spirit (Cuitláhuac, Cuauhtémoc). I attribute a further unifying thematic principle to Sigüenza's choice of the epigrama: he employs it to chart and commemorate his version of (nothing less than) the origin, apogee and fall of the Mexica dynasty. Sigüenza created octavas reales for those rulers to whom

Mexica Lord	Mexica Glyph and/or Baroque portrait painting	Virtue	Castilian verse form
Huitzilopochtli	Left arm holding torch and flowering branch with bird	Reverence for divinity	Epigrama
Acamapichtli	A hand holding reeds	Hope	Octava
Huitzilihuitl	Hummingbird's head	Clemency	Octava
Chimalpopoca	Smoking shield	Self-sacrifice for the homeland	Octava
Itzcoatl	Serpent with back studded with blades of obsidian	Prudence	Décima
Motecuhzoma Ilhuicamina	Diadem	Piety	Epigrama
Axayacatl	'Water face' (profile of man's head with water streaming in front of it). Portrait painting of Axayacatl, with globe on his shoulders, standing atop a column	Fortitude	Décima
Tizoc	Rock punctured by pointed instrument or leg pierced by an arrow	Peace	Octava
Ahuitzotl	Aquatic, marsh-dwelling rodent with stream of water flowing down its back	Wise counsel	Décima
Motecuhzoma Xoyocotzin	Diadem, also a portrait painting of Motecuhzoma atop a column, richly dressed, pulling riches from the mouth of a lion	Magnanimity	Décima
Cuitláhuac	Portrait painting of Cuitláhuac wearing toga on which hands are printed to allude to the breaking of the Gordian knot	Magnanimity and boldness of defence of the *patria* under adversity	Epigrama
Cuauhtémoc	Portrait painting of Cuauh-témoc standing atop a column	Constancy, perseverance; unbreakable spirit	Epigrama

TABLE 1.1. Sigüenza's Baroque Display of the Mexica Dynasty

he attributed the exercise of the solemn virtues of hope (Acamapichtli [first ruler, in traditional Mexica chronologies]), clemency and gentleness in the formation of laws (Huitzilihuitl [second ruler]), sacrifice for the homeland (Chimalpopoca [third ruler]), and the virtue of peace (Tizoc [seventh ruler]). We can perceive the unifying principle of Sigüenza's octavas reales to be the Mexica creation of civil and social order (the first three rulers) and the enduring value of its peace (the seventh).

Sigüenza composed décimas for the emperors whom he characterized as exercising prudence (Itzcoatl [fourth ruler]), fortitude or courage (Axayacatzin [sixth ruler]), the importance of taking wise counsel (Ahuitzotl [eighth ruler]), and magnanimity or generosity (the second Motecuhzoma, Motecuhzoma Xocoytzin [ninth and final pre-Spanish-conquest Mexica ruler]). Citing prudence as the 'principal virtue' and the 'aggregate of all the others', Sigüenza (p. 102) signals the value he places on this virtue by inaugurating his use of the décima for its exemplar, the fourth Mexica ruler, Itzcoatl, and follows it up by celebrating other civic virtues among his successors. Taken together, we see that Sigüenza's 'quartet' of décimas constitutes a mini-*florilegium* whose wisdom is presented appropriately in the third-person voice in contrast to the first-person octava and epigrama in which Sigüenza's other Mexica rulers 'speak'.

Remarkably, Sigüenza creates, through the use of these three poetic forms, a still larger *florilegium* consisting of three 'bouquets' centred on series of carefully related themes: the mythical-historical origins and historical endings of the Mexica dynasty (the epigrama); the foundations of the Mexica civil order and its achievement of peace (the octava real); and the Mexica exercise of time-honoured principles of governance and statecraft (the décima). We now turn to Huitzilopochtli, which is the most crucial and most controversial of Sigüenza's arch-to-*Teatro* portraits.

Huitzilopochtli, Mexican Moses

On casting Huitzilopochtli as the 'caudillo y conductor' [leader and guide] (p. 67) who led the Mexica peregrination from Aztlán to Anáhuac, Sigüenza argued that Huitzilopochtli's followers and subsequent generations venerated him as a god only after his death because they did not know how to repay him except through apotheosis. Sigüenza here follows the hermeneutical tradition of 'euhemerism, the ultimate source of which was Euhemerus (*c.* 300 BC), a Greek mythographer who theorized that the ancient gods were actually heroic human beings who, at some point in the past, had been elevated to the status of gods by the gratitude of successive generations who venerated them.[36]

To characterize the personage of Huitzilopochtli, as well as the nine preconquest dynastic rulers, Sigüenza submits their names to philological analysis. The name Huitzilopochtli, Sigüenza (p. 68) tells us, was derived from '*huitzilín*', the little bird called flower-sucker [chupa-flores], the *colibrí*, that is, the hummingbird, and 'tlahuipochtli', or necromancer. Citing Fray Antonio de la Calancha's history of the Augustinian order in Peru, Sigüenza (p. 68) insists that the term means neither sorcerer nor shaman but rather an individual who produces wonders, a maker of marvels or portents and, instead of 'pochtli', he proposes 'o̱pochtli', meaning the left hand. Sigüenza (p. 69) tells us that Huitzilopochtli led his people by following the song of a bird that took them from their birthplace in Aztlán to their destination: the site of Tenochtitlan in Anáhuac (Mexico's Central Valley).[37]

Sigüenza chose his representation of Huitzilopochtli carefully and, as we will see, he implicitly threads through his account the sagas of the Old Testament patriarchs Abraham and Moses. The valorous Huitzilopochtli, Sigüenza (69–70) noted, was often dressed in the costume of the ancient Chichimecas, and he revealed what he saw in the clouds and exhorted his people to undertake the journey from Aztlán, proposing to them a goal and reward in the words of Genesis, *Ingentem magnam* [I will make of you a great people]. This motto is taken from the account of God's covenant with Abraham.[38] The image of Huitzilopochtli that Sigüenza (p. 69) commissioned for his arch was a left arm coming forth out of the clouds, grasping a lighted torch and accompanied by a flowering branch on which a bird rested; he chose the motto 'Ducente deo' [God is my guide] from Virgil, *Aeneid* II.

Sigüenza (pp. 70–71) had requested the left (not right) arm to be painted, he wrote, not so much because it suggested the name of this remarkable leader but because it conveyed the symbol's recondite and mysterious meanings: the torch held by the left hand was not only a symbol expressive of divinity (he gives the example of the Persians, venerating the fires of their daily hearth as a sign of divinity) but also inferred from it the 'apellido también de nuestro Dios verdadero' [a name of our true God]: 'Dominus Deus tuus ignis consumens est' [The lord God of yours is a consuming fire], he added, citing Deuteronomy 4. 24. Significantly, this declaration comes straight from one of Moses's final speeches to the Israelites before his death in sight of the Promised Land.

Leaving implicit this allusion to Moses in his reference to Huitzilopochtli, Sigüenza (p. 71) asserts that even in pagan times the plumes of fire that fell to the left side of its source augured that great events would follow (he has in mind the creation of the Mexica empire). Von Kügelen has suggested some European emblematic sources (Juan de Horozco y Covarrubias, Joachim Camerarius, Georgette de Montenay) that may have inspired Sigüenza to use the familiar motif of a celestial hand reaching down through the clouds.[39] If so, Sigüenza skilfully drew together a familiar Western icon (typically featuring a right hand) and a Mexican motif, the latter consisting of the left hand (*opochtli*) and the *huitzilín*, both associated with his representation of Huitzilopochtli. At all events, the *colibrí* plumes typically forming the headdress of Huitzilopochtli's engraved images or costumed reenactors suggest that the viewers of the arch would have known that the bird perched on Sigüenza's emblem's flowering branch represented Huitzilopochtli.[40]

The explanation Sigüenza gives of the emblem's meaning in *Teatro* is one thing, but conveying its intended message in the public spectacle was another. In particular, Sigüenza had the task of conveying that Huitzilopochtli was guided by God, not Satan. This was the role of the *epigrama*, compactly presented in two stanzas of four eight-syllable verses:

> Acciones de fe constante
> que obra el príncipe jamás

> se pueden quedar atrás
> en teniendo a Dios delante.
>
> Los efectos lo confiesan
> con justas demostraciones,
> pues no tuercen las acciones,
> que solo a Dios se enderezan. (p. 70)

[The worthy actions of the prince can never be lacking or left behind if God is in the lead. The results are revealed through just demonstrations, because only actions directed to God do not go awry].

Sigüenza (pp. 73–74) concludes his discussion of Huitzilopochtli by citing authorities from Lucius Apuleius ('Apuleyo') to Aristotle to Paul's letter to the Romans to Solomon's Proverbs and, via his favoured authority Farnese, 'Varron' (Marcus Terentius Varro, 116–27 BC), specifically Varro's chronology of Roman consuls on the governance of the Roman Republic: 'Quotiescumque Senatum Magistratus coegisset nulla causa tam praepropera erat, quin primae partes divino cultui darentur' [As many times as the magistrate pressured the Senate, nothing required action so urgently that the Senate did not first pay homage to the divine].[41]

In the epigrama and *Teatro*'s argumentation, Sigüenza claims for Huitzilopochtli a divinely inspired orientation. The references to Abraham and Moses are indirect but clear: Huitzilopochtli, like Abraham, acted on a divine promise; like Moses, he leads, but he does not rule, bringing the Mexicas only to the threshold of the promised land of Anáhuac. Sigüenza's treatment of each of the nine Mexica rulers, plus their two post-conquest successors, follows the same pattern of convergence between Mexican and European images and ideas.[42] Too extensive to take up here, we now move 'fast forward', from the contemplation of the northern façade of Sigüenza's commemorative arch to its southern side.

The Mexica Lords' Zodiacal Light

Sigüenza (pp. 140–43) pauses in his narration of events to describe the southern façade of his arch. Its contents displayed a condensed 'summary' of what the northern façade had presented. It consisted of a final painting ('este último lienzo') and a sonnet that he describes as prophetic (Sigüenza, pp. 141, 142). On this final canvas appear the insignias that have served as the emblems of the twelve Mexica lords (see Table 1). These icons emit rays of light that terminate in a cornucopia which the viceroy, pictured seated on a Mexican eagle that serves as his throne, is emptying over a landscape of the city of Mexico. Thus seated high among beautiful clouds in this painting, the viceroy is accompanied by the motto is 'De sursum est' [He is elevated] as well as the declaration: 'Et quae divisa beatos efficient, collecta tenes' [All that which has been given individually to the blessed is brought together in you] (p. 141).[43] In his right hand the viceroy holds the ancient arms of the city, that is, the Mexican prickly pear cactus (*nopal*).

But the light of the Mexica princes still shines, and to emphasize their sustained luminescence, Sigüenza (pp. 142–43) accompanies this tableau with the aforementioned 'prophetic' sonnet addressed to the viceroy. Here Sigüenza introduces the metaphor of light, which will be the persistent image throughout the panegyric. I call this light, as it pertains to the Mexica lords, 'zodiacal'; 'zodiacal light' is not the powerful, generative light of a sun but is known as a diffuse glow commonly seen in the west after twilight and in the east before dawn. Sigüenza presents the twelve crowned heads of Mexico as constituting a Zodiac:

> De las coronas doce poderosas,
> que fueron de Occidente honor temido,
> si ya no a su Zodíaco lucido
> de imágenes sirvieron luminosas,
>   al círculo que forman misteriosas
> faltaba el centro, a tanta luz debido,
> hasta que en ti, señor esclarecido,
> lo hallaron tantas líneas generosas.
>   Goza, príncipe excelso, ese eminente
> compendio de virtudes soberanas,
> pues las regias divisas del Occidente,
>   que a tanto rey sirvieron mexicano
> de dilatados triunfos en la frente
> son abreviadas glorias de tu mano.

[Of the twelve crowned heads who were the feared 'honour of the Occident', if they no longer serve to illuminate their Zodiac, they still form a circle which, lacking an illuminated centre, is now being filled by you, illustrious lord. Enjoy, lofty prince, the compendium of the sovereign virtues of those lords whose brows were graced with the royal insignia of the Occident; these are the virtues, the abbreviated glories that you, as viceroy, now hold in your hand].

Here appears another formulation of Sigüenza's dynasty of twelve lords: The order of the past, having lost its centre (its sovereign rulers), has disappeared, and it will now be occupied by a new centre or sun (the viceroy). Nevertheless, the virtues of that Zodiac still glow, still project their 'zodiacal light', which is the enduring legacy of the Mexica lords' virtues, whose 'abbreviated glories' the viceroy now holds in his hand.

As we contemplate these verses and acknowledge the enormous discrepancy between the colonial world of every day and this exalted visual and verbal rhetoric, we ask, with Paz, if its artistic practitioners were sincere, if they took their assertions at face value.[44] Paz's answer is both affirmative and negative: 'no' because they did not take literally such correspondences, but 'yes', Paz argues, inasmuch as such hyperbolic expressions seemed 'natural' in their era. I agree with that assessment; Sigüenza and Sor Juana did not take such hyperbole literally, while those who could not see through its 'transparent disguises' probably did. At the same time, in the realm of poetic signification and the attendant desire to believe in the integrated harmonies of the divine, social and natural orders, such articulations must have held hopeful symbolic value. Sigüenza's prophetic sonnet is a clear expression of such (barely hopeful) hope.

Sigüenza now moves to wrap up his exposition: 'De esta manera salí (como pude) del empeño en que me puso mi patria en ocasión tan grande' [With these actions

I discharged the duty to which my *patria* obliged me on that so great occasion] (p. 143). In doing so, he cites Barthelemy de Chasseneux's ('Casaneo') *Catalogus gloriae mundi* [Catalogue of the Glories of the World] (1529) to the effect that the perfect tribute is the one that describes the origins of things, narrates events of the present, and presages those of the future.[45] This harks back to Sigüenza's (p. 102) discussion of prudence, in reference to the Mexica ruler Itzcoatl, as the principal virtue, and the prognosticating sonnet that places the responsibility for the enduring legacy of the Mexica lords' 'zodiacal light' emphatically in the viceroy's hands. The full weight of his new responsibilities, previewed in the sonnet, will be elaborated in the panegyric.

Sigüenza (p. 143) makes a final, unexpected observation to his readers, the relevance of which will become obvious in 'Neptune, Figural Foreshadower'. Although in Preludio II (pp. 12–22) he had given well-argued and authoritative reasons for refusing to rely on fables, moral tales, or parables, he now seems to do an 'about-face'. Although he (p. 143) reiterates his conviction that it is a great crime [crimen enorme] to intersperse 'disguised truths' with lies, he closes *Teatro* proper with a Latin citation from *Commentaria in Pentateuchum* [Commentary on the Pentateuch of Moses] (Lisbon, 1556–58) by the Portuguese Dominican friar and Inquisitor Jerónimo de Azambuja (*c.* 1505–1563), who was known as Oleaster [Oleastro] (pp. 143–44).[46] Wondering why the holy prophets spoke in parables and made up imaginary comparisons [semejanzas], especially when they addressed kings and princes, and also querying why Christ spoke in parables to the multitudes, Azambuja determined that, since not only the general populace but also kings and princes looked upon truth with suspicion while gladly giving credence to lies, and because it was necessary for all people to hear the naked truth, the saints wrapped it up in parables — 'veils of lies' — so that, at the very least, the truth would be heard (even if not accepted or understood).[47] On this note, the surprised reader of *Teatro* forges ahead to the long-awaited panegyric, which Sigüenza presents as a re-enactment.

Mexico Personified and her Panegyric

We return to the live performance: now the doors of the archway open, and we join the viceroy and the vicereine as they pass through it. They have now either turned to view its southern façade — which Sigüenza has just now described to us — or they are standing in front of it, facing the assembled citizenry to receive its welcome and listen to young Mexico's recitation of the panegyric. High above them 'among the clouds' [entre unas nubes] and standing at the apex of the arch, the young woman allegorically representing Mexico would have turned around on her perch overlooking the northern façade of the arch and walked some ten or eleven feet to preside over its southern face.[48]

Dressed in simple, traditional garb and wearing a 'corona murada' [an encircling crown], she teeters high above the crowd and 'rests' (probably holding on for support!) against (a simulacrum of?) a prickly pear cactus (*nopal*) that serves, as we know, as the original royal insignia of the city (p. 144). All those viewing this spectacle, as Sigüenza (p. 55) had written, were aware that this was the archway of the Mexican kings and emperors and, knowing that the flower of the prickly pear was shaped like a crown, were not surprised when they saw the accompanying motto, a quotation from Virgil's third eclogue, 'Inscripti nomina regum nascuntur flores' [The flowers come forth with the names of kings inscribed on them].[49] As he recalls events as though they were now taking place, Sigüenza (p. 144) offers, on the authority of Chasseneux [Casaneo], the reminder to the assembled throng that, upon a new governor's entry into some celebrated city or provincial capital, its citizens should listen to and ratify with respect the praises sung to him.[50]

Lovely Mexico now prepares to recite the seventeen-stanza panegyric to the viceroy. As she takes a deep breath before beginning, we pause to recall that the public events featuring panegyrics were those that were formally staged for the benefit of their aristocratic honourees and that, as a result, excessive, exorbitant praise was the norm in such orations; they 'were often little more than a declaration of active loyalty to the regime in power', not the 'gratuitous action of an enthusiastic citizen'.[51] The poet's challenge was to show how excessive such praise could be while still remaining within the bounds of decorum and restraint. This was surely Sigüenza's aim, and Sor Juana would comment on it (see 'Sor Juana's "Sweet, sonorous Mexican swans"'), just as Sigüenza would remark on *Neptuno alegórico* (see 'Neptune, Figural Foreshadower'). Young Mexico's recitation of the panegyric concludes the formal theatrics of the public event, and its text, accordingly, appears last in *Teatro*. This means that to the viewers of the live performance, as to the readers of the printed memoir, the viceroy's formal entry is the dominant theme (stanzas one to ten, thirteen to sixteen) but near its end (stanzas eleven and twelve), as we will see, the Mexica rulers come into view. Along the way (stanza five) there is a small amusement.

Allegorical Mexico now recites Sigüenza's panegyric, which is staged as a dramatic declaration; I paraphrase its contents here:[52] Mexico begins by feigning surprise when the viceroy appears. 'What! Who? Oh, what effort! Oh, what great glory!' She proclaims that the peace and silence of Mexico have been broken but happily, by 'clauses of love' — a 'contract' of love, we might say — that is, the viceroy's royal appointment. She mentions the benefits that the sacred, purple imperial East offers to the West (in the immediate case, what Rome and Spain bestow on America), one of those gifts being the appointment of the new viceroy who brings to the city the abundance of his great, not fleeting light.[53] In the second stanza Mexico confesses to being timid before the viceroy, but then asks herself why she should be so, since he has come here to favour her: 'But you here, my lord? My pale timidity stops me in my tracks! What is it that frightens me if the great light of your august presence, which is here to favour me, inflames me, just as a glow is cast on a lesser celestial body by a greater one?' The metaphor of light continues: the lofty light of the viceroy illuminates and inspires the city. The noun 'influjos' contributes to the elaboration of the metaphor, because it speaks to the influence or effect of celestial bodies or stars, suggesting a kind of refracted light emanating from them to illuminate others.[54] Related to the imagery of light in the previous stanza, the viceroy is characterized as a star that casts its light over Mexico. (This verbal image of the viceroy also recalls its counterpart — the Mexica princes — in the southern façade's painting's rays of light, emanating from them and converging on the viceroy and the cornucopia that he empties over the water-surrounded city; it also resonates with the 'prophetic' sonnet's image of the Mexica lords casting their now-diffuse zodiacal light.)

The third stanza addresses the praise to be offered to the viceroy in the successive ones: he will be 'carried' by the 'voice' of the city, which will incline him toward that which is divine. Continuing the metaphor of the previous stanzas, the viceroy, as it were, will be the 'heavenly body' that holds sway over the city, thus occupying an earthly but celestially inspired space. He will be venerated by Mexico, by the Abyssinian, the Scythian, the Greek, and the whole deep sea, to the very ends of the earth.[55] Stanzas 4 and 5 begin with an anaphora, the vocative subject 'tú', initiating the celebration of the Marqués's virtues. In the fifth stanza lively, lovely Mexico narrates the origin of the illustrious Cerda lineage:

> Tú, que de coronados ascendientes,
> que a pesar del imperio del olvido
> brillaron oro en imperiales frentes;
> tú, genial duración has construido;
> tú, en quien las reales púrpuras ardientes
> unión lograron que inmortal ha sido,
> pues la voz de la historia nos acuerda
> que dos coronas penden de una cerda.
> (p. 145 [fifth stanza])

[You, of crowned ancestors on whose imperial foreheads the brilliance of gold shone forth in spite of the force of oblivion; you, who have become in yourself a worthy continuation; you, in whom the ardent royal purples achieved a union that has been immortal inasmuch as — the voice of history reminds us — two crowns are suspended from a single cord.]

Two crowns hanging from a single cord [cerda]? In true Baroque style, this odd image depends on the two meanings of 'cerda' that Sigüenza clearly had in mind: the Marquis's surname Cerda and a literal cord from which objects can be suspended. Period sources made similar associations between this proper name and the common noun. Covarrubias, for example, defined 'cerda' as the term denoting the long hair of horses' or mules' manes and tails, and he also explained that the illustrious surname Cerda was taken by the descendants of the prince, Fernando de la Cerda, who was the son of Alfonso X (r. 1252–84), the Wise, adding that Fernando's surname had its origin in his nickname: he was born with a mole on his back from which hung a long, thick hair like those of horses or mules.[56]

Fernando de la Cerda (1255–1275) was the primogenitor of Alfonso X. After Fernando's premature death, Alfonso named as his heirs his grandsons, the sons of Fernando ('los Infantes de la Cerda'), but the monarch's second son Sancho had himself proclaimed king of Castile and León in 1284, and became known as Sancho IV, el Bravo (r. 1284–95).[57] Since the House of the Cerdas did not produce kings, Sigüenza's mention of two crowns may refer to the two kingdoms of Castile and León, which had been united since 1230, or to his confusion about the Alfonsine succession. But his 'penden de' [hanging from] suggests that Sigüenza may have permitted himself the indulgence of a double entendre. If not by authorial intention but only by readers' inferences (because we have read Covarrubias), there is a slight hint of humour which, in turn, alludes to a phenomenon that was common at the time. Alfonso Méndez Plancarte refers to such instances as 'autoburla de escuela' [the self-parody of a guild or 'school' by its members], to which we will turn in 'Sor Juana's "Sweet, sonorous Mexican swans"'.[58] But let's listen to the rest of Mexico's praiseful performance.

She asks that she be permitted to construct this praise poem if its subject, that is, the new viceroy, is disposed to being drawn forward, to being immortalized in history, and to having his name carried on the wind to the most remote regions of the earth (sixth stanza). Mexico raises her voice to seek assistance from the deity (is it a generalized idea, is it the Christian God?) that is her muse, evoking that muse's rare beauty, which is worthy of adoration, she says, just as the sea adores Venus and as the mountains revere Cynthia (Artemis, Diana) with her bow (seventh stanza). Mexico turns again to the familiar convention of feigning inability to create this praise poem and again evokes that unnamed deity that is the sum of all the graces, revealing in its face an 'entire heaven' [todo un cielo].[59] Mexico knows that her poetic endeavour will fail like a truncated flight; here she evokes Icarus by mentioning a 'vida alada' [winged (airborne) life] that ends in a 'líquida muerte' [liquid death] (eighth stanza).

Yet if her poetic efforts should make her mortal life eternal, and if she receives applause for the 'riesgo tan glorioso' [glorious risk] she is taking, despite the fact that she will suffer mortality's fall, she desires to be consumed [abrasarse] by the viceroy's glorious fame (flame?). Thus, though extinguished, her efforts, now 'difuntos' [stilled], will continue to have life and breath [alientos] (ninth stanza). Because of the viceroy's great glory, Mexico erects this 'trofeo' [trophy], this panegyric; it will never be able to do its honouree justice because it is merely an outline, able only to cast pale reflections or to sound distant echoes of those attributes that in the viceroy himself can be fully observed and admired (tenth stanza).[60]

The eleventh stanza introduces into the panegyric a new theme, that is, the Mexica lords. The 'mármoles de lino' [marbles made of canvas] depict the Mexica rulers (Mexico says 'mis héroes'), who are worthy of veneration [han debido veneración]. She cautions that the canvases displayed on the arch are not flimsy, ephemeral walls constructed of illusory virtues, but that, rather, if polished they can be like mirrors that faithfully reproduce objects divinely inspired; thus the radiance of these Mexica heroes will triumph over the ashes of oblivion (eleventh stanza). Rescued from death by the arch's paintings, these heroes aspire to imitate the light of the viceroy, which is a lasting light that owes its being to the rays emanating from him and that, although he is mortal, will allow his name to live on (twelfth stanza).

On the threshold of concluding her praise poem, Mexico now envisions the viceroy's entrance into the city: its gates open, 'not by violence or need but voluntarily', and the whole city ('mi emporio', Mexico declares) submits itself to the viceroy as a 'víctima suave', that is, like a gentle offering. The city's love, shown also in its obedience, is the key to the gratitude that the hearts of all Mexico's peoples feel toward their new lord (thirteenth stanza). The viceroy is invited to enter the city. Emphasizing the generosity and gratitude of Mexico's citizens, the following three stanzas open with an anaphora, the exhortative 'Entra' [Enter], which purposefully calls attention to the civic rite being carried out, signifying the mutual obligations that existed between the lord and his vassals.[61] The metaphor of light continues; the viceroy is referred to as a star [astro], a light that Mexico, with the 'ocaso denigrado' [defamed defeat] of its reviled pagan past, now reveres.

The Marquis is again invited to come forth, for the heavens already hold a 'constellation of fixed stars' [lucido asterismo], that is, Mexico and, by inference, the Mexican emperors, all awaiting the sovereign genius of the viceroy, who is, nevertheless, a greater star than theirs (fourteenth stanza). For a third time the viceroy is invited to enter, knowing that heaven itself will serve as the 'paper' on which his deeds will be 'written'; for this purpose, the phoenix (the Mexican *quetzal*) will offer the feathered quill pens, and the kingdoms of Spain, the ink. Thus the Marquis's nobility will be immortalized. Heaven will be the enduring 'marble' that, if softly polished, will be bright, displaying the unique achievements of the viceroy which, while being timeless, are also current and modern (fifteenth stanza).

Enjoining the viceroy for a fourth time to enter, Mexico once again invokes the mutual obligations that ideally define the relationship between lord and vassal: she proclaims that the city's commoners as well as the nobles of the viceregal court await him, to take his measure, to see if in him resides the greatness of the empire that 'el Jove Hispano' [Spain's 'Jupiter', the Spanish king] has entrusted to him. The glory of the viceroy will be applauded by all — the learned and the unschooled, the labourer, the friar and the priest — and, being celebrated by all, needs no other admirers or adherents (sixteenth stanza). At the conclusion of this stanza, the voice of Mexico falls silent.

The final stanza is delivered like a stage direction, in the third person. It announces the end of the recitation and offers a prognostication: we are told that the voice — that of beautiful, dutiful Mexico — that sang softly like a melodious [canoro] instrument to the rhythm of the movement of the celestial bodies, was followed by celestial applause. The echoes of this strain have been carried on the wings of the wind to all the domains presided over by the goddesses of sea and land so that Fame, accompanied by her tuneful cithara, can eternally sing the viceroy's praises (seventeenth stanza).[62] Here the live performance, and *Teatro*'s text, draw to a close.

Sor Juana's 'Sweet, sonorous Mexican swans'

In the final stanza of Sigüenza's panegyric, the Latinate 'canoro', typically connoting sweet birdsong, and 'alas', wings, are avian associations that may well have inspired Sor Juana's sonnet, the incipit of which is 'Dulce, canoro cisne mexicano' [Sweet, sonorous Mexican swan].[63] This is the sonnet that appears on the verso of the frontispiece of Sigüenza's separately published *Panegírico*:

> Dulce, canoro cisne mexicano,
> cuya voz, si el estigio lago oyera,
> segunda vez a Eurídice te diera,
> y segunda el delfín te fuera humano;
>   a quien, si el teucro muro, si el tebano,
> el ser en dulces cláusulas debiera,
> ni a aquél el griego incendio consumiera,
> ni a éste postrara alejandrina mano:
>   no el sacro numen con mi voz ofendo,
> ni al que pulsa divino plectro de oro
> agreste avena concordar pretendo;
>   pues, por no profanar tanto decoro,
> mi entendimiento admira lo que entiendo
> y mi fe reverencia lo que ignoro.

[Sweet, melodious Mexican swan | if the Stygian lake [river] had heard your voice, | Eurydice would have been returned [to Orpheus] a second time | and for a second time, the dolphin, with generous kindness, would have saved Arion; | if to the swan's sweet strains, instead to those of Apollo and Amphion, the walls of Troy and Thebes had been erected, Troy would not have been consumed by Greek fire, | nor Thebes humbled by Alexander's hand: | I neither want to offend the sacred spirit of poetry with my voice, | nor do I pretend to equal, with my rustic flute, the one who strums [the lyre] with a golden pick, | thus, to avoid dishonouring such greatness | my mind admires what I understand | and my faith reverences that which is beyond me.]

This poem has been interpreted, on one hand, as being not merely ironic but also biting and vengeful toward Sigüenza and, on the other, as an expression of Sor Juana's ambiguous praise of him.[64]

To me, this sonnet, and more generally the 'back and forth' between Sigüenza and Sor Juana on the subject of their commemorative commissions, is a more subtle engagement; it represents, I argue, a meeting of literary minds. I characterize 'Dulce, canoro cisne mexicano' as an instance of Méndez Plancarte's 'autoburla de escuela'.[65] In their own guild, that is, within their artistic sub-set of the elite society of church and viceregal palace, the poets' hyperbolic expression and flamboyant examples of verbal mastery were no doubt 'inside jokes' that to many auditors and readers were opaque but which to their authors and intended readers were perfectly transparent and, I will wager, much enjoyed. The target in such cases is the poet's craft, not his or her personal character.

The conventionality (and the levity) of Sor Juana's 'Dulce, canoro cisne mexicano' of 1680 can be appreciated by comparing it with her 'Suspende, cantor cisne, el dulce acento' of 1668, created for the dedication of the cathedral of Mexico City in 1667. On that occasion, the poet Diego de Ribera took the literary lead, writing an account of the proceedings.[66] Ribera was praised by Sigüenza in *Triunfo parténico* (1683) as an 'Orfeo numeroso' [an abundantly talented Orpheus] and as a 'singular gloria de nuestra patria' [singular glory of our homeland], and his poetry was the subject of the following sonnet by Sor Juana:

> Suspende, cantor cisne, el dulce acento:
> mira, por ti, al señor que Delfos mira,
> en zampoña trocar la dulce lira
> y hacer a Admeto pastoril concento.
>   Cuanto canto süave, si violento,
> piedras movió, rindió la infernal ira,
> corrido de escucharte, se retira.
> Y al mismo templo agravia tu instrumento:
>   que, aunque no llega a sus columnas cuanto
> edificó la antigua arquitectura,
> cuando tu clara voz sus piedras toca,
>   nada se vio mayor que tu canto;
> y así como le excede tu dulzura,
> mientras más le agrandece, más le apoca.[67]

I follow Alatorre's paraphrase of the sonnet:[68] if Ribera continues to write such wonderfully musical verses, Apollo will have to renounce his lyre to take up the rustic flute and become a shepherd, just as Admeto, the king of Thessaly, was once made to do when punished by Jupiter. Orpheus, whose songs made stones tremble and captivated the gods of Averno will have to retire![69] Our cathedral itself will be put to shame: although superior to the works of Greek and Roman architects, its stones (its 'songs', that is, its art) will not be able to compete with the power and beauty of Ribera's poetic praise.[70] Thus, Sor Juana proclaims, Ribera's verses overshadow or reduce the cathedral's art, even as they enlarge it by celebrating the cathedral's greater glories: 'mientras más le engrandece, más le apoca'.

The apparent antithesis contained in this final verse of 'Suspende, cantor cisne, el dulce acento' anticipates the contrast she draws between ignorance and understanding of the final tercet of 'Dulce, canoro cisne mexicano'. There we read 'mi entendimiento admira lo que entiendo | y mi fe reverencia lo que ignoro'; Sor Juana tells us that her mind registers what she understands but takes on faith that which she does not. This final tercet is often interpreted to mean that Sor Juana rejected Sigüenza's Neptune myth-into-history argument, finding it to be preposterous. (On its face, this assertion assumes that she would have read Sigüenza's *Teatro* when she read the panegyric, but this is not necessarily the case.) In any event, Sigüenza's claim about Neptune is no more preposterous than Sor Juana's transformation of the Roman sea god into the prefiguration of the Marqués, and she would have been the first to recognize that fact. (Both Sigüenza and Sor Juana subscribed to the theory of figural interpretation, to which I will return.)

Additionally, it is a stretch to suppose that Sor Juana brought up in this final tercet a topic that she had not addressed in the previous eleven verses. Her topic in 'Dulce, canoro cisne mexicano' has been Sigüenza's poetry, for which she has expressed jocular, extravagant praise, just as she had done earlier for Ribera. With a wink and a nod, she proclaims that to avoid offending the 'sacred spirit of poetry' of Sigüenza's panegyric, she will not attempt to equal it with her own rustic flute ('agreste avena'). Here we recall the one ('zampoña') that, she had assured us, Apollo would be shamed into taking up, forsaking his golden lyre when humbled by Ribera's 'poetic greatness'. The same applies here: It is now she who is 'humbled' by the 'greatness' of Sigüenza's poetry and so holds in 'reverence' its unfathomable character.

But what about the absence of 'Dulce, canoro cisne mexicano' from Sor Juana's later published works? Paz suggests, prudently, that it could have been purposeful or simply an oversight.[71] I agree: we will never know. Like 'Dulce, canoro cisne mexicano', the sonnet honouring Ribera did not make it into *Inundación castálida*, and such editorial decisions suggest that Sor Juana may simply have found that in selecting works to include in her poetic 'flood from the font of the Muses', the merely 'occasional' poems had to be sacrificed. This is a more likely scenario than suggesting that the stern hand of self- or external censorship was at work (we are always too quick, these days, to attribute dark motives to practices that, in their own time, were often simple pragmatic choices).

Did Sigüenza proscribe the publication of 'Dulce, canoro cisne mexicano' in *Teatro*? No, again. Sigüenza refrained from the convention of including any preliminaries (in verse or in prose) by others; his dedication to the viceroy, which occupies the first four unnumbered pages of his quarto-size book, is the only adjunct to the following eighty-eight pages of text.[72] The usually overlooked admonition on the first unnumbered leaf of *Teatro* makes clear Sigüenza's objective: it admonishes the reader to keep one's own faults in mind when trying to assess those of others, 'it being easier to judge others than to hold oneself accountable, and easier, from the security of a fortress, to be unmoved by the dangers befalling others, who are below'.[73] We might think of this epigraph as targeting the vicious, arbitrary critics that Sigüenza called out at the conclusion of Preludio II, but the epigraph's reference to looking down on others from the security of a high fortress suggests that the viceroy is the object of this admonition. He, as the intended reader of this unconventional, controversial 'mirror for princes', is admonished to be generous in his assessment of *Teatro*'s (Mexica) subjects and the efforts of its author. The epigraph underscores Sigüenza's single-minded objective in having *Teatro* printed: to get his work into the hands of the new viceroy as soon as possible after his installation in hopes of receiving some useful professional recognition or appointment from him.[74]

On this point it was clear that Sor Juana's sonnets, 'Dulce, canoro cisne mexicano' and 'Suspende, cantor cisne, el dulce acento', were not intended to curry the favour of higher authorities, as her *Neptuno alegórico* (and Sigüenza's *Teatro*) did. With both sonnets Sor Juana sought instead to 'take a break' from writing commissioned works to relish a few light moments with 'guild members' like Sigüenza and Ribera.[75] In sum, if the challenge to writers of ceremonial panegyrics was to offer praise sufficiently high to satisfy the expectations of their aristocratic honorees but not so high as to seem ridiculous or absurd (or so clever as to be unrecognizable by them), the games played among the virtuoso members of the poets' guild (the 'autoburla de escuela') pulled out all the stops. The display of poetic virtuosity could be as arcane and as witty as the author's talent could make it. Sor Juana was the dean of the guild and its master practitioner; her often-discussed sonnet to Sigüenza, like the one to Ribera that anticipated it, are masterpieces of the genre.

Neptune, Figural Foreshadower

Sigüenza and Sor Juana were united on two fronts: their common use of hyperbolic Baroque literary expression and their adherence to the symbolic doctrines of interpretive prefiguration. Working with the Mexican historiographic tradition, Sigüenza has made Huitzilopochtli the heroic human leader of the migration from Aztlán to Anáhuac. It seems clear that, upon learning about Sor Juana's homage to the Marqués de la Laguna as Neptune, Sigüenza composed his Preludio III (pp. 23–39) that made the Roman sea god the post-diluvian patriarch of the peoples of the Americas. It seems almost certain that he made this move after reading (or at least knowing about) Sor Juana's *Neptuno alegórico*, and that he did so after having completed (he thought) the composition of his prefatory texts as well as the body of *Teatro*.

Taking this premise, we can understand Prelude III in its apparent contradiction to Prelude II and why, at the very end of *Teatro*, that is, in the final utterance Sigüenza makes in his own, authorial voice, he cites Jerónimo de Azambuja, 'Oleaster'. In both cases, he seems to override his earlier (Preludio II) arguments about relying on history instead of myth, but what he actually does is make adjustments so that the case fits the principle to which he adheres. He achieves this in Preludio III by making Neptune the father of the natives of the New World and, at the end of *Teatro*, by citing Azambuja to justify the use of myths and fables in interpreting history and, on the authority of the holy prophets and Christ himself, to justify wrapping truths in 'veils of lies'. It seems to me that Sor Juana provided the stimulus for Sigüenza's reworkings. Here's why:

Both Sigüenza's and Sor Juana's respective accounts of Huitzilopochtli and Neptune call into play the principles and techniques of euhemerism and figural interpretation. Like Sigüenza in *Teatro*, Sor Juana in *Neptuno alegórico* followed the precepts of euhemerism, as she makes clear: 'Las fábulas tienen las más su fundamento en sucesos verdaderos; y los que llamó dioses la gentilidad, fueron realmente príncipes excelentes a quienes por sus raras virtudes atribuyeron divinidad' [Fables generally have their origin in historical events; and those whom antiquity called gods were actually outstanding princes to whom, because of their rare virtues, divinity was attributed].[76]

Sor Juana also explicitly expressed her understanding of the interpretive method of figural interpretation. She declared that it seemed to her that Nature, for the lack of power to do so, did not dare to materialize, even in shadows, anything that divine Providence would bring into the world in its perfect original but that, nevertheless, Providence allowed the mind to form an idea as to how to 'draw or sketch' it, because, although such phenomena could not be produced within the bounds of Nature, the human mind was given the necessary latitude to imagine them.[77] She observed that there was nothing very remarkable, even in Scripture, that had not already been presaged by various 'figures', 'que como en dibujo las representen' [presented as if in outline or sketch], and that this marvellous invention obliged her to seek among the heroes of antiquity the deeds most comparable to the illustrious virtues of the Marquis; she insisted that although she had looked high and low, from the most well-known classical heroes to the most obscure, she found none that even minimally compared with the incomparable talents of the Marqués de la Laguna.[78]

In this hyperbolic mode Sor Juana presents the Marquis not only as the heir to Spanish kings but also to the mythical-historical figure of Saturn, the father of Neptune, to whom she likewise attributes historical as well as mythical antecedents. She cites the *Mythologiae sive explicationum fabularum libri X* [Mythologies, or the explanation of fables in ten books] (1581) of Natale Conti (1520–1582), who was one of the Renaissance mythographers favoured by both Sor Juana and Sigüenza. Sor Juana writes that not only Virgil but also the ancient Greeks believed that Saturn was the first ruler of mortal man. She asserts that Conti affirmed that the Erythraean Sibyl had proclaimed 'Primus mortales inter Saturnus at olim regnavit' [The first one to reign among mortals in ancient times was Saturn].[79] This is the essential picture that Sor Juana paints to honour the new viceroy: even those who prefigured him in ancient times were of mortal origin. Sigüenza picks up the thread and follows suit in *Teatro*, taking up his pen to match or exceed Sor Juana's claims by arguing that Neptune was the origin of all the New World's peoples. He does so in the freshly minted Preludio III and then, at the end of *Teatro*, follows up with a justification, citing Oleaster on the authoritative use of myths and parables in interpreting history (pp. 23–39, 143–44).

What does it mean that, as devoted practitioners of figural interpretation, Sigüenza casts Neptune as the progenitor of the Indians of America, while Sor Juana, more modestly, has Neptune prefigure the Marqués de la Laguna? In Sor Juana's formulation the Marquis would become, on that November day in 1680, the ruler of New Spain. In Sigüenza's presentation, Huitzilopochtli had made possible, long centuries before the arrival of Tomás de la Cerda, the foundation of Anáhuac. If Sor Juana's Neptune prefigured the Marqués, Sigüenza's Neptune turned out to be nothing less than the progenitor of all the native inhabitants of the New World. Here we have a neat correspondence or, rather, a sequence of prefigurations: Sor Juana's prefigural genealogy goes from Neptune to the Marqués, and Sigüenza ups the ante, going from Neptune to Acamapichtli-through-Cuauhtémoc to the Marqués. In this synthetic (syncretic) figural gesture, Sigüenza adds the intermediate missing link to Sor Juana's mythical-historical genealogical chain by introducing into it the ancient lords of Mexico.

In their remarkable 'Baroque contredanse', Sigüenza's Neptune, though introduced belatedly in *Teatro*, prefigures Sor Juana's. This interpretation is made persuasive (and was easily executed) because Sigüenza had already built his entire inaugural commemoration around the pre- and post-Columbian Mexica rulers as models of moral political virtue for the viceroy to follow. Thus the meritorious conduct of the rulers of Anáhuac prefigured, and now prophesy, the new Spanish viceroy's anticipated governance. Together and in sum, Sor Juana and Sigüenza have articulated the traditions of the ancient classical West, the pre-Columbian world of Mexico, and the Spanish creole viceroyalty, creating of them a single overarching, globalizing vision embracing the past, present, and future. In inspiration and execution, the successive 'steps' of their ultimately collaborative work resulted in an artistic, literary apotheosis that transcended the works of each. The 'sweet, sonorous Mexican swans', which were the creation of them both, sang in panegyric and in sonnet their celebratory but not final song.

For Wallace Stevens the poem was 'the cry of its occasion'. In the Baroque festival's public performance in 1680, as well as in Sigüenza's *Teatro* published as the year ended, that 'cry' expressed the occasion's deepest meanings, its deepest hopes. Neither frivolous nor extraneous, the place that poetry occupied in civic spectacle (Stevens' 'part of the res itself and not about it') was fundamental. The fact that Sigüenza and Sor Juana were mutually engaged in one such grand commemoration has offered us a glimpse into the Hispanic Baroque world where the foreshadowing, the anticipation of a larger, more just and ultimate order, though not realized, could be richly imagined.

Notes to Chapter 1

1. Wallace Stevens, *Collected Poetry and Prose* (New York: Library of America, 1997), p. 404.
2. Carlos de Sigüenza y Góngora, *Teatro de virtudes políticas que constituyen a un príncipe* (México: Coordinación de Humanidades UNAM/Miguel Ángel Porrúa, 1986). All parenthetical textual citations of Sigüenza's *Teatro* follow the modern pagination used in this facsimile edition. All translations from Spanish texts to English are my own, including renderings from the Spanish translations of Latin texts, which will be identified as such.
3. Octavio Paz, *Sor Juana o las trampas de la fe* (Mexico City: Fondo de Cultura Económica, 1997), pp. 251–52.
4. Paz, *Sor Juana*, p. 251.
5. Paz, *Sor Juana*, pp. 96–97, presents convincing documentation for the birth date of 1648.
6. Paz, *Sor Juana*, pp. 251–53.
7. Their personal relationship has long been the object of speculation. Paz, *Sor Juana*, pp. 345–46, has suggested that their relationship was probably akin to many whose members lived in a closed society, saw one another with frequency, read the same books, shared intellectual interests, and had the occasional personal or professional spat.
8. Vicente de P. Andrade, *Ensayo bibliográfico mexicano del siglo XVII* (Mexico City: Imprenta del Museo Nacional, 1899), pp. 479–80, identified the pamphlet publication: *Panegyrico con que la muy noble e imperial Ciudad de México aplaudió al Excelentíssimo Señor D. Thomas Antonio Lorenço Manuel de la Cerda [...] al entrar por la triumphal Portada, que erigió con magnificencia a su feliz venida. Y que ideó D. Carlos de Sigüenza y Góngora, Cathedrático de Mathemáticas en la Real Universidad de esta Corte. En México, por la Viuda de Bernardo Calderón. Año de 1680.* José Toribio Medina, *La imprenta en México (1539–1821)*, 8 vols (Santiago de Chile: Impreso en casa del autor, 1907–12), II, 526, noted that the sonnet by Sor Juana appeared, 'as a sign of the regard in which she held the author' on the verso of the frontispiece, and he (II, 416) transcribed the sonnet, citing as his source the early nineteenth-century Mexican bibliographer José Mariano Beristáin de Souza. Francisco de la Maza, 'Sor Juana y don Carlos: explicación de dos sonetos hasta ahora confusos', *Cuadernos Americanos*, 145.2 (1966), 190–204 (p. 199), who examined *Teatro* and 'Dulce, canoro cisne mexicano' in tandem, suggested that Beristáin possessed a manuscript copy of Sor Juana's sonnet.
9. Dr Ken Ward, former Maury A. Bromsen Curator of Latin American Books at the John Carter Brown Library, Providence, Rhode Island, and a specialist in Mexican bibliography, finds Sigüenza's author's mark to be unique among Mexican imprints.
10. Émile Benveniste, *Problems in General Linguistics*, trans. by Mary Elizabeth Meek (Coral Gables, FL: University of Miami, 1971), pp. 201–15.
11. Sigüenza employed the term 'mexicano' to refer to the Mexica, that is, the people who settled Tenochtitlan after their migration from Aztlán; he (p. 69) used the term 'azteca' [Aztec] only

once, to refer to the origin of that migration. See R. H. Barlow, 'Some Remarks on the Term "Aztec Empire"', *The Americas*, 1.3 (1945), 345–49 (pp. 345–46).

12. Sebastián de Covarrubias, *Tesoro de la lengua castellana o española*, ed. by Martín de Riquer (Barcelona: Alta Fulla, 1998), p. 764.

13. I have adopted the conventional modern spellings of the names of Sigüenza's dynastic heroes.

14. Early sources, such as the Codices Aubin and Boturini, the *Historia de los Mexicanos por sus pinturas*, and the *Anales de Quauhtitlan*, treated Huitzilopochtli exclusively as the god of the people of Aztlán (Barlow, 'Some Remarks', p. 345).

15. Sigüenza (p. 48) here cites Góngora's 'Soledad segunda' [Second Solitude]. See Luis de Góngora, *Obras completas*, ed. by Juan Millé y Giménez and Isabel Millé y Giménez (Madrid: Aguilar, 1961), p. 684. Only in *Teatro* does Sigüenza mention his familial relationship to the great Cordovan poet, to whom the creole polymath was a 'sobrino segundo' (in English-language tradition, a 'first cousin once removed'). See Irving A. Leonard, *Don Carlos de Sigüenza y Góngora: un sabio mexicano del siglo XVII*, trans. by Juan José Utrilla (Mexico City: Fondo de Cultura Económica, 1984), pp. 17–18.

16. Notable scholars of Sigüenza's emblems, his triumphal arch, and/or *Teatro* include, among others: Antonio Bonet Correa, José Pascual Buxó, Jaime Cuadriello, Pablo Escalante Gonzalbo, Pablo García Loaeza, Helga von Kügelgen, Antonio Lorente Medina, Sigmund Jádmar Méndez Bañuelos, and Anna More.

17. I first made this argument in 'Aztecs and Allegory: the Baroque in Colonial Mexico' at the international symposium, 'Colonial Intersections: Reconsidering the Historical, the Literary, and the Visual Archives', United States Library of Congress, Washington, DC, 12 October 2012. See Rolena Adorno, 'El México antiguo en el Barroco de Indias: don Carlos de Sigüenza y Góngora', *Anales de Estudios Latinoamericanos*, 35 (2015), 1–42.

18. My emphasis. This is one of *Teatro*'s most difficult (but key) passages; I have paraphrased it here.

19. I translate to English Rojas Garcidueñas's Spanish rendering of Sigüenza's quotation of Farnese's Latin text: 'Pues así como los ríos se arrojan al mar en precipitado e inclinado curso, así los jeroglíficos son arrebatados por su arte, hasta la sabiduría: la virtud y la inteligencia son sus metas'; in Carlos de Sigüenza y Góngora, *Teatro de virtudes políticas*, in *Obras históricas*, ed. by José Rojas Garcidueñas (Mexico City: Editorial Porrúa, 1983), pp. 225–361 (p. 269).

20. Paz, *Sor Juana*, pp. 56–57.

21. See Leonard, *Don Carlos*, pp. 23–24. The reasons for Sigüenza's expulsion have long been a topic of speculation.

22. Allan P. Farrell, SJ (trans. and ed.), *The Jesuit 'Ratio Studiorum' of 1599* (Washington, DC: Conference of Major Superiors of Jesuits, 1970), pp. 127–28, note 58.

23. Farrell (ed. and trans.), *Ratio*, p. 128, note 58.

24. Farrell (ed. and trans.), *Ratio*, pp. 72–73.

25. Nigel Griffin, 'Enigmas, Riddles, and Emblems in Early Jesuit Colleges', in *Mosaics of Meaning: Studies in Portuguese Emblematics*, ed. by Luís Gomes (Glasgow: Glasgow University Press, 2009), pp. 21–39 (pp. 22–23).

26. Farrell (ed. and trans.), *Ratio*, pp. 75, 82.

27. Leonard, *Don Carlos*, pp. 24–26.

28. See Rolena Adorno, 'Carlos de Sigüenza y Góngora (1645–1700): "el amante más fino de nuestra patria"', *Hispanófila*, 171 (2014), 11–27 (p. 22), and Adorno, 'El México antiguo', p. 25.

29. Erich Auerbach, 'Figura', in *Scenes from the Drama of European Literature: Six Essays*, trans. by Ralph Manheim (Gloucester, MA: Peter Smith, 1973), pp. 11–76 (pp. 34, 37, 44).

30. Góngora, *Obras completas*, pp. 578–79. The sonnet that Sigüenza cites was Góngora's tribute in 1606 to Don Francisco de Guzmán y Zúñiga (1564–1607) upon his appointment as viceroy of New Spain; Guzmán died before taking up the post.

31. Housed at the Museo de América, Madrid, the painting features a male reenactor precariously standing on top of the triumphal arch; he wears a plumed headdress and lace-encrusted sleeves and tunic, which was a fairly common eighteenth-century version of royal Inca vestments.

32. I paraphrase Rojas Garcidueñas' Spanish translations of Plutarch and Philip of Harvengt (in

Sigüenza, *Teatro*, p. 279). For the identification of the twelfth-century abbot of the Abbey of Good Hope in Hainault (present-day Belgium), I thank José Cárdenas Bunsen.

33. Zoilo, a grammarian of ancient Alexandria, was a detractor of Homer, Plato, and others; by extension, the term connotes any person who criticizes the works of others with malevolence.

34. To my knowledge, this detailed articulation has not been previously attempted.

35. The epigram, realized as a double redondilla, consisted of two stanzas of four eight-syllable verses in consonant rhyme, *abba cddc*; the octava real was a stanza of eight eleven-syllable verses in consonant rhyme, *ababab cc*, and the décima's stanza was composed of ten eight-syllable verses in the complex consonant rhyme pattern of *abbaaccddc*.

36. See John Daniel Cooke, 'Euhemerism: A Medieval Interpretation of Classical Paganism', *Speculum*, 2.4 (1927), 396–410 (pp. 397, 401–03).

37. The image in Sigüenza's mind was surely the pictorial narration of that migration, contained in the artefact today called 'el mapa de Sigüenza', so named because it had been in Sigüenza's possession at the time of his writing. See María Castañeda de la Paz, *Pintura de la peregrinación de los culhuaque-mexitin (Mapa de Sigüenza): análisis de un documento de origen tenochca* (Zinacantépec, Estado de México: El Colegio Mexiquense, AC, and Conaculta: Instituto Nacional de Antropología e Historia, 2006), p. 24.

38. Helga von Kügelen, 'Carlos de Sigüenza y Góngora, su *Theatro de Virtudes Políticas que constituyen a un príncipe* y la estructuración emblemática de unos tableros en el Arco de Triunfo', in *Juegos de ingenio y agudeza: la pintura emblemática de la Nueva España* (Mexico City: Patronato del Museo Nacional de Arte, AC, 1994), pp. 151–61 (p. 159, note 31), corrects Sigüenza's citation of Genesis as well as the mistranscription 'ingentem' to 'in gentem'.

39. Von Kügelen, 'Carlos de Sigüenza y Góngora', pp. 154–55, 159.

40. See Elizabeth H. Boone, *Incarnations of the Aztec Supernatural: The Image of Huitzilopochtli in Mexico and Europe* (Philadelphia, PA: Transactions of the American Philosophical Society, 1989).

41. 'Cuantas veces el magistrado apremiaba al Senado, nada era tan urgente que no se diera antes el primer lugar al culto divino' (Rojas Garcidueñas in Sigüenza, *Teatro*, p. 290).

42. See also Adorno, 'El México antiguo', pp. 11–20.

43. 'Lo que dividido hace a los bienaventurados, tiéneslo tú reunido' (Rojas Garcidueñas in Sigüenza, *Teatro*, p. 355).

44. Paz, *Sor Juana*, pp. 253–55.

45. I owe the identification of Chasseneux, in Sigüenza's (p. 143) 'Casan, in Cathal. parte I. Consid. 50' and 'Casaneo part I, Consid. 32', to Teodoro Hampe Martínez, 'La biblioteca del arzobispo Hernando Arias de Ugarte', *Thesaurus*, 42.2 (1987), 337–51 (p. 352).

46. Azambuja is thus identified by H. P. Salomon and I. S. D. Sassoon, 'Introduction to the English Edition', in António Jose Saraiva, *The Marrano Factory: The Portuguese Inquisition and its New Christians, 1536–1765*, trans. by H. P. Salomon and I. S. D. Sassoon (Leiden: Brill, 2001), pp. ix–xiv (p. xiii, note 10).

47. I translate the Spanish rendering of Oleaster's Latin text (Rojas Garcidueñas in Sigüenza, *Teatro*, pp. 356–57).

48. The arch soared to a height of ninety feet and had a depth of twelve, from façade to façade (Sigüenza, *Teatro*, p. 42). Measured in 'pies geométricos' [geometric feet], which was the old Roman foot; it was slightly longer than the Castilian linear foot of 28 centimetres.

49. I translate from Rojas Garcidueñas in Sigüenza, *Teatro*, p. 274.

50. I paraphrase Rojas Garcidueñas' translation in Sigüenza, *Teatro*, p. 357.

51. James J. O'Donnell, *Cassiodorus* (Berkeley and Los Angeles: University of California Press, 1979), p. 34.

52. I thank Stephanie Rohner Stornaiuolo for her brilliant analysis of this difficult, often opaque seventeen-stanza panegyric. I follow its modernized transcription by Daniel Torres in Carlos de Sigüenza y Góngora, *'Dulce canoro cisne mexicano': la poesía completa de Carlos de Sigüenza y Góngora*, ed. Daniel Torres (Barcelona: CECAL, 2012), pp. 122-129.

53. '¡Cómo! ¿quién? ¡Oh, qué empeño! Oh, cuánta gloria | con cláusulas de ardor rompe el profundo | alto silencio, en que se ejecutoria [se garantiza] | la paz tranquila que me envidia el mundo. | Piélago de luz es, no transitoria | volante exhalación, cuanto el fecundo | purpúreo

imperio del sagrado Oriente | obsequios tributa a mi Occidente' (Sigüenza, *Teatro*, p. 144 [first stanza]).

54. '¿Pero tú aquí Señor? ¡Qué me suspende | pálida timidez! De qué me asusta | si a influjos de ti mismo más me enciende | la excelsa luz, de tu presencia augusta. | Si hibleas suavidades de ti aprende | cuanto hay del polo hasta la zona adusta, | a tu dictamen deba mi esperanza | de tu culta excelencia la alabanza' (Sigüenza, *Teatro*, pp. 144–45 [second stanza]).

55. 'Llevado así en la voz de mis acentos | ese tu heroico espíritu divino | fueras entre celestes movimientos | genio inmortal al orbe cristalino | mientras entre suavísimos concentos [armonía de voces], | venerando tu nombre el abisino, | el scita, el griego y todo el mar profundo | me atendieran los términos del mundo' (Sigüenza, *Teatro*, p. 145 [third stanza]).

56. Covarrubias, *Tesoro*, pp. 408–09.

57. Jesús P. Martínez, *Historia de España, I: Edades antigua y media* (Madrid: EPESA, 1963), pp. 96–98.

58. Alfonso Méndez Plancarte, 'Notas', in *Obras completas de Sor Juana Inés de la Cruz, I Lírica personal*, ed. by Alfonso Méndez Plancarte (Mexico City: Fondo de Cultura Económica, 1976), pp. 361–617 (p. 559), referred to poetic self-parody in discussing Sor Juana's ovillejo, 'El pintar de Lisarda la belleza'.

59. The implicit, larger question is whether Sigüenza here anticipated a convergence of classical and Scriptural traditions.

60. In this tenth stanza, the panegyric itself is posed as a figural interpretation; I paraphrase the verse: the panegyric is merely an outline, a mere construction, of what eternity has bestowed on you, the viceroy [Cuanto en él [el panegírico] es bosquejo, en ti adelanta | la eternidad que en él [el panegírico] se te construye] (Sigüenza, *Teatro*, p. 146).

61. Mexico's repeated invitation to the viceroy to enter the city emphasizes that passing through the arch (metaphorically, the city's gates) was both a capitulation and a triumph, signalling the mutual obligations between lord and vassal in the earthly order and foreshadowing the anticipated arrival to celestial Jerusalem in the divine; see Jaime Cuadriello, 'Los jeroglíficos de la Nueva España', in *Juegos de ingenio y agudeza: la pintura emblemática de la Nueva España* (Mexico City: Patronato del Museo Nacional de Arte, AC, 1994), pp. 84–113 (p. 101).

62. 'Siguió a esta voz del estrellado asiento | aplauso celestial, que en voz sonora | a compás del celeste movimiento | suave articuló trompa canora: | El eco entero en alas fue del viento | por cuanto Thetis baña y Cinthio dora, | para que tanto aplauso eterna cante | veloz la Fama en cítara sonante' (Sigüenza, *Teatro*, p. 148).

63. Sor Juana Inés de la Cruz, 'Dulce, canoro cisne mexicano', in *Obras completas de Sor Juana Inés de la Cruz, I. Lírica personal*, ed. by Antonio Alatorre (Mexico City: Fondo de Cultura Económica, 2012), p. 446 (poem 204).

64. Maza, 'Sor Juana y don Carlos', p. 199; Alatorre, in Sor Juana, *Obras I*, p. 446.

65. Méndez Plancarte, 'Notas', p. 559.

66. Ribera's *Poética descripción de la pompa plausible que admiró esta nobilísima ciudad de México en la sumptuosa dedicación de su hermoso, magnífico y ya acabado templo, celebrada jueves 22 de diciembre de 1667 años [...] Con licencia: en México por Francisco Rodríguez Lupercio. Año de 1668* is catalogued by Medina (*La imprenta en México*, II, 412), who describes it as including poems of praise for Ribera by Sor Juana and also Sigüenza.

67. Sor Juana, 'Suspende, cantor cisne, el dulce acento', in *Obras I*, ed. Alatorre, p. 444 (poem 202). Sigüenza's remarks are cited by Méndez Plancarte, 'Notas', p. 548.

68. See Alatorre in Sor Juana, *Obras I*, p. 444.

69. Averno, a crater lake in Italy, was for the ancient Romans the threshold to the underworld.

70. Méndez Plancarte, 'Notas', p. 549, likened the songs of Ribera to the 'bellas piedras' [beautiful stones] of the great cathedral.

71. Paz, *Sor Juana*, p. 346.

72. Andrade, *Ensayo*, pp. 480–81; Medina, *La imprenta en México*, II, 525–26. Dr Kenneth Ward has confirmed this by examination of the John Carter Brown Library's *Teatro* imprint.

73. I translate from Rojas Garcidueñas (in Sigüenza, *Teatro*, p. 2, unnumbered): 'Consideren lo suyo los que se empeñan en considerar lo ajeno: es más fácil juzgar que obrar, y más fácil mirar desde la seguridad de la fortaleza los peligros'. I acknowledge with thanks José Cárdenas Bunsen's

identification of the source, which is Sedulius's epistle to Macedonius in Sedulius's fifth-century paschal poem, *Carmen Paschale*.

74. If Sor Juana succeeded in being favoured by the new viceroy and the vicereine during the eight years of their tenure (1680–88), Sigüenza had no such luck, despite his repeated efforts (see Paz, *Sor Juana*, pp. 254–55).

75. Paz (*Sor Juana*, pp. 249–50) pointed out that more than half of Sor Juana's literary production consisted of works commissioned for specific events and personages.

76. Sor Juana Inés de la Cruz, *Neptuno alegórico*, in *Inundación castálida*, ed. by Georgina Sabat de Rivers (Madrid: Castalia, 1982), pp. 365–447 (p. 372).

77. Sor Juana, *Neptuno alegórico*, pp. 371–73.

78. Sor Juana, *Neptuno alegórico*, p. 371.

79. My translation of Sabat de Rivers' Spanish rendering of Sor Juana's Latin citation of Virgil (Sor Juana, *Neptuno alegórico*, pp. 385–86). Sor Juana follows Conti's chapter 2 of book 2; see Natale Conti, *Mythologiae*, trans. by John Mulryan and Steven Brown, 2 vols (Tempe, AZ: Arizona Center for Medieval and Renaissance Studies, 2006), I, 96.

CHAPTER 2

Luis Jerónimo de Oré (1554–1630): Poetry and Proselytism in the Andes[1]

Raquel Chang-Rodríguez

In memoriam Carlos Araníbar Zerpa (1928–2016)

The Franciscan Luis Jerónimo de Oré, together with Inca Garcilaso de la Vega and Guaman Poma de Ayala, is one of the most prominent personalities of the first generation of intellectuals born in the viceroyalty of Peru. Oré catechized Andean natives, travelled to Europe (Spain and Italy), trained priests to missionize in La Florida, lived in North America and Cuba, and was appointed Bishop of Concepción (in today's Chile) where he died. He wrote several manuals to Christianize the natives; a biography of Saint Francis Solano (Madrid, *c.* 1614); *Symbolo Catholico Indiano* [Indian Catholic Symbol] (Lima, 1598); *Corona de la Sacratísima Virgen María Madre de Dios Nuestra Señora* [Crown of the Most Holy Virgin Mary Mother of God Our Lady] (Madrid, 1619) and an account of his time in La Florida (Madrid? *c.* 1619), then a vast territory that went beyond the state now bearing that name. Oré composed hymns in Quechua praising the Virgin Mary and various aspects of Catholic dogma. They are considered the largest body of poetry written in that language in colonial Peru.

In my discussion of the contributions and poetic compositions of this insufficiently studied Franciscan priest, I will focus on three areas. First, I will offer an overview of the early part of his career when he was a missionary in the Peruvian highlands and composed his main book, *Símbolo católico indiano*.[2] I will then move on to major events shaping catechization in the Andean region: the Lima Church Councils, particularly the third, summoned in 1581 and held in 1582–83. This will allow for the contextualization of Oré's major book, *Símbolo católico indiano*, and the hymns included therein. Finally, I will review the content of a group of seven 'cánticos' or hymns recently translated into Spanish, and conduct an analysis of important features of two of these compositions.[3]

Early Education

Oré was born into a deeply religious and well-to-do Spanish family in Guamanga (today Ayacucho) in southeastern Peru. His father, Antonio de Oré, was an *encomendero* or land-owner with a large number of native wards. Testimony of the period shows Antonio de Oré to have been cultured, pious, well-versed in Latin, a language he taught his sons and daughters, and also fluent in Quechua, which he acquired in daily contact with the area's native population. Luis Jerónimo's childhood was spent in an atmosphere imbued with religious fervour. He learned Gregorian chant and to play the organ. When remembering the importance of music in his own education, he later recommended it as a key tool in evangelizing the native population. The boy also grew up in contact with several languages. He spoke Spanish with his family, learned Latin from his father and from listening to religious services, and acquired Quechua and Aymara in exchanges with household helpers and other native speakers. These linguistic skills marked Oré's career and set him apart from other ecclesiastics.

Missionizing in the Andes and Beyond (1582–1613)[4]

Oré's religious vocation manifested itself early. He began his studies around the age of fourteen in 1568 at the Franciscan monastery in Cuzco and then continued at the Franciscan convent in Lima and at the University of San Marcos. He was ordained a priest in Lima on 31 March 1582,[5] by Archbishop Toribio de Mogrovejo, who presided over the Third Lima Church Council that same year.[6] Luis Enrique Tord has brought to our attention events that likely had an impact on his sensibilities in this early period — the nativist movement of Taqui Onqoy [dance sickness] that erupted in 1565 in the areas of Parinacochas, Lucanas and Soras (all near Oré's home in Guamanga), and the decapitation of Tupac Amaru in the central square of Cuzco in 1572.[7] The followers of Taqui Onqoy wanted to return to the worship of the ancestral *huacas* (revered objects or shrines) and rid the Inca territory of Spaniards. The viceroy Francisco de Toledo (1569–81) had ordered the execution of Tupac Amaru I, the last Inca leader who had held out against Spanish rule from the Andean stronghold of Vilcabamba. These events represented the clash of two worlds, and it is no wonder that they caused this young man from a wealthy family to reflect on his personal responsibility to bridge the gap between the two.

According to Franciscan sources, during the Third Council of Lima, Oré was invited to participate in preparing a trilingual catechism in Spanish, Quechua and Aymara, *Doctrina cristiana y catecismo para instrucción de los indios* [Christian Doctrine and Catechism for the Instruction of Indians] (1584), the first book printed in Lima. It is unclear how much Oré contributed to this publication. Again, Franciscan sources indicate that he worked on it with other *lenguaraces* or experts in Amerindian languages and with a group of theologians; however, his name is absent from any document.[8] It has been speculated that the venture brought Oré into contact with the Jesuit José de Acosta (who had acquired some knowledge of Quechua in his travels in Peru) and with Guaman Poma de Ayala, the indigenous author and illustrator of the landmark *Primer nueva corónica y buen gobierno* [First New Chronicle and Good Government] (1615). However, Rolena Adorno has cautioned that it is not certain that Guaman Poma attended the Council or knew Oré personally.[9]

Shortly after his ordination (1582), Oré was assigned to preach among the Spanish population of Cuzco. While there, he ministered to eight Indian parishes under the jurisdiction of that bishopric. Between 1583 and 1585, he moved to the province of Collaguas where he preached among the natives and served as guardian of the Convent of Santiago in Coporaque, the first Spanish city in the area. From here, Oré went to Jauja, where between 1595 and 1598 he was guardian of the convent and preached in Indian villages and among unbaptized natives. In 1600, we find him in the convent of San Francisco de Potosí ministering to *mitayos*, the indigenous labourers assigned to work in the silver mines of Potosí. During his stay in this mining town, his skills impressed the Hieronymite friar Diego de Ocaña (c. 1570–1608), the author of another illustrated chronicle who travelled in the region between 1599 and 1606 and who commented on the Franciscan's linguistic ability and Marian devotion:

> Y el milagro le predicó a todos los indios en su lengua el muy reverendo padre fray Luis de Oré, predicador de la orden de San Francisco, el cual, todos los domingos que predicaba a los indios, les contaba algún milagro de los que estaban en el libro de Nuestra Señora de Guadalupe. Y con esto se dio fin al octavario [periodo de ocho días] y se colocó en el altar mayor la imagen, sobre el sagrario, adonde ahora está, con mucha veneración; con quien toda la villa tiene tanta devoción, que en teniendo alguna necesidad, luego acuden a ella a pedir remedio della. Y ofrecen sus limosnas, las cuales recogen los mayordomos y con esto quedan perpetuas en esta villa.[10]

> [And the most reverend father Friar Luis de Oré, preacher of the order of Saint Francis, preached about the miracle every Sunday to all the Indians in their language and related one of the miracles in the book of Our Lady of Guadalupe. When the octave ended, the image of Our Lady was placed with great reverence on the high altar, above the shrine where it is now; and the whole town is so devoted to this image that when in need they go and pray to Her to request a remedy for their problem. And they give alms, which the stewards collect and which remain in perpetuity in this town.]

Oré continued to perfect his knowledge of Quechua and Aymara and, in addition to *Símbolo*, produced two manuscripts which circulated in several areas of the vice-royalty: *Sermones del año* [Sermons of the Year], and *Arte y vocabulario en romance y en las lenguas generales deste reino, quechua y aimara* [Grammar and Vocabulary in Romance [Spanish] and in the General Languages of this Kingdom, Quechua and Aymara].[11] Because of their importance to the task of evangelization, Church notables and colonial administrators recommended that Oré's manuscripts be published. As a result, his *Símbolo católico indiano* appeared in Lima in 1598, and later they gave him licence to publish his manuscripts in Spain.

While in Cuzco, Oré developed close ties with Bishop Antonio de la Raya (1594–1606) who appointed him Procurador [Attorney] of that diocese. Admiring Oré's missionary work and recognizing his intellectual qualities, but also wishing to see Oré's manuscripts published, the Bishop of Cuzco had him sent to Europe in 1604. When he left, Oré took three manuscripts with him — the collection of sermons also called the *Sermonario*, a work titled the *Manual de administrar los sacramentos con las traducciones necesarias en las cuatro lenguas generales quechua, aymara, puquina y guaraní* [Manual for Administering the Sacraments with the Necessary Translations in the Four General Languages Quechua, Aymara, Puquina and Guarani], and the *Arte y vocabulario* or grammar and vocabulary. He also hoped to have published there a new edition of *Símbolo*. His efforts in Europe soon bore fruit. Cook states that on 22 March 1605, the Royal Council of the Indies authorized the publication of the *Manual*.[12] Beginning to move in important administrative and ecclesiastical circles, Oré went on from Spain to Rome by the end of 1605. Since the *Manual* had not yet been published in Spain, he submitted the manuscript to Pope Paul V for publication in Italy. Two years later it was printed in Naples as *Rituale seu Manuale Peruanum et forma brevis administrandi apud Indos Sacrosancta Baptismi poenitentiae, Eucharistiae, Matrimonij & Extremae unctionis Sacramenta*.[13] This work contained prayers in Quechua, Aymara, Puquina, Mochica, Guaraní and in Brazilian languages.

Upon returning to Spain, Oré was given two main commissions: to prepare missionaries for evangelizing in La Florida and to travel to Venezuela. However, this latter charge was interrupted as he was preparing to sail on 20 June 1613,[14] when he was asked to gather material on the life of the Spanish friar Francisco Solano,[15] missionary to the Calchaquíes of Tucumán (in present-day northern Argentina). Early in 1612, travelling from Madrid to Cádiz, Oré stopped in Córdoba and met his fellow countryman, el Inca Garcilaso de la Vega (1539–1616). This meeting between the two Peruvians — one a *criollo*, the other a mestizo — was significant for both. Garcilaso was an accomplished chronicler who had already published his major books, *La Florida del Inca* (1605) and *Comentarios reales* [Royal Commentaries] (Part I, 1609). Oré particularly wanted to discuss with his compatriot *La Florida del Inca*, a chronicle he was familiar with and which he thought would be helpful for his missionaries to read before leaving for work there. Garcilaso described Oré's visit in the second part of *Comentarios reales* (1617), characterizing him as a 'gran teólogo' [great theologian]. He gave Oré three copies of *La Florida del Inca* and four of *Comentarios reales* and wished him success in his missionary work: '[que] la Divina Majestad se sirva de ayudarles en esta demanda, para que aquellos idólatras salgan del abismo de sus tinieblas' [May the Divine Majesty help you in the task of bringing those idolaters out of the abyss of their darkness].[16]

La Florida, Cuba and Concepción (Chile) (1614–1630)

The Franciscans arrived in La Florida in 1572. At first they limited their efforts to the area around San Agustín, but later they attempted to extend their radius. Wanting to expand into other areas of this region, Franciscan superiors asked Oré to prepare catechists for preaching on the new frontier. When Oré first arrived, La Florida was a territory where rival European powers competed and where Spanish religious and civil authorities squabbled. Oré left Seville for Havana on 27 June 1614, and arrived in La Florida that same year.[17] He immediately tried to establish contact with its diverse native populations, inspected the missions, and called a chapter meeting in

San Agustín. He then went on to Havana, returning in 1616 to visit all the missions in the Franciscan province of Santa Elena, and to hold another chapter meeting in San Buenaventura de Guadalquini in December. Upon his return to Havana he probably began writing the *Relación de los mártires de La Florida* [An Account of the Martyrs in the Provinces of La Florida] (*c.* 1619). In 1617 Oré was in Spain to attend the General Chapter of the Order of Saint Francis, held in Salamanca in June of 1618. The following year, he published *Corona de la Sacratísima Virgen María Madre de Dios Nuestra Señora* in Madrid, in the press of Cosme Delgado. It is very likely that *Relación de los mártires* appeared in the same year and was published by the same printer.

Oré's administrative career took another turn when, on 17 August 1620, King Philip III appointed him Bishop of Concepción, at that time the southern-most bishopric of the Church in present-day Chile. In Concepción, the diocesan seat, he established a seminary to train priests. Although the king had asked for Oré's counsel as to how to pacify the Arauco region, his advice to withdraw the army and allow missionaries to catechize the Mapuche was not followed.[18] Instead, war continued and the rebellious natives were imprisoned, branded and sold as slaves in Lima and other parts of the viceroyalty. Oré died on 31 January 1630 at the age of 76.

Catechization in Quechua

The emphasis of the Council of Trent (1545–63) and the Second Church Council of Lima (1567–68) on catechization in the native languages prompted the Jesuit Colegio de San Pablo to begin offering instruction in Quechua in 1569.[19] Ten years later, viceroy Francisco de Toledo created a chair or *cátedra* for studying Quechua at Lima's Universidad de San Marcos.[20] He also decreed that priests could not be ordained unless they knew Quechua, and university students were unable to graduate from San Marcos without taking courses in this language. Also following the dictates of Trent, the Second and Third Church Councils in Lima established that all adults had to be taught in their native language.[21] A frequently quoted passage from the Third Lima Church Council summarizes the spirit of these regulations: 'cada uno ha de ser de tal manera instruido que entienda la doctrina, el español en romance, y el indio también en su lengua' [Each one should be instructed in a manner that enables him to understand the doctrine, the Spaniard in romance [Spanish] and the Indian also in his own language].[22] Thus the *vulgarem linguam* and the Indian languages were elevated and equated to Latin when missionizing and teaching Church doctrine. And, as was to be expected, this legal and institutional backing opened the door for the preparation of grammars (*artes*), vocabularies, catechisms, prayers, sermons, and guides to confessors in the native Andean languages. In addition, the bishops were charged with publicizing the decrees of the Third Lima Council.

As Alan Durston has pointed out, soon after these councils, synodal legislation also called for increased participation of the native population in worship centred on the liturgy of the canonical hours. In the 1580s, under the direction of Archbishop Mogrovejo, several forms of prayers were standardized: 1) the responsive Angelus

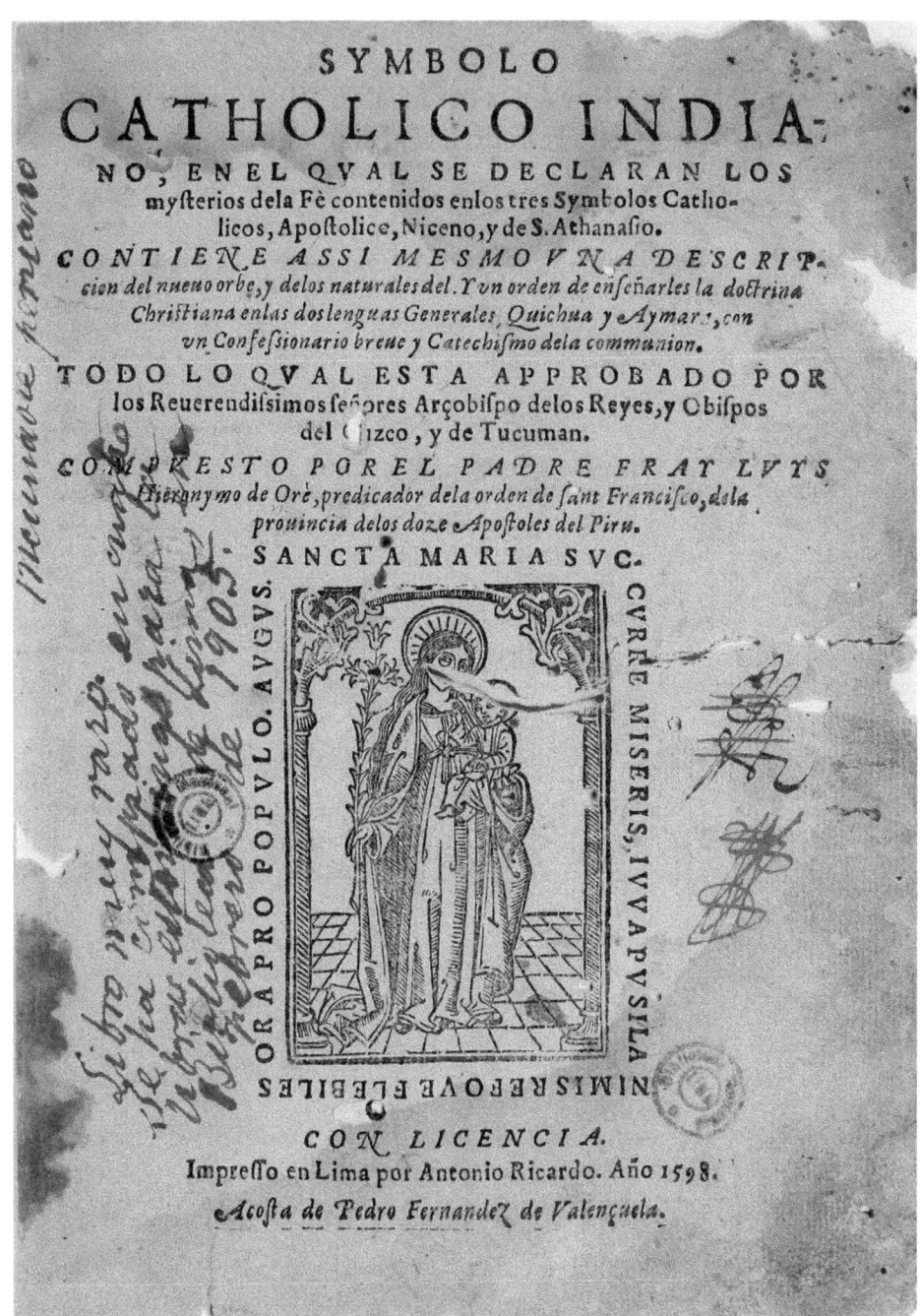

FIG. 2.1. Fray Luis Jerónimo de Oré, *Símbolo católico indiano* (Lima: Antonio Ricardo,
a costa de Pedro Fernández de Valenzuela, 1598), title page. Courtesy of the
Biblioteca Nacional del Perú (Lima).

prayer, recited every day at noon; 2) the prayers for the souls in purgatory, recited on Saturdays after the last prayer at the end of the day (Compline); and 3) the Salve Regina, also recited after Compline. In addition, the Marian cult acquired unique importance in the *pueblos de indios*.[23] To comply with these and other regulations, in several synodal jurisdictions such as Cuzco, natives were trained to sing hymns and responses for masses and feasts days.[24] Thus, worship and catechetical instruction gradually acquired a performative character and were marked by greater participation of the native population.

Trent also recognized the importance of images to strengthen the Evangelical message and teach illiterates. The proceedings of its 25th session stated: 'when this is beneficial to the illiterate, the stories and narratives of the Holy Scriptures should be portrayed and exhibited'.[25] This new policy of visual communication, in tandem with the increased engagement of the native population in worship and the publication of key tenets of Catholic dogma in the local vernaculars, changed the way Christianity was taught in the Andean region. The manuscript of *Símbolo*, Oré's principal book, was directed towards all literate new Andean Christians and particularly towards *indios ladinos*, the native interpreters who aided priests in teaching doctrine and the various stages of liturgy. Its publication in 1598 responded to the new attempts by the Church to reach the native population in the viceroyalty of Peru (the printing press in Lima having been established in 1584 with this aim), and, as previously stated, it had ample circulation in the Peruvian highlands.[26]

Símbolo católico indiano, a Book for Andean Neophytes (Fig. 2.1)

When approaching Oré's book, it should be remembered that the creeds or symbols referenced by its title (the Apostles', Nicene and Quicumbe creeds) appear at a time of religious tension; in addition, the formulation of a creed serves to distinguish those who follow or reject a particular doctrine. Two previous creeds, the Nicene and the Quicumbe or Athanasian, address doctrinal issues in dispute. The former emerged to counter Arian ideas on the divinity of Jesus and their threat to the concept of the Trinity (as stated in its 381 version). The latter, whose importance Oré recognized by offering it in Latin and translating it into Quechua in his book, reaffirms the equality and divinity of the three persons of the Trinity; however, unlike the Nicene Creed, it adds condemnations or anathemas for those who disagree. Probably the most immediate influence on Oré's book was *Introducción del Símbolo de la Fe* [Introduction of the Symbol of Faith] (Salamanca, 1583), written by the Dominican Luis de Granada (1504–1588) in a period in which Protestant ideas threatened Catholic unity in the Iberian Peninsula.[27]

Símbolo católico indiano also appears in a critical period when the church in America is in a time of transition, eager to attract and evangelize peoples of diverse cultures. Addressing the challenge of this evangelization head on, Oré's book codifies the precepts to be followed by those who accept Catholic teaching. In so doing he recognizes the ability of the new Indian Christians to master Western cultural tools (including reading and writing), and read about, understand and put into practice dogma. In the preliminary section of the book, a sonnet by the

Dominican Jerónimo de Valenzuela, Prior of the Convent of Parinacocha, confirms the targeted readership of *Símbolo*:

> Inculta gente del oculto mundo,
> de niebla oscura hasta aquí cercada
> y en el tartáreo piélago anegada
> del satánico reino furibundo,
>   despierta ya de sueño tan profundo
> y con la luz deífica guiada
> al mar tranquilo sal muy confiada
> de llegar a aquel puerto sin segundo.
>   Y si saber quisieres el camino
> deste plácido, ameno e impíreo puerto,
> aunque no tengas guía ni piloto,
>   fray Luis Hierónimo de Oré, qu'es digno
> de ecelsa loa, te lo muestra abierto
> en tu lenguaje con su libro docto.[28]

> [Uneducated people from the hidden world
> up to now fenced in by dark fog
> and drowning in the sea of hell
> of the furious Satanic kingdom,
>   Wake up now from such a deep sleep
> and guided by Divine light,
> sail into the tranquil sea, confident
> of arriving at that peerless port.
>   And if thou want to know the way
> to this placid, pleasant, and heavenly port
> even though [you are] without a guide or pilot,
>   Fray Luis Hierónimo de Oré, who is worthy
> of the highest praise, opens it for you
> in your language with his learned book.]

Thus, *Símbolo* and its author become guide and pilot for the Quechua-speaking Christians of Peru. Oré's book opens the road to Heaven — to the 'plácido, ameno, e impíreo puerto' [placid, pleasant, and heavenly port] — for the Andean neophytes. In this treatise they will find the key tenets of the faith as well as the principal ideas that informed Oré's thinking when codifying dogma in prose and poetry. The poems or *cánticos* are there and, in their learned beauty and complex imagery, they combine cultural insights from Europe and the Andes to make the Gospel accessible. Since in their curiosity and desire to master Christian teachings neophytes will want to go beyond the poems, the notations on the right hand side of the hymns lead to the Old and New Testament, to the writings of key figures of the Church, and continue clearing the road to Paradise (Fig. 2.2).

In *Símbolo* Oré relates the origin of the Indians to the Biblical story of man's fall from God's grace. He indicates their participation in a common humanity and emphasizes this in the introduction to the fifth *cántico*: 'Nuestro primer principio fue de Adán y de Eva, y después, cuando Dios castigó el mundo y perecieron todos los hombres, de solos estos cuatro, de Noé y de sus tres hijos nos hemos propagado y multiplicado' [Our first beginning was in Adam and Eve. Then since

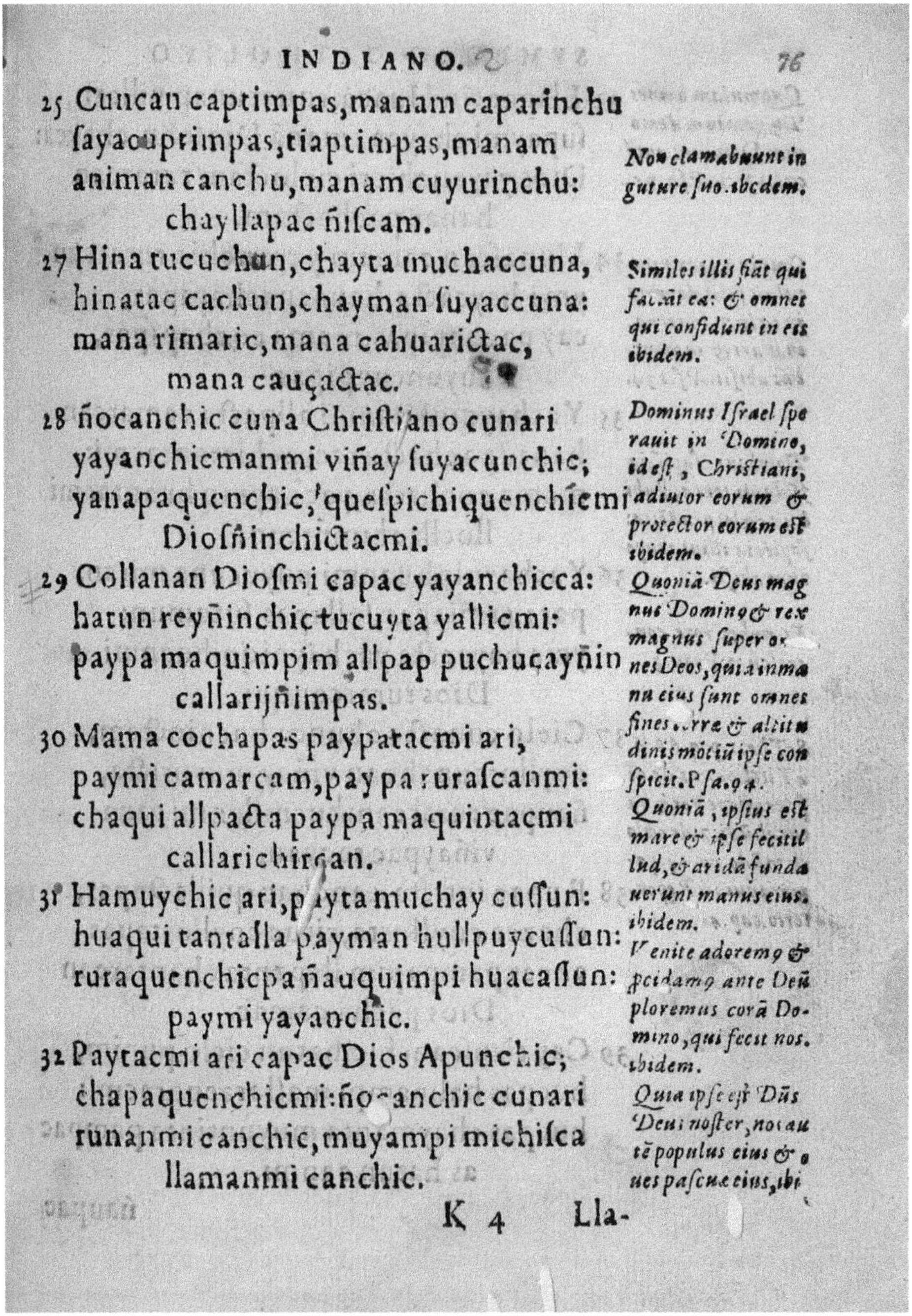

INDIANO.   76

25 Cuncan captimpas, manam caparinchu
sayacuptimpas, tiaptimpas, manam
animan canchu, manam cuyurinchu:
chayllapac ñifcam.

Non clamabunt in guture fuo.abcdem.

27 Hina tucuchun, chayta muchaccuna,
hinatac cachun, chayman fuyaccuna:
mana rimaric, mana cahuariⅽtac,
mana cauçaⅽtac.

Similes illis fiat qui faciat ea: & omnes qui confidunt in eis ibidem.

28 ñocanchic cuna Chriſtiano cunari
yayanchicmanmi viñay fuyacunchic;
yanapaquenchic, quefpichiquenchicmi
Dioſñinchiⅽtacmi.

Dominus Ifrael fperauit in Domino, ideft, Christiani, adiutor eorum & protector eorum eſt ibidem.

29 Collanan Dioſmi capac yayanchicca:
hatun reyñinchic tucuyta yallicmi:
paypa maquimpim allpap puchuçayñin
callarijñimpas.

Quonià Deus magnus Domino & rex magnus fuper omnes Deos, quia in manu eius funt omnes fines terræ & altitudinis mötiu ipfe cöfpicit. Pfa.94.

30 Mama cochapas paypatacmi ari,
paymi camarcam, paypa rurafcanmi:
chaqui allpaⅽta paypa maquintacmi
callarichircan.

Quonià, ipſius eſt mare & ipfe fecitil lud, & aridã fundauerunt manus eius. ibidem.

31 Hamuychic ari, payta muchay cuffun:
huaqui tantalla payman hullpuycuffun:
ruraquenchicpa ñauquimpi huacaffun:
paymi yayanchic.

Venite adoremg & pcidamg ante Deu ploremus corã Domino, qui fecit nos. ibidem.

32 Paytacmi ari capac Dios Apunchic;
chapaquenchicmi: ñocanchic cunari
runanmi canchic, muyampi michifca
llamanmi canchic.

Quia ipfe eft Dũs Deus noſter, nos au tẽ populus eius & ○ ues pafcue eius, ibi

K 4   Lla-

FIG. 2.2. Fray Luis Jerónimo de Oré, *Símbolo católico indiano* (Lima: Antonio Ricardo, a costa de Pedro Fernández de Valenzuela, 1598), f. 76. Courtesy of the Biblioteca Nacional del Perú (Lima).

God punished the world and all men perished except four — Noah and his three children — we have spread and multiplied] (p. 294 [fol. 108ᵛ]). Oré distinguishes between polytheistic and monotheistic practices and translates a prayer attributed to Inca Capac Yupanqui associated with the cult of Pachacamac or the supreme creator, citing it as evidence of native monotheism (pp. 157–58 [fols 40–42ᵛ]). He identifies the Devil as responsible for the outrages that he sees in native practices (pp. 161–62 [fols 42–42ᵛ]). In *Símbolo*, he condemns the Spanish for their exploitation of the native population and specifically criticizes their failure to provide good shepherds to instruct their flock in Catholic doctrine. If Christianity is to flourish, he proposes, every Indian village must have a school, a teacher, and singers. The natives, Oré argues, are fully able to understand and assimilate Christian doctrine along with other Western cultural tools:

> Que haya escuela y maestro de ella, y cantores diputados y pagados con salario suficiente, donde sean enseñados los muchachos a rezar la doctrina, y a leer y escribir, cantar y tañer. Y de la escuela salgan hábiles en la doctrina, para enseñarla a todo el pueblo. Finalmente, la escuela es como ánima de todo un pueblo para ser mejor doctrinado y regido, y donde no la hubiere, faltará todo lo dicho: de doctrina, música, ornato y servicio de las iglesias, altar y coro. (p. 189 [fol. 56])

> [Let there be a school and a teacher, and also singers who are appointed and paid sufficient wages, where they teach the boys to say the doctrine and to read and write, sing and play [stringed instruments]. And they [the boys] will come out of the school ready to teach it to the entire village. Finally, the school is like the soul of a people, [needed] in order for them to be better taught and governed. And where there is no school, everything mentioned will be lacking: doctrine, music, decoration and service of the churches, altar and choir.]

At the same time, *Símbolo* encourages devotion to the Marian cult — there are two poems dedicated to the Virgin — and recitation of the rosary.[29] Also it calls for punishing those who do not learn the basic tenets of the Faith. Oré shows his conviction that the Franciscan mission will elevate Indians to a new level in understanding Catholic dogma, and equates preaching the Gospel in the New World with the work of the Apostles bringing the teachings of Jesus to the Gentiles.[30] Ministers must preach the true doctrine, live a saintly life and behave with the piety of a father towards the Indians.[31] Oré balances this example of a good minister with criticism of those who are more interested in profit than in preaching. His *Símbolo*, then, goes beyond a creed. Addressed to a new and multilingual population which he deems capable of reading, writing, singing and fully understanding the Christian message, it codifies the essential aspects of dogma while establishing the routine of necessary rituals. It is a creed but also a primer; it is a catechism but also a book of songs. Its Quechua hymns and the manner in which he presents them are an integral part of the new context in which missionizing should take place. While *Símbolo* can be characterized, following Raúl Porras Barrenechea, as 'la primera prosa científica' [the first scientific prose] written in Quechua, its *cánticos* or poems also represent the largest body of poetry written in that language during the colonial period.[32]

Oré harks back to Church tradition to explain their composition and inclusion in *Símbolo*:

> [...] de estos misterios [de la fe] hay compuestos himnos en latín por san Ambrosio y san Gregorio [...] y por otros autores. Y en romance y en toscano, y en las demás lenguas de las naciones que han recibido la cristiandad, hay versos y composturas diferentes en octavas, sonetos y tercetos, canciones y en otros metros de los que encierra la poesía latina, italiana y castellana, lo cual ayuda a asentar la devoción de los documentos y doctrina cristiana [...] y nos causa alivio de las continuas molestias de esta vida, dar gracias a Dios cantando de corazón salmos y cánticos espirituales. (pp. 202–03 [fols 62^v–63])

> [[...] about these mysteries [of the faith] there are Latin hymns composed by St Ambrose, and St Gregory [...] and [others]. And in romance and in Tuscan, and in the other languages of the nations that have adopted Christianity, there are verse lines and different compositions in octaves, triplets and sonnets, songs and other metres of Latin, Italian and Spanish poetry which contribute to establishing devotion to the tenets of Christian doctrine [...] [they help to] alleviate the persistent problems of this life, to thank God from our heart by singing psalms and spiritual songs.]

Thus, following an accepted practice since the time of the Apostles, and as had been done by the great teachers of the Church, Oré, through these hymns, aims to offer aid and comfort to the Andean neophytes. They too must have access in their own language to the same catechetical and devotional tools as parishioners across the centuries and cultures.

Oré first justifies his proposal to compose his hymns in Sapphic metre by reviewing — starting with Horace — who has used it and on what occasions.[33] He further adds that singing moves the Indians 'Porque [con el canto los Indios], se muevan a devoción, con la letra principalmente, y el tono les sea ayuda y parte para lo mesmo' [to devotion particularly the lyrics; the melody is also helpful and contributes to achieving the same aim] (p. 204 [fol. 63^v]). Oré admits composing the hymns of *Símbolo* after much study and 'no sin trabajo grande' [not without great effort] (p. 203 [fol. 63]), hoping that by word and example the Indians will be 'induced' to praise God 'en los templos y en toda parte, y en las procesiones [...] resuene con vociferación en las bocas, almas y corazones de todos el santísimo nombre de Jesucristo' [in the temples and in every place, and in processions [...] so that the name of Jesus Christ resounds vociferously in the mouths, souls and hearts of everyone] (p. 205 [f. 64]). Thus, by way of these compositions, Oré again dignifies the Quechua language and its speakers. He aims to use rhyme metres harking back to classical poetry written in Latin and mastered by none other than Horace. The Peruvian natives, like Christians in other latitudes, will now be able to affirm their faith through poetry, by singing the message of the Gospels in their own language and invoking it beyond the Church walls.

Like other missionaries — particularly the Jesuits — Oré recognized the importance of incorporating into Christian worship elements from indigenous cultures such as dancing and singing.[34] Bearing this in mind, in *Símbolo* he stipulates the hour and manner in which these and other hymns should be sung as well as how worshippers should participate. He offers a true choreography for each liturgical occasion in order to enhance learning and enable the participation of neophytes (pp. 182–83 [fols 52ᵛ–53]).

The Cánticos or Poems: Their Structure and Themes

The seven major *cánticos* or poems are preceded by an 'argument and a statement'. Each has a varying number of verse lines, treats different aspects of dogma and should be sung on a given day of the week. Aiming to address the concerns of literate speakers of Spanish and Quechua, in the right margin the author carefully indicates the sources supporting the argument detailed in the poem. Often he refers the reader to the Old or New Testament; there are many references to the Psalms as well as to the leading Doctors of the Church. On several occasions Oré makes reference to Andean culture and behaviour patterns and carefully associates them with Christian dogma, thus facilitating understanding for the neophytes. At other times he expands on specific ideas through vocabulary or lexical markers. As for the Quechua language of the *cánticos*, Gerald Taylor has pointed out that it follows the guidelines or linguistic models proposed by the Third Lima Church Council in which, according to Franciscan sources, Oré participated. Let us now turn to the content of the poems.[35]

Preceded by a Quechua translation of the *Symbol* of Saint Athanasius, the first song or poem is dedicated to the mysteries of the Holy Trinity (Sunday). In the second, the poet praises God who dwells in the empyrean together with the angels. He is loved and adored for his many attributes as well as for being the creator of the universe (Monday). The third hymn praises the Father for the creation of man and for saving him through Christ's sacrifice (Tuesday). It includes a rich characterization of Mary in her capacity of virgin-mother of Christ. She has defeated the devil and is presented as the protectress of humankind. A sign from heaven has portrayed her, 'vestida del Sol resplandeciente, y la Luna la tenías debajo de tus pies, y en tu cabeza una corona de doce estrellas' [clothed with the shining Sun, and the Moon under her feet, and on her head a crown of twelve stars]. She is described as 'aventajada a la luna y a las estrellas' [superior to the moon and the stars], as a 'tierra bendita y fértil, monte de Dios, hermoso y grueso, cuajado de flores, azucenas y lirios' [blessed and fertile land, mountain of God, beautiful and vast, covered with flowers, lilies and irises] (p. 242 [fol. 82ᵛ]). Following St Athanasius, the fourth hymn shows the embodiment of Jesus as saviour of all men as well as Mary's virtues (Wednesday). The fifth song deals with the origin of humanity and responds to native ideas about the provenance of all peoples underscoring their common roots (Thursday). It also stresses the Ten Commandments and the condemnation of all who transgress them. It ends with the institution of the sacrament of the Eucharist. The sixth poem focuses on the passion, death and resurrection of Christ (Friday). The cruelties committed against Jesus are presented through bloody images associated, according to Margot Beyersdorff, with the Hispanic literary tradition of describing the Passion in realistic terms.[36] The poem ends with a touching portrait of the crucified Christ and the idea of salvation through Holy Communion. The last hymn is dedicated to the resurrection of Christ and the descent of the Holy Spirit (Saturday). It explains how Jesus is head of the Church and the Pope his vicar on earth. It depicts the glories of paradise attained through divine love as well as the pains of hell reserved for those who do not follow the commandments. The content of the *cánticos* can be summarized as follows:

1st   Holy Trinity (Sunday)
2nd   Creation of the World (Monday)
3rd   Creation of Man, Sin and Redemption (Tuesday)
4th   Incarnation of Christ (Wednesday)
5th   Origin of Humanity and Life of Christ (Thursday)
6th   Lamentations for the Passion and Death of Christ (Friday)
7th   Resurrection and Glorification of Christ. The Holy Spirit.
       The Establishment of the Church (Saturday)

These poems are followed by others dedicated, for example, to Saint Ambrose and Saint Augustine, Doctors of the Church, creeds, prayers, commandments of the law of God and of the Church offered in Quechua, Aymara, Spanish, and sometimes in Latin. Others, like a song or *lira* to Our Lady of the Rosary and a poem praising the Most Holy Virgin, are presented only in Quechua. Concentrating on poems six and two, I will now comment on some lexical and cultural features which will enable us to glimpse how the poems yield their meaning.

Lexical and Cultural Aspects

Oré, a learned individual, was well aware of Catholic liturgy and how lexicon could enrich or even transform the meaning of a poem or a particular verse line. Quechua language scholars have drawn attention to 'code switching' or 'code mixing' in his poetry.[37] For example, Alan Durston has studied an important example of code switching in the following verse lines of poem 6, 'Lamentations for the Passion and Death of Christ': 'cay huañay caliz Abba Pater Yaya | yachacuprinca, ñocamanta richun | upiayta ama ypyashacchu | munaptiiquica' [Abba Pater Yaya if it is possible, let this chalice of death go away from me, if you so wished, I would not drink the drink of death].[38] He points to the use of the word 'Father' in Aramaic (*Abba*), Latin/Greek (*Pater*) and Quechua (*Yaya*). Referencing Augustine of Hippo's suggestion that Christ used the word Father in both Greek and Aramaic at this critical time, Durston indicates that by doing so Christ wished to establish the church incorporating Gentiles and Jews. Following this reasoning, he further elaborates that by adding Yaya, Oré proposes to include the Quechua people in the church while preserving indexical icons of the translation process that refer us to a particular language and culture.[39] This is just one example where the notion of 'code switching' helps us to understand the thoughtful manner in which Oré gave the poems a new theological twist to involve the Andean people in the Church. To his mind, they counted as much as the groups that were traditionally considered the pillars of the institution. It also shows, as Durston has proposed, an inclusive Christ, calling the Father in three languages at such a crucial juncture.

In the second poem of the collection, 'Creation of the World', several stanzas are devoted to the origin of the universe and to praising God's ability to make it out of nothing. Specifically, the lyrical voice draws a parallel with the construction of a house: friends and relatives get together, bring the material, and build walls and ceilings with a lot of effort:

> Runakuna wasikta ruraŝpa,
> rumiktam ñawpaq maymantapaŝ tawqaq,
> humpi ŝaykuŝpa apamuŝparaqmi
> tipsinta qallap
>
> Ayllu masinwan yanapanakuŝpam
> pirqanta llamkaq kurkuwanpaŝ chakap
> qatanqankama ñakaymantaraqmi
> puchukakuqpaŝ.[40]

[Men when they build their homes, first [take] the stones from somewhere and put them together; immediately, with great effort, sweating, they bring them to the place where they lay the foundations

Their companions from the *ayllu* help them, they all put up the walls, they put the beams and, finally, with great difficulty, they complete [the house] placing the roof.]

The poem stresses how many people are needed to build a dwelling and how difficult it is. In contrast, God created the universe and populated it from nothing, with just a word from his mouth.[41] The poem praises God and recognizes him as the architect of the universe. Nevertheless, in the allusion to building a house the Andean parishioners surely were able to recognize the *ayni* or system of mutual aid. It was used then and now to construct houses, roads and communal edifices with the cooperation of relatives and friends from the same *ayllu*. Also known as *minka* or reciprocity, the *ayni* is one of the singular markers of Quechua culture. Indeed, community members aided others in agriculture and home construction; when members of a family received help to complete a task, the only condition was to reciprocate when others called. *Ayni* and *minka* are about the good of the community and how to achieve it collectively. Those who sang Oré's lyrics or listened to them surely appreciated the collective effort which went into building a house and certainly were familiar with *ayni*. As they respected those who participated in *ayni*, they were able to evaluate and admire the work of God as the single architect of the universe. I contend that in the poem Oré used the building imagery with its cultural markers to underscore to the neophytes that they were part of creation as God's people, and thus they felt engaged, bound to reciprocate by spreading the tidings of the Gospel and constructing the new church in Peru.

The poem also includes the story of the angels who joined God in the 'Empyrean heaven'.[42] He distributed them into nine *ayllus* and three *suyus* or hierarchies: angels and archangels are in the first *suyu* while virtues, cherubim and seraphim are in the superior *suyu*, closest to the Creator; the others are in between. Most angels worshipped God; others, elated at their situation, wanted to be like him. The lyrical voice takes advantage of this narrative to highlight the issues of free will, transgression and punishment. God wants us to love him willingly and not by force, and this is why he gave angels — and humans — the ability to choose between good and evil.[43] But there is also punishment: the proud angels, who thought they were like God, 'illapahina *rayo* qapchahinam | uraykumurqan' [with a flash of lightning | came down] and, led by Satan, went straight to hell.[44] Other demons remained in the air, hiding in the dark to tempt us. The poet mentions the names of the archangels Michael and Gabriel who expelled and defeated the traitor angels, and Raphael, who heals the sick. Then we return to the narrative of origins and, through elegant references, the lyric voice reviews the creation of heaven, earth, the angels, the sun, the moon, the stars, the streams, the hills, the chicks, the dove, the *amancaes* and the Andeans.[45] Even stones, minerals and pearls owe their beauty to the Creator:

> Umiñakuna, nina qiŝpi rumi
> allpap ŝunqunpi quyllurhina situq
> quchap ukunpi llipyaq *perlas*kuna
> sumachiŝqaykim (Taylor, *El sol*, pp. 144–45)

> [You give their beauty to the emeralds,
> To the fire-coloured crystals which shine as stars
> in the bowels of the earth,
> To the shining pearls in the sea]

The poem presents free will as a divine gift, the tragic consequences of transgression, and also love as a precious bond between God and his creation. It concludes by highlighting Divine power and, in my view, the advantages of following the almighty Christian God, for those who accept the Gospel will have His protection and also that of the powerful archangels Michael, Gabriel, Raphael. All must worship the Creator because He is superior to the *huillcas*, objects made by men of gold, silver, copper, stone and wood and thus with no power to see and hear; and lacking the sense of smell or touch, the ability to walk, scream, or the 'ánima' to move. In God's hands rest the beginning and the end of the earth. And let those who do not follow the Christian God become like the old idols, without word, sight or life.[46]

★   ★   ★   ★   ★

In this essay I have reviewed key points of Luis Jerónimo de Oré's biography; the missionary context in which *Símbolo católico indiano* developed; why Oré used song and poetry in proselytizing the native population, and some distinct aspects of the *cánticos*. For the Franciscan from Guamanga, Quechua was on a par with Latin and Spanish. The Andean people, like other Christians before them, deserved to have the right tools to affirm their faith: an accessible book, an intelligible creed, and poems or *cánticos* to establish and spread devotion, to 'alleviate the persistent problems of this life, and to thank God from our heart by singing psalms and spiritual songs'.[47] The poetry written by this *lenguaraz* deserves to be further studied and brought to the attention of the scholarly community for its beauty and sophistication. In addition, through its analysis it is possible to perceive Oré's attempts to equalize the groups from Europe and America that came into contact in the Andean highlands more than five centuries ago.

Notes to Chapter 2

1. My gratitude to Nancy Vogeley for her friendship and generosity in sharing insights into the Lima church councils and Franciscan missionary work in the larger context of European ecclesiastical politics. I am indebted to Ramón Mujica Pinilla, Director of the Biblioteca Nacional del Perú (2010–16), for facilitating my investigation on Oré at this institution. My thanks to the Reed Foundation for its unfailing support of my research on Oré and his missionary work in La Florida and Cuba.
2. Hereafter I will use the modernized spelling of this title. All translations are my own unless otherwise indicated.
3. The translation was done by Felicita Domínguez and its style was reviewed by Julia Beatriz Benavidez, both native speakers of Quechua from Ayacucho. It appears in Miguel Ángel Espinoza Soria, *La catequesis en fray Luis Jerónimo de Oré, OFM. Un aporte a la nueva evangelización* (Lima: Provincia Misionera de San Francisco Solano del Perú, 2012), pp. 97–240. The book has circulated mainly in Peruvian ecclesiastical circles.
4. The sources for this summary of Oré's career are: Federico Richter, 'Primera parte: Fray Luis Jerónimo de Oré (biografía) 1554–1630. Segunda parte: Información de oficio en la Real Audiencia de La Plata del Perú, de los méritos del biografiado (tres piezas)', in *Anales de la Provincia Franciscana de los Doce Apóstoles de Lima* (Huamanga: Imprenta de la Universidad de San Cristóbal de Huamanga, 1986), pp. 1–41; Noble David Cook, 'Luis Jerónimo de Oré: una aproximación', in *Symbolo Catholico Indiano*, ed. by Antonine Tibesar (Lima: Australis, 1992), pp. 35–63; and Margot Beyersdorff, 'Luis Jerónimo de Oré', in *Guide to Documentary Sources for Andean Studies, 1530–1900*, ed. by Joanne Pillsbury, 3 vols (Norman: University of Oklahoma Press, 2008), III, 472–75.
5. Richter, 'Primera parte', p. 4.
6. Bishop Toribio de Mogrovejo was canonized by Pope Benedict XIII on 10 December 1726. Following Richter, the dates for Oré's ordination are: auxiliary deacon, 23 September 1581; deacon, 3 March 1582. Oré was ordained a priest (1582) together with Ludovico Bertonio, a Jesuit later famous for his studies of the Aymara language.
7. Luis Enrique Tord, 'Luis Jerónimo de Oré y el *Symbolo catholico indiano*', in *Symbolo Catholico Indiano*, ed. by Antonine Tibesar (Lima: Australis, 1992), pp. 22–24.
8. Alan Durston, *Pastoral Quechua. The History of Christian Translation in Colonial Peru, 1550–1650* (Notre Dame, IN: University of Notre Dame Press, 2007), p. 98.
9. Rolena Adorno, *Guaman Poma: Writing and Resistance in Colonial Peru* (Austin: University of Texas Press, 2000), p. xlviii. For Oré and Guaman Poma and their shared intellectual concerns, see my 'Felipe Huaman Poma de Ayala y Luis Jerónimo de Oré, dos ingenios andinos', *Libros & Artes* (Revista de Cultura de la Biblioteca Nacional del Perú), 13.78–79 (2016), 11–14.
10. Diego de Ocaña, [c. 1607], *Memoria viva de una tierra de olvido: relación del viaje al Nuevo Mundo de 1599 a 1607*, ed., introduction and notes by Beatriz Carolina Peña (Barcelona: CECAL/Paso de Barca, 2013), pp. 497–98.
11. Cook, 'Luis Jerónimo de Oré', pp. 42–44.
12. Cook, 'Luis Jerónimo de Oré', p. 45.
13. The sections in Quechua and Aymara were translated by Dominican, Franciscan, Augustinian, Mercedarian and Jesuit priests. Alonso de Barzana, a Jesuit, was in charge of the segment in Puquina and there were additions after he died in 1597; the section in Mochica was translated by secular and regular priests and approved by the Archbishop of Lima. Father Luis de Bolaños took charge of the section in Guaraní and it was approved by the Río de la Plata ecclesiastical authorities. The section on 'Brazilian languages' (Tupi) was attended to by monks of San Benito and Jesuit priests from Portugal. I have consulted a copy of the 1607 edition of the *Rituale* at the Biblioteca Nacional del Perú.

14. Following the passenger list in Archivo General de Indias [henceforth, AGI], Contratación, 5538, L.2. fols 125^V–126^V.

15. Francisco Sánchez-Solano Jiménez (1549–1610), beatified in 1675, and canonized in 1726. See Oré's book on his life and missionary work in America.

16. Inca Garcilaso de la Vega, *Historia general del Perú*, ed. by Ángel Rosenblat and José de la Riva Agüero, 3 vols (Buenos Aires: Emecé, 1944), III, Book 7, Chap. 30, p. 182.

17. Passenger list for the ship *Nuestra Señora de los Remedios* (AGI, Contratación, 5538, L.2, F. 128–128^V.).

18. Cook, 'Luis Jerónimo de Oré', pp. 57–58. See also Espinoza Soria, *La catequesis*, p. 15.

19. It is worth remembering that before these regulations, under the auspices of the Lima cathedral, Quechua was taught there since 1551. Every Sunday the natives gathered in the Cathedral square and listened to sermons in Quechua; see Raúl Porras Barrenechea, 'Prólogo', in Diego González de Holguín, *Vocabulario de la lengua general de todo el Perú llamada lengua qquichua o del Inca* (Lima: Instituto de Historia, Universidad Nacional Mayor de San Marcos, 1952), pp. v–xliv (pp. viii–ix).

20. The first *catedrático* was Dr Juan de Balboa. The chair functioned for 200 years until an edict by viceroy Agustín de Jáuregui, after Tupac Amaru's rebellion in 1780, proscribed it in 1784 (Porras Barrenechea, 'Prólogo', p. ix).

21. 'Que el credo y oraciones de la Iglesia y mandamientos se digan a los indios en su lengua, [...] que los curas de indios aprendan con cuidado su lengua' [That the Apostle's Creed and church prayers and commandments be said to the Indians in their language; [...] that priests ministering to the Indians learn their language with great care], Rubén Vargas Ugarte, *Concilios Limenses (1551–1772)*, 3 vols (Lima: Talleres Gráficos de la Tipografía Peruana, 1951), I, Parte 1ra, art. 48, p. 230; Parte 2da. Capt. 1, item 3, p. 240. For a review of these policies and their impact, see Juan Carlos Estenssoro Fuchs, *Del paganismo a la santidad: la incorporación de los indios del Perú al catolicismo, 1532–1750*, trans. by Gabriela Ramos (Lima: Instituto Francés de Estudios Andinos and Fondo Editorial, PUCP, 2003).

22. Vargas Ugarte, *Concilios*, I, 325.

23. It was further strengthened by a 1605 decree from Paul V — obtained by Oré — which granted indulgence to Spaniards and Indians who practised it in Peru (Cook, 'Luis Jerónimo de Oré', p. 45).

24. Durston, *Pastoral Quechua*, pp. 139–40.

25. H. J. Schroeder, OP (trans. and introduction), *Canons and Decrees of the Council of Trent* (Rockford, IL: Tan Books, 1941), p. 216.

26. Margot Beyersdorff, 'Rito y verbo en la poesía de fray Luis Jerónimo de Oré', in *Mito y simbolismo en los Andes: la figura y la palabra*, ed. by Henrique Urbano (Cuzco: Centro de Estudios Regionales Andinos 'Bartolomé de las Casas', 1993), pp. 215–37 (p. 219).

27. As the Dominican explained: 'Pues contra esta ponzoña, así de herejes [protestantes] como de malos cristianos, servirá como de triaca un pedazo desta escritura, en la cual declararemos cuán altamente sientan los católicos de este soberano misterio de nuestra Redención, y cuánto magnifiquen y engrandezcan este sumo beneficio' [Against this poison coming from heretics [Protestants] as well as from bad Christians, a piece of this writing in which we will declare how highly Catholics hold this sovereign mystery of our redemption, and how they magnify and exalt this supreme benefit, will serve as an antidote]; Fray Luis de Granada, *Introducción del Símbolo de la Fe*, ed. by José María Balcells (Madrid: Cátedra, 1989), p. 107 (Dedication).

28. Oré, *Símbolo*, p. 74 [fol. 6^V]. In quoting from *Símbolo* I use the modern pagination and indicate in brackets the folio number of the 1598 edition; punctuation and spelling have been modernized.

29. Both poems, 'Lira a Nuestra Señora del Rosario' (p. 434, [fol. 179^V]) and 'Alabanza a la Sacratísima Virgen' (p. 435, [fol. 180]), are in Quechua.

30. Oré, *Símbolo*, p. 153 [fol. 38]. For Marian cult, see Cook, 'Luis Jerónimo de Oré', p. 45.

31. Thus this ideal minister 'será idóneo ministro de Cristo y podrá con segura conciencia, si la obediencia le encargare alguna doctrina, tomarla y amarla como esposa' [will be able with a clear conscience, if required by his vows of obedience to discharge the requirements of this doctrine, to receive it and love it as if it were his wife] (p. 165 [fol. 44]).

32. Porras Barrenechea, 'Prólogo', p. x.

33. Oré further explains: 'que consta de troqueo, espondeo y dáctilo y dos troqueos' [consisting of trochee, spondee and dactyl and two trochees] (pp. 203–04 [fols 63–63$^\text{v}$]). Probably because of the characteristics of Quechua, he is unable to follow this rhyme pattern.

34. For a historical discussion, see Berta Ares Queija, 'Las danzas de los indios: un camino para la evangelización en el virreinato del Perú', *Revista de Indias*, 44.174 (1984), 445–63.

35. Gerald Taylor, *El sol, la luna y las estrellas no son Dios... La evangelización en quechua (siglo XVI)* (Lima: Instituto Francés de Estudios Andinos/Fondo Editorial, PUCP, 2003), pp. 14, 120.

36. 'Rito y verbo', pp. 215–37.

37. Durston, *Pastoral Quechua*, p. 294.

38. Durston, *Pastoral Quechua*, p. 295. The rendition in Quechua and the translation into English are by Durston. The translation into Spanish as it appears in Espinoza Soria, *La catequesis*, p. 191, offers Abba, Pater and Yaya as 'Papacito, Padre, Papá', and doesn't stress the different languages of the original.

39. Durston, *Pastoral Quechua*, p. 295.

40. For the analysis of this poem, I have used the bilingual Quechua–Spanish translation of Oré's *cántico* by Taylor, *El sol*, pp. 123–47. For my translation into English of the quoted verse lines, I have been guided by Taylor's Spanish version.

41. Taylor, *El sol*, pp. 130–31.

42. Angels were frequently depicted in church murals and paintings as powerful figures, often carrying weapons. The church of Andahuaylillas, in the area where Oré missionized, is famous for its murals and oils representing angels. See José de Mesa and Teresa Gisbert, *Historia de la pintura cuzqueña*, 2 vols (Lima: Fundación Banco A. N. Wiese, 1982), I, section 4, and more recently Ananda Cohen Suárez, *Heaven, Hell and Everything in Between: Murals of the Colonial Andes* (Austin: University of Texas Press, 2016).

43. Taylor, *El sol*, p. 141.

44. Taylor, *El sol*, p. 140.

45. The *amancae* or *ismene amancaes* flowers in Lima around 24 June, St Johns the Baptist's Day.

46. Taylor, *El sol*, pp. 134–35.

47. Oré, *Símbolo*, p. 203 [fol. 63].

PART II

Satire, Balladry and Burlesque Poetry

Radical Visions of Post-Conquest Mexico: Humanism and Experience in the Poetry of Fray Cristóbal Cabrera[1]

Andrew Laird

Barely ten years after the fall of the Aztec capital of Tenochtitlan to Hernán Cortés in 1521, an intellectually gifted teenager from a humble family in Burgos voyaged across the Atlantic to New Spain. He was taken in and educated by the first Franciscan bishop of Mexico City, Fray Juan de Zumárraga, who had only arrived there himself a couple of years before. The bishop's choice of *protégé* soon paid off: Cristóbal Cabrera joined the Franciscan order, proving to be an accomplished translator of patristic Greek and a dedicated missionary. He worked in the region of Michoacan under the direction of Bishop Vasco de Quiroga, who was inspired by the utopian thought of Erasmus and Thomas More to establish residential communities for groups drawn from some native populations. Cabrera also spent time in Cuernavaca, in central Mexico, apparently in the service of the family of Hernán Cortés.

The Franciscan priest was a prolific author, whose poems are the earliest known from colonial Mexico. Two years after his return to Spain in 1546, he published the *Meditatiunculae* [Little Meditations], a volume of acrostic verses composed in the Indies which he dedicated to the future Philip II.[2] After being appointed by Philip to translate the Tridentine catechism from Latin into Castilian, Fray Cristóbal Cabrera settled in Rome in the 1560s, as a Spanish envoy attached to the Papal Palace and as a Master of Sacred Theology.[3] By the time of his death, in 1598, he had written more than forty works of poetry and devotional literature, by far most of which were in Latin.[4]

This chapter will examine three poems Cabrera produced during his early career in New Spain: the 'Dicolon icastichon', his first publication (and the first poem to be printed in the New World); a verse epistle surviving in manuscript which excoriates the Spaniards for their conduct in the Indies; and the 'Ecstasis', an ingenious autobiographical fiction which is nothing short of a masterpiece. Before turning to those Latin compositions, the discussion will open with a dedicatory letter Cabrera penned to Cortés's wife. Though on this occasion he was writing in the vernacular, the author indicated his preference for Latin, a preference which was widely shared by Spanish humanists — for all that Antonio de Nebrija had idiosyncratically championed Castilian as the 'companion of empire' nearly half a century earlier.[5]

I

During the period Fray Cristóbal Cabrera spent in Cortés's fief of Cuernavaca, probably in the early 1540s, the friar translated a collection of moral maxims for the conquistador's wife, the Marquesa Juana de Zúñiga. The collection, entitled *Flores de consolación* [Flowers of Consolation] and later published in Valladolid in 1550, is lost, although it is evident from an early Italian translation of the work that it consisted of excerpts from the writings of patristic authors.[6] The dedication of the original Spanish volume, however, has been preserved.[7] There Cabrera makes a show of his humanist learning as he reflects on the difficulty of rendering the Latin of his source into Spanish, and professes that he is not adept at using the vernacular, or *romance*:

A la muy ilustre y muy generosa señora, la Señora D.ª Juana de Zúñiga, marquesa del Valle. El intérprete, salud: *Las flores de consolación*, que el señor obispo de Méjico envió a vuestra señoría como ilustre señora, y vuestra señoría me mandó traducir de latín en castellano, traduje de corrida en aquellas horas que pude hurtar a mi familiar estudio. No fui tan supersticioso intérprete, que dejase de quitar o poner, o mudar algo cuando el tiempo y lugar lo requería; porque todo era menester para poner en concierto las escobas desatadas que topé. Tal era el estilo; era tan conciso y mal ceñido, que pudiera con más razón decir dél el emperador Calígula lo que dijo del de Séneca, que parecía arena sin cal. El libro vino a mis manos escripto de mano y de tal letra, que algunas veces era menester el ingenio de Delio el nadador, o la adevinanza de Edipo para acertar lo que quería decir. No fue menos trabajo buscar los originales destas *Flores* para sacar a la luz la verdad... De buena gana hice lo que puedo en la traducción de este libro; si no va mi romance tan polido como lo hilan algunos retóricos castellanos, no es de maravillar, porque al cabo de tanto tiempo como ha que peregrino por estas tierras y naciones bárbaras, donde se tracta más la lengua de los indios que la española, y donde se tiene por bárbaro el que no es bárbaro entre los bárbaros, no es mucho que esté olvidado de la elegancia de la lengua castellana. Cuanto más que no soy muy curioso del romance; véolo poco, trátolo poco, sé bien que no lo sé bien. Tomemos el tronco, que es la doctrina; dejemos las ramas, que son las palabras... En Cuernavaca, o como los indios dicen, Cohaunauac, el más fresco y apacible pueblo de la Nueva España, 25 de mayo.

[To the very illustrious and very generous Lady, Doña Juana de Zúñiga, Marquesa del Valle. The translator's greetings. *The Flowers of Consolation*, which the Lord Bishop of Mexico sent to your ladyship, as an illustrious lady, and which your ladyship bade me to translate from Latin into Castilian, I translated hurriedly in those hours that I could steal for my personal study. I have not been so deferential a translator that I have refrained from omitting, adding or moving something when the time and place requires it; because it was necessary to place in order the loose ends I encountered. Such was the style: it was so compact and awkwardly tight that I could say of it what the emperor Caligula said of Seneca's style — and with more justification — that it seemed like sand without lime. The book came to my hands written by hand, and the lettering was such that at times the genius of a Delian diver or Oedipus's skill at riddles was necessary to hit on what it meant. It was no less work to find the originals of these 'Flowers' to bring the truth to light... Very willingly I did what I could in the translation of this book: if my vernacular is not as polished as what some Castilian rhetoricians can spin, it is not surprising: since, after so much time as a wanderer in these lands and among these barbarous peoples, where the language of the Indians is used more than that of the Spaniards, and where one who is not a barbarian is regarded as a barbarian among the barbarians, it is of little account that I should be forgetful of the elegance of the Castilian tongue. More significantly, I am not very interested in the vernacular: I rarely see it, I rarely use it, I know well that I do not know it well. Let us keep the trunk of our education; let us leave the branches which are the spoken words... In Cuernavaca, or as the Indians say, *Cohaunauac* [sic], the most refreshing and peaceful town in New Spain, 25 May.]

Cabrera's complaints about the unwieldy style and poor legibility of the manuscript he was translating were embellished with classical *exempla* — all purloined from Erasmus of Rotterdam. It was Erasmus who had first taken Caligula's remark that Seneca was 'sand without lime' to be a verdict on Seneca's prose style, when (according to Suetonius) the emperor had meant it of the man himself.[8] And it had been Erasmus who, tellingly in the context of making his own translations of Euripides, complained that the Greek choruses were 'so obscure that they needed an Oedipus or a Delian [diver] rather than an interpreter'.[9]

But once Cabrera turns to discuss his lack of facility with vernacular Spanish, he makes far more direct and innovative use of ancient sources. His observation that he is 'regarded as a barbarian among barbarians' reprises Ovid's lament that he could not make himself understood in the language of the Getic people amongst whom he had been exiled.[10] The Roman poet's fear that he might be losing the ability to speak Latin is also recalled, along with Saint Jerome's anxiety that his Latin had rusted away after reading so much Hebrew.[11] The Franciscan's claim here that he was losing his proficiency in Castilian could be genuine: he really had been living in places where Amerindian languages were predominant, and at least one other missionary in Mexico reported that he had forgotten all of his native language.[12]

Yet Cabrera makes no suggestion that his predicament of being a *bárbaro entre los bárbaros* has done any damage to his Latin. The implication might be that everyday spoken languages, whether they are European or native American, may come and go, whilst knowledge of Latin is of a different order and more deeply rooted. That implication is corroborated by what follows. The image of the tree-trunk and its branches indicates a conception of language in which what can be taught or learnt is fundamental, of far more importance than the spoken word.[13] Thus the trunk of 'doctrina' corresponds to the acquired *langue* of Latin, and the branches of 'palabras' [words] are everyday spoken languages, Amerindian as well as European. The interchangeability of those vernacular 'palabras' is illustrated in the final sentence, as Cuernavaca and its indigenous name 'Cohaunauac' are set in equivalence. The meaning of that name in the Mexican language of Nahuatl, 'place beside the trees', might be connected to the conceit of language as a tree, with Latin as the trunk.[14]

The very suggestion that Nahuatl and Spanish alike could be viewed as offshoots from the trunk of Latin appears bizarre by our own lights — but even by the sixteenth century, the idea now taken for granted of Latin as the precursor of Romance languages had little currency. Latin was not seen as the source of the vernaculars, but as an artificial medium which had been refined *from* them.[15] The perceived universality of Latin, commonly referred to in Spanish simply as 'gramática' [grammar], partly explains why Latin was being studied and promoted in the Peninsula more than ever before, and its importance increased over the course of the 1500s.[16] Cabrera's comments on the Castilian texts he wrote much later in his life, long after his return to Europe, indicate that he considered writing in the vernacular as a kind of sacrifice he was making for the benefit of Spanish readers.[17]

II

A humorous Latin epigram on how to baptize an Indian was the first poem — in any language — to be printed in the Americas.[18] The 'Dicolon icastichon' appeared as a coda to the *Manual de adultos*, a handbook on administering baptism which was published in Mexico City in 1540:

> Christophorus Cabrera Burgensis ad lectorem sacri baptisimi ministrum:
> Dicolon Icastichon
>
> Si paucis praenosse[19] cupis: uenerande sacerdos:
>   Ut baptizari quilibet Indus habet:
> Quaeque prius debent ceu parua elementa doceri:
>   Quicquid adultus iners scire tenetur item:
> Quaeque sient priscis patribus sancita: per orbem   [5]
>   Ut foret ad ritum tinctus adultus aqua:
> Ut ne despiciat (fors) tam sublime Charisma
>   Indulus ignarus terque quaterque miser:
> Hunc manibus versa: tere: perlege: dilige librum:
>   Nil minus[20] obscurum: nil magis est nitidum   [10]
> Simpliciter docteque dedit modo Vascus acutus
>   Addo Quiroga meus praesul abunde pius.
> Singula perpendens nihil[21] inde requirere possis:
>   (Si placet) omne legas ordine dispositum.
> Ne videare (caue) sacris ignauus abuti   [15]
>   Sis decet aduigilans: mittito desidiam.
> Nempe bonum nihil unquam fecerit oscitabundus.
>   Difficile est pulchrum: dictitat Antiquitas.
> Sed satis est: quid me remoraris pluribus: inquis.
>   Sit satis: et facias quod precor atque uale.   [20]

[Cristóbal Cabrera of Burgos to the reader, minister of holy baptism: a
Dicolon Icastichon

If you yearn to know, in just a few words, reverend priest,
   How any Indian is to be baptized,
And what he ought to be taught as some short basics,
   Indeed whatever a lethargic adult is supposed to know
And what was ordained by the early fathers, for all the world   [5]
   That an adult is to be intincted ritually with water,
That Grace so exalted is not to be scorned (as it may be)
   By an unwary little Indian three and four times wretched,
Then turn in your hands, thumb, read through, cherish this book:
   Nothing is less obscure, nothing is more bright.   [10]
In a direct and learned way, sharp Vasco has just granted this
   — I add 'Quiroga' — my overwhelmingly devout bishop.
Weighing each point, you should then need nothing more,
   (If you don't mind) read everything set out, in order.
(Take care) Don't show yourself lazy and thus abuse the rite: [15]
   Be appropriately vigilant, send slackness on its way.
For nothing good has ever been done by one prone to idleness.
   Difficult is fine: Antiquity tells us again and again.
But this is enough. 'Why detain me with more?' you say.
   May it be enough, and may you do as I ask, and fare well.]   [20]

Such occasional verses in elegiac couplets routinely accompanied publications of all kinds. At first glance this example appears unremarkable, apart from the caveat about the potential irreverence of the Indian whose abject state, 'terque quaterque miser' [three times and four times wretched], pointedly inverts the condition of the defeated Trojans in Virgil who were 'terque quaterque beati' [three and four times blessed] for dying under Troy's walls before their fathers' eyes.[22]

Other allusions throw more light on the temper of this short text. The opening and closing lines recall pagan Greek and Roman verse epitaphs which began by requesting the attention of whoever might read them and ended by expressing thanks for their compliance.[23] The last couplet anticipates any complaint from the reader who is now being subjected to more than the 'few words' indicated at the start, whilst the tone of the final farewell is also in keeping with that of many classical funerary inscriptions.[24] For humanist Latin poets, as for their Roman forebears, it was common to begin a short elegy or epigram with the word *Si*, 'If'. But Cabrera's opening words, '*Si* paucis prae*nosse* cupis...' [*If* you yearn to *know* in a few words...] ('Dicolon Icastichon', 1), more specifically bring to mind the very first line of a more notorious 'manual for adults', Ovid's *Ars amatoria* [The Art of Love]:

> *Si* quis in hoc artem populo non *nouit* amandi
>   hoc *legat* et lecto carmine *doctus* amet. (*Ars amatoria* 1.1–2)
>
> [*If* anyone in this throng has not *known* the art of loving,
>   Then let him *read* this poem, and after reading it, be *learned* in love.]

The diction of Ovid's second line, above, is picked up too, but only after Cabrera's long opening conditional clause (verses 1–8) has finally come to an end:

> Hunc manibus versa: tere: per*lege*: dilige librum:
>   Nilminus obscurum: nil magis est nitidum
> Simpliciter *docte*que dedit modo Vascus acutus
>   ('Dicolon Icastichon', ll. 9–11)

> [Then turn in your hands, thumb, *read* through, cherish this book
>   Nothing is less obscure, nothing is more bright.
> In a direct and *learned* way, sharp Vasco has just granted this.]

The evocation of the controversial *Ars amatoria* is purely structural and lexical — not thematic.[25] Its function was to signal clearly to a Latinate reader the lighter tenor of the present verses. The flippant disparaging of the Indian as 'iners' [lethargic], 'ignarus' [unwary] and 'miser' [wretched] in this lengthy sentence is thus not in earnest: such use of humour or hyperbole as a vehicle for serious concerns was an Erasmian trait which is also exhibited in the remaining texts to be examined in this chapter.

After echoing Horace and Martial, Cabrera tactfully identifies the author of the *Manual de adultos* as Vasco de Quiroga — who was his own director and mentor.[26] Quiroga expressed his enthusiasm for both Erasmus and Thomas More in his own writing.[27] Tendencies characteristic of both authors can be seen in the 'Dicolon Icastichon'. The Latinization of Greek terms in that very title was a frequent practice in the *Utopia* and in other works by Thomas More — who himself wrote some 250 elegiac epigrams, many of which have the kind of ironic tone Cabrera adopts here.[28] Erasmus played an important part in promoting early church authors or 'prisci patres' whose prescriptions are accentuated in verse 5; and 'Difficile est pulchrum' [Difficult is fine] in verse 18 derives from a coinage in 'Venatio' [Hunting], a dialogue in his *Colloquia familiaria* [Discussions among friends]:

> Laurentius: Difficile est sectari volantia.
> Bartholus: *Difficile, sed pulchrum*; nisi pulchrius esse ducis sectari lumbricos
>   aut cochleas, quia carent alis.[29]

> [Lorenzo: It is difficult to hunt things that fly.
> Bartolo: *Difficult, but fine*; unless you think it's finer to hunt worms or snails,
>   because they have no wings.]

'Difficile, sed pulchrum' translates an expression in Plato's *Sophist* and the Greek maxim 'Difficult things are fine', was indeed reiterated in antiquity as Cabrera affirms, in Platonic literature.[30]

The *Colloquia familiaria*, published in 1518, were primarily to provide models of Latin usage, but they referred to topical or intellectual concerns. 'Venatio' in fact evoked a whole section of the *Sophist* in which Socrates and his companions in the dialogue reviewed different methods of hunting to illustrate the various strategies a sophist could employ. Plato's interlocutors went on to consider the nature of representational art — which can be either *phantastic* (completely imaginative) or *icastic* (precisely imitative of its object).[31]

The notion of icastic representation helps to explain the title of Cabrera's epigram, 'Dicolon Icastichon'. The Greek 'díkōlos' denotes two cola or metrical units — but in medieval rhetoric the term 'dicolon' referred to the doubling or synonymic repetition of a phrase — the sense more pertinent here.[32] As 'Icastichon' appears to be derived from 'eikastikón', an adjective from the Greek noun 'eikasía' [precise imitation], the title as a whole could mean something like 'A Precisely Imitative Reduplication'.[33] Such a pleonasm suits a poem which formulates so many of its propositions in two different ways — and which recapitulates the content of the *Manual* to which it was appended. The first poem to be printed in Mexico City anticipated later colonial Latin literature in its deft application of humanist *imitatio* to American themes.

III

Cabrera's manuscripts of 'ex tempore' poetry from Mexico included more than a hundred epigrams on a variety of classical, patristic and Renaissance humanist authors, ranging from Homer and Herodotus to Prudentius and Pico della Mirandola. There were also two longer epistolary poems conveying personal opinions and observations about the missionary experience of New Spain.[34] One, taking after Ovid's *Tristia*, was written to another friar named Hieronymus and sought to alleviate his loneliness as a 'barbarian among barbarians'.[35] The other verse epistle, to be surveyed here, was entitled 'Ad Emmanuelem Florez sanctae Mexicanensis Ecclesiae Decanum Extemporalis Epistola' [An *Ex Tempore* Letter to Manuel Flores, Dean of the Holy Church of Mexico].

The addressee, Dean Manuel Flores, had testified in support of Vasco de Quiroga in 1536 and took part in the Mexican Synod of 1544.[36] A 1547 letter from Bishop Zumárraga to Prince Philip of Spain reveals that damp and the environment of Mexico City were having an adverse effect on Flores's health, to which Cabrera refers in the opening lines:[37]

> Emmanuel Florens, Christum mihi nomine signans,
> Vt valeas nunc scire velim, nam saepe timemus
> Ne male sana tibi sit Mexicus, atque rebellet
> In caput illa tuum nebulis infecta palustris.
> ('Ad Emmanuelem Florez', ll. 8–10)

> [Emmanuel Flores — your first name signifies *Christ* to me —
> I would like to know you are well now, as I often fear
> Mexico City is not at all good for you, and that it is punishing
> For your head, as the place is tainted with fog from the marshes.]

As well as calling attention to the meaning of Flores's Christian name, the poet plays covertly on the similarity of his surname to *Florus*, the addressee of two verse epistles by the Roman poet Horace. Horace's complaints to Florus in *Epistles* 2.2 that the rowdiness of Rome made it an unsuitable location for a poet are transformed by Cabrera into a sustained diatribe: Mexico City, with its noise and insalubrious marsh vapours, is set in contrast to the peacefulness of the countryside where he is writing. In a prose letter to Bishop Zumárraga, Cabrera had made a similar objection to the capital 'ubi nihil non est obstreperum, turbulentum et clamosum, vulcanicam officinam dicas rectius quam literariam' [where everything is clattering, chaotic and clamorous: you'd be right to say it is more like Vulcan's workshop than a literary one].[38]

But in this poem he goes further. Contempt for the noisiness of the urban *vulgus* leads him to liken the city to Babylon, just as the first Epistle of Peter in the New Testament had used Babylon as a vehicle for Rome:[39]

> Mexicus est Babylon, similet mea cella Sionem.
> Quisquis amat miseri Babylonica flumina mundi
> Obrutus, heu, pelago mersusque peribit in vndis
>   ('Ad Emmanuelem Florez', ll. 19–21)

> [Mexico City is Babylon, but may my own cell take after Zion.
> Anyone who loves Babylon's rivers in this wretched world,
> Overcome, alas, by an ocean, will perish plunged in its waves.]

The inhabitants are denounced for their greed, their tendency to brag like Terence's comical character Thraso — even to boast of an ancestry going back to Cecrops, the mythical king of Athens. The old men in the city show folly and vanity: an ageing man thinks he is as beautiful as Narcissus, Nereus or Astur, when really he is uglier than Homer's Thersites or Brotheus.[40] Such greed and indecorousness might amuse Democritus, the laughing philosopher, but should prompt tears from a follower of Christ. Even pagan Rome, with all the vices which Horace, Persius and Juvenal recorded in their satires, was not as corrupt as Mexico City — which is again characterized as a Babylon ruined by *bruta voluptas*:

> Quot tibi sunt, rogito, meretrices? Quot tibi lenae?
> Innumerae Hispanae non hûc remeare verentur
> Auri auidae, magni quas quaestus fama coegit
> Vt vasti Oceani sulcarent nauibus aequor
> Et peterent indos semotos orbe. quid oro
> Turpius hoc fingi queat aut audacius vnquam?
>   ('Ad Emmanuelem Florez', ll. 59–64)

> [How many whores have you, Babylon? I ask, How many bawds?
> Countless are the Spanish women who have no fear to come here
> Greedy for gold, compelled by talk of great gain
> To furrow the waters of vast Ocean in their ships.
> What, pray, more disgusting or rash than this could be imagined?]

The harangue against women continues for another fifty lines — the longest section of the epistle, amounting to a quarter of the entire text. Cabrera compares the unjustified elevation of women to that of the biblical idol of Baal, Beelphegor.[41] Many wives claim the respectable title of *matrona*, but they do not deserve the name:

> Illud enim claret perpaucas esse modestas
> In cute curanda, faciéque et corpore fucis
> Vt nimia cura nitidis et olentibus illae
> Vestibus ornantur molles, crispante capillo?
>   ('Ad Emmanuelem Florez', ll. 80–84)

> [Shouldn't it be clear that very few women are modest
> In the way they look after their skin, and colour their faces and body,
> Like those taking too much trouble over their shiny and scented
> Outfits to dress up alluringly, crimping their hair?]

The women falsely claim to be adorning themselves to please their husbands, who are really worn down by their shrieking and demands, while 'vetulae', old crones, make themselves ridiculous by dyeing their hair and smearing their decaying bodies with ointment. Returning to the association with idolatry, the poet deplores the wantonness and pride of women who are decked out like goddesses in temples, when Christ taught mortification of the flesh by his own example.

There were comparable comments and condemnations from priest and members of religious orders who sought to regulate social and sexual mores in the Indies.[42] But Cabrera's insistence that 'countless' [Innumerae] Spanish women were arriving in New Spain during the 1530s and 1540s is an exaggeration. Even by the end of the sixteenth century women constituted only one third of the population of Spaniards in the Americas.[43] The poet's tirade was inspired by ancient pagan and Christian traditions of invective against women rather than by anything he really witnessed. Moreover, Cabrera was no misogynist: his earliest biographer Nicolás Antonio reveals that at the end of his life he supported the widowed wife of his brother and her daughter, and he endowed a 'hospitalis domus' or residential home for women pilgrims in Rome.[44] The likely motive for incorporating the diatribe against women was to provide a memorable diversion, softening the impact of the shorter but more seditious polemics which are to follow.

The poet then turns to the males in the colony: he has seen for himself how youths and men in their prime imitate women by decorating themselves in gold and gems, like the Assyrian king Sardanapalus. They ride around on horseback as they look for houses with windows, to serenade girls with their guitars, to entrap as many victims as they can. The menfolk show no temperance in dining and their gluttony knows no bounds. In elaborating upon the 'Plague of Greed' [Avaritiae pestis] (146) brought by the Spaniards to the Indies, the poet's reference to gold, silver and jewels as the 'idols served by mankind' would have been provocative at a time when the extirpation of Indian idolatry remained the pretext for the Spaniards' accumulation of wealth in the Indies. Just as avarice, pride and lust had been standard themes for the Roman satirists, so too was the idea of imitation as the basis of moral conduct:

> Hispani hîc peccant, peccare docentur et indi.
> Quod deploro nefas. Hi quae sunt praua sequuntur
> Moribus ex nostris, vt simiae quaeque facessunt.
> ('Ad Emmanuelem Florez', ll. 161–63)

> [The Spaniards here are sinful, the Indians are taught to sin too.
> An evil I deplore, as the Indians follow what is depraved
> From our behaviour just as apes are inclined to act things out.]

Peter Martyr d'Anghiera's *De orbe novo Decades* [Decades on the New World], first published in Seville in 1516, had popularized an image of the original state of the native Americans drawn from Ovid's description of the classical Golden Age.[45] That may have in turn provided a model for Cabrera's description of the native Americans before their contact with the Spaniards:

> sine vestibus ante
> Degebant, vitam naturae legibus omnes

> Metantes, tenui victu, tenuique paratu
> Contenti (quibus esse animus qui possit auarus?)
>   ('Ad Emmanuelem Florez', ll. 164–67)

>   [before without clothes
> They subsisted, all measuring their life by Nature's laws,
> And with minimal diet and minimal preparation of food they were
> Content (who among these could be a greedy soul?)]

Cabrera, though, was more directly influenced by Vasco de Quiroga, whose idea of the primitive innocence of the Indians can be found in his official letters and reports. On the other hand, the ensuing attack on the integrity of the missionaries in the New World could be compared to the reprimands Fray Bartolomé de las Casas would issue in the 1540s:

> Crede mihi non est syncerus Apostolus Indis.
> Quisne rogo Christi diuina negotia curat?
> Quin sua quisque magis quaerit, per fasque nefasque
> Tenditur in lucrum. Argentum dominatur et aurum,
> Tale sibi idôlum charum vir auarus adorat.
> Pro quo non dubitat cum Juda vendere Christum,
> Nomine et ore tenus quem profert corde negauit.
> Per nostrûm multos, heu, blasphematur ab indis
> Nomen adorandum Christi Dominique Deique.
>   ('Ad Emmanuelem Florez', ll. 173–81)

> [Believe me, there is not a genuine Apostle in the Indies.
> Who, pray, sees to Christ's divine work?
> Rather each one looks out for himself: by fair means or foul
> Profit is the target. Silver and gold rule.
> Such is the dear idol the greedy man adores for his own lot.
> For that, he doesn't hesitate, with Judas, to sell Christ,
> Whose name he pays lip-service to but has denied in his heart.
> Because of many of us, alas, the Indians blaspheme
> The beloved Name of Christ, and of our Lord and God.]

In fact, the poet was really imitating the scathing polemics of Erasmus who had, for instance, declared that impious popes were really the true enemies of the church.[46] The aspersions Cabrera had cast on *all* the Spaniards in Mexico in this epistle may have prepared the ground for this invective against the missionaries, but his bitter comparison of the apostles in the Indies to Judas Iscariot remains highly inflammatory.

The final part of the epistle is more optimistic. The poet lists all the healthy activities that could be pursued in the country: hunting, tilling the earth, playing the shepherd's pipe, horse-riding and reading. He himself enjoys the pursuit of 'sapientia', and books provide him with company in his rural solitude. His Muse is able to devote herself to sacred texts and to take pleasure in the contemplation of nature — even mulling over the insights of the natural historians from Greco-Roman antiquity as she does so — to refresh his spirit for further work. The Muse is a tactful projection of the poet himself: by attributing to her his dispositions and his forms of recreation, he can avoid appearing sanctimonious and self-satisfied as he presents positive *exempla* from his own way of life.

The text ends by reaffirming its opening assertion: the countryside is safer than the city, and a better place to struggle against the world, the flesh and the devil. The initial greeting of verses 1–2 is recalled in the very last lines, as the writer prays that Christ may save him and Emmanuel from the devil for God's kingdom and a life of blessedness.

IV

The 'Ecstasis', a first-person narrative in 236 hexameters, fuses the discourses of confession, prayer, vision literature, satire and epic to construct a harrowing psychodrama. It appears at the end of the *Meditatiunculae*, a collection of acrostic verses and *carmina figurata* which Cabrera had composed in New Spain and which he dedicated to Prince Philip in 1548.[47]

The 'Ecstasis' begins with the poet's expression of remorse for reading profane rather than sacred literature, in a manner very reminiscent of Saint Augustine's *Confessions*. He explains that in the twelve years following his arrival in the New World he has long been devoted to 'humana volumina', books on the humanities. But after being instructed by a dream to turn his back on pagan classical literature, he dedicates himself to the intensive study of Christian works, fasting with such zeal that he becomes ill and suffers a premonition that the City of Mexico will be destroyed by God. In this state he runs 40 miles from the villa of Cuernavaca towards Mexico City, staying overnight with some monks before hurrying on. He refuses the offer of food from some Indians, begging them to revere God, but they persist in their rituals of scattering flowers and dancing.

The poet then has a Vision of Judgment in which he sees clergy, doctors, merchants and women — the over-strict and over-indulgent alike — being dragged down to hell, and glorious knights on white horses ascending to heaven. At nightfall he is found by the monks who were anxiously searching for him; when he still refuses to eat, they take him to the Bishop in Mexico City. The Bishop, appalled at the state his former pupil is in and recognizing that he is mentally ill, disregards his warnings of an apocalypse and orders him to be locked up and forcibly medicated. The patient is eventually restored to full health. But the poet tells us that what he had feared in his delusions did come about after all: Mexico was devastated by a plague, a calamity without precedent.

The 'Ecstasis' confirms that Erasmus provided Cabrera with far more than a repertory of *exempla* and *bons mots*: the Dutch humanist's *Moriae encomium* or *Stultitiae laus* [Praise of Folly], first published in 1511, was foundational for the conception of this poem. In his popular work of philosophical satire, Erasmus had presented Christianity as a kind of madness, arguing that enraptured Christians enjoyed an experience similar to dementedness. Ancient Platonic traditions of conceiving madness or 'ecstasy' as a route to mystical understanding had been influential and there were analogues in patristic interpretations of scripture.[48] In that context, three biblical books shape the story Cabrera tells: the book of Jonah, which inspired the premonition of Mexico City 'appearing as Nineveh once did'; the book of Revelation, which informs the poet's Vision of Judgment; and an excerpt from the 'book of consolation' in Jeremiah which offered hope that Jerusalem would be restored.[49]

There are also clear traces of classical epic design in the 'Ecstasis'. Virgil began the *Aeneid* with a geographical description of Carthage to explain Juno's resentment of the Trojans, and a comparable transition launches Cabrera's small-scale verse narrative:

> Sed quo gesta modo res est, est dicere. dicam:
> Indorum regio procul hoc quae distat ab orbe
> Nostro, quae oceani vasti concludit abyssum,
> Ductu continuo, longe lateque vagata,
> Orbem quippe nouum latio[50] quam nomine dicunt,
> Me quo[n]dam excepit. ('Ecstasis', ll. 45–50)

> [But it remains to tell how this came about. I shall tell it:
> The realm of the Indies which lies far away from the world
> Of ours, the realm marking the end of the vast ocean's abyss,
> Spreading far and wide with a long shoreline,
> Which indeed they call the 'New World' in Latin,
> Once took me in.]

The anger of Virgil's Juno ('irae', *Aeneid* 1.11) is later paralleled by Cabrera's anticipation of God's wrath ('Dei [...] iras' ['Ecstasis', l. 90]) coming upon the Spaniards and Indians in Mexico. The poet's reaction to the vision he beheld also has an epic colouring:

> Isthic persistens occasum solis adusque
> *Attonitus* simulacra *hominum variasque figuras*
> *Mirabar.* tunc visa mihi nunc nolo profari.
> *Eloquar an taceam?* ('Ecstasis', ll. 135–38)

> [Remaining there steadfast right until sunset, I was
> Astounded *by images of* men and various figures
> *I wondered at.* I do not wish to tell now of things I saw then.
> *Should I speak or keep silent?*]

Virgil's Aeneas had been 'astounded' [attonitus] at the apparitions of the divine Penates and Mercury, and he too had hesitated about whether to 'speak or be silent' [Eloquar an sileam?] on hearing the ghostly voice of Polydorus. A description of a tapestry '*varied* with the ancient *figures of men* [...] with *wonderful* art' [vestis priscis *hominum variata figuris* [...] *mira* [...] arte], from Catullus's poem 64, a miniature epic on the marriage of Peleus and Thetis, is in play too.[51]

But Catullus's poem 63, about the mythical Attis, has far more in common with the language and theme of the 'Ecstasis'. Both works involve protagonists who make a journey overseas before excessive religious zeal leads them into a state of agitation in which they lose their judgment and identity. Catullus's Attis, a young devotee of the goddess Cybele, sailed to Phrygia and castrated himself in an ecstatic frenzy, but briefly repented of his actions, before again being driven 'mad' [demens] (63.89) by one of the goddess's lions whom she commanded to 'suffer [its] own lashes' [tua verbera patere] (63.8). Cabrera's narrator, having voyaged to the New World, repents of his enthusiasm for profane literature, to find that his 'mad state of mind has been displaced by a mad state of mind' [mens mea demens | Mente repulsa fuit demente] (ll. 30–31), so that he comes to 'know [God's] lashes' [tua verbera noui] (l. 33).

His 'swift hurry to celebrate Mass' [citus propero feruens ad sacra synaxis] (l. 109) parallels Attis's hastening with 'the swift chorus on hurrying feet' [citus [...] properante pede chorus] (63.30) to the Bacchic rites on Mount Ida; and the Franciscan's likening of himself to 'an unbroken foal or a horse that has cast off its bridle' [veluti indomitum pullum effrenemque caballum] (l. 229) parallels Catullus's comparison of Attis to a untamed heifer shirking the yoke ('veluti iuvenca [...] indomita' [63.33]).[52] At the end of the 'Ecstasis' the narrator admits that the virtue and piety he possessed have left him barren ('me sterilem fugit' [l. 221]), just as the emasculated Attis complained that he was 'a sterile man' [ego uir sterilis] (63.69) at the close of Catullus 63.

Cabrera's debt is obvious but it is hard to account for. Catullus's poetry barely circulated in peninsular Spain in the sixteenth century, let alone in the Indies. The only Spaniard to have known the Attis poem in this period had been the soldier-poet Garcilaso de la Vega, who encountered it in the early 1530s, not in Spain but in Naples, where he imitated it in a Latin ode which remained in obscurity until 1898.[53] How Garcilaso's *recherché* Catullan model reached Cabrera in Mexico only a few years after the soldier's death in Nice in 1536 is a mystery, but Garcilaso's widow, Elena de Zúñiga, was from the same family as Cortés's wife, Juana de Zúñiga. Such well born Spanish women were sometimes afforded a humanist education: possibly Doña Juana had a part in making the text of Catullus available to Cabrera when he was in Cuernavaca.

Classical models for the 'Ecstasis' can be closely interwoven with biblical sources. The poet's description of the site of his vision is a striking example:

> Sub fruticem quendam, quem indi dixere magaeum,
> Tensus humi iaceo *meditans resupinus ad umbram*. ('Ecstasis', ll. 118–19)

> [Under a sort of bush, which the Indians have called a maguey,
> I lie stretched out on the ground *meditating, reclining in the shade*.]

That is an evocation of Virgil's first *Eclogue*:

> Tityre, tu patulae *recubans sub tegmine* fagi
> silvestrem tenui Musam *meditaris* avena. (Virgil, *Ecl.* 1.1–2)

> [Tityrus, *recumbent under the cover* of a spreading beech,
> You meditate upon your woodland Muse on a slender pipe.]

By resting in the shade to see what would happen to the city of Mexico, the poet is also following the example of Jonah who sat in the shade of a large plant to see what would befall Nineveh (Jonah 4. 5–6). Here the shade is provided by a maguey plant — a dig at Saint Jerome's notorious decision in his Vulgate bible to translate the Hebrew for 'gourd' in this passage with 'hedera', the Latin for ivy. By inserting the Mexican plant in his evocation of the episode in Jonah, Cabrera sidesteps the controversy even as he calls attention to it.

The maguey contributes to the reality effect of the story. Other details reflect the poet's experience of New Spain: Mexico City and Cuernavaca are named; the vignette of the Indians dancing and scattering flowers evokes authentic ritual practice; and the plague which fulfilled the poet's premonition really did occur. The epidemic, known in Nahuatl as 'matlazahuatl' [green rash], killed approximately 800,000 Indians in 1545.[54] Some friars had predicted that such a scourge would come upon Mexico City as divine retribution for the Spaniards' greed and corruption, although the 'Ecstasis' is not a straightforward expression of that millenarian creed.[55] It is not clear whether the premonitions and visions in the text were divinely prompted or delusions brought on by a frenzy of reading, sleep deprivation and fasting. The reader is obliged to hesitate over whether what is recounted can be *naturally* explained (because the narrator had gone mad) or *supernaturally* explained (because God really was forewarning him of a disaster).

The solution lies in an amazing formal feature of the poem: it is the longest acrostic in western literature. The first letters of each of the 236 hexameter lines spell out the words of Jeremiah 31. 18–19:

> Castigasti me Domine et eruditus sum, quasi iuvenculus indomitus: converte me et convertar; quia tu Dominus Deus meus. Postquam enim convertisti me, egi poenitentiam: et postquam ostendisti mihi, percussi femur meum. Confusus sum, et erubui, quoniam sustinui opprobrium adolescentia mea.

> [Thou hast chastised me, Lord, and I was chastised, as a bullock unaccustomed to the yoke: turn thou me, and I shall be turned; for thou art the Lord my God. Surely after thou didst turn me, I repented; and after thou didst instruct me, I smote my thigh: I was confused, yea, even ashamed, because I bore the reproach of my youth.]

The diction of the vertical acrostic consistently reflects the theme of the horizontal text it accompanies. For example, the first letters of the lines which related the poet's revelatory vision of judgment spell 'postquam enim convertisti me' [after thou didst instruct me]; while the acrostic 'percussi femur meum' [I smote my thigh] aligns with the poet's self-destructive fasting which prompted the monks to abduct him for his own good. The word 'confusus' in the text of Jeremiah could not better reflect the poet's erroneous belief that the monks who wanted to help him were agents of an evil demon:

> C redideram secum qui me disperdere vellent.
> O mnes qui dicto nollent audire putabam
> N on ex parte Dei, sed daemonis esse maligni.
> F irmiter abstineo triduum ieiunus ab escis.
> V ectus postridie perque indos raptus in urbem,
> S enis distantem miliis, ad praesulis aedes
> V t mihi prospiceret, deponor. Episcopus horret.
> S alve, dico, Pater. Salve quoque, dixit, amice. ('Ecstasis', ll. 178–85)

> [I had believed they wanted to destroy me with themselves.
> All who were unwilling to pay heed to my words I thought
> Were not on God's side, but that of an evil demon.
> I firmly abstain from food, fasting for three days.

Seized the next day I was carried by Indians to the city,
A distance of six miles, to the Prelate's residence
For him to examine me, I am set down. The Bishop shudders.
'Greetings Father' I say. 'Greetings to you, friend' he said.]

That acrostic helps to solve the conundrum which is almost a Cretan paradox: *should we believe the narrative of a poet who claims he was insane?*

The answer lies in the association of acrostics with prophecy and madness in a text from pagan Rome which was available in sixteenth-century Spain.[56] Cicero's *De divinatione* discussed the Sibylline books in which the first letters of each line of an oracular poem spelled out the subject of its prophecy. Cicero's *porte-parole* in his dialogue affirmed that such acrostics has to be the work of a writer 'who is not in a frenzy, but one who takes pains, not a madman' [hoc scriptoris est, non furentis, adhibentis diligentiam, non insani].[57]

Cabrera must have got the whole idea of combining the acrostic verse form with *content* about madness and prophecy from Cicero's insistence that only a sane person can compose acrostic poetry. The acrostic of the 'Ecstasis' can thus be taken as a signal that its author — in contrast to the unstable narrator — is not mad at all. Such a contrast, between the narrator of the 'Ecstasis' and the poem's actual author works against reading its content as any kind of veridical testimony. That narrator, in verses 69–70, deemed pagan literature 'friuola prorsum nulliusque usus' [really silly and of no use], yet the author was *de facto* making effective use of classical sources in the poem. What is more, Cabrera made clear to Prince Philip in a prose *peroratio* following the 'Ecstasis' that 'the principle for [his] poems was taken from certain authors of antiquity' [haec carminum ratio a priscis quibusdam autoribus vsurpata].[58]

The original and primary meaning of the Greek word *ecstasis*, 'standing outside oneself', nicely signals the position of the poem's narrator in relation to its author. That disjunction subverts the seriousness of the story told in the poem. The story is a clever caricature of the belief some Franciscans held that the millenarian prophecies of destruction were soon to be fulfilled in the New World.

V

Cristóbal Cabrera is now all but forgotten, but his accomplishments won him acclaim in the sixteenth-century Atlantic world. As a young man he worked closely with Zumárraga and others who had a pivotal role in the early history of post-conquest Mexico. After his return to Europe, the Franciscan's talents were later recognized by Philip II and a succession of popes: his final publication in Rome, the *Rosarium Beatae Mariae*, in Latin, Spanish and Italian verse, contained an engraving which depicted the poet receiving the blessing of Gregory XIII.[59]

The present chapter has sought to highlight the innovative quality of Cabrera's poetry of the 1540s as well the unique perspective it affords on belief and society in New Spain at the time. The friar's formidable learning served as a vehicle for addressing contemporary concerns — in his tactful and finely crafted praise of the reformer Vasco de Quiroga, in his invective against the corruption and greed of the Spaniards in the Indies, and in his use of proto-Baroque artifice to challenge the credibility of Franciscan millenarianism. The 'Ecstasis', in particular, was a remarkable achievement, its ambitious acrostic eclipsed by the realistic fiction it generated.

The texts surveyed in this chapter are in different genres and address a range of subjects, but currents of Erasmus's thought and writing pervade them all. The poet's explicit preference for Latin was in line with this tendency — even the vernacular letter to Juana de Zúñiga deployed the same kind of *exempla* from the *Adagia* which adorned and amplified his Latin verse. Other missionaries in post-conquest Mexico, Dominicans and Franciscans alike, sought to apply the principles of Erasmian radical political theology and the *Philosophia Christi* [Philosophy of Christ] in the New World, with a corresponding emphasis on the models of the early church. Fray Cristóbal Cabrera gave expression to these values, advocating a practical religion, rooted in study of the Christian fathers. But the mordant wit and dark, paradoxical humour of Erasmus's satire is also evident in these poems which censured the greed and mocked the irrationalism of his fellow churchmen.

Erasmus of Rotterdam had made an immense contribution to the 'Christian turn' which propelled sixteenth-century humanism in Europe. That tendency, though, was losing its momentum even before the Council of Trent and the Counter-Reformation — to a large degree because Erasmus's followers began to be persecuted in Spain from as early as the 1520s.[60] By the following decade, literary productions in Latin and the vernacular were already becoming escapist and remote from the realm of praxis. Cabrera's early writings are an exceptional case. Intense Catholic religiosity and an Erasmian formation fused to endow his poetry with a caustic energy, so that the flawed ideals, injustices, and hypocrisies of a colonial environment inspired genuine poetic innovation.

Notes to Chapter 3

1. The initial research for this paper was done with the support of a Leverhulme Trust Major Research Fellowship. I am grateful to the staff of the Biblioteca Nacional de España (BNE), the Bodleian, the John Carter Brown Library and the Warburg Institute. Translations of quoted passages (and italicizations for emphasis) are my own.

2. Cabrera, *Meditatiunculae ad Serenissimum Hispaniarum Principem Philippum* (Pinciae [Valladolid]: Franciscus Ferdinandez Cordubensis, 1548): a copy is in the BNE [R/11385].

3. Pedro Rodríguez, *El Catecismo Romano ante Felipe II y la Inquisición española* (Madrid: Rialp, 1998), pp. 89–95, 101–05.

4. The following are detailed studies specifically devoted to Cabrera's work in New Spain: E. J. Burrus, 'Cristóbal Cabrera (*c.* 1515–98), First American Author: A Checklist of his Writings in the Vatican Library', *Manuscripta*, 4 (1960), 67–89; Idem, 'Cristóbal Cabrera on the Missionary Methods of Vasco de Quiroga', *Manuscripta*, 5 (1961), 17–27; Elisa Ruiz, 'Cristóbal Cabrera, apóstol grafómano', *Cuadernos de Filología Clásica*, 12 (1977), 59–147; Juan F. Alcina Rovira, 'Cristóbal Cabrera en Nueva España y sus *Meditatiunculae ad principem Philippum*', *Nova Tellus*, 2 (1984), 131–63; Andrew Laird, 'Franciscan Humanism in Post-Conquest Mexico: Fray Cristóbal Cabrera's Epigrams on Classical and Renaissance Authors (*Vat Lat* 1165)', *Studi Umanistici Piceni*, 33 (2013), 195–216; Idem, 'Classical Letters and Millenarian Madness in Post-Conquest Mexico: The *Ecstasis* of Fray Cristóbal Cabrera (1548)', *International Journal of the Classical Tradition*, 24.1 (2017), 78–108.

5. Nebrija made this affirmation in his Castilian grammar which was barely known: Hans-J. Niederehe, 'La *Gramática de la lengua castellana* (1492) de Antonio de Nebrija', *Boletín de la Sociedad Española de Historiografía Lingüística*, 4 (2004), 31–42.

6. The Italian translation, mentioned by Cabrera in his *Instrumento espiritual*, did not credit or name him at all: Ruiz, 'Cristóbal Cabrera', p. 103, considered it lost but it is in the BNE [R/30316]: *Fiori di consolatione ad ogni fedel Christiano necessarii [...] tradotti dallo Spagnolo per M. Pietro Lauro Modone* (Vinegia [Venice]: Gabriele Giolito de' Ferrari, 1562).

7. The dedication, not found in the Italian version, is quoted here as it was transcribed by Bartolomé José Gallardo, *Ensayo de una biblioteca española de libros raros y curiosos*, 4 vols (Madrid: M. Rivadeneyra, M. Tello, 1863–89), II, cols 164–65, and copied in Ruiz, 'Cristóbal Cabrera', pp. 102–03. According to Gallardo the 97 octavo pages of the *Flores de Consolación* contained 89 'stoical' maxims.

8. Erasmus, *Adagia* 2.3.57, in *Opera Omnia*: II.3, ed. by M. Szymański (Amsterdam: Elsevier Science, 2005), p. 276 (probably the source of the Spanish saying 'una de cal y otra de arena'). D. Wardle, *Suetonius' Life of Caligula. A Commentary* (Brussels: Collection Latomus, 1994), pp. 343–44 explains the original sense of '*harenam esse sine calce*' in Suetonius, *Caligula* 53.

9. Erasmus, *Hecuba et Iphigenia, Latinae factae* (Paris: J. Bade, 1506), preface to *Hecuba* [= Letter 188 to William Warham], in *Opera Omnia*: I.1, ed. by J. H. Waszink (Amsterdam: North-Holland, 1969), pp. 193–359 (p. 217): 'adeo obscuros, vt Oedipo quopiam aut Delio sit opus magis quam interprete'. Diogenes Laertius, *Lives of the Philosophers* 2.22 attributed to Socrates a remark about a book by Heraclitus which 'needed a Delian diver not to drown in it'.

10. Ovid, *Tristia* 5.10.37–8: 'Barbarus hic ego sum [...]' [Here I am the barbarian].

11. Ovid, *Tristia* 5.7.55–64; Jerome, *Epistulae* 29.7; compare *Epistulae* 7.2 and Jerome's preface to Book 3 of his commentary on Galatians. G. J. M. Bartelink, 'Hieronymus und Ovid', *Greek, Roman and Byzantine Studies*, 4 (1975), 13–19.

12. Peter of Ghent, 'Carta de fray Pedro de Gante a los Padres y Hermanos de la Provincia de Flandes, 27 de junio de 1529', in Ernesto de la Torre Villar, *Fray Pedro de Gante, maestro y civilizador de América* (Mexico City: Seminario de Cultura Mexicana, 1973), p. 71.

13. A tree illustrates Latin morphology, declensions and syntax in Juan Pastrana's *Grammatica* (Lisbon, 1497); for Ramon Llull the tree symbolized encyclopaedic knowledge: Linda Baéz Rubí, *Mnemosine novohispánica* (Mexico City: Universidad Nacional Autónoma de México, 2005), pp. 88–91.

14. James Lockhart, *Nahuatl as Written* (Stanford, CA: Stanford University Press, 2001), p. 23: 'Quauhnahuac = "close to the woods" (Cuernavaca)'.

15. Angelo Mazzocco, *Linguistic Theories in Dante and the Humanists: Studies of Language and Intellectual History in Late Medieval and Early Renaissance Italy* (Leiden: Brill, 1993).

16. Richard Kagan, *Students and Society in Early Modern Spain* (Baltimore, MD: Johns Hopkins University Press, 1974), pp. 31–61.

17. Ruiz, 'Cristóbal Cabrera', p. 108 quotes relevant comments in Cabrera's prologues to his 1567 *Escuela de la disciplina y doctrina Cristiana*: 'por sólo su amor y caridad del prójimo me aficioné a hacer' [I set myself to do so out of [God's] love and charity for my neighbor]) and to his *Instrumento espiritual* (1575–1594).

18. Joaquín García Icazbalceta, *Bibliografía mexicana del siglo XVI* (Mexico City: FCE, 1981), pp. 58–61; Román Zulaica Gárate, *Los franciscanos y la imprenta en México en el siglo XVI* (Mexico City: Pedro Robredo, 1939), pp. 31–32; Josep Closa Farrés, 'Notas sobre el primer texto latino publicado en América', *Universitas Tarraconensis*, 1 (1976), 143–54, and Joaquín Quiñones Melgoza, *Poesía neolatina en México en el siglo XVI* (Mexico City: Universidad Nacional Autónoma de México, 1991), p. 40 present Latin texts with Spanish translations.

19. García Icazbalceta, *Bibliografía*: 'paucis praenosse'; Closa Farrés, 'Notas': 'pauciser nosse'; Quiñones Melgoza, *Poesía neolatina*: 'paucis pernosse'.

20. *Manual* (1540): 'nilminus'.

21. Quiñones, *Poesía neolatina*: 'nil'.

22. Virgil, *Aeneid* 1.94.

23. Richmond Lattimore, *Themes in Greek and Latin Epitaphs* (Urbana: University of Illinois, 1942);

Iiro Kajanto, *Classical and Christian Studies in the Latin Epitaphs of Medieval and Renaissance Rome* (Helsinki: Suomalainen Tiedeakatemia, 1980); Hans Walter, *Initia carminum ac versuum Medii Aevi posterioris Latinorum* (Göttingen: Vandenhoeck and Ruprecht, 1959).

24. Cabrera wrote his own epitaph in elegiacs: Nicolás Antonio, *Biblioteca Hispana Nova*, 2 vols (Madrid: Joaquín de Ibarra, 1783), I, 239.

25. The *Ars* was a source for other Latinists in New Spain; compare Ignacio Osorio Romero, *La enseñanza del latín a los indios* (Mexico City: Universidad Nacional Autónoma de México, 1990), p. 13. Gaspar de Quiroga's post-Tridentine Index of 1583 prohibited vernacular translation of the *Ars* but not the Latin text, indicating its continuing importance as a stylistic model: *Index et catalogus librorum prohibitorum mandato Illustriss. Inquisitoris D. D. Gasparis a Quiroga Cardinalis Archiepiscopi Toletani, ac in regnis Hispaniarum Generalis Inquisitoris, denuo editus* (Madrid: Alphonsus Gomezius, 1583), p. 70.

26. Horace, *Ars poetica* 269: 'nocturna *versate* manu, *versate* diurna'; *Epistles* 2.1.92: 'quod *legeret tereretque* viritim publicus usus'. Martial, *Epigrams* 8.3.4: '*teritur* noster ubique *liber*'. Jaime Lara, 'Roman Catholics in Hispanic America', in *Oxford History of Christian Worship*, ed. by Geoffrey Wainwright and Karen B. Westerfield Tucker (Oxford: Oxford University Press, 2006), pp. 633–50 (p. 637), reasonably assumes Quiroga wrote the *Manual*. Burrus, 'Cristóbal Cabrera'; Leopoldo Campos, 'Métodos misionales y rasgos biográficos de don Vasco de Quiroga según Cristóbal Cabrera, Pbro.', in *Don Vasco de Quiroga y el Arzobispado de Morelia*, ed. by Manuel Ponce (Mexico City: Jus, 1965), pp. 107–58.

27. Ross Dealy, *Vasco de Quiroga's Thought on War: Its Erasmian and Utopian Roots* (Bloomington: Indiana University Press, 1975).

28. *The Latin Epigrams of Thomas More*, ed. by Leicester Bradner and Charles Arthur Lynch (Chicago, IL: Chicago University Press, 1953).

29. Erasmus, *Colloquia*, in *Opera Omnia*: I.3, ed. by L.-E. Halkin, F. Bierlaire and R. Hoven (Amsterdam: North-Holland, 1972), p. 181.

30. Plato, *Sophist* 259c: καὶ χαλεπὸν ἅμα καὶ καλόν; compare *Republic* 435c; Plato, *Hippias Major* 304e, *Cratylus* 384b; Helius Eobanus Hessus, *Medicinae Laus* (Paris: apud Simonem Colinaeum, 1533), 103a: 'Si quod *difficile est, pulchrum...* est.' Hessus' versification of Erasmus's *Encomium medicinae* was first published in 1530.

31. Michael Allen, *Icastes: Marsilio Ficino's Interpretation of Plato's Sophist* (Berkeley and Los Angeles: University of California, 1989), pp. 117–204. Erasmus's appreciation of Ficino is expressed in Epistle 862 (1518) to Bonifacius Amerbach; see *Opus Epistolarum*, ed. by P. S. Allen, 12 vols (Oxford: Clarendon Press, 1906–58), III, 384.

32. Robert L. Politzer, 'Synonymic Repetition in Late Latin and Romance', *Language*, 37.4 (1961), 484–87.

33. García Icazbalceta, *Bibliografía mexicana*, p. 58, n. 1 suggested that the title signifies a composition of twenty verses, relating 'Icastichon' with 'eikosi' (Greek for 'twenty') and 'stichos' [verse]. José Quiñones Melgoza, *Poesia neolatina*, p. 53 rejects this on the basis that Cabrera would have written 'Icostichon', but ignores Cabrera's use of 'ch' (equivalent to Greek letter chi) instead of 'c' (for Greek kappa) which could refer to the verse lines of this composition.

34. All these poems are in the same Vatican Library manuscript: Vat Lat 1165. The *In philosophorum, oratorum, historicorumque classicorum opera extemporalia epigrammata* are edited and examined in Laird, 'Franciscan Humanism'; the texts of the epistles anthologized (with Spanish translations) in José Quiñones Melgoza (ed.), *Hispana seges nova* (Mexico City: Universidad Nacional Autónoma de México, 2012) should be compared to the manuscript facsimiles appended to Ruiz, 'Cristóbal Cabrera'.

35. Andrew Laird, 'Migration und Ovids Exildichtung in der lateinischen Kultur Kolonialmexicos', in *2000 Jahre Wiederkehr der Verbannung des Ovid: Exil und Literatur*, ed. by Veronika Coroleu and Gerhard Petersmann (Horn and Salzburg: Berger, 2011), pp. 101–18 (pp. 111–14).

36. Mariano Cuevas, *Historia de la Iglesia en México*, 5 vols (Mexico City: Ediciones Cervantes, 1942), I, 350, 486.

37. Zumárraga, *Carta al Príncipe Don Felipe*, 4 December 1547, in Joaquín García Icazbalceta, *Don Fray Juan de Zumárraga, primer obispo y arzobispo de México*, 4 vols (Mexico City: Porrúa, 1947), IV, 208.

38. Cabrera, Dedication of *Argumenta* to Fray Juan de Zumárraga, 1 December 1540, ed. by Campos, 'Métodos misionales', pp. 116–23 (p. 117).

39. 1 Peter 5. 13: 'salutat vos quae est in Babylone cumelecta' [The church that is in Babylon, elected together with you, saluteth you].

40. The Narcissus story in Ovid, *Metamorphoses* 3.339–510 was well known; Erasmus, *Institutio Principis Christiani* [Education of the Christian Prince], in *Opera Omnia*: IV.1, ed. by O. Herding (Amsterdam: North-Holland, 1974), pp. 95–219 (p. 172) alludes to the beauty of Nereus; Astur is mentioned only in Virgil, *Aeneid* 10.180–81. The ignoble appearance and nature of Homer's Thersites were a Renaissance topos; in Ovid, *Ibis* 517, Brotheus burned himself to death to avoid ridicule for his deformity.

41. Numbers 25. The Baal of Mount Phogor was associated with immoral sexual rites.

42. Sergio Ortega, 'Teología novohispana sobre el matrimonio y comportamientos sexuales, 1519–1570', in *De la santidad a la perversión, o por qué no se cumplía la Ley de Dios en la sociedad novohispana*, ed. by Sergio Ortega (Mexico City: Grijalbo, 1986), pp. 19–48; Patricia Seed, *To Love, Honor, and Obey in Colonial Mexico* (Stanford, CA: Stanford University Press, 1988); Asunción Lavrin, 'Sexuality in Colonial Mexico: A Church Dilemma', in *Sexuality and Marriage in Colonial Latin America*, ed. by Asunción Lavrin (Lincoln: University of Nebraska, 1989), pp. 47–95.

43. Nicolás Sánchez-Albornoz, 'The Population of Colonial Spanish America', in *The Cambridge History of Latin America. Volume II: Colonial Latin America*, ed. by Leslie Bethell (Cambridge: Cambridge University Press, 1984), pp. 3–35 (pp. 15–19); Magnus Morner, 'Spanish Migration to the New World Prior to 1800: A Report on the State of Research', in *First Images of America: The Impact of the New World on the Old*, ed. by Fredi Chiappelli, 2 vols (Berkeley and Los Angeles: University of California, 1976), II, 737–82.

44. Antonio, *Biblioteca Hispana Nova*, I, 238; Thomas James Dandelet, *Spanish Rome* (New Haven, CT, and London: Yale University Press, 2001), pp. 144–45.

45. Petrus Martirius Anglerinus, *De orbe novo*, *Decades I–III* (Basel, Ioannem Bebelium: 1533), I, 3, 10A: section entitled *Admiranda vitae innocentia* [Admirably innocent way of life]; Ovid, *Metamorphoses* 1.189–93.

46. Erasmus, *Moriae encomium id est Stultitiae Laus*, in *Opera Omnia*: IV.3 ed. by Clarence H. Miller (Amsterdam and Oxford: North-Holland, 1979), p. 174. The gist of Erasmus's argument here was recalled by Vasco de Quiroga: see Dealy, *Vasco de Quiroga*, pp. 14–15.

47. Cabrera, *Meditatiunculae*, fols 73–77[v]. Alcina Rovira, 'Cristóbal Cabrera', pp. 160–63 and Laird, 'Classical Letters and Millenarian Madness' (a full survey, text and translation of the 'Ecstasis', from which the present discussion has drawn) are the only treatments of the poem to date.

48. 'Ecstasy', in *Oxford Dictionary of the Christian Church*, ed. by F. L. Cross and E. A. Livingstone (Oxford: Oxford University Press, 1997), p. 528; M. A. Screech, 'Good Madness in Christendom', in *The Anatomy of Madness: Essays in the History of Psychiatry, I: People and Ideas*, ed. by W. F. Bynum, Roy Porter and Michael Shepherd (London: Routledge, 2004), pp. 25–39.

49. 'Vt Niniue quondam, apparet', 'Ecstasis' 96; Revelation 19. 14; Jeremiah 26–52.

50. Scansion precludes emending 'lătĭō' to 'latīnō; and 'latio' evokes Virgil's proem (*Aeneid* 1.6): 'Latio, genus unde Latinum' [Latium, source of the Latin race].

51. *Aeneid* 3.172, 4.282; 3.39 (compare Erasmus, *Moriae encomium* 30: 'eloquarne, an sileam? Cur autem sileam, cum sit vero verius?' [Should I speak or be silent? But why be silent about something truer than the truth?].

52. 'quasi iuvenculus indomitus' [like a bullock unaccustomed to the yoke], from Jeremiah 31. 18 is also the acrostic text of *Ecstasis*, 32–55.

53. Eugenio Mele, 'Una oda inédita de Garcilaso de la Vega y tres poesías a él dedicadas por Cosimo Anisio', *Revista Crítica de Historia y Literatura Españolas, Portuguesas e Hispanoamericanas*, 3 (1898), 362–68.

54. Bernardino de Sahagún, *Florentine Codex: Introductions and Indices*, trans. by Arthur J. O. Anderson and Charles Dibble (Salt Lake City: University of Utah, 1982), pp. 93–94, 98.

55. D. A. Brading, *The First America: The Spanish Monarchy, Creole Patriots and the Liberal State, 1492–1867* (Cambridge: Cambridge University Press, 1991), pp. 102–27; John Leddy Phelan, *The Millenial Kingdom of the Franciscans in the New World* (Berkeley: University of California, 1970); Georges Baudot, *Utopia and History in Mexico* (Niwot: University of Colorado, 1995).

56. Ángel Escobar Chico, 'La pervivencia del corpus teológico ciceroniano en España', *Revista Española de Filosofía Medieval*, 4 (1997), 189–202.

57. Cicero, *De divinatione* 2.54.112.

58. Cabrera, *Meditatiunculae*, fol. 78$^\mathrm{v}$.

59. *Rosarium Beatae Benedictæq[ue]; & Almæ Virginis Dei genitricis Mariæ... Meditatione Trilingui meditatum* (Rome: Vincentius Accoltus, 1584).

60. Marcel Bataillon, *Erasmo y España: estudios sobre la historia espiritual del siglo XVI*, trans. by A. Alatorre (Mexico City: FCE, 2007), pp. 432–93.

CHAPTER 4

Popular Balladry in
Colonial Latin America

Miguel Martínez

No Time for Songs

That was no time for songs, according to Bernal Díaz del Castillo; 'Dejemos estas
pláticas y romances, pues no estábamos en tiempo de ellos' [Let us leave aside these
conversations and ballads, since that was no time for them].[1] He was referring to
the two famous ballads that were reportedly sung while Cortés and his men looked
down to Tenochtitlan from a temple in Tacuba: the traditional 'Mira Nero de
Tarpeya' and 'En Tacuba está Cortés', newly composed on the occasion, according
to Bernal:

> En Tacuba está Cortés
> con su escuadrón esforzado,
> triste estaba y muy penoso,
> triste y con gran cuidado,
> la una mano en la mejilla,
> la otra en el costado.[2]

> [Cortés is in Tacuba with his zealous battalion; he was sad and melancholy, sad
> and with great worry, with one hand on his cheek, the other on his waist.]

In the context of colonial warfare, Bernal Díaz del Castillo deemed the ballads
('romances') that Cortés's soldiers exchanged while preparing for a new conquest
of the capital insubstantial or superfluous. He was not alone in pointing to the
tension between the urgency of warfare and lyric writing — or ballad-singing —
as a light exercise that appears not to belong in the colonial battlefield. Despite
Bernal's passing dismissal, however, as incompatible with the pressing demands
of conquest war, ballad-singing and writing, in many different forms, was indeed
one of the dearest literary modes among the sailors, peasants, artisans and low
hidalgos that soldiered in the conquistadors' *huestes*, the 'armada de hombres pobres'
that according to Bernal invaded Mexico. Indeed, Bernal himself records in his
chronicle at least four other instances in which Cortés and his men exchange lines
from famous ballads in the course of the conquest. 'No parece', said Ricardo Palma
much later, 'sino que en cada español soldado de la conquista hubiera encarnado un
coplero' [it just seems that every Spanish soldier of the conquest is a balladier].[3]

In 1445, popular ballads ('romances' and 'cantares') were regarded by a noble writer such as the Marquis of Santillana as the lowest form of poetry, only enjoyed by people of servile and lowly condition: 'ínfimos [...] estos romances y cantares de que las gentes de baxa y servil condición se alegran'.[4] Although there is enough evidence to contest the restricted social distribution of *romances* as characterized by Santillana and later writers of the Golden Age, ballads did indeed circulate widely among commoners.[5] The rich orality of popular culture was also ingrained in the conquistadors' reading and writing practices, as we shall see. As Raquel Chang suggests, 'los primeros versos [españoles] escuchados en América como parte de una tradición oral fueron muestras de la poesía popular, en especial villancicos, coplas y versiones de antiguos romances' [the first Spanish verses heard in America as part of an oral tradition were samples of popular poetry, particularly *villancicos*, *coplas*, and versions of old ballads].[6]

The romantic 'discovery of the people', to use Peter Burke's felicitous phrase, gave way to the intellectual development and academic institutionalization of folk-lore, philology and literary history during the nineteenth and the first decades of the twentieth century which, in the case of Spain, contributed greatly to the compilation and study of songs and ballads. The oral patrimony of popular poetry in Spanish has also been carefully collected in different regions of Latin America.[7] Regarding the oral poetry of the first moments of the conquest, however, we only have scattered references and even more sparse texts that were precariously and fragmentarily recorded, for the most part, in the chronicles. The foundational work was done by José Toribio Medina and Marcelino Menéndez y Pelayo. Menéndez Pidal complemented Medina's work by culling the ballads used or mentioned in the chronicles of the conquest. The same anecdotes have been recorded and explored by a number of other scholars.[8] Drawing from the work of these and other scholars, this chapter is an attempt to review and contextualize the small number of oral songs and ballads of the conquest that have been preserved in relation to the literary and political culture of the Spanish conquistadors. The original archive of oral and written ephemeral and circumstantial poetry was disproportionately vaster than the surviving minimalist corpus of scattered lines and allusions. In this chapter I will argue that this group of *coplas* and *romances*, however small, is crucial for understanding the political and literary culture of the conquistadors. The vast majority of these songs emerged in a context of political turmoil and tension between the main commanders and rank-and-file conquistadors. Rather than celebrating the feats of the conquest, as could have been expected from the traditions of genres such as the *romance*, these songs often reveal pre-existing or new fractures in conquistador society, a highly volatile and contingent social formation for which the peculiar interaction of material and oral practices of poetry was particularly well suited. The forms and vocabularies of traditional lyric and narrative poetry, as well as their performative and material traditions, will be constantly reappropriated and reinvented in relation to the political languages and practices of the conquest.

It was also Bernal who recorded the tight connection between the practices of ephemeral poetry and the traditional political culture of the conquistadors. After the conquest of Tenochtitlan, the soldiers and their captains quarrelled about the treasures of the city recently sacked. Some discontented soldiers started circulating rumours about Cortés's keeping all the gold for himself: 'Y como Cortés estaba en Coyoacán y posaba en unos palacios que tenía blanqueadas y encaladas las paredes, donde buenamente se podía escribir en ellas con carbones y con otras tintas, amanecía cada mañana escritos muchos motes, algunos en prosa y otros en metros, algo maliciosos, a manera de mase-pasquines' [While Cortés was in Coyoacán lodging in some palaces that had their walls plastered and white-washed on which it was easy to write with charcoal and other inks, numerous rather malicious sentences appeared on them every morning, some written in prose and others in verse, in the way of lampoons].[9] Although Bernal warns the reader that the graffiti contained 'palabras que no son para poner en esta relación' [words that cannot be put in this account], he readily summarizes some of these *coplas*.

First Cortés answered the accusations 'por buenos consonantes y muy a propósito' [by good rhymes much to the point], since the captain 'era algo poeta' [was something of a poet himself]. When the *coplas* became too impudent, Cortés famously wrote: 'pared blanca, papel de necios' [a blank wall is the paper of fools]. To which the restless soldiers replied: 'aun de sabios y verdades, y Su Majestad lo sabrá muy presto' [and of wise men, and of truths and his majesty would soon know it]. The mention of the king was a way of implicitly questioning the legitimacy of the captain's authority, and thus a signal that an open rebellion might have been brewing. Vivas to the king were a frequent way of crystallizing or heralding popular uprisings and even soldierly mutinies. Vargas Machuca, a later, experienced conquistador, would advise strongly against 'chismes', or gossip, that emerged among the soldierly mass.[10] No wonder Cortés ended up threatening the satirists with serious punishment. The political protagonism of the rank and file in the Indies, who actively participated through collective deliberation in the decision-making process, often led to conflicted negotiations with, if not open mutiny against, the commanders of the conquest. 'En las Indias hay muchos soldados y pocas cabezas', complained Vargas Machuca, who nonetheless remarked: 'la presunción que en aquella milicia tienen los soldados de que se les puede fiar y encargar a cada uno el gobierno de las Indias y de dar su voto; y así es que en esta milicia lo tienen todos. Y cuando se ofrece la ocasión al soldado decir lo que siente, se debe admitir, unas veces por el provecho que de él resulta y otras por cumplimiento' [In the Indies there are many soldiers but few commanders; among those soldiers it is assumed that anyone can be trusted and given the responsibility of the government of the Indies and of giving their vote, and so it is that in this militia they all have it. And when the opportunity presents itself for the soldier to say what he feels, it should be allowed].[11] The tension between the *heads* and the mass of rank-and-file conquistadors is often mediated through the written and oral practices associated with ephemeral poetry, which seem to be constitutive of the political practices and beliefs of these Spaniards. The Roman Pasquino soon reached the New World, and its ways proved as dangerous for the precarious order of conquistador society as they were for the heavenly and mundane arrangements of the capital of the orb.

In 1527, in a critical moment of the expedition in search for Peru, and after being repelled by indigenous resistance, Pizarro and Almagro withdrew from mainland South America to the so-called Isla del Gallo. From there, Almagro was sent back to Panama in order to man up the enterprise and return to support the exhausted conquistadors who stay with Pizarro. Among Pizarro's men, one Saravia, in his secret correspondence with the governor of Panama, used the satirical circumstantial *coplas* that allegedly circulated in the Isla del Gallo, verses that openly criticized Almagro ('el recogedor') and Pizarro ('el carnicero'):[12]

> Pues, señor Gobernador,
> mírelo bien por entero:
> que allá va el recogedor
> y acá queda el carnicero.[13]

[So, Governor, look at this carefully: there goes the gatherer, here stays the butcher.]

Versions differ significantly about the circumstances in which this *copla* was created and some doubts have been raised about the authenticity and chronology of the episode reported, since the first mention of the 'coplas de la Isla del Gallo' occurs in Gómara's chronicle of 1552.[14] Yet all of them hint to the satirical, even libellous, potential of a *redondilla* that emerged in the context of generalized discontent and turmoil among the famished troops, who 'comenzaron a desabrirse con los capitanes, y ellos, especialmente Pizarro, a tratarlos con algún rigor' [started to get embittered with the captains, and they, particularly Pizarro, to treat them rigorously], as Miguel Cabello Valboa, among other chroniclers, pointed out.[15] Garcilaso de la Vega el Inca claimed to have heard this and other *coplas* many times when he was growing up. His testimony hints to the existence of a rich oral culture that included the circulation of popular, ephemeral poems such as these: 'Estos versos oí muchas veces en mi niñez a los españoles que contaban estos sucesos de las conquistas del Nuevo Mundo y los traían de ordinario en la boca como refrán sentencioso [...]. Después cuando los topé en España, en la corónica de Francisco López de Gómara holgué mucho verlos, por la recordación de mis tiempos pasados' [As a child, I heard these lines many times from the Spaniards, who often recounted the events of the conquests of the New World and they usually brought them in their mouths like sententious proverbs [...]. I was very happy to see these lines later in Spain, in Francisco López de Gómara's chronicle, because they brought me good memories from my previous days].[16]

In the context of Peru's civil wars, the chroniclers recorded a number of instances in which verses of popular stock were used in direct connection with the political events of the period. Pizarro and Almagro met for talks in Mala in 1537. While the latter allegedly sued for peace, the former had planned to ambush Almagro with the help of his brother Gonzalo. According to the colourful version of the story told by Herrera y Tordesillas, Almagro saved his head when Francisco de Godoy (a cavalryman in Pizarro's camp) started muttering to his ear the lines of one of the most famous Iberian *romances*: 'Tiempo es el caballero | tiempo es de irnos de aquí | que me cresce la barriga | e se me acorta el vestir' [It is time, my knight, to leave this place, because my belly is growing and my garments shorten].[17] The ballad was in the memory of every Spaniard, but it also circulated in a *pliego suelto* or broadsheet printed around 1524. While dealing with a secret pregnancy, 'the men of Cajamarca' would certainly recall the ambiguity about the knight's social origins in the *romance*, which no doubt applied to some of the conquest commanders, and particularly to the Pizarros:[18] ' — Parildo infanta, parildo, | que assí hizieron a mí: | hijo soy de un labrador, | que de cavar es su bivir' [Give birth, infanta, give birth, I was born just like that: I am the son of a peasant who earns his living by ploughing]. The lines of the ballad allegedly sung by Godoy became almost proverbial, and they would also be quoted by soldiers of the army of Flanders in the 1570s and 1580s. In one of these cases, the same lines of the ballad in the mouth of a soldier's weeping wife serve to remind him that it may be about time to desert his post in Antwerp's citadel.[19]

The improvisational skills and malicious use of traditional songs by the caustic Francisco de Carvajal — a feared old veteran soldier of commoner background who was field marshal of Gonzalo Pizarro during Peru's civil wars in the late 1540s — were also proverbial. His *greatest hits* have been duly collected by historians. When Gonzalo was losing to La Gasca, many of his soldiers seem to have rushed to change camps, to which Carvajal is claimed to have sung: 'Estos mis cabellicos madre | dos a dos se los lleva el aire' [These locks of mine, mother, the wind takes two by two].[20] Medina took the notice from Gómara and Diego Fernández de Palencia, but Margit Frenk's *Nuevo corpus* identifies many other colonial and Peninsular sources that recorded the usage of this traditional, and extremely popular, lyric distich, which can also be found in authors such as Gil Vicente or Correas.[21] Beyond pure sarcasm, the same wind that in many traditional lyric songs often signified flimsiness and passion must have evoked here the radical contingency and ephemerality of colonial politics in the context of the civil wars.

Similarly, when some captains flocked to Pizarro's camp, Carvajal is reported to have sung, while air-drumming, 'Para mí me los querría, | madre mía, | para mí me los querría' [I would like them for myself, mother, I would like them for myself].[22] The *copla*, of which we possess many witnesses, can be traced back to the fifteenth century, as in the case of the previous song. Its enunciative structure and its theme (a young woman in dialogue with her mother openly expressing her sexual desires) are characteristic of traditional Iberian lyric. Mary Gaylord has summarized the thematic universe of a large section of popular Iberian lyric as 'the world of the girl who is growing into womanhood'. In the rough times of the Peruvian civil wars, 'the homely stuff of life at hand' and the 'rhetorical code of intimacy' of traditional lyric served quite another purpose when actualized by the occasional enunciation of an unruly soldier.[23] I have little doubt, moreover, that the queer twist of this ephemeral actualization of the *copla* was part of Carvajal's salacious mockery.

Even such a cautious historian as James Lockhart considered Carvajal an 'evil' man with 'pathological tendencies'.[24] The most famous sociopath of the conquest, Lope de Aguirre, was also considered, in line with Carvajal, 'chocarrero y hechicero, y grande amotinador' [a clown, a sorcerer, and a bad rioter].[25] There seems to be a very interesting connection between the oral and poetic creativity of the *chocarerro* kind — 'hombre gracioso y truhán [...] porque es hombre de burlas, y con quien todos se burlan, y también se burla él de todos' [amusing and shameless man, because he likes joking, and everyone likes joking with him, and he makes fun of everyone] — and the proneness to political rebellion in the Indies.[26] All the portraits of Aguirre by fellow soldiers and enemies coincide in describing the mad soldier as 'de agudo y vivo ingenio para ser hombre sin letras' [of sharp and alert wit for an illiterate man].[27] Aguirre's idiosyncratic idiom throughout his letters and reported sayings is built with the materials of a rich oral culture that relies on proverbs, blasphemy, expletives and morphologically creative insults.[28] Aguirre's letters, with their defiant forms of address, subvert 'the narrative armature of conquest', as Pastor argued, and the discursive formation of the matters of the Indies.[29] By debasing and even carnivalizing the rhetorical structure of address ('mira, mira rey español' [look, look, Spanish king]), the rebel's texts open the way to a radical challenge to the institutional and discursive arrangements of the conquest enterprise. Similarly, the idiom of blasphemy and soldierly speech ('voto a Dios de no dejar en esta tierra cosa que viva sea' [I swear to God that I will not spare anything alive in this land]) put down in official writing alters the codes of the *relación* and the *probanza*. 'Vuestro gobierno es aire y viento' [your government is air and wind] he tells the king in a new rehearsal of Carvajal's lyric and political winds.[30]

Lope de Aguirre's seemingly demented rebellion gave way to the composition of new songs recorded in writing by other soldiers, such as Gonzalo de Zúñiga. 'De Sevilla y cejijunto', Zúñiga was also, according to Aguirre himself, a 'gentil chocarrero' [from Seville, unibrowed; a vulgar joker]. And the uttermost tyrannical rebel of colonial Latin America, Aguirre, does not forget to remind one of his interlocutors, Fray Francisco de Montesinos, that the *coplero* Zúñiga had himself been 'in rebelión y alzamiento contra su rey' [in open rebellion against his king] in Popayán.[31] Zúñiga's *romance* is not wholly lacking in humour: 'Riberas del Marañón | do gran mal se ha congelado | se levantó un vizcaíno | muy peor que andaluzado' [By the riverbanks of the Marañón, where great evil has congealed, a Biscaian rebelled, a much worse one than if he were Andalusian]. Otherwise, the ballad is mostly a list of Aguirre's atrocities and killings, all of them confirmed by other *relaciones* of the time. Perhaps most famous among his victims is 'la linda doña Inés | que a Policena ha imitado' [the pretty doña Inés, who has emulated Polyxena]. The killing of the Peruvian mestiza Inés de Atienza, the lover of Pedro de Ursúa, Juan Alonso and Lorenzo de Salduendo, is likened to that of the Trojan princess Polyxena, a character in Ovid's *Metamorphoses* and other sources of antiquity, and one of Boccaccio's heroines in *De mulieribus claris*. More importantly, however, she was the protagonist of a number of Spanish ballads, one of which was certainly in Zúñiga's memory when finding a known analogy for the cruel murder of a loving woman.[32]

Aguirre, however, was not universally hated only because of his cruelty, a trait he generously shared with many official heroes of the conquest. Matthew Restall and

Felipe Fernández-Armesto have convincingly argued that we should not readily dismiss Lope de Aguirre as an impenetrable madman. Even though 'wars nurture sociopaths', it was not the 'orgy of violence' that he generated that troubled the imperial authorities.[33] In his apparently erratic actions, which include the slaughter of thirty-seven of his men and the cold-blooded murder of his own daughter, we can easily find 'the same spectrum of origins, experiences, and actions as the other conquistadors', which in their turn can be related to the practices and discourses of popular soldiery of early modern Europe.[34] The rationale of the uprising is not different from those in Peru during the civil wars. Soldierly mutiny in the Old World becomes political rebellion in the Americas.

Peru's political turmoil was widely sung in ballads and occasionally written on the walls, and there are a few more examples than the ones reviewed above. After the first of the civil wars, Alonso Enríquez de Guzmán wrote a *romance* on the death of Diego de Almagro, 'el cual se ha de cantar al tono del "Buen conde Fernán González"'[35] [which should be sung to the melody of 'Buen conde Fernán González']. The rebellion of Francisco Hernández Girón was also sung in a couple of anonymous romances: 'En el Cuzco, esa ciudad | grande gente se juntó' [In that city of Cuzco, many people gathered] and 'De ese fuerte de Pucará | Francisco Hernández salía' [From that fort of Pucará, Francisco Hernández was leaving]. In the early twentieth century, Ciro Bayo collected in Bolivia some romances of oral transmission that also dealt with Pizarro's rebellion ('Non creyades, rey Felipe | lo que acaso os contarán' [Do not believe, King Philip, what they may tell you]).[36] The imaginative fancies that we associate with the world of the *romancero* fit well with the alleged madness and exceptionality of some of these men. But their seeming insanity had much to do with their political audacity. Rather than the conquest, the popular poetry of the New World seems to sing of 'alteraciones', and this contrasts sharply with the frontier ballads of the Iberian Peninsula, which have been assumed to be their natural precedent.

All these episodes show how the practice of oral poetry and improvised *coplas* is inserted in a context of political upheaval, linked to the social practices of a mutinous soldiery. This becomes clearer if we compare these examples with the chroniclers' reporting on Taino *areitos* and other forms of indigenous oral poetry, which are in turn explicitly compared to Spanish literary practices such as the *romance*. 'Tenían estas gentes', says Oviedo, 'una buena e gentil manera de memorar las cosas pasadas e antiguas; e esto era en sus cantares e bailes, que ellos llaman *areito*, que es lo mismo que nosotros llamamos bailar cantando [...]. ¿Qué otra cosa son los romances e canciones que se fundan sobre verdades sino parte e acuerdo de las historias pasadas?' [These people had a good and elegant way of remembering their ancient past; this was done in their songs and dances, which they call *areito* — to dance while singing [...]. What else are the ballads and songs that are based on true events, if not memorials of past history?]. Gómara, on his part, insisted that *areito* 'es como zambra de moros, que bailan cantando romances en alabanza de sus ídolos y de sus reyes, en memoria de victorias y acaecimientos notables y antiguos' [is like the Moors' zambra, in which they dance while singing ballads in praise of their idols and their kings, and in memory of ancient and notable events].[37] The satirical actualizations of traditional ballads and songs, the composition of new ones on the rebel par excellence — el Loco Aguirre — and the anonymous *pasquines* against Pizarro or Cortés seem all to be quite far from the *areito*'s epic memory of 'kings and victories'. *Romances* and *coplas* were also used effectively by the soldiers in the struggle for their share of the loot and to mock the captains, all of which usually pitted them against their military superiors, and even in ambitious rebellions of an overt political character, as is also the case with the soldiers in Cortés's and Pizarro's camps.

Orality, Print and Popular Literacies

Popular balladry, moreover, was never purely *oral*, and this is another difference with indigenous epic and ritual poetry such as the *areito*. Orality and the written word have always interacted in complex and perhaps unexpected ways, and perhaps more so in early colonial America, where letter writing, rumour, the publication of manuscript pamphlets, the oral culture of soldierly jokes, mural poetry and pasquinades seem to be intimately related political and literary practices.[38] The social and cultural world these anecdotes depict, its peculiar form of publicity, was built, as I have already mentioned, upon a complex interaction between the spoken and the written word, between oral and written poetry of an anonymous and popular nature. *Popular* poetry is certainly not the same as oral balladry. In sixteenth-century Spain, *romances* were not only in everyone's memory, but also in everyone's pockets, and thus they were carried along across the Atlantic. And in this regard, we have to keep in mind that what makes poetry *popular* is not *orality* but rather the social distribution of its uses, regardless of the media of circulation, and its insertion in a certain social hierarchy of cultural practices. Popular balladry in the New World is not the residue of culturally deprived commoners, but a common cultural background and a shared political language among men who, before (or while) conquering the New World, have also conquered letters.

Fortunately, we possess strikingly systematic and reliable surveys of the con-quistadors' literacy rates and class background. Numerically, the vast majority of them were commoners of different trades, although some of the leaders were *hidalgos*. In the case of the conquest of Mexico, only about 5% of Cortés's men were hidalgos (120 out of 2,200), and yet most of them could read and write. In Veracruz, 75% of the signers of a petition by Cortés must have been literate, even though only 4 to 8% were of noble origin. In the case of the conquest of Peru, 77% of Lockhart's 'men of Cajamarca' could sign their names (108 out of 168). Strikingly similar figures have been estimated in the case of Tierra Firme, Chile and New Granada, where 70 to 80% of the soldiers seem to have been at least partially literate.[39] Even though scholarship on popular literacies is continuously revising literacy rates upwards, these figures are significantly higher than those of the conquistadors' social counterparts back in Europe.[40]

It has been shown that ballads had a crucial role as a locus of mediation between orality and writing in early modern Spain. The ABCs and *cartillas*, or primers, used in the teaching of the first letters included well-known *romances* as exercises in reading practice.[41] And Menéndez Pidal, tracing the pervasiveness of the *romancero*'s idiom in both colloquial and literary speech, found examples of the pedagogical usage of ballads in the primary schools of the period.[42] Moreover, the products of popular print, particularly one-sheet *pliegos de cordel*, were produced cheaply and massively. Hernando Colón, who was Cristóbal's second son, and one of the most important book collectors of Renaissance Europe, could have been, for obvious reasons, a crucial agent in the distribution of European popular pamphlets in early colonial America. According to his notes, most single-sheet *pliegos* would sell for as little as one or two *maravedís* or *quatrines* in the 1500s to 1530s — less than a loaf of bread or half a dozen eggs.[43] The lowest salary of a European soldier would buy him between 1000 and 1200 one-sheet *pliegos*, but a soldier in the Indies, according to Vargas Machuca, could make ten times as much money as his counterpart in the Old World.[44] Virtually anyone could afford the printed poetic word.

As early as 1529, Jacobo Cromberger, a famous printer in Seville who traded heavily, and at times monopolistically, with New Spain, had in stock 50,500 'pliegos de coplas' [poetic broadsheets]. Later on, *romanceros* and *cancioneros* would figure prominently among the cargoes of the Atlantic book trade, reaching Mexico, Panamá and Perú. In 1583, Lima's bookseller Juan Jiménez del Río ordered '20 resmas de menudencias' [20 reams of broadsheets (literally 'trifles')], which might have amounted to around 1000 *pliegos*. When bookseller Pedro Durango died in the same Ciudad de los Reyes in 1603, he had in stock 595 'libros de diferentes historias' [books of different stories] which have been identified as *pliegos*, making up almost 50% of his catalogue. And in 1608 a cargo of 'cuatrocientos [libros de] coplas de todas suertes' [four hundred books of all kinds of songs] was sent to Cartagena de Indias from Seville.[45]

The rich interactions between written and oral, popular and literate cultures can also be seen in one of the most imposing monuments of conquest literature, one that covers a less studied territory of early colonial Latin America. In Juan de Castellanos's *Elegías de varones ilustres* oral and written ballads are found at several moments of the conquest of New Granada. The son and brother of farmers from a small village near Seville, Juan de Castellanos attended the city's Estudio General, or college, and travelled to the Indies in 1539. Alonso de Ercilla, who wrote the *aprobación* of the second part, found in Castellanos's massive narrative poem 'fielmente escritas muchas cosas y particularidades que yo vi y entendí en aquella tierra [de las Indias], al tiempo que pasé y estuve en ella: por donde infiero que va el autor muy arrimado a la verdad' [many truthfully written accounts and particularities that I have myself seen in that land when I was there, and thus I infer that the author always keeps close to the truth].[46] Castellanos also records in his *Elegías* the usage, during the conquest of New Granada, of at least six other traditional ballads, namely those of the Marquis of Mantua, Montesinos, Gómez Arias, 'Mira Nero de Tarpeya', 'Mis arreos son las armas', and Gaiferos and Melisenda.[47] At one moment during Alonso de Lugo's campaigns in New Granada in 1540, in which Castellanos participated as a footman, he praises his old-time friend and veteran captain Lorenzo Martín as an accomplished poet in the old Castilian style:

> Este fue valentísimo soldado
> y de grandes industrias en la guerra,
> el cual bebió también en Hipocrene
> aquel licor que manar hizo
> la uña del alígero Pegaso,
> con tan sonora y abundante vena,
> que nunca yo vi cosa semejante
> según antiguo modo de españoles,
> porque composición italiana,
> hurtada de los metros que se dicen
> endecasílabos entre latinos,
> aun no corría por aquestas partes.[48]

[This one was a truly valiant soldier and very skilled in warfare, who also drank from Hippocrene that liquor which the winged Pegasus caused to spring out with his hoof; this one had such a sonorous and abundant vein that I have never seen anything similar in the old mode of the Spaniards, since the Italian composition, stolen from the metres that the Latins called hendecasyllable, had not yet arrived in these parts.]

Famous for his 'gracias y facecias' [jokes and facetiae] not unlike those *burlas* of Carjaval and Aguirre, Castellanos tells us that the *chocarrero* Martín intends to cheer up the melancholic survivors of starvation during an exhausting *entrada* in the New Granadan northwest; so he recited 'torrentes | de coplas redondillas repentinas', 'como buen oficial de las que entonces | usaban por acá' [streams of improvised *redondillas*; as a good crafter of those which were then used around here] — *oficial*, or artisan, suggests that poetic writing and singing is conceived of as closer to manual labour than we usually tend to think.[49] Castellanos reproduces only six that someone had copied for him, giving Martín the necessary credit ('quiérolas poner aquí por suyas' [I want to put them here as his]):

> Sus, sus, hermanos míos;
> trastornemos y busquemos
> algo con que reformemos
> los estómagos vacíos.
> Sacad de flaqueza bríos,
> aunque estáis puestos del lodo,
> si no queréis que del todo
> nos quedemos patifríos.
>
> Tenemos las camisetas
> flojas y anchos los jubones;
> pretinas de los calzones
> encogen las agujetas.
> Todos bailamos gambetas
> al son de los estrompiezos,
> y tenemos los pescuezos
> más delgados que garcetas.

> Quedan de los cerviguillos
> solamente los hollejos;
> los más mancebos son viejos
> en rostros y colodrillos.
> Nuestros vientres tan sencillos
> que ternía cada uno
> por liviano desayuno
> menudo de dos novillos. (II, 50–51)

[Go, go, my brothers, let's return and look for something to restore these empty stomachs. Make strength from weakness, even though you're ruined, if you don't want us all to kick the bucket. | Our shirts grow loose and our doublets wide; the laces tighten our waistbands. With the rhythm of our stumbling we dance *gambetas* and our necks are thinner than an egret's. | Only the peel remains of our napes, the youngest are old in face and skull. Our bellies are so plain that they would take the stuffed tripe of two heifers as a light breakfast.]

Martín's stanzas poke fun at some of his famished comrades, one of whom had just devoured with delight a tallow candle. Their clothes have grown large at the same rate their bodies shrank; the stumbling movement of the undernourished is likened to the popular *gambeta* dance; their napes are all peels (*hollejos*). Later on, their empty bowels happily sing *villancicos*, a form of Castilian popular verse ('las tripas que nos hacen villancicos' [our bowels sing *villancicos*]). Martín resorts to the scatological humour so dear to Renaissance culture, popular or otherwise, to laugh at his comrades Valderrama and Francisco de Henao, who cannot stop farting after sustaining themselves with only stems of the *bijao* plant for two weeks:

> Y ansí dicen Valderrama
> y Francisco de Henao
> que con tallos de bihao
> la parte baja les brama.
> Y quieren ir do los llama
> algún cuesco de palmicha
> cuando no hallaren chicha,
> yuca, batata y auyama. (II, 51–52)

[And so Valderrama and Francisco de Henao say that, because of the *bijao*'s stems, their lower parts roar. And since they can't find maize, yuca, sweet potato, or pumpkin, they are even attracted to the stones of the silver palm fruit.]

Irony and joyful pranking were already present in some of the ballads recorded by Bernal or those of Carvajal. The discourse of hunger, or more generally of the conqueror's travails, could also be deployed in the code of Renaissance *facetiae* and popular carnivalization, emphasizing degradation and the material bodily principle.[50] It entails a different kind of *somatography*, as Luis Fernando Restrepo called his study of bodily representations in the *Elegías*.[51] The suffering of the conquering soldier, which in most instances bestows honour and legitimacy upon the bodies and voices of the conquistadors — and certainly in most of Castellanos' *Elegías* — is degraded here with a bodily imagery of popular stock. There is a thin line between the self-mocking satire of the famished conqueror and the languages of social and political rebellion that were also articulated in poetic form, as we have seen. Indeed, many of the so-called 'subsistence riots' of the early modern world used the language of hunger and deprivation to legitimize revolt.

Conclusions: Popular Poetry and the 'Rebel Imagination'

The rich, tumultuous oral culture of the conquest period, which clearly included ballad-singing and the writing of ephemeral *coplas*, is crucial for understanding not only the social lives of the conquistadors but also the traditional political culture of popular upheaval. The brutal reality of the conquest contributed, logically, to the erasure of social difference and conflict on the Spanish side. The institutional and discursive production of colonial difference was largely based on a clear realignment of national and ethnic affiliation, which helps explain why Spaniards proverbially aspired to becoming *hidalgos* as soon as they set foot on American territory. Yet the rich repertoire of popular poetic practices reviewed in this chapter allows us to see through the cracks that divided Spanish society whether in the New World or back in the Old.

The late fifteenth and early sixteenth centuries were times of social and political turmoil in Europe and in Spain. Conflicts between lords and peasants, cities and monarchy, artisans and the urban patriciate were so pervasive that they came to define a period. The commoners who formed the bulk of the Spanish *huestes* in America, 'the people of servile and lowly condition' who liked romances according to Santillana and later intellectuals, lived through these conflicts and carried with them the vocabularies and the cultural practices associated with these struggles. The vitality of the oral and written practices that mediated these conflicts, with particular emphasis on the *pasquín*, have been analysed in a number of studies.[52] Dramatist Guillén de Castro reminded a tyrannical king that 'de las calles las paredes | tienen bocas, tienen lenguas | para que de ti se quejen | entre el confuso alboroto | que se levanta en la gente' [the street walls have mouths and tongues to complain about you in the midst of the confusing tumult that raises from the people].[53] Early modern Spain was characterized, according to Michele Olivari, by 'a polyphonic public life', the vitality of which, I argue, only intensified in the Indies.[54] A series of important studies by Natalia Silva Prada and others have contributed to emphasize the centrality of certain cultural practices, such as rumour, songs, *pasquines* and carnival in the political culture of the colony at a later period. *Pasquines* were regularly posted on walls and doors of the lettered cities of the New World with occasion of metropolitan investigative *visitas*; in factional quarrels in viceregal capitals; and in subsistence riots, large and small, including the most important and threatening of all, which occurred in Mexico in 1692 — and it should be possible to trace the continuities and discontinuities, in a non-linear genealogy, that linked the ballads of the first conquistadors with some of the popular cultural practices of the great 'tumulto'.[55]

From the anonymous pamphlets reported by Bernal or the *coplas* of the evil Carvajal, to the ballads on The-Wrath-of-God Aguirre and Girón, the forms and the material practices involved in the production and distribution of ballads, regardless of the content of the poems themselves, were many times associated with discontent, rebellion, political opposition, social protest and mutiny. Many conquistadors were as much 'chocarreros' — clownish and shameless, yes, but also witty and creative improvisers — as they were 'grandes amotinadores', or dangerous rioters. A textual portrait of 'el loco Aguirre' connected these two traits in the same sentence.[56] Songs and ballads were part of the 'repertory of themes and acts ready for use by people of a variety of social levels (not necessarily in like fashion);' they were central not only to the 'rebel imagination' of European peasants as crucial tools of mobilization when uprisings broke out, but also to that of the different social groups of New World early societies.[57] Popular poetry was constitutive of the spaces of public opinion that allowed for the expression of dissent and the articulation of resistance.

Notes to Chapter 4

1. Bernal Díaz del Castillo, *Historia de la verdadera conquista de Nueva España*, ed. by Joaquín Ramírez Cabañas (México: Porrúa, 1994), p. 324. The episode in Bernal's narrative may indeed be targeting Las Casas, who had also reported the use of *romances* by the conquistadors in a context that highlighted their brutality. See Bartolomé de las Casas, *Brevísima relación de la destruición de las Indias*, ed. by José Miguel Martínez-Torrejón (Barcelona: Círculo de Lectores, 2009), pp. 44–45. See also Winston A. Reynolds, *Romancero de Hernán Cortés: estudio y textos de los siglos XVI y XVII* (Madrid: Ediciones Alcalá, 1967).

2. Díaz del Castillo, *Historia*, p. 324. For an accessible version of 'Mira Nero de Tarpeya', see Giuseppe Di Stefano (ed.), *Romancero* (Madrid: Castalia, 2013), pp. 217–20.

3. Díaz del Castillo, *Historia*, p. 7. Menéndez Pidal gathered references in Bernal's chronicle to romances being mentioned, said, or sung by Cortés and his men, in *Romancero hispánico (hispano-portugués, americano y sefardí): historia y teoría*, 2 vols (Madrid: Espasa-Calpe, 1968), II, 226–29. Palma quoted in José Toribio Medina, *Los romances basados en La Araucana* (Santiago: Imprenta Elzeviriana, 1918), pp. vii–viii.

4. Marqués de Santillana, *Obras completas*, ed. by Ángel Gómez Moreno and Maxim P. A. M. Kerkhof (Barcelona: Planeta, 1988), p. 444.

5. On the complex, but often dismissive attitudes of Golden Age authors towards the *romancero*, see Maxime Chevalier, 'La Fortune du romancero ancien (fin du XVe–debut du XVIIe siècle)', *Bulletin Hispanique*, 90.1 (1988), pp. 187–95.

6. Raquel Chang-Rodríguez, 'Introducción' to *Venid, ninfas del sur, venid ligeras: voces poéticas virreinales* (Madrid and Frankfurt: Iberoamericana/Vervuert, 2008), p. 25.

7. Peter Burke, *Popular Culture in Early Modern Europe* (Burlington, VT: Ashgate, 2009), pp. 23–48; Margit Frenk, 'Un siglo de especulaciones', in *Las jarchas mozárabes y los comienzos de la lírica románica* (Mexico City: El Colegio de México, 1985), pp. 3–43. Significant collections of Latin American folk poetry can be found in Margit Frenk (ed.), *Cancionero folklórico de México*, 5 vols (Mexico City: El Colegio de México, 1975–1985); Mercedes Díaz Roig, *Romancero tradicional de América* (Mexico City: El Colegio de México, 1990). See also Mercedes Díaz Roig, *Del romancero hispánico* (Mexico City: El Colegio de México, 2008); Aurelio González Pérez, *El romancero en América* (Madrid: Síntesis, 2003); and Aurelio González (ed.), *La copla en México* (Mexico City: El Colegio de México, 2007). For a historical survey of the twentieth-century collection of oral ballads in America see González Pérez, *El romancero*, pp. 65–81.

8. See Marcelino Menéndez y Pelayo, *Historia de la poesía hispanoamericana*, 2 vols (Madrid: V. Suárez, 1911–13), II; Medina, *Romances*; Horacio Urteaga, 'Los copleros de la conquista', *Mercurio Peruano*, año IV, 6.32 (1921), 120–41; Ramón Menéndez Pidal, *Los romances de América y otros estudios* (Buenos Aires: Espasa-Calpe, 1939), pp. 13–52; and Menéndez Pidal, *Romancero hispánico*,

pp. 226–35, 341–56; Guillermo Lohmann Villena, 'Romances, coplas y cantares de la conquista del Perú', *Mar del Sur*, 9 (1950), 18–40; more systematically comprehensive in Óscar Coello, *Los inicios de la poesía castellana en el Perú* (Lima: Pontificia Universidad Católica, 1999). See also the systematization of the standard references in 'Romances sobre la conquista de América', *Archivo Digital del Romancero*, <http://fundacionramonmenendezpidal.org/archivodigital/collections/show/22> [accessed 10 April 2016].

9. Díaz del Castillo, *Historia verdadera*, pp. 375–76; trans. by Alfred Maudslay: *The Conquest of New Spain*, 5 vols (Nendeln: Kraus Reprint, 1967), IV, 198–99. I have slightly modified Maudslay's translation.

10. Bernardo de Vargas Machuca, *Milicia y descripción de las Indias* (Madrid: Pedro Madrigal, 1599), ff. 79v–80.

11. Vargas Machuca, *Milicia*, fol. 12^v; trans. by Timothy Johnson: *The Indian Militia and Description of the Indies*, ed. by Kris Lane (Durham, NC: Duke University Press, 2008), pp. 32–33.

12. James Lockhart, *The Men of Cajamarca: A Social and Biographical Study of the First Conquerors of Peru* (Austin: University of Texas Press, 1972), pp. 127, 143, 398.

13. Medina, *Romances*, p. ix.

14. For a thorough review of these problems and a useful collection of sources, see Coello, *Los inicios*, pp. 319–50.

15. Miguel Cabello Valboa, *Miscelánea Antártica*, ed. by Isaías Lerner (Seville: Fundación José Manuel Lara, 2011), p. 471.

16. Garcilaso de la Vega el Inca, *Comentarios reales de los incas*, ed. by Ángel Rosenblat (Buenos Aires: Emecé, 1945), book 1, ch. 8; quoted in Coello, *Los inicios*, p. 343, who also questions el Inca's reliability in this regard.

17. Medina, *Romances*, p. ix, refers to Palma, who seems to take it from Prescott, although the ultimate source is Pedro Cieza de León, *Guerras civiles del Perú*, ch. 38, or Antonio de Herrera y Tordesillas, *Historia general de los hechos de los castellanos en las Islas y Tierra Firme del mar Océano que llaman Indias Occidentales* (Antwerp: Juan Bautista Verdussen, 1728), dec. 6, lib. 3, cap. 4 (2: dec. 2, p. 56).

18. Lockhart, *Men of Cajamarca*, pp. 135–57.

19. A version of the ballad can be found in Di Stefano (ed.), *Romancero*, p. 132. See also Miguel Martínez, *Front Lines: Soldiers' Writing in the Early Modern Hispanic World* (Philadelphia: University of Pennsylvania Press, 2016), p. 172.

20. Medina, *Romances*, p. x.

21. Margit Frenk, *Nuevo corpus de la antigua lírica popular hispánica*, 2 vols (Mexico City: UNAM/El Colegio de México/Fondo de Cultura Económica, 2003), #975, I, 665–66, who quotes all the chronistic sources where the song is found.

22. Frenk, *Nuevo corpus*, #1547, II, 1091.

23. Mary Gaylord, 'The Grammar of Femininity in the Traditional Spanish Lyric', *Revista Interamericana*, 12.1 (1982), 115–24. See also Margit Frenk, *Poesía popular hispánica: 44 estudios* (Mexico City: FCE, 2006), pp. 353–86.

24. Lockhart, *Men of Cajamarca*, pp. 183–84.

25. 'Relación de Gonzalo de Zúñiga', in Beatriz Pastor and Sergio Callau (ed.), *Lope de Aguirre y la rebelión de los marañones* (Madrid: Castalia, 2011), p. 147.

26. Sebastián de Covarrubias, *Tesoro de la lengua castellana o española*, ed. by Ignacio Arellano and Rafael Zafra (Madrid and Frankfurt: Iberoamericana/Vervuert, 2006), p. 522.

27. Pastor and Callau (ed.), *Lope de Aguirre*, p. 273.

28. See, for instance, Pastor and Callau, *Lope de Aguirre*, pp. 75, 254–55, 260, 270, 273.

29. Beatriz Pastor, *The Armature of the Conquest: Spanish Accounts of the Discovery of America, 1492–1589*, trans. by Lydia Longstreth Hunt (Stanford, CA: Stanford University Press, 1992), pp. 168–204.

30. 'Carta de Lope de Aguirre a Felipe II', in Pastor and Callau (ed.), *Lope de Aguirre*, pp. 66, 73.

31. 'Carta de Lope de Aguirre al provincial Montesinos', in Pastor and Callau (ed.), *Lope de Aguirre*, p. 63. Although the ballad, on pp. 148–49, was recorded by Zúñiga after his 'Relación', he makes no explicit claim of authorship. In this regard see Coello, *Los inicios*, pp. 307–13.

32. Ovid, *Metamorphoses*, trans. by David Raeburn and Denis Feeney (London: Penguin Classics,

2004), 13.448–80 and 13.494–532. Policena is a character, among others, in 'Oh cruel hijo de Arquiles', 'Triste estaba y muy penosa', in Di Stefano (ed.), *Romancero*, pp. 205–07; and 'En las obsequias de Héctor', 'A la que el sol se ponía', in Antonio Rodríguez Moñino (ed.), *Silva de varios romances (Valencia: 1561)* (Valencia: Castalia, 1953), pp. 156–58, 172–73.

33. Matthew Restall and Felipe Fernández-Armesto, *The Conquistadors: A Very Short Introduction* (Oxford: Oxford University Press, 2012), pp. 50–51.

34. Restall and Fernández-Armesto, *The Conquistadors*, p. 51.

35. For pasquines on the walls see Winston Reynolds, *Hernán Cortés en la literatura del Siglo de Oro* (Madrid: Editora Nacional, 1979), p. 20. Enríquez de Guzmán's ballad in Coello, *Los inicios*, pp. 259–64. 'Buen conde Fernán González | el rey envía por vos', in Di Stefano (ed.), *Romancero*, pp. 362–63.

36. See Medina, *Romances*, pp. xviii–xxxii, xlii–li, for some of these notices. See also Coello, *Los inicios*, pp. 315–18 and 209–64; and Emilia Romero, *El romance tradicional en el Perú* (Mexico City: El Colegio de México, 1952).

37. Gonzalo Fernández de Oviedo, *Historia general y natural de las Indias*, 4 vols (Madrid: Real Academia de la Historia, 1851–55), I, 127; Francisco López de Gómara, *Historia general de las Indias*, in *Historiadores primitivos de Indias I*, Biblioteca de Autores Españoles 22 (Madrid: Rivadeneyra, 1852), pp. 155–294 (p. 174).

38. See Margit Frenk, *Entre la voz y el silencio: la lectura en tiempos de Cervantes* (Mexico City: FCE, 2005); Aurelio González Pérez, 'El romance: transmisión oral y transmisión escrita', *Acta Poética*, 26 (2005), 221–37; María Cruz García de Enterría, 'Romancero: ¿cantado, recitado, leído?', *Edad de Oro*, 7 (1988), pp. 89–104, a special issue that contains other essays on the topic.

39. John F. Schwaller and Helen Nader, *The First Letter from New Spain: The Lost Petition of Cortés and His Company, June 20, 1519* (Austin: University of Texas Press, 2014), pp. 109–15, 137–39; Lockhart, *The Men of Cajamarca*, pp. 34–35. Although these men must have achieved different levels of literacy, Lockhart points out that signing one's name in the sixteenth century indicated some formal instruction, however basic, in reading and writing. For Tierra Firme, see Mario Góngora, *Los grupos de conquistadores en Tierra Firme (1509–1532)* (Santiago de Chile: Editorial Universitaria, 1962), pp. 68–90. For Chile, see Tomás Thayer Ojeda and Carlos Larraín, *Valdivia y sus compañeros* (Santiago: Imprenta Universitaria, 1951). And for New Granada, José Ignacio Avellaneda, *The Conquerors of the New Kingdom of Granada* (Albuquerque: University of New Mexico Press, 1995), p. 74 and Appendix 2.

40. I discuss this in more detail in *Front Lines*, pp. 12–21. For a survey on literacy figures in the Spanish context, see the recent work by Michele Olivari, *Avisos, pasquines y rumores: los comienzos de la opinión pública en la España del siglo XVII* (Madrid: Cátedra, 2014), pp. 102–03.

41. Olivari, *Avisos*, p. 103.

42. Menéndez Pidal, *Romancero hispánico*, II, 184–89.

43. See Antonio Rodríguez Moñino, *Pliegos poéticos de la Biblioteca Colombina* (Berkeley: University of California Press, 1974); Clive Griffin, *The Crombergers of Seville: The History of a Printing Dynasty* (Oxford: Clarendon Press, 1988), pp. xvii–xviii. About Hernando Colón, see now Edward Wilson-Lee, *The Catalogue of Shipwrecked Books: Young Columbus and the Quest for a Universal Library* (London: William Collins, 2018).

44. Vargas Machuca, *Milicia indiana*, fol. 32.

45. Irving Leonard, *Books of the Brave: Being an Account of Books and of Men in the Spanish Conquest and Settlement of the Sixteenth-Century New World* (Berkeley and Los Angeles: University of California Press, 1992), pp. 96, 223–24, 280; González Pérez, *El romancero en América*, p. 49; Jaime Moll, 'Los surtidos de romances, coplas, historias y otros papeles', in *Actas del Congreso Romancero-Cancionero. UCLA (1984)*, ed. by Enrique Rodríguez Cepeda, 2 vols (Madrid: José Porrúa Turanzas, 1990), I, 205–16. Carlos Alberto González Sánchez, *Los mundos del libro: medios de difusión de la cultura occidental en las Indias de los siglos XVI y XVII* (Seville: Universidad de Sevilla, 1999), pp. 124–30. On broadsheets in the carrera de Indias, see Pedro Rueda Ramírez, *Negocio e intercambio cultural: el comercio de libros con América en la carrera de Indias (siglo XVII)* (Seville: Universidad de Sevilla/ CSIC, 2005), pp. 191–217 (especially p. 195).

46. José Toribio Medina, *Vida de Ercilla* (Santiago: Imprenta Elzeviriana, 1917), p. 240.

47. See González Pérez, *El Romancero en América*, p. 53; Gisela Beutler, *Estudios sobre el romancero español en Colombia en su tradición escrita y oral desde la época de la Conquista hasta la actualidad* (Bogotá: Instituto Caro y Cuervo, 1977).

48. Reproduced and discussed by Medina, *Romances*, pp. lxii–lxiii. I quote Castellanos from *Historia del Reino de Nueva Granada*, ed. by Antonio Paz y Meliá, 2 vols (Madrid: Pérez Dubrull, 1886). See II, 49–52; and also I, 365–68.

49. Castellanos, *Historia*, II, 50.

50. Mikhail Bakhtin, *Rabelais and his World*, trans. by Helen Iswolsky (Bloomington: Indiana University Press, 1984), pp. 20–21.

51. Luis Fernando Restrepo, 'Somatografía épica colonial: las *Elegías de varones ilustres de Indias* de Juan de Castellanos', *MLN*, 115.2 (2000), pp. 248–67.

52. See, mainly, Fernando Bouza, *Corre manuscrito: una historia cultural del Siglo de Oro* (Madrid: Marcial Pons, 2001), especially pp. 109–35; Antonio Castillo Gómez, *Entre la pluma y la pared: una historia social de la escritura en los Siglos de Oro* (Madrid: Akal, 2006), pp. 225–51; and Olivari, *Avisos*.

53. Quoted in Olivari, *Avisos*, p. 26.

54. Olivari, *Avisos*, pp. 313–38. Javier Castro-Ibaseta's 'Monarquía Satírica. Poética de la caída del Conde Duque de Olivares' (unpublished PhD dissertation, Universidad Autónoma de Madrid, 2008), and his forthcoming book *Beware the Poetry. Political Satire and the Emergence of the Spanish Public Sphere (1600–1645)*, are the key studies on the relation between satire, political culture, and public life in early modern Spain.

55. Natalia Silva Prada, 'Pasquines contra visitadores reales: opinión pública en las ciudades hispanoamericanas de los siglos XVI, XVII y XVIII', in *Cultura escrita y espacio público en la ciudad hispánica del Siglo de Oro* (Gijón: Trea, 2010), pp. 373–98; 'Cultura política tradicional y opinión crítica: los rumores y pasquines iberoamericanos de los siglos XVI al XVIII', in *Tradición y modernidad en la historia de la cultura política: España e Hispanoamérica, siglos XVI y XVII*, ed. by Riccardo Forte and Natalia Silva Prada (Mexico City: Universidad Autónoma Metropolitana, 2009), pp. 89–141; and *La política de una rebelión: los indígenas frente al tumulto de 1692 en la Ciudad de México* (Mexico City: El Colegio de México, 2007), pp. 229–31, 411–510.

56. 'Relación de Gonzalo de Zúñiga', in Pastor and Callau (ed.), *Lope de Aguirre*, p. 147.

57. Roger Chartier, *The Cultural Origins of the French Revolution*, trans. by Lydia Cochrane (Durham, NC: 1991), pp. 142–43. The 'rebel imagination' is a coinage by Yves-Marie Bercé, *History of Peasant Revolts* (Ithaca, NY: Cornell University Press, 1990), pp. 278–79.

CHAPTER 5

Laughter between Spain and New Spain: The Poetics of Zeuxis in the Burlesque Poetry of Agustín de Salazar y Torres

Raquel Barragán Aroche

For many reasons, the *Cítara de Apolo* [Zither of Apollo] of Agustín de Salazar y Torres might be considered a poetic bridge between Spain and New Spain. Juan de Vera Tassis, the editor of this work, emphasized this idea in his posthumous eulogy to it when he suggested that its poetic heights had scaled both the Old World and the New.[1] Salazar y Torres arrived in New Spain when he was just under nine years old with his uncle Marcos de Torres, bishop of Yucatán and later viceroy of New Spain (1647), and probably returned to the Peninsula when he was twenty-four, dying there fifteen years later.[2] His work occupies a privileged position as a link between two worlds, becoming a catalogue of voices and styles which translate and disseminate the Hispanic canon and its art of wit from the other side of the Atlantic. For example, it must be remembered that Sor Juana, in addition to completing *La segunda Celestina* [The Second Celestina], imitates him in several poetic compositions, some of which will be alluded to here.[3] Also worth mentioning here, from the world of theatre and the other side of the Atlantic, is Francisco Bances Candamo, who, according to Alfonso Méndez Placarte, was Salazar's pupil.[4]

It is no coincidence that the work is entitled *Cítara de Apolo*, since semantically it brings to mind a Parnassian universe, very much in fashion in the poetic titles of the period, including poems which varied in metrics, styles, genres and imitations of different authors. As Aurora Egido points out, the proliferation of works 'con el sello castálido o hesperiano, como con el de Apolo y las musas, es casi abrumadora' [with the seal of Castalia or Hesperia, or that of Apollo and the muses, is almost overwhelming]; these editions of the second half of the seventeenth century, like the *Ocios de Castalia en diversas rimas* [Leisure of Castalia in Different Rhymes] (1663) of Juan de Ovando, all have the signature of *varietas*. Sor Juana's *Inundación Castálida* [Castalian Flood] (1689) would also count under this heading, carrying its significance to the extremes.[5]

It is curious that in this second half of the century, alongside the proliferation of this series of Parnassian titles, one finds an exaggeration of their semantic meaning. These characteristics correspond to a period which we can term 'ultra-baroque' — following the terminology of Antonio Alatorre — in which poets, in virtue of that quality of variety, showed in their works 'más y más elaboración, más y más ingenio, más y más barroquismo, hasta llegar, si posible era, al *non plus ultra*' [more and more elaboration, more and more wit, more and more excess, until reaching, if it were possible, the point at which one can go no further].[6] This attitude is more evident in the colonial poets, who carried their Peninsular models to the limits of their possibilities, for good or for ill. The paradigmatic example is their imitation of the work of Góngora. As is well known, the poetry of Salazar y Torres also bore the imprint of Gongorism.[7] For obvious reasons, scholarly attention has turned more to his practice of imitation, underplaying the variety and dynamism of his oeuvre, into which he ingeniously weaves other models for both humorous and serious effect.[8]

This perspective extends to many studies of colonial poetry, which depart from the principle that all roads lead to Góngora — true in part, but not sufficiently so as to frame the entire canon which was assimilated on the other side of the Atlantic. As Joaquín Roses points out, this is not the only way to explain the richness of either Góngora or the poets of the Americas.[9] The relevant question, therefore, must be: what other poets did Salazar y Torres imitate directly or indirectly? Vera Tassis himself gives us a sense of Salazar's readings in another part of his poetic eulogy, in which he relates the qualities of the poetry of canonical authors to those of which Salazar y Torres's can boast:

> Formó don Agustín nuevo Parnaso
> en su capaz gloriosa poesía,
> pues de Homero alcanzó la melodía
> con la erudita locución del Taso,
> lo lírico, de Lope y Garcilaso;
> de Góngora, lo culto y lo elegante;
> de Quevedo, lo agudo y lo picante;
> de Virgilio, lo heroico y lo elevado
> de Marcial, lo juicioso y lo salado;
> del Petrarca, lo sabio y lo eminente
> de Ovidio, la inventiva y lo elocuente;
> de Camoens, lo dulce y lo amoroso;
> de Calderón, la idea y lo ingenioso:
> del Marino, lo docto y lo süave;
> de Argensola y de Zárate, lo grave;
> de Lucano, la frasi y la sentencia;
> del Dante la facundia y la elocuencia;
> de Pantaleón y Hortensio, lo divino [...]. (sig. ¶¶3)[10]

> [Don Agustín formed a new Parnassus
> in his vast and glorious poetry,
> since he blended the melody of Homer
> with the erudition of Tasso,
> the lyricism of Lope and Garcilaso,
> the elegance and refinement of Góngora,

> the sharpness and bite of Quevedo,
> the heroic and exalted verse of Virgil,
> the level-headedness and wit of Martial,
> the wisdom and eminence of Petrarch,
> the invention and eloquence of Ovid,
> the sweetness and seductiveness of Camões,
> the intelligence and ingeniousness of Calderón,
> the learnedness and evenness of Marino,
> the gravity of Argensola and Zárate,
> the language and maxims of Lucan,
> the ease and eloquence of Dante,
> the heavenly Pantaleón and Hortensio]

Again, it is evident that his poetic microcosm incorporates a literary Parnassus due to the variety of Greek, Latin, Italian, Portuguese and Spanish poets invoked. Having said that, it is interesting that this Parnassian allegory — a common one within the literary establishment, which defines the canon of classical and contemporary authors — itself involves another, subtler, one, which remains hidden at first sight. Vera Tassis depicts Salazar's poetry based on a selection of the most appealing qualities in the poetry of canonical authors, which finds a symbolic correspondence in the anecdote concerning Zeuxis's painting of Helen. The acclaimed Greek painter based his portrait of her on the most perfect features of five women, as Pliny recounts in his *Naturalis Historia* (XXXV, 64) and Cicero in *De inventione* (II, 1). The anecdote was a popular one not only in manuals of painting, but also in poetry, since it proposed a more dynamic method of composition which selected the best from each author.[11] For now, it will suffice to mention the Jesuit Pedro Zapata's description of Sor Juana in the preliminary material to the *Poemas de la única poetisa americana* [Poems of the Unique Poetess of America] (1692), in which he claims that the design of Zeuxis's Helen was comparable to that which nature achieved in making of Sor Juana a compendium of the knowledge of many other illustrious women. Likewise, the presentation of the work of Salazar through the poetic virtues of others, based on adjectives which evoke particular genres and styles, not only assembles fragmentary elements which converge on the notion of Parnassus, but also suggests a method of composing ideal poetry which is not constructed on the basis of a single model. This is a vision of lyric founded on the *imitatio multiplex* which Cicero postulated in the aforementioned work as the conclusion to the anecdote, and which would take shape in the debate between Poliziano and Cortese, Pico and Bembo, Erasmus and the Ciceronians, among others. There is nothing surprising about this by the second half of the seventeenth century, by which time the debate about imitative eclecticism in the Hispanic world, extolled in the work of Garcilaso, had been more than won. Nevertheless, we often lose sight of the fact that this method of composition remained active to the point of acquiring 'ultra-baroque' characteristics. It is, therefore, a very significant allegory, one to which scholars of the literature of New Spain must pay greater attention, since it is fundamental to an understanding of the structure of a work in which the sources overlap in a dynamic fashion. In this case, it helps us to articulate the objective of this article, since Salazar y Torres follows this kind of 'poetics', that of

Zeuxis, which in its journey from painting to writing preserves the meaning of a more ambitious kind of mimesis, one which constructs something new (an ideal) through a selection of different elements. It is precisely through the variety of his jokes that his wit can establish a dialogue with a variety of models. This reveals one element of the poetic Parnassus of New Spain which has remained hidden.

Therefore, the following analysis of some of Salazar's burlesque compositions aims to sketch out, on the one hand, the models which he imitated and, based on that, which Peninsular authors of humorous and burlesque poetry could have been known in New Spain, and on the other, to establish the radical characteristics of the eclectic method for writing burlesque poetry, which might in itself have influenced the poets of its day. The so-called 'poetics' of Zeuxis, therefore, is manifest on two levels: in a general way, in the selection of a variety of authors — from whom I will pick out only a few — who form the basis of his burlesque style, and in particular, in the compositions of burlesque portraits and self-portraits, which abound in his work, since they are constructed through a variety of paradigms of comparison which reflect this poetics on a small scale with burlesque implications.

Burlesque *idea artificis*: Anastasio Pantaleón de Ribera and Gerónimo de Cáncer

The burlesque poems of Salazar y Torres, which comprise more than half of his work, could be defined in a general way as a constant reflection on how to compose a poem based on the play between fiction and authorship, which evokes or reveals the tradition which is being imitated. These poetic games, in which readers are involved in an immediate way, acquired value in a social and collective space which found its identity in those models considered to be canonical. Salazar's poetry was far from being addressed primarily to the individual, since the epigraph to many of his poems reveals their relationship with one of the literary academies, and his poetry found a wide audience through performance at poetic contests, spaces which shape the features of the New Spanish canon in ways which we still do not entirely understand.

Salazar took part in the poetic competition on the theme of the Immaculate Conception convened by the Real y Pontificia Universidad de México (1654), where Juan de Guevara presented him as 'a second *Anastasio Pantaleón* for our times' (my emphasis) on awarding him one of the two first places which he achieved in the competition. The first composition to win a prize was a *romance de equívocos* [punning ballad] dedicated to the shield of Mary. The second were 'doce redondillas de pie quebrado, significando en ellas el miedo con que quedó el demonio después de vencido' [twelve rhyming quatrains with shorter lines interspersed, on the subject of the devil's fear after his defeat]. This presentation indicates that there was an institutionalized space for laughter, just as in Spain, in which the canonical status of an author was recognized by juxtaposing his identity with an imitator who, in turn, is elevated to the same category of canonicity. From the perspective of the literary establishment, it was not enough to be part of Parnassus, but to incarnate Parnassus itself, and this could only function through a previous process of fragmentation.

Doubtless, this comparison with a fully burlesque author marked the coordinates of his identity as a writer and mapped out certain convergences between the two authors to which Vera Tassis would also allude, in all seriousness, in his posthumous eulogy. Both poets admitted to being followers of Góngora and actively participated in contests and literary academies. It was common to recall Pantaleón in these competitions as a paradigm of a burlesque author.[12] In this case, his name had become a kind of honorary title on the other side of the Atlantic, where his work was indeed read: Sor Juana mentions him in her ballad which began 'Ilustrísimo don Payo' [Most illustrious don Payo], revealing that if Fray Payo had not read Pantaleón, she could have taken a line from the latter for herself. Méndez Plancarte adds four more references from a New Spanish context: in the 1673 competition at the church of Saint Philip of Jesus there was a call for *sextillas de quebrados* in imitation of Pantaleón; Sigüenza wrote some *quintillas* in the style of Pantaleón in the *Fuegos* [fireworks] of the *Triunfo parténico* [Parthenon Triumph] (1683); Ignacio de Santa Cruz Aldana mentioned him in his jocular *romance* 'Aquí con nuestro Anastasio [...] que esta vez Pantaleonizo' [Here with our Anastasio [...] whom I Pantaleonize at this time], dedicated to the 'Reales fiestas' [royal festivities] on the coronation of Charles II (1677); and Ramírez de Vargas had invoked Pantaleón's 'musa chocarrera' [uncouth muse] in his *Fuegos de san Bernardo* [Fireworks for Saint Bernard] (1691).[13]

Apart from these, compositions were also published in the *Cítara de Apolo* which showed imitative correspondences with those of Pantaleón. There is, for example, the opening of the *romance* in which the poetic persona declares himself to have syphilis and recounts his sufferings in his own voice: 'Selvas, yo vengo a quejarme | que las yerbas me cansan, | pues desde que tuve bubas | las Catalinas me matan' [Woods, I come to lament, | for the herbs weary me, | and since I had bubos | the Catalinas kill me].[14] This is quite similar to the famous epistle 'Al duque de Lerma en esta enfermedad' [To the Duke of Lerma in this illness], in which Pantaleón declares himself to have syphilis and complains of the treatment he is receiving.

In the second composition which received a prize in the aforementioned poetic contest, there are more correspondences than the honorary title, since in the first line Salazar evokes and transforms the well-known opening of the *romance* 'Poeta soy gongorino' [I am a Gongorine poet] with which Pantaleón inaugurated the competition of April 1625, commissioned by the Marquis of Velada, and which he uses again in his introduction to another burlesque *romance* on the wedding of a tailor. Salazar also recreates it with different intent as a *captatio benevolentiae* to introduce his *redondillas* on the defeat of the devil:

> Poeta soy desdichado,
> pues cuando quiero escribillas
> con mis proprias redondillas
> he quebrado.
>
> Y de hacellas, aunque veo
> que en haciéndolas tendré
> mil que conozcan el pie
> que cojeo.

> Ea, ya estoy empeñado;
> empiézolas, vaya pues:
> (por dios que el asumpto es
> endiablado).[15]

> [I am a hapless poet,
> since when I want to write them
> on my very own *redondillas*
> I have broken.
>   And in making them, though I see
> That in making them I will have
> A thousand who know the foot
> I limp on.
>   Well, I am committed now;
> I'm starting them, let's get going:
> (by God, the topic is
> bedevilled)]

Salazar exchanges a poetic filiation for a complaint about the exercise of writing: from Gongorine poet to hapless poet, ridiculing in the process the whole *captatio benevolentiae*. Nevertheless, the simultaneity of the phrase which is alluded to and its recreation demonstrates the imitative process which refers to a chain of models which the reader might recognize: Pantaleón as imitator of Góngora, Salazar as imitator of Pantaleón. Beneath this burlesque identity, which is enunciated in the first person, he achieves the equivalence of the poetic discourse with the *pie quebrado* [broken foot] of the verse, resulting in a visual illustration of the content and making possible a joke at his own expense: he is a hapless poet (no longer a Gongorine poet), since his very own redondillas have 'broken' and hinder his poetic enterprise. The same semantic and visual overlap is played with in the 'broken foot' of the second stanza, whose meaning alludes to the fact that the foot he limps on is his lack of virtuosity, which is exposed to his readers. Finally, the third quatrain of this introduction closes with the pun on 'endiablado', which despite not having a semantic correspondence with the metre, does refer to the difficulty or ugliness of the subject which will, literally, speak of the devil.

As has been observed, the true challenge of the proposed topic lay in its form, and is highlighted in the introduction to this winning poem: 'metro que por su gracia y garbo le han estimado los mayores ingenios de España, y por lo que tiene de tirar a la chanza, que escribirla como se debe escribir no es cosa de chanza, sino de muchas veras' [a metre which for its grace and elegance has been esteemed by the greatest wits of Spain, and because of its tendency to jest, writing it as it should be written is no laughing matter, but a very serious one]. This *idea artificis* — which allowed a very serious game to be played out between content and form — would remind the readers of another burlesque model, that of Jerónimo de Cáncer, who was the precursor of the witty piece above in his famous *redondillas de pie quebrado* dedicated 'A san Francisco' [to Saint Francis]:

> Pues Francisco al más baldado
> sana sin que afán le cueste,

cúreme ahora de aqueste
pie quebrado.[16]

[Since Francis heals the most crippled
without breaking sweat,
may he cure me now of this
broken foot.]

Salazar employs exactly the same pun ('quebrado') in his first stanza, which demonstrates that Cáncer's metrical joke is the missing piece that sets in motion the burlesque artifice, although with different semantic implications. The famous theorist Juan Caramuel reveals the success of this metre of Cáncer's in his *Rhytmica* (1665), affirming that those 'tetrásticos de pie quebrado' [quatrains with a broken foot] had been 'editados en España una y otra vez, leídos y aprobados por ingenios doctísimos, merecieron alabanza en el orbe literario' [published in Spain time and again, read and approved by the most learned wits, earned praise throughout the literary world].[17] This statement, very similar to the one in the epigraph of the *certamen*, explains the positive reception that the metre had in New Spain, making it one of the favourite metres in some competitions, since it was ideal for visually transmitting the burlesque discourse exposed in the ephemeral constructs which adorned the festivities.

Sor Juana also used this form in her *villancico* — with some humorous elements — dedicated to Saint Joseph.[18] She probably also knew, directly or indirectly, the model of Cáncer, since, according to an epistolary eulogy of the Peruvian poet Luis Antonio de Oviedo, Count of La Granja, Sor Juana had absorbed the wit (literally, 'sucked off the salt') of Cáncer and Quevedo.[19] The juxtaposition of the burlesque qualities of two well-known poets therefore recurs in Sor Juana, a mechanism which as well as being an established way of legitimating the poet can be considered an instance of Cáncer's influence on the poetry of religious contests, in the viceroyalties of both New Spain and Peru[20]. This influence is more significant than we think, since the work of Juan del Valle Caviedes also coincides at several points with that of the Zaragozan Cáncer, a filiation which is demonstrated in the humorous allusion which he makes to the latter in two quatrains of his humorous *romance* which begins '¿Qué médico llamará?' [Which doctor will call?], in which he refers to Cáncer among various other authors in the Hispanic canon. Moreover, this was not the only time Salazar y Torres used the *pie quebrado* metre, since it appears again in what is probably an academy poem entitled 'A cierta dama purgada, a quien otras daban vaya en el día que se purgó' [To a certain lady who was purged, to whom other ladies gave a damn on the day she was purged], in which he weaves in several scatological euphemisms which Góngora employed in his famous *letrilla*, or refrain poem, '¿Qué lleva el señor Esgueva?' [What's the matter with Mr Esgueva?].

Furthermore, from these stanzas we can deduce that beyond the fact that the literary establishment itself defined the burlesque canon of New Spain, since it proposed the metres to be used and awarded the canonical title which concurred with the author's choice, poets themselves protected the space of invention as a bastion of their ingenuity, based on a comprehensive practice of *imitatio* which combined the most significant characteristics of different models. In the case of Salazar, we can observe the parody of a line which proposes an identity and a form with different possibilities of burlesque expression. This method, which we can define as a kind of 'poetics' of Zeuxis, proposes that variety of elements whose compositional principal shares characteristics with the famous Horatian metaphor (*Ep.* I 3, 21) in which the poet is like the bee which makes honey from the pollen of a variety of flowers, an allusion which, curiously, the Italian poet Marino linked to the Zeuxis anecdote in his encomium of painting *Dicerie sacre* (1614).[21] Nevertheless, the difference between the two metaphors consists in that what we might call the 'poetics' of Zeuxis allows for the construction of more *visible* intertextualities, since the models are still recognizable. Its objective does not only consist in exhibiting these models as fragments, but also in uniting them to favour the novelty of this hybrid which does not correspond with any real model, but only with the ingenious invention of the author. In this case, through the *idea artificis*, which links Pantaleón with Cáncer, Salazar constructs a hybrid which seeks to show how complicated it is to write a poem. The intention is to make present his fictionalized voice in order to elaborate metapoetic reflections through a humorous framework.[22] This is an aspect of burlesque poetry which finds antecedents in Baltasar del Alcázar, Góngora, Quevedo, Lope, Polo de Medina and Calderón, among others. Nevertheless, this rhetorical device is taken to its extremes and used most recurrently by Jacinto Polo de Medina. His name is no novelty in New Spain, since Sor Juana's famous *ovillejo* shows the influence of his *Apolo y Dafne* (1634), which she also imitates in other compositions. Although there is no epigraph in the work of Salazar y Torres which directly links him with Polo de Medina, the structure of the poem — *epanorthosis*, *erotema* and *dubitatio* — establishes the link between both, a link which is affirmed on numerous occasions in Méndez Plancarte's anthology of *Poetas novohispanos* [Poets of New Spain], especially since several of Polo de Medina's works were known in New Spain. This is clearer in the allusions to the difficulty of writing the poem, which are already present in the *redondillas de pie quebrado* and which Salazar develops masterfully in his poem entitled 'Cuatro estaciones del día...' [Four seasons of the day...]. I will not explore this relationship in detail, but it is worth highlighting that this characteristic creates a direct link between Salazar and Sor Juana in the Hispanic canon, since both their poems incorporated these humorous notes, which reveal the intertextual horizon which structured their work: they became their own commentators. The old reproach against Francisco de las Brozas for demonstrating in his commentaries the 'thefts' of Garcilaso was now a burlesque practice. It corresponded with a context in which the burden of creating novelties through *imitatio* left no other way than to expose the process of the dismemberment of the models and the reconstitution which made apparent the author's invention, legitimated his poetry within the canon and created a dialogue with readers.[23] Thus, eclectic imitation in a burlesque vein is exploited to its furthest limits and creates a poetic bridge with Peninsular poets. Therefore, we are presented with a trajectory of radicalization of eclectic imitation which must be defined based on the intertextual dialogue which in each work proposes a kind of poetics similar to the assemblage carried out by Zeuxis. It is, therefore, not coincidental that in just one composition for a competition Salazar has imitated the distinct qualities of three of the great burlesque poets to construct an *idea artificis* based on identity, form and content.

A Burlesque Zeuxis: The Construction of Portraits and Self-Portraits

The 'poetics' of Zeuxis did not only serve to compose a dynamic Parnassus within the works of the poets, but for obvious reasons had a more concrete development within the tradition of the female portrait, especially the image which poets favoured for a long time based on Petrarch's *Canzoniere*.[24] As is well known, the Petrarchan description set out a semantic field composed of metaphorical fragments which described ideal beauty based on the selection of distinct elements of nature: gold, suns, stars, rubies, crystal, roses, and snow, among others. It is worth remembering that Petrarch himself, in his *De inventione et ingenium*, of clear Ciceronian inspiration, had defended compound imitation. This same mechanism of construction through dispersion gave rise to the parodies of Francesco Berni and his followers, who affirmed that such metaphors, in their literalness and diversity, constituted a monstrosity.[25] It was a process of accumulation which, in surpassing itself and breaking its harmony through the disparity of elements, favoured the burlesque. In his *Ars poetica*, Horace described a similar mechanism in which he assured that a painter could only succeed in eliciting laughter if he joined a human head with a horse's neck, with uneven limbs full of feathers and the figure of a beautiful woman which ended in a black fish (*Ep.* II 3, 1–5). It is interesting that it is these same lines which bring us closer to a definition of parody as a process of chimerical imitation disproportionate to the original model.

Salazar's work offers a variety of examples of which we will select only two: the parody of the tradition of portraits and self-portraits through fragmentation and accumulation to the point of radicalizing the semantic fields to elicit laughter. It might be said that this was a method based on the principle that the laughable was a consequence of ugliness and deformity — the model was deformed through fragmentation — as Aristotle and later Cicero had taught.[26] Nevertheless, in this, too, some compositional paradigms can be traced. For example, one of the burlesque self-portraits in which Salazar imitates one of Lope's sonnets in the *Rimas humanas y divinas del Licenciado Tomé de Burguillos* [Human and Divine Rhymes of the Licentiate Tomé de Burguillos] (1634) — which has come to be considered the last Spanish anthology in Petrarchan style, albeit a parodical one — allows us to speculate on the impact of this dimension of Lope in the burlesque Parnassus of New Spain. Lope's *Rimas* are not only a constant in the work of Salazar, but we also know from other sources that they circulated, since two copies from the second half of the seventeenth century are preserved in the Biblioteca Nacional de México.[27]

The sonnet in question is 'Da noticia de sus gracias para que de ellas infieran las de su dama' [He recounts his own graces so that those of the lady might be inferred from them], composed in imitation of Lope's Sonnet 66 entitled 'Díjole una dama que le enviase su retrato' [A lady told him to send her his portrait]:

(Salazar y Torres)
Si de alguna taberna en los tapices
visteis al Cid sin calza o pedorrera;
si al Moro Abindarraez de Antequera
sin marlota, turbante, ni terlices;
si visteis a Catón (con más narices)
colgado de un figón en la espetera;
visteis, Cintia, la efigie verdadera
de mi cara, colores y matices.
Demás de esto, soy tonto un tanto cuanto,
y tan puerco, que puedo ser poeta;
y hay, con todo esto, quien por mí se muere.
De insulso a nadie quiero sin ser santo;
siendo yo tal, juzgad como discreta,
que tal debe de ser la que me quiere (p. 63).

[If, in the hangings of some tavern
you have seen El Cid without breeches or riding shoes;
or the Moor Abindarraez of Antequera
without tunic, turban, or girdle;
if you have seen Cato (the nosier)
hanging from a rack in the larder;
you have seen, Cynthia, the true effigy
of my face, colour and complexion.
Apart from this, I am something of an idiot,
And so boorish, that I can be a poet;
And, for all this, there is someone who dies for me.
I love no one dull without being a saint;
Since dull I am, use your better judgement,
Since thus must be the woman who loves me.]

(Lope de Vega)
Si habéis visto al Sofí sin caperuza
en dorado cuartel de boticario,
o a Barbarroja el ínclito cosario
y en nariz de sayón tez de gamuza;
si habéis visto a Merlín, si al moro Muza
o a Juan Francés vendiendo letuario,
si el rostro de un corito cuartanario
que quiso ser lechón y fue lechuza:
ese soy yo, que a la virtud atento
sólo concedo a su vitoria palma,
que todo lo demás remito al viento.
Pero supuesto que el argén me calma
tengo con ropa limpia el nacimiento,
la cara en griego y en romance el alma.[28]

[If you have seen the Shah without his turban
in the golden quarters of the apothecary,

or the illustrious corsair Barbarroja
and his executioner's nose the colour of chamois;
if you have seen Merlin, or the moor Muza
or Juan Francés selling candied fruits,
or the face of a group of sufferers of ague
Who wanted to be a piglet and turned out an owl:
that's what I am, since attentive to virtue
I only concede the palm to virtue's victory,
all the rest can be taken by the wind.
But since argent calms me
I'm born with clean clothes,
My face in Greek and my soul in Spanish.]

The two compositions have many similarities in the two quatrains; Salazar imitates, on the one hand, the anaphorical use of the subordinate conditional clause (protasis) to generate expectations, and on the other, the variety of portraits of historical figures who act as similes, since both poets suggest that their faces — of Morisco features — are like theirs, but ridiculed to the point that they have lost the features by which they might be recognized. The Cid, who is embroidered on the tapestry of a tavern, has no breeches or riding shoes, and the *sofi*, or Persian prince, who appears in one section ('cuarto') of the heraldic shield of an apothecary, has no turban ('caperuza'). Both poets appeal to the sense of sight through the *verba videndi*, since the portraits which are mixed together come from two lower-class establishments, the tavern and the apothecary. Lope also alludes to the famous corsair Barbarroja who is described through textilic puns — almost like Góngora's Pyramus — since he continues referring to the heraldic shield: he has a big 'executioner's' nose ('de sayón'), referring to the garment worn by executioners, to whom, by metonymy, the same name was applied, as well as to the Jews, the 'executioners' of Christ par excellence, and the complexion of a chamois based on the texture of goatskin and the yellow colour which will be linked, a few lines on, with the 'corito' with ague (a yellow face).[29] In turn, Salazar describes the moor Abindarraez of the Abencerrajes without the typical Moorish garments (tunic, turban and girdle) in order to support the idea of his ridiculous and ordinary image. Nonetheless, in the following quatrain he refers to the size of his nose — like Lope but without the anti-Semitic jest — with the allusion to a portrait of Cato the censor ('con más narices', with more nose) hanging from a meat hook ('espetera') in an inn or tavern ('figón'). The other figures to whom Lope alludes (Merlin, the moor Muza, Juan Francés and the 'corito') serve to create a ridiculous effect based on the accumulation of anodyne faces which adorn an apothecary (thus the sale of candied fruits or syrup), a conjunction which will result in a chimera or an incomprehensible face (a face 'in Greek'). Salazar, unlike Lope, anticipates the punchline by introducing the main clause in the final lines of the second quatrain in which he reveals that he is the mix of all those degraded characters ('cara, colores y matices'), in addition to humorously announcing, in the following tercet, that he is dirty enough to be a poet. He therefore wittily changes the meaning of Lope's final tercets — who closes with reference to the ugliness of the face but the beauty of the soul (including purity of blood) — since, as the epigraph ironically declares, he uses his own portrait so that the supposed graces and discretion of the lady might be inferred, a discursive strategy which adds an extra element, since it is really two poems in one. The burlesque self portrait-sonnet takes shape as a kind of burlesque Zeuxis — an idea taken from Lope — which depicts itself bringing together incongruous features from historical figures made ridiculous in order to present the ideal ugliness of poet and lady.

From this composition we can establish two important characteristics which will be exploited in his work: on the one hand, the search for novel terms of comparison to compose the *descriptio*, and on the other, the proliferation of planes of reading within a single poem. Regarding the first characteristic, he composed portraits of women based on distinct semantic fields such as tailoring or poetic metres, among others. Just as in painting, the concept of invention played an important role here, overburdening the imagination with new semantic fields which opened a space for new forms and themes. Be that is it may, this radicalized kind of portrait was a popular one in the canon of poets from the Spanish colonies. Sor Juana composed a poem dedicated to the Countess of Galve comparing her with various heroes and used musical metaphors in the *redondillas* entitled 'Pinta la armonía simétrica que los ojos perciben en la hermosura, con otra música' [She paints the symmetrical harmony which eyes perceive in beauty, with another music]. Juan del Valle Caviedes also follows this mechanism in various burlesque compositions, in which he depicted ladies through metaphors of war, doctors and surgeons, astrology and playing cards, in addition to experimenting with a different metrical form in each one. It is an application of the 'poetics' of Zeuxis in which there is a multiplication of the parameters of comparison with the most dissimilar semantic fields, which we might compare to the paintings of Arcimboldo.

In all this search for metaphorical conceits there is a strong desire to dialogue with the Petrarchan model which favours parody as an inverse imitation: fragmentation continues to be fundamental, but also a quest to surpass the model in the confrontation of heterogeneous elements, hence the proliferation of planes of reading. Salazar offers us a powerful example of this in a *romance* entitled 'Para que una hermosura se vincule en la última perfección, ha de tener facciones como están en este retrato, señalándose con letras versales' [In order that a beauty be associated with the ultimate perfection, she must have features as they are in this portrait, indicated with capital letters], in which both characteristics are brought together, since there are two simultaneous meanings and a proliferation of elements of comparison; it is another visual game which renews the concept of the Petrarchan portrait, since it competes with the model:

> DEIdad SABE aL sol narcisa,
> saCAndo lo BELLO a plaza,
> a LAs luces, FRENTE a frente,
> DE INdignACIon Apagarlas,
>   Y DECLARÁndoSE, hACE
> queJArSe a las SOBERANAS
> DEidades, y JIMEN nEZias
> de enOJOS de no igualarla.

LAs flechas NARcIsa aguZa,
y al esgrimirlas CON GRACIA,
DEspidiéndoLAS sU ALiENto,
esCUdos dEL Amor pasa... (p. 159)

[Narcisa, a deity with a taste of sun,
Bringing beauty to light,
Face to face with its lights,
Putting them out with indignation,
      And revealing herself, she makes
The sovereign deities complain
And they foolishly groan
In anger at not equalling her.
      Narcisa sharpens her arrows,
And brandishing them with grace,
Her breath shoots them out,
She passes the shields of love...]

The poem continues for six quatrains more, in which Narcisa is described, a chaste woman who surpasses in beauty any deity and natural power, of whom Love himself is enamoured; but in the hidden message in capitals a chimeric revelation is read composed of three *quintillas* (6–6-11–6-6) and two final lines (6–5): 'De Isabel cabello, | la frente de Inacia | y de Clara sea cejas soberanas; | de Jiménez ojos, | la nariz con gracia | de las Valenzuela,[30] | la tez de Bernarda, | de Luisa sea la boca de nácar, | manos de Teresa, | süaves y blancas; | piernas de la Sernas, | cintura de Anarda, | con sus tres hoyos el blanco de Antandra,[31] | lo demás oculto | y que se recata, | de cualquiera tomo | y cualquiera basta' [Isabel's hair, | Inacia's forehead | and the high eyebrows of Clara; | eyes of Jiménez, | the graceful nose of the Valenzuela sisters, | the complexion of Bernarda, | let the mother-of-pearl mouth be Luisa's, | hands of Teresa, | smooth and white, | legs of Sernas, | waist of Anarda, | the whiteness of Antandra with her three holes, | the rest which is hidden and guarded, | I'll take anyone's | and anyone's will do]. Salazar y Torres introduces a subversive portrait beneath the Petrarchan *descriptio* of the most beautiful lady: a selective process to construct ideal beauty, but based on the limbs of twelve women. There is doubtless an allusion not only to the anecdote of Zeuxis, but also to the 'poetics' of Zeuxis which favours fragmentation or enumeration — in a very self-consciously experimental metric — in which the reader perceives the invention which by contrast makes a mockery of the model by representing the Narcisa who contemplates herself as the only beauty.[32] Salazar is converted into another burlesque Zeuxis who with his eclecticism breaks with traditional moulds both in form and content.

In this context, it is worth mentioning that in spite of the fact that references to the composition of Zeuxis are frequent in the poetic works of this period, Lope, with whom the Sorian poet is in dialogue, is one of the authors who alludes to it most frequently and who transforms it in a novel way by inverting its sense: he compares those five beauties with the only model who surpasses them, that of his lady.[33] This mechanism appears in the sonnet dedicated to Ángela Vernegali, and in another of the *Rimas de Tomé de Burguillos* which begins 'Bien puedo yo pintar una hermosura' [I can paint a beauty very well] and which closes with the memorable line: 'basta que para mí tan linda seas [it is enough that you are so beautiful to me].

However, Salazar y Torres does not only show his artistic personality in this 'ultrabaroque' game of comic and serious planes, since he does not only reveal how Narcisa fragments into several women who delineate a discursive geometry, but, in a parallel manner, uncovers the two ways of making poetry in the period: on the first plane, the imitation of a model, and on the second *imitatio multiplex*. The poem is a dialogue between both imitative methods, but above all it is a miniature allegory of the eclecticism which he preferred and which populated his Parnassus with muses of different provenance: those of Góngora, Lope, Anastasio Pantaleón, Jerónimo de Cáncer and Polo de Medina. From all of them he took specific qualities of mechanisms, forms and contents. This is precisely what the burlesque poetry of Salazar y Torres was: a style which could contain a mixture of authors considered first- and second-rate, if indeed that categorization really existed, since poets like Anastasio Pantaleón had more success than is usually realized. We can deduce, therefore, from the clues that appear in Salazar's poetry — and from those in Sor Juana and Caviedes — who were the most read and who belonged to the Parnassus of colonial poetry. Likewise, we can deduce a kind of 'poetics', which, through the pictorial allegory of Zeuxis, allows us to assemble not only a variety of models, but the mechanisms of creation which mark out a method: metapoetic reflection and the multiplication of metaphorical fields, metric forms and planes of reading. Authors like Salazar reveal the interest of the public in New Spain in the humorous style, since there was indeed an institutional space for this type of wit in the seventeenth century. One might also suspect the influence exerted by the anonymous anthology *Flores de varia poesía*, compiled in New Spain around 1577, since the fourth book, now lost, was dedicated 'a lo de las burlas' [to burlesque]. Furthermore, although there is much still to be explored, we can say that Salazar y Torres's burlesque poetry gives us several insights towards a concept of poetry in its spatial and temporal context, which delineates a constant poetics — that of Zeuxis — in which the burlesque is based on fragments projected onto that chimeric 'harmony' which becomes a display of baroque — or ultrabaroque — aesthetics carried to the extremes and linking both continents.

Notes to Chapter 5

1. Agustín de Salazar y Torres, *Cítara de Apolo, varias poesías divinas y humanas, que escribió Don Agustín de Salazar y Torres; y saca a luz D. Juan de Vera Tasis y Villarroel, su mayor amigo [...]. Primera parte* (Madrid: Antonio González de Reyes, 1694), sig. ¶¶2.

2. José Ignacio Rubio Mañé, *Introducción al estudio de los virreyes en Nueva España 1535–1746*, 4 vols (Mexico City: Universidad Nacional Autónoma de México, 1955–63), I, 149; Thomas O'Connor, 'Antecedentes inmediatos de la "Aprobación" del padre Guerra: el "Discurso de la vida y escritos de don Agustín de Salazar y Torres" de Vera Tassis', in *El escritor y la escena VII: estudios sobre teatro español y novohispano de los Siglos de oro: Dramaturgia e Ideología*, ed. by Ysla Campbell (Ciudad Juárez: Universidad Autónoma de Ciudad Juárez, 1999), pp. 159–67.

3. Agustin de Salazar y Torres left this comedy unfinished (also known as *El hechizo sin hechizo* [Enchantment without Enchantment]). It was written to commemorate Mariana of Austria's birthday.

4. Alfonso Méndez Plancarte (ed.), *Poetas novohispanos: segundo siglo (1621–1721)*, 2 vols (Mexico City: Universidad Nacional Autónoma de México, 1944–45), I, 180. Salazar was one of Mariana of Austria's favourite playwrights; see Gabriel Maura y Gamazo, Duque de Maura, *Vida y reinado de Carlos II*, 2 vols (Madrid: Espasa-Calpe, 1954), I, 200.

5. Aurora Egido, 'Góngora y la batalla de las musas', in *Góngora hoy*, ed. by Joaquín Roses (Córdoba: Diputación de Córdoba, 2002), pp. 95–126 (pp. 120–21).

6. Antonio Alatorre, 'Avatares barrocos del romance', in *Cuatro ensayos sobre arte poética* (Mexico City: El Colegio de México, 2007), pp. 55–85 (p. 55).

7. It is customary for those who study his work to recount the famous anecdote which Vera Tassis recalls concerning the precocious age at which he recited and commented on the *Soledades* and *Polifemo* — at twelve years old — in order to establish him as one of the most fervent followers of the Cordoban poet. If we consider O'Connor's information referred to above, actually Salazar was eighteen years old.

8. See Martha Lilia Tenorio, 'Agustín de Salazar y Torres: discípulo de Góngora, maestro de sor Juana', *Nueva Revista de Filología Hispánica*, 57 (2010), 157–89; Jesús Ponce Cárdenas, 'El oro del otoño: glosas a la poesía de Agustín de Salazar y Torres', *Criticón*, 103–04 (2008), 131–52.

9. Joaquín Roses, 'Góngora en la poesía hispanoamericana del siglo XVII', in *Parnaso de dos mundos: de literatura española e hispanoamericana en el Siglo de Oro*, ed. by José María Ferri and Juan Carlos Rovira (Madrid and Frankfurt am Main: Universidad de Navarra/Iberoamericana/Vervuert, 2012), pp. 161–88 (p. 66).

10. The praise that Vera Tassis accords Pantaleón might seem strange, in that, despite the latter being a poet of the burlesque, he is related with sacred literature and, consequently, with Fray Hortensio Paravicino, preacher to Philip IV. Nevertheless, on the one hand, one must recall that Pantaleón had Paravicino as his teacher both in literary and spiritual pursuits, as Pellicer reveals in his edition of his works, and on the other, he was also recognized for his participation in competitions of religious poetry and praised, by authors such as Gracián, for his serious works. See Kenneth Brown, *Anastasio Pantaleón de Ribera (1600–1629): ingenioso miembro de la República literaria española* (Madrid: Studia Humanitatis/José Porrúa Turanzas, 1980).

11. On this anecdote and its cultural development, see Elizabeth Mansfield, *Too Beautiful to Picture: Zeuxis, Myth, and Mimesis* (Minneapolis: University of Minnesota Press, 2007).

12. Luis Vélez de Guevara, who was president of the Academia burlesca del Buen Retiro (1637), paid an underhanded tribute to Pantaleón in his contest rules: 'Yten, que nadie lea sus versos en idioma de jarave ni en lengua *pantaleona*, sino en el que Dios le dio, pena de no ser oído segunda vez' [Item, that no one should read his verses in syrupy language nor in Pantaleonian, but in the language which God gave him, on pain of not being heard a second time]; *Academia burlesca que se hizo en Buen Retiro a la majestad de Filipo cuarto el Grande*, ed. by María Teresa Julio (Madrid and Frankfurt: Universidad de Navarra/Iberoamericana/Vervuert, 2007), p. 58.

13. Méndez Plancarte (ed.), *Poetas novohispanos*, I, 216.

14. Salazar, *Cítara*, p. 117.

15. *Certamen poético* (Mexico City: Viuda de Bernardo Calderón, 1654), s.f.

16. Jerónimo de Cáncer, *Obras varias* (Lisbon: Henrique Valente de Oliveira, 1657), p. 150.

17. Juan Caramuel, *Primer Cálamo. Rítmica*, ed. by Isabel Paraíso (Valladolid: Universidad de Valladolid, 2007), p. 192.

18. Sor Juana Inés de la Cruz, *Obras completas*, ed. by Alfonso Méndez Plancarte and Alberto G. Salceda, 4 vols (Mexico City: Fondo de Cultura Económica, 1951–57), n. 301, II, 145. In this case, she did without the ingenious union of form and content which she would employ in a *décima de pie quebrado* which began 'Tersa frente, oro el cabello' [Smooth forehead, golden hair]. See Tenorio, 'Agustín de Salazar', p. 182. Also regarding Salazar's influence on Sor Juana, see Chapters 3 and 6 by Edna Margarita Benítez Laborde, 'La poesía de Agustín de Salazar y Torres' (unpublished PhD dissertation, SUNY, Albany, 1998), pp. 80–90, 170–91.

19. Sor Juana, *Obras*, n. 49bis, I, 151.

20. The Biblioteca Nacional de México has a copy of the Madrid 1651 edition of *Obras varias*, which might be an indication of its diffusion in New Spain.

21. Giambattista Marino, *Dicerie sacre* (Venice: Nicolò Pezzana, 1674), p. 57.

22. Regarding the burlesque speaker in Baroque poetry, see Samuel Fasquel, *Quevedo et la poétique du burlesque au XVIIe siècle* (Madrid: Casa de Velázquez, 2011), p. 188.

23. Antonio Gallego Morell, *Garcilaso de la Vega y sus comentaristas* (Madrid: Gredos, 1972), p. 23.

24. See François Lecercle, *La Chimère de Zeuxis: portrait poétique et portrait peint en France et en Italie à la Renaissance* (Tübingen: Narr, 1987).

25. See Silvia Longhi, *Lusus. Il capitolo burlesco nel Cinquecento* (Padova: Antenore, 1983), pp. 218–21.

26. See Mary Beard, *Laughter in Ancient Rome: On Joking, Tickling and Cracking up* (Berkeley: University of California, 2014).

27. Another indication is the imitation of Lope's sonnet 'A la muerte de una dama, representanta única' [On the death of a lady, a unique actress] which the New Spanish Luis Sandoval y Zapata (born *c.* 1618–29, died 1671) carries out in 'A una cómica difunta' [To a dead actress] (Méndez Plancarte, *Poetas novohispanos*, I, 147).

28. Lope de Vega, *Rimas humanas y divinas del licenciado Tomé de Burguillos*, ed. by Macarena Cuiñas Gómez (Madrid: Cátedra, 2008), p. 247.

29. On this Ignacio Arellano explains: '*corito*: apodo dado a los asturianos, que solían ser aguadores y llevaban odres de agua; es referencia jocosa en la literatura áurea. Se les atribuía el ser planos de cogote; *cuartanario*: que sufre de cuartanas, fiebres que dan cada cuatro días' [*corito*: a nickname given to Asturians, who were often water-sellers and carried skins of water; it is a humorous reference in Golden Age literature. They were thought to have a flat back of the neck; *cuartanario*; one who suffers from *cuartanas*, fevers which recur every four days]; *El ingenio de Lope de Vega: escolios a las Rimas Humanas y divinas del Licenciado Tomé de Burguillos* (New York: Idea, 2012), p. 119.

30. I infer *ope ingenii* since the text is not clear.

31. I am not sure of the meaning of this fragment, but there is possibly a salacious undertone.

32. Antonio Alatorre ('Avatares barrocos', pp. 87–191) emphasized the novel and 'ultrabaroque' metrical schemes of Salazar y Torres.

33. Lope de Vega, *Rimas de Tomé de Burguillos*, p. 133; Boscán in his poem 135 in *octavas reales* introduces the reference which he probably took from Castiglione's *Il cortegiano*. In Gutierre de Cetina we can find two allusions to this method of Zeuxis in the *estancia* 'Sobre la cubierta de un retrato' [On the cover of a portrait] and in his sonnet dedicated to Laura Gonzaga. There is also a similar perspective in Góngora's *décima* which begins 'No os diremos, como al Cid' [We will not tell you, as El Cid].

PART III

Religious Culture, *villancicos* and Music

CHAPTER 6

❖

Royal Deaths and Viceregal Rule: Diego de Hojeda's *La Christiada*, Epic Agonies and Colonial Government in Seventeenth-Century Peru

Arantza Mayo

The journey of this essay begins in 'el viejo mundo' [the Old World], at the ultimate symbolic site of Spanish imperial religious and political power, resting place of almost eight thousand relics and mausoleum for the Hapsburg dynasty: San Lorenzo del Escorial. In July 1598, Philip II of Spain made a slow and painful last journey to the palace where he would die, following a protracted agony, on 13 September, the eve of the Feast of the Exaltation of the Cross.

Philip's subjects and contemporaries got to know the particulars of the monarch's final weeks in minute detail. Within a week of the king's passing, a documentary investigation into his agonic drama was commissioned by the primate of Spain, the Archbishop of Toledo. Witnesses were interviewed and testimonies taken by one of Philip's chaplains, Antonio Cervera de la Torre. An official report was published within months.[1] Several other publications and versions, very similar in content, would be issued over the course of the following two decades, both in Spain and abroad.[2]

Cervera de la Torre's account included detailed information about the steady deterioration of the king's body.[3] What a twenty-first-century reader might interpret as a set of un-dignifying and gruesome revelations was presented, by contrast, as an edifying narrative. Philip took great care to model his last days on Christ's Passion.[4] His strength, patience, prudence, serenity and unshakeable faith amidst such terrible suffering provided confirmation of what had been — according to the chaplain — the king's defining qualities in the running of his empire. His keen interest in the Passion followed in the footsteps of earlier Spanish monarchs who had also sought, in life as well as in death, moral guidance in explicit representations of Christ's suffering. The influential and descriptive *Vita Christi* by Ludolph of Saxony had been translated into Spanish at the request of Philip's great-grandparents, the Catholic Monarchs; his great-grandmother had owned a significant collection of devotional paintings on Passional themes and Philip himself used the crucifix held by his father, Charles V, at his own death.[5] This, somehow, coexisted with an established tradition in the Spanish court which dictated that kings, and indeed heirs, should not witness death or anything related to the dying process.[6] Philip dispatched with this custom and demanded the presence of the future Philip III at his bedside during the administration of the last rites.[7] He was adamant that his son should witness his Christomimetic agony as he readied himself to take the Spanish Crown and his advisors were keen to ensure that there was a written record of what the monarch expected of his successor.[8]

The numerous accounts of Philip's death, including the *Testimonio*, are essentially a collection of treatises on the qualities of a good Christian monarch which take Jesus's Passional sufferings as its basis.[9] They had a dual purpose: on the one hand, they glorified the figure of the dead king, underlining the links between Christ's Passion and his rule; on the other hand, they served, at a time of looming crisis and in a court which held reservations about the capabilities of the new king, as a guide for the young monarch on how to face the challenges of his new political role.[10]

Diego de Hojeda, who had left Seville around 1590 to profess as a Dominican friar at the prestigious convent of Our Lady of the Rosary in Lima, must have been aware of Philip's spiritually inspired rule as well as the details of his 'exemplary' passing when he set out to compose his *magnum opus*, *La Christiada*.[11] Although, surprisingly, there is no record of royal exequies for the monarch in Lima, it seems inevitable that one or more of the descriptive accounts of the king's 'heroic' death would have made it into the friar's hands, not least since several of the sermons which included details of the agony had been preached by relevant members of his own order, such as Alonso de Cabrera. The poem was finished no later than 1608, although the text would only be published in Seville in 1611.[12] Hojeda's work is a very extensive and detailed elaboration of the most royal death in Christian history, that of the Son of God, in the period's most prestigious poetic form.[13] Its main narrative plot, aside from a number of substantial digressions, spans from the Last Supper to the descent of Christ's body into his sepulchre and, as many contemporary works, it engages with Jesus's painful death in piecemeal graphic detail.[14] *La Christiada* may be formally described as a 'religious epic' in so far as its 'epic structure, imagery and general stylistic technique are used to restate the truths and recorded facts of Christian history'.[15] Yet while it is essentially based on the biblical narrative and partakes of a particular tradition of devotional writing, Hojeda's own apparent conception of the work suggests a politico–didactic aim that goes beyond the heroic retelling of events and relates it to formally very different works, such as treatises on governance and the accounts of Philip II's death which have been briefly considered above.

Hojeda dedicates his poem to the new viceroy of Peru, Juan de Mendoza y Luna, 3rd Marquis of Montesclaros, who had been appointed to the prestigious post in 1606 following a stint in the viceroyalty of New Spain.[16] The young marquis arrived in Lima just before Christmas 1607 and must have been presented with *La Christiada* shortly afterwards; the manuscript would have served as an inauguration gift, probably intended to gain patronage.[17] In his missive to the marquis, described as a 'Príncipe tan justo y misericordioso' [a Prince so fair and merciful], Hojeda explains his decision noting three reasons, all related to virtue in government: firstly, because of the viceroy's 'sabiduría y gran conocimiento' [wisdom and great knowledge]; secondly, because to 'quien ha gobernado los dos reinos de las Indias Ocidentales y el archivo de sus tesoros, Sevilla, con tanto acertamiento y prudencia, es justo se le ofrezca por espejo la fundación y acrecentamiento y premio del Reino del Salvador, Rey de reyes verdadero' [it is only fair to offer as a mirror the foundation, expansion, and reward brought by the Kingdom of our Saviour, true King of Kings, to him who has governed the two kingdoms of the Indies as well as Seville, the archive of its treasures, with such accomplishment and wisdom]. Thirdly, the poet notes that Montesclaros is 'aficionado a pobres' [a friend of the poor] and a 'recto distribuidor de la justicia' [upright provider of justice], features which set out the relationship between Christ and the work's dedicatee which will be developed in the epic.[18]

Beyond the customary obsequiousness, Hojeda's choice of terms is significant and points to a goal beyond patronage: his epic is presented as a mirror which sets out a model target, clearly superior to Montesclaros, and provides the means to achieve it. According to this dedication, the poem will reveal to the newly-appointed dedicatee how he should procure the foundation and expansion of a kingdom as well as the rewards that this will bring. The words that describe the three-step process shown on the mirror — foundation, expansion, and reward brought by the Kingdom of our Saviour — describe, in theological terms, the meaning and purpose of Christ's Passion. Nonetheless, they are also poignantly relevant to the colonial context of the early years of the viceroyalty of Peru, which had been established in 1542 and was under expansion, to the nature of the viceroy's developing role and responsibilities as well as to the rewards, both at a personal and imperial level, derived from the successful fulfilment of the post's duties.[19] It is in the light of the above that the present chapter will delve into Hojeda's epic with a double aim: to understand the politico-religious substrate of its composition and to trace its insights into the conception and formulation of viceregal power in Peru in the first half of the seventeenth century. The following pages will thus examine the implications of Hojeda's conception of La Christiada as a mirror by exploring how and to what effect the links suggested in the dedicatory epistle between the Passional and the colonial contexts — Christ's Passion and Montesclaros's tenure — are developed in the body of the epic poem.

★ ★ ★ ★ ★

In simple optical terms, a looking glass offers a faithful reflection of what lies opposite it; since Hojeda identifies Montesclaros as both fair and merciful, it is possible to read his words straightforwardly as an underscoring of the young man's merits through a flattering association with the virtues displayed by the Son of God in his last hours. Literary mirrors, however, are usually never merely reflective and, by means of a sort of double vision, also offer exemplary, aspirational images for the reading onlooker.[20] This is best exemplified by the books of political advice for royal princes, specula principum or mirrors for princes, which abounded across Europe

from the Middle Ages.[21] These texts, from their classical origins, expounded the
key qualities of a sovereign as heroic and virtuous and, in the process, developed
conceptualizations of the figure of the good ruler: the image they presented was an
ideal model which the onlooker-reader must aim to match. The meaning of virtue
in early modern Spain was, inevitably, very much coloured by the religious context:
a Christian, and indeed Catholic, prince's main qualities had to be wisdom as well
as justice.[22] But despite the religious element, Spanish prose *specula* remained, above
all, political treatises: although they touched on matters of faith and insisted on
the importance of Christian virtues, they did not provide religious programmes
for their princely dedicatees' lives. Their advice was chiefly focused on matters
of administration and strategy, often within a clear moral framework, but not of
spiritual practice. Although they were meant to be instructive to a wide readership,
their dedicatees were those in positions of absolute authority: monarchs or royal
heirs, rather than their deputies or representatives.[23]

Hojeda's identification of his work as a mirror ostensibly suggests that *La
Christiada* should be considered as part of the *specula* tradition, yet the poem does
not, at first glance, appear to share the strictly defined characteristics of such
treatises. While obviously focused on the importance of Christian virtue in a
viceroy, its focus on the Passional subject — with a strong emphasis on its physical
details — and devotional language, by contrast, suggest closer links with private
meditative practices ultimately rooted in the *devotio moderna* than with any guide to
political practice. Furthermore, while the poem's dedicatee is in a position of power,
he is technically an emissary from the real king, to whose authority he is legally
subject, rather than a reigning monarch himself or his heir. These divergences
raise the question of whether Hojeda's definition of his work as a mirror should be
considered with reference to Montesclaros's political task. Is it possible to reconcile
the contemplative dimension of the poem, indeed its focus on the sensory and
physical, with its supposedly politico-didactic aims? If *La Christiada* is a political
work crafted for the American context, what does it tell us about the nature of
viceregal rule at the turn of the seventeenth century as seen by the Dominican?[24]

The oft-quoted fifth stanza of Book I, in which the Dominican develops his
dedication suggests that his mirror metaphor is not a casual image:

> Verás clavado en cruz al Rey eterno:
> míralo en cruz, y hallarás qué aprendas;
> que es una oculta cruz el buen gobierno
> y en tu cruz quiere que a su cruz atiendas.
> Aquí el celo abrasado, el amor tierno,
> de rigor y piedad las varias sendas
> por donde al cielo un príncipe camina,
> te enseñará con arte y luz divina. (p. 2)

> [You will see the eternal King nailed upon a cross:
> behold him upon the cross and you will find what to learn;
> good government is a hidden cross
> and [Christ] wants you to heed his cross from yours.
> From this cross, his burning zeal and tender love

will show you, with divine care and knowledge,
the various paths of rigour and mercy
which lead a prince to heaven.]

The stanza gives a developed view of the specular landscape in which the viceroy is placed by virtue of his position, offering a condensed key to its optics: the figure of the crucified Christ nailed to the cross is presented for the prince to gaze and learn ('míralo en cruz, y hallarás qué aprendas' [behold him upon the cross and you will find what to learn]). The viceroy's memory — as the first power of the soul — focused on the crucifix, should prepare the ground for his understanding to unfold.[25] It is in the course of the mindful consideration of what the poem shall expound that the mirror-crucifix shall reveal a second cross to the attentive viceregal onlooker. This hidden cross is not an object made of wooden beams which can be perceived with the physical eyes, nor does it refer to a concealed dimension of Christ's Passional narrative; rather, it is a metaphor which refers to the painful task of governing well.[26] That Hojeda chooses to qualify the viceregal position in such terms is significant: *La Christiada*'s dedicatee must look beyond the prestige, wealth and pomp inherent to his new appointment — clearly at odds with the physical and spiritual humiliations of the Passion — to reflect upon and realize the full extent of the sacrifices demanded by good governance. The discovery of something hidden requires effort and diligence just as good rule, in Hojeda's view, is the result of a leader's understanding and application — enacted by the third power of the soul, the will — of the virtues displayed by the suffering Christ.

Christ's rule is linked to viceregal government and Montesclaros must carefully consider ['atender'] the events of the Passion in order to understand the sacrifices implicit in his challenging political mission. Just as Philip II wanted his heir to draw a lesson in good governance and upright Christian living from his own Christomimetic death, the narrative of Jesus's heroic last hours, defined by his burning zeal and tender love, can teach the king's alter ego how to walk down the right path and to muster the 'rigor' [rigour] and 'piedad' [mercy] essential to a good and Christomimetic rule.[27] The exercise of such virtues will not only be good for the realm but also lead the viceroy to his own heavenly afterlife — the reward of the Kingdom of our Saviour alluded to in the paratextual dedication. In this specular landscape, the Prince must learn to reflect the image provided by the Eternal King, just as an heir must heed his reigning father's example. Although Hojeda's deployment of the term 'prince' should not be taken literally as an identification of Montesclaros as a secular king's heir — but rather in the more general sense of a ruling aristocrat — the ambiguity implicit in his use of the title invites a direct link between the marquis and Christ to the exclusion of others.[28] This contrasts with the fact that viceroys, as royal agents, were meant to have, in formal terms, a direct specular relationship not with the Divinity but rather with the metropolitan monarch who appointed and rewarded them, on whom they ultimately depended and whose image and power they represented.[29] As monarchs were divinely appointed, viceroys could only be a secondary reflection of the main specular link between God and real king. While there has been a historical tendency to consider these men as colonial bureaucrats or imperial administrators, their status, in actual terms, was significantly more complex: they were treated with all the ritual pomp and verbal reverence due to the king whose image they officially personified and embodied but, simultaneously, were often reminded by local elites eager to assert their own power that they were a mere reflection of their greater metropolitan superior.[30] This gap between concept and practice in the construction and understanding of the viceregal figure was made more acute throughout the sixteenth century by a dearth of theoretical writings which might moderate or settle the equivocality implicit in the role, as well as provide more precise guidance on how the inherent powers of the position might be exercised.

That *La Christiada* was written just over seven decades after the formal establishment of the American viceroyalties — New Spain in 1535 and Peru in 1542 — when the figure of these subject-bureaucrats — the king's living images — was still in the process of being defined, is significant. While the poem's epic form and religious subject may initially discourage twenty-first-century readers from considering the work's dimension as a contribution to the definition of the viceregal figure at the turn of the seventeenth century, it is worth bearing in mind other ways in which early modern colonial society — or at the very least its elites — sought to typify the role. Alejandro Cañeque argues that the lack of textual conceptualizations of the viceregal office, not just up to the start of the 1600s but also in the following decades, is counterbalanced by a particular form of ephemeral architecture, namely the triumphal arches customarily erected to welcome viceroys into the capitals cities of Mexico and Lima.[31] These inaugural displays, inspired by those produced in Europe for royal entries, were material statements which spelled out, through a combination of emblems, hieroglyphs and references to classical and biblical exempla, what was expected of the incoming rulers by the local secular and religious elites.[32] They offered a flattering compendium of the dedicatee's qualities as well as outlining an aspirational model ruler on which the incoming viceroy could map his existing virtues, developing and deploying them for the benefit of the realm. They were, in Cañeque's words, exemplary mirrors 'in which the viceroy could gaze at the personification of an idea, the Christian prince, who at the same time was a reflection of the viceroy's own image'.[33] Viceroys of Peru were required to take their oaths of service in the vicinity of these ephemeral structures and would have had to behold what were essentially conceptualizations of both themselves as rulers and their imminent rule before formally accepting their role; they would only enter their capital city after reading their own bespoke 'visual treatise' which Cañeque relates to the *specula* genre.[34]

Indeed, there is evidence that these structures were seen in precisely those terms by those who conceived them. For instance, Carlos de Sigüenza y Góngora, in the description of an arch of his own design erected to welcome the viceroy Tomás de la Cerda y Aragón to Mexico City in 1680, defined arches as an 'espejo en donde [los virreyes] atiendan a las virtudes con que han de adornarse' [a mirror in which [viceroys] can consider the virtues with which they must adorn themselves]. Once enriched by the sight of profitable examples presented to them, viceroys could initiate the 'ejercicio de la autoridad y del mando adornados de cuantas perfecciones se les proponen para ejemplar del gobierno' [exercise of authority and rule adorned of all those perfections that are shown to them as exemplary of government].[35] Sigüenza y Góngora's understanding of the mechanics and purpose of triumphal arches is thus closely mapped onto the aims and function of literary mirrors: one the one hand, the arch/mirror represents the existing qualities of their chief intended viewer/reader while, on the other, it lays out an aspirational programme in which virtues will be enhanced and applied to the task of government.

La Christiada's similarities with early modern American ephemeral arches not only underline its declared aim as mirror, but also draw attention to how Hojeda, in a role of poet-advisor, contributed to the conceptualization of the viceregal role. The poem was presented at the beginning of the viceroy's tenure and it also offers the customary combination of praise and aspiration typical of inaugural arches.[36] The first lines of the fourth *octava* of Book 1 highlight Montesclaros's virtues:

> Tú, gran marqués, en cuyo monte claro
> la ciencia tiene su lugar secreto,
> la nobleza un espejo en virtud raro,
> el Antártico mundo un sol perfeto,
> el saber premio y el estudio amparo
> y la pluma y pincel dino sujeto. (p. 2)

> [You, great marquis in whose clear mountain
> science holds its secret seat
> the nobility has a rare mirror of virtue
> the Southern world, a perfect sun
> knowledge is afforded reward, and learning, protection
> and the quill and the brush have a worthy subject.]

The new viceroy is flatteringly associated with wisdom ('ciencia' [science], 'saber' [knowledge], 'estudio' [learning]), model leadership ('sol perfeto' [perfect sun]), and presented as a worthy subject of artistic pursuits, whether literary ('pluma' [quill]) or painterly ('pincel' [brush]). Hojeda's fascination with the specular is again evident when the poetic voice describes the aristocrat as an aspirational role model for other members of the nobility ('espejo en virtud raro' [rare mirror of virtue]). Yet his poem does not dwell on the viceroy's existing virtue; indeed, such praise is swiftly tempered by the implicit assertion in the following *octava* that these qualities do not suffice to carry out the political task ahead. The emphasis changes from celebrating his position as mirror for noblemen to the challenge of replicating the heroism illustrated by the Son of God.

The cross was, of course, the model for every Christian and not just for rulers although the specular relationship between earthly and heavenly kings made it of specific relevance to the former.[37] That the cross is a life-guiding symbol for all Christians may however distract from the remarkable nature of the direct relationship which *La Christiada* establishes between viceroy — not only as an individual person but as ruler — and the Son of God. It is important to remember that there is a marked difference between matters of individual faith — the personal relationship that Christians are encouraged to develop with the Divinity — and hierarchical correspondences between the kingdom of Heaven and earthly realms. The power of the King of kings is echoed in that of a divinely appointed monarch and, just as the Lord of Heaven delegates some important tasks to his most trusted representatives, the archangels, the earthly king appoints viceroys to act on his behalf. This equivalence was clearly evident in New Spain, where the association between viceregal authority and divine power was channelled via the widespread cult of the Archangel Michael; the highest ranking of all angelic creatures was the most obvious model for royal deputies.[38] Archangels were also extremely popular in the viceroyalty of Peru, yet Hojeda's work establishes no obvious link between the various angelic figures, such as Michael himself, who have prominent roles in his poem, and Montesclaros.[39] Hojeda envisages no intermediaries or secondary reflections between Christ and the viceroy, whose official status as the king's deputy is consistently unheeded throughout the poem.

While *La Christiada*'s dedication and first *octavas* of Book 1 state the political aims of the work, the devotional emphasis of the narrative as the poem develops lessens the overt engagement with aspects of governance. This is particularly obvious in those segments in which the reader is prompted to engage at an emotional level with Jesus's Passional sufferings. This type of spiritual meditation was promoted by the influential Ludolph of Saxony's *Vita Christi* in the fourteenth century and by the *Imitatio Christi*, attributed to Thomas à Kempis, in the fifteenth, which would in turn shape key works such as Loyola's *Spiritual Exercises* and much of Luis de Granada's writings in the sixteenth. It encouraged readers to position themselves as witnesses to Christ's sacrifice and, crucially, to acknowledge themselves as guilty sinners.[40] *La Christiada* is an evident heir to that tradition and displays many of its defining stylistic characteristics. There is, for instance, no shortage of meditative reflections uttered in the first person:

> Mas ¡ay, Jesús! ¡Ay, Dios!, que mis pecados
> los poros abren de tu carne pura:
> ellos son los cuchillos afilados
> en mi mal corazón y piedra dura. (p. 120)

> [Oh Jesus! Oh God! My sins
> open the pores of your pure flesh
> they [sins] are sharp knives
> in my evil, stone-hard heart.]

The poetic voice guides the readers through intense confessional assertions, forcing them to enunciate their repentance in the very act of reading. Nonetheless, the poem includes various voices and the penitent first person is, in more exhortative sections, replaced by a third person orator who levels dogmatic reminders and accusations at the reader:[41]

> No te digo, ¡oh, cobarde!, que padezcas
> semejante pasión, igual trabajo.
> Ni que a la muerte por su amor te ofrezcas,
> si eres de ánimo vil, de pecho bajo;
> solo pido, ¡oh, cristiano!, que agradezcas,

y será un breve y provechoso atajo
su gran pasión, y pienses con gran pausa
quién la lleva y por quién y por qué causa. (p. 311)[42]

[I am not telling you, oh coward, that you must endure
such Passion or the same travails.
Nor am I telling you to offer yourself up to death for the sake of his love
if you have a base mind or ill will;
I am only asking, oh Christian, that you are grateful,
 — and that would be a short and profitable shortcut —
for his great Passion and consider mindfully
who bears it, and for whom and for what reason.]

The emotional engagement of the reader is keenly encouraged through interrogative leads which invite consideration of Christ's own feelings: '¿Qué sentiste, Señor, cuando te viste | roto el cuerpo y en partes mil abierto?' [What did you feel, Lord, when you saw | your body broken and torn in a thousand places] (p. 454). More often, however, Hojeda attempts to captivate his reader's emotions through the protracted detailing of physiological damage sustained by Christ in his Passion: the flagellation, the falls under the weight of the cross and the actual process of having his body nailed to the wooden beams are drawn in full colour. As the cross is raised in place, Hojeda describes in videographic detail how blood gushes out of Jesus's hand wounds as they expand under the weight of his body ('abriéronse las llagas de las manos') and his flesh becomes extricated from the bones ('de los huesos las carnes desasidas'); he goes as far as noting how the detached flesh continues to register heart beats ('palpitar') (p. 461).[43] The author's interest in physical torment even moves him to include episodes extraneous to the biblical narrative. In Book 8, as Jesus cries in pain after his scourging at the column, a group of heavenly creatures, led by the archangel Michael, arrives to offer consolation and revive his strength. In the course of forty two *octavas* (pp. 321–30) they present him with a summary of the sufferings that numerous martyrs will endure in future centuries.[44] Their song is revealed as an ekphrastic account of shields ('tarjas') in which the martyrs' tortures, mirror images of Christ's Passion, are vividly painted:[45]

Y en tarjas de concetos dibujaban
al Verbo de inmortal sabiduría
los hechos de los mártires valientes
de varios tiempos y diversas gentes. (p. 330)

[And they drew concepts in shields
for the Word of immortal wisdom.
They drew the acts of the brave martyrs
of various periods and diverse peoples.]

These reflections on guilt, exhortations to repentance and explicit descriptions of physical suffering, both of Christ himself and the martyrs and saints, contrast with the initial political notes and appear to encourage Montesclaros to engage in physical penance rather than the effective running of a Christian viceroyalty, yet *La Christiada* is neither an *ars moriendi* nor an invitation to martyrdom. As Philip

II's agony and its accounts demonstrate, political lessons may not only be rendered in the philosophical terms of traditional treatises but can also be embodied in the representation of physical suffering. Although the poem is a written text, its reader must deploy the eyes of the mind, and then his understanding, to access its teachings. An important key to the poem's intended application as a politico-spiritual guide does indeed lie in the ekphrastic accounts of the angels' shields: the viceroy, like Christ himself did, must heed the highly visual representations of these heroic examples of fortitude to face challenges (physical or otherwise) of his office as well as to remind himself of the importance of the successful fulfilment of his task for his own spiritual welfare as well as that of his people.[46]

Although the emphasis on physical representation remains present throughout the poem, Hojeda also devotes significant attention to elaborating those instances of psychological struggle which are part of the biblical story and which bear clearer relevance to the challenges of the viceregal post. Doubt, for instance, is exemplified in the narrative relating to Christ's vigil at the Garden of Olives at Gethsemane — which Philip II requested to have read to him during particularly painful episodes of his agony — that is protractedly developed by the Dominican in Book 1.[47] The focus is on Jesus's human fear. The Son of God is fully aware of his fate — 'Mi nombre es Salvador y hostia mi oficio' [My name is Saviour and my job is to be the Host] — and insists that he must deliver on the promise he made in his mother's womb ('debólo y pago' [I owe it and I shall settle it]) just as Montesclaros should prove himself worthy of the viceregal title he has sworn as he takes on his own 'gravíssimo ejercicio' [most serious task] (p. 22). Yet, a few pages later, Christ is shown as a struggling human being who asks his Father to have his burden lessened. Anxious feelings, variously expressed as 'temor' [fear], 'pavor' [dread] and 'horror' [horror], besiege him throughout the episode. Later, in an elaborate digression from the canonical gospels and in which the visual plays a key role, Christ is visited by the disturbing figure of Death whose wounded body and distorted countenance reflects his prospective suffering:

> Y el amarillo gesto y las manos gualdas
> a los pechos más bravos y animosos
> pone pavor, y a Cristo se le pone. (p. 39)

> [The yellow countenance and the yellow hands
> put fear into the bravest and most courageous hearts,
> and they put it into Christ's.]

As the Son literally beholds the details of his impending torture in the towering figure of Death, he collapses under the weight of fear: 'Sudó, tembló, cayó en tierra asombrado; | que aún Dios teme a la muerte y al pecado' [He sweat, shook and fell in shock to the ground | for even God fears death and sin] (p. 40). Jesus, nonetheless, finds the strength to face his ordeal when the Father — in another episode of physical revelation — appears in his full glory. The Son's 'entendimiento' [understanding] is lifted and fertilized by his Father's presence in which he can now see 'el mundo hecho y el posible mundo' [the created world and the possible world] (p. 44). Christ's three powers of the soul — memory, understanding and will

— come into action to dispel his anxiety. From his willingness to bear the cross depends that 'el mundo hecho' [the created world] tarnished by man's sin — perhaps reflected in old Europe — may become 'el posible mundo' [the possible world], which Montesclaros's Peruvian rule should aim to reflect. The Son overcomes crippling fear and accepts his duty — 'el tedio y el pavor de sí destierra' [he banishes despair and terror from himself] — as he readies himself to be captured by the guards of the Sanhedrin (pp. 119, 123).

   La Christiada does not limit itself to the Son's salutary triumph over fear, presenting, as contrast, cautionary illustrations of failure when rulers buckle under Satan's pressures. As with the episode in Gethsemane, Hojeda uses figures from the gospel as the basis to develop a warning to Montesclaros. In book 10 he engages with the case of the Roman prefect Pontius Pilate, who decided on Jesus's fate; the reader is presented with a ruler who finds himself struggling to decide whether to free Jesus or to condemn him. The evil 'Luzbel', described as 'el rey cobarde' [the coward king], realizes the potential afforded by Pilate's doubt and swiftly dispatches 'hórrido Temor' [horrid Fear] to the scene. Fear, as Hojeda carefully describes and warns the viceroy, can obstruct the best of intentions:

> Tropiezos finge a los principios buenos
> y lo bien comenzado desalienta;
> hace que vaya el vivo ardor a menos
> y el desmayado spíritu acrecienta:
> ciega los ojos al mirar serenos
> y las nubes que tiene les aumenta. (p. 373)

> [It undoes good starts
> and discourages what begins well;
> he weakens fervour
> and fosters weary spirits:
> he blinds the gaze of tranquil eyes
> and their clouds of doubt.]

In direct contrast with Jesus's triumphant victory over dread, Pontius Pilates is unable to handle the moral weight of his power. In Hojeda's poem, the ruler weakens physically in a manner akin to Christ's in Gethsemane — he blanches, loses his voice and his knees tremble — as his moral compass, broken by Fear's action, fails to function under the pressure of his advisors and subjects:

> Temió las amenazas y rencillas
> de aquellos en mentiras hombres sabios;
> [...]
> y déjase rendir, aconsejado
> dellos y del temor, a su pecado. (p. 374)

> [He feared the threats and the arguments
> of those masters of deceit;
> [...]
> and he yields to their advice and to fear,
> and resigns himself to sin.]

As Pontius Pilate turns down the hidden cross attached to his political duty by listening to those who seek their own personal gain at the cost of injustice — a scenario recurrently faced by Montesclaros in Peru — sin triumphs and he fails his people and himself. While it is not remarkable that Hojeda includes these two biblical episodes in his poem, his treatment of Christ's and Pilates's reactions to Fear indicates a conscious interest in highlighting the difficulties inherent to governance. Rather than merely concentrating on undiluted virtue and seamless salutary examples, as triumphal arches did, the Dominican also engages with the moral and emotional vulnerability of those in power, enriching his guide for the new viceroy.[48]

★   ★   ★   ★   ★

Montesclaros, as viceroy, must then concentrate on deploying a Christomimetic rule based on the reflection upon and acceptance of meaningful and ultimately redemptive suffering that can inform both the 'rigour' and 'mercy' essential to 'good government'. Hojeda does not suggest that Montesclaros should seek martyrdom in his new post, ('de cruz muerte terrible' [a terrible death on the cross]) but that the viceroy lead a 'vida de cruz' [sacrificial life] for the sake of both realm and soul (p. 463).[49] Christ's heroic death must illuminate Montesclaros's viceregal life just as Philip II's own agony, modelled on that of Jesus as befit a divinely appointed monarch, was to provide his heir with an illustrated guide to good kingship.[50] The necessary virtues of a viceroy are not presented through the disquisitions typical of *specula* but literally embodied in the challenges experienced by a vulnerable human body. Such hardships, metaphors for all the challenges of government, must be endured and distilled into profitable political and spiritual outcomes for both the individual and their realm. In Hojeda's work, as in the meditative frame around which he weaves his mirror-epic, contemplation leads to discovery and must result in action.

La Christiada also makes an important conceptual statement about the viceregal office, for it not only defines the ideal parameters of virtue in an incumbent, as inaugural arches did, but also underlines the burden of his task in terms equal with those of the metropolitan monarch.[51] Through its consistent exclusion of superiors or intermediaries, it establishes a direct link between viceroy and Christ and, as result, effectively conceptualizes viceregal power, at the very least in its moral dimension, as independent from that of the metropolis. Hojeda's heroic viceroy does not need to seek to be the metropolitan king's reflection: he should be Christ's direct reflection. The poet may not have been fully conscious of the implications of his specular model and there are no reasons to suspect that he questioned metropolitan royal power. To suggest that the he was engaging in a conscious act of state-making would be disproportionate, but to ignore the implications of Hojeda's design of a viceregal model of direct reflection of the divine misses a crucial part of his epic's contribution to the literature and history of its period.

We cannot possibly know whether Montesclaros's reading of *La Christiada* guided his Peruvian rule or armed him with the spiritual fortitude required to fulfil at least some of the Dominican's ambitious hopes. We do, however, know that the prestigious jurist and prosecuting attorney of the Royal Council of the Indies, Juan de Solórzano Pereira, praised Montesclaros's legal dispositions as models of 'suma destreza y prudencia' [great skill and wisdom].[52] We also have a record of the Marquis's own retrospective summary of his tenure: in a candid account addressed to his successor, the Prince of Esquilache, Montesclaros offers information, advice and a probing view of the viceregal office.[53] It is perhaps not surprising that he likened some of the challenges attached to the role to an instrument of torture: his mention of a wooden 'tormento' [rack] operated by metal 'clavijas' [keys] bears a clear echo of the cross and nails.[54] Montesclaros's final account brings us back to and corroborates what Hojeda had cautioned in the opening stanzas of his inaugural gift: 'que es una oculta cruz el buen gobierno' [good government is a hidden cross].

Notes to Chapter 6

1. Antonio Cervera de la Torre, *Testimonio auténtico, y verdadero de las cosas notables que pasaron en la dichosa muerte del Rey nuestro Señor Don Phelipe segundo* (Valencia: Pedro Patricio Mey, 1599).

2. Carlos M. N. Eire, *From Madrid to Purgatory: The Art and Craft of Dying in Sixteenth-Century Spain* (Cambridge: Cambridge University Press, 1995), pp. 302–05.

3. As well as the symptoms of malarial tertian fevers, the chaplain describes suppurating bed sores, festering skin infections, the lancing of a pus-oozing knee, and a persistent diarrhoea which tormented king and retinue with its stench (Cervera de la Torre, *Testimonio*, pp. 1–37).

4. Cervera de la Torre affirms that the crucifix was Philip's main source of consolation throughout his life. The monarch had always shown intense devotion to the cross and, in his bed, 'he resembled a new Saint Andrew or Saint Helen'. His small bedchamber was surrounded by crucifixes and, in the hours leading up to his death, he held one close (*Testimonio*, p. 30). Philip is said to have repeated aloud Christ's last words and even recited whole biblical passages on the Passion. He asked his confessor to recite Matthew's Passion, paying particular attention to the episode of Jesus's agony in Gethsemane while his infected knee was being lanced and requested Ludovicus Blosius's meditations to be read, with emphasis on the same event (pp. 60–68). He also bade his confessor to read John's Passion (p. 127). In his funeral sermon, Alonso de Cabrera, went as far as affirming that Philip was 'crucified' by his agony; *Sermón que predicó el maestro fray Alonso de Cabrera, predicador de su Majestad del Orden de predicadores. A las honras de nuestro Señor el serenísimo y católico Rey Filippo Segundo, que esté en el Cielo: que hizo la Villa de Madrid en S. Domingo el Real último de octubre 1598* (Roma: Luis Zaneti, 1599), p. 33.

5. Ludolphus of Saxony, *Vita Christi cartujano romanzado por fray Ambrosio* (Alcalá de Henares: Estanislao Polono, 1502–03); José Manuel Pita Andrade, 'Pinturas y pintores de Isabel la Católica', in *Isabel la Católica y el arte*, ed. by Gonzalo Anés and Alvarez de Castrillón (Madrid: Real Academia de la Historia, 2006), pp. 13–72 (pp. 35–39); Cervera de la Torre, *Testimonio*, p. 123.

6. Eire, *From Madrid to Purgatory*, p. 275.

7. Cervera de la Torre, *Testimonio*, pp. 107–08.

8. The *Testimonio* also includes the transcription of a letter — originally from saint Louis of France to his son — which Philip II gave to his heir 'instruyéndole en lo que debía saber para su salvación y gobierno político destos Reinos' [instructing him in what he needed to know for his own salvation and political rule of these realms]; Cervera de la Torre, *Testimonio*, pp. 109–18 (p. 112).

9. As late as 1628, Baltasar Porreño's popular *Dichos y hechos del rey don Felipe II* dwelt on his minutely described death as illustration of the monarch's life-long virtues and example to others (Eire, *From Madrid to Purgatory*, pp. 304–05).

10. The *Testimonio* is dedicated to Philip III; Cervera de la Torre, frontispiece and sigs ¶¶–¶¶3^{v}.

11. Mary Helen Patricia Corcoran (ed.), *La Christiada* (Washington, DC: Catholic University of America, 1935), p. xxiv.

12. The book must have been completed between 21 December 1607, when the dedicatee — the Marquis of Montesclaros — entered Lima as viceroy of Peru, and May 1608, when Hojeda began to use the title of master. The licence from his local prior, Francisco de Vega, which appears in the 1611 edition is dated 28 March 1609. The two accompanying licenses issued in Lima are from 27 March 1609; Diego de Hojeda, *La Christiada* (Seville: Diego Pérez, 1611), fols 2ᵛ, 3. See also Corcoran (ed.), *La Christiada*, pp. xli–xlii.

13. The 1611 edition has 1974 *octavas* (heptasyllabic eight-line stanzas) divided into twelve books. Corcoran's edition — based on a probably earlier manuscript version of the poem held at the Bibliothèque de l'Arsenal in Paris, which she considers a ' "corrected" copy of Hojeda's original manuscript' — has one less; Corcoran (ed.), *La Christiada*, pp. xl, lxxv.

14. As Vélez Marquina notes, supported by evidence provided by Frank Pierce and Cayetano Rosell, several epic poems on the life of Christ were published in the years before *La Christiada* was printed: the most relevant examples are Girolamo Vida's *Christias* (1535), Juan de Quirós's *Christo Pathia* (1552) and Francisco Hernández Blasco's *Universal redempción, pasión, muerte y resurreción de nuestro Redemptor Iesu Christo* (1598), which is also identified as a source by Frank Pierce in his edition of *La Cristiada* (Salamanca: Anaya, 1971), pp. 20–21; Elio Vélez Marquina, 'Posicionamiento discursivo del narrador épico colonial de *La Christiada*, de Diego de Hojeda', in *Eros divino: estudios sobre la poesía religiosa iberoamericana del siglo XVII*, ed. by Julián Olivares (Zaragoza: Universidad de Zaragoza, 2010), pp. 421–33 (p. 422).

15. Frank Pierce, 'Some Aspects of the Spanish "Religious Epic" of the Golden Age', *Hispanic Review*, 12.1 (1944), 1–10 (p. 6).

16. Montesclaros was the first viceroy appointed by Philip III (1603). From the 1550s, many of those appointed to the Peruvian viceroyalty had served first in New Spain; Pilar Latasa Vassallo, *Administración virreinal en el Perú: Gobierno del Marqués de Montesclaros (1607–1615)* (Madrid: Centro de Estudios Ramón Areces, 1997), p. 5.

17. It was, of course, customary to dedicate works to those in prominent positions, yet, Hojeda's request is rather coy. Compare, for example, his dedication to the viceroy with the bolder approach of Juan de Miramontes Zuázola in his *Armas antárticas: hechos de los famosos capitanes españoles que se hallaron en la conquista del Perú*, where he bides Montesclaros to favour and support his work 'con la benignidad y grandeza de su generoso ánimo'; ed. by Paul Firbas (Lima: Pontificia Universidad Católica del Perú, 2006), p. 163.

18. Hojeda, *La Christiada*, ed. by Corcoran, p. 506. All translations of Spanish texts are my own. Translations of poetic texts prioritize content over aesthetics. I modernize the spelling and punctuation of the Spanish text. I have, however, decided to retain the original spelling of the title, *La Christiada* as it is customary among scholars. All quotations from the poem are taken from Corcoran's edition.

19. Hojeda's terms echo those of the law, signed by Philip II in 1588 and ratified by his son in 1614, which states that viceroys should ensure that their provinces are 'aumentadas y ennoblecidas' [augmented and ennobled]. *Recopilación de leyes de los reinos de las Indias*, 4 vols (Madrid: Julián de Paredes, 1681), II, Book 3, fol. 12.

20. For a survey of mirror metaphors, see Herbert Grabes, *The Mutable Glass: Mirror-Imagery in Titles and Texts of the Middle Ages and English Renaissance*, trans. by G. Collier (Cambridge: Cambridge University Press, 1982). See also Edward P. Nolan, *Now through a Glass Darkly: Specular Images of Being and Knowing from Virgil to Chaucer* (Ann Arbor: University of Michigan Press, 1991).

21. Quentin Skinner, *The Foundation of Modern Political Thought*, 2 vols (Cambridge: Cambridge University Press, 1978), I, 118–28, 213–43.

22. Pedro de Ribadeneyra's treatise for the future Philip III, *Tratado de la religión y virtudes que debe tener el príncipe cristiano para gobernar y conservar sus estados: contra lo que Nicolás Machiavelo y los políticos deste tiempo enseñan* (Madrid: P. Madrigal, a costa de Juan de Montoya, 1595), includes chapters on 'clemencia' [mercy], 'liberalidad y magnificencia' [generosity and magnificence], 'templanza' [temperance], 'prudencia' [wisdom] and 'fortaleza' [strength].

23. Ribadeneyra's treatise was a mirror for Philip III who was in turn meant to become a model

looking glass ('todo el mundo tiene hoy puestos los ojos en vuestra alteza' [everyone has their eyes on your highness today], sig. †3^{v}) for all his subjects.

24. Vélez Marquina ('Posicionamiento discursivo', p. 426) affirms that *La Christiada* takes on the hermeneutical role of *specula principum* in order to update the political interpretation of Christ's struggle with the Devil for the early modern context, yet his work does not engage with the peculiarities and implications of Hojeda's approach which are the focus of this essay.

25. The importance of sculptures and depictions of the crucified Christ as support objects for spiritual reflection was patent in Philip II's display of crosses in his bedchamber as well the role played by his father's crucifix in his own agony; Cervera de la Torre, *Testimonio*, p. 30.

26. The identification of any difficult but ultimately virtuous challenge with a cross has a biblical basis; Luke 9. 23 and Matthew 16. 24.

27. Hojeda's references to Montesclaros's justice and mercy in the dedicatory epistle are echoed here.

28. It is noteworthy that Hojeda makes no reference, however oblique, to the Spanish monarch in the paratextual material or the poem itself, something unusual amongst contemporary works: Juan de Miramontes Zuázola does not mention the king in his dedication of his *Armas antárticas* to Montesclaros, but references to the metropolis are explicit throughout the poem. Diego Dávalos y Figueroa's *Miscelánea austral* (Lima: Antonio Ricardo, 1602) refers to 'the king our Lord' in his dedication to the viceroy Luis de Velasco (sig. ¶5).

29. Viceroys were legally referred to by the Spanish monarch as 'personas que representan la nuestra' [individuals who represent our person]; *Recopilación de leyes*, III, Book 3, fol. 12. Matías de Caravantes, a canon in Trujillo, indicated that 'Bien podremos decir que el virrey no es distinto de la persona real, pues en él vive por translación y copia con tal unión e igualdad que la mesma honra y reverencia que se debe a Su Majestad se debe a Su Excelencia, y la injuria que se les hace es común a entrambos' [We could correctly say that the viceroy is no different from the royal person, as [the monarch] lives in him by transmission and as a copy with such unity and equality that the same honour and reverences that is owed to His Majesty is owed to His Excellency, and that when one is offended both are offended]; Pilar Aguirre Zamorano, 'Poder ordinario del virrey del Pirú sacadas de las cédulas que se han despachado en el Real Consejo de las Indias', *Historiografía y Bibliografía Americanistas*, 29.2 (1985), 15–97 (p. 15).

30. Alejandro Cañeque, *The King's Living Image: The Culture and Politics of Viceregal Power in Colonial Mexico* (New York and London: Routledge, 2004), p. 28.

31. Cañeque, *The King's Living Image*, p. 26. Although his study applies to New Spain, the observations regarding arches considered in this piece are equally applicable to the viceroyalty of Peru.

32. Although ultimately based on Roman practice, the religious frame for these structures was biblical: 'the king as Christ or one of his scriptural prototypes, takes possession of the New Jerusalem, in which the earthly state is directly presented as a mirror of the heavenly'; Roy Strong, *Art and Power in Renaissance Festivals, 1450–1650* (Woodbridge: Boydell and Brewer, 1986), p. 10.

33. Cañeque, *The King's Living Image*, p. 34.

34. In Peru, the triumphal entry through the arch happened immediately after the swearing of the oath; Víctor Mínguez, Inmaculada Rodríguez Moya, Pablo González Tornel and Juan Chiva Beltrán (eds), *La fiesta barroca: los virreinatos americanos (1560–1808)* (Castellón de la Plana: Universitat Jaume I and Universidad de las Palmas de Gran Canaria, 2012), p. 98. See also Alejandra Osorio, 'La entrada del virrey y el ejercicio del poder en la Lima del siglo XVII', *Historia Mexicana*, 55.3 (2006), 767–831 (pp. 769–70). Montesclaros's biographer describes his oath as follows: 'desmontó del caballo, subió al tablado erigido a tal efecto, y luego, hincado de rodillas ante un bufete en el que se hallaban un misal y un crucifijo, prestó el juramento' [He dismounted his horse, climbed onto the platform erected to that effect and swore the oath on his knees before a desk with a missal and a crucifix']; Aurelio Miró Quesada, *El primer poeta-virrey en América* (Madrid: Gredos, 1962), pp. 64–65.

35. Carlos de Sigüenza y Góngora, *Teatro de virtudes políticas, que constituyen a un príncipe advertidas en los monarcas antiguos del mexicano imperio, con cuyas efigies se hermoseó el arco triunfal que la muy noble,*

muy Leal, imperial Ciudad de México erigió para el digno recibimiento en ella del excelentísimo señor virrey Conde de Paredes, Marqués de La Laguna (México: viuda de Bernardo Calderón, 1680), pp. 3–4.

36. Interestingly, Pierce points to *La Christiada*'s visual qualities by variously speaking of the work as 'a versification of those feelings and inspirations obtained from a contemplation of church "retablos"' and a 'Baroque façade'; these observations further the links between the poem and ephemeral arches. Frank Pierce, 'La Christiada of Diego de Hojeda: A Poem of the Literary Baroque', *Bulletin of Spanish Studies*, 17 (1940), 203–18 (pp. 207, 215).

37. The poem was conceived to be of specific value to Montesclaros as well as spiritually edifying for a much wider readership. Hojeda describes the cross as a 'fuente abierta' [open fountain] and a 'dichosa puerta' [joyful door] for both 'justos' [righteous] and 'pecadores' [sinners] (p. 419).

38. Cañeque, *The King's Living Image*, p. 239.

39. Escardiel González Estévez considers the devotion to the archangels in the American viceroyalties in 'De fervor regio a piedad virreinal: culto e iconografía de los siete arcángeles', *Sémata*, 24 (2012), 111–32.

40. Granada's work was particularly influential throughout the seventeenth century. See, for example, Keith Whinnom, 'The Problem of the Best-Seller in Spanish Golden Age Literature', *Bulletin of Hispanic Studies*, 57 (1980), 189–98. Hojeda was, of course, a member of the same order as Granada and would inevitably have been familiar with his works.

41. The Dominicans were also known as the Order of Preachers. Elizabeth B. Davis considers the narrator's 'shifting positionality' the consequence of author's dual goal: to recount Christ's history with 'epic objectivity' and to 'instruct and reform his readers'; 'The Politics of Effacement: Diego de Hojeda's Humble Poetics', *Bulletin of Hispanic Studies*, 71.3 (1994), 339–57.

42. Although Hojeda is not suggesting that Montesclaros must literally die for the sake of his subjects to be a good ruler, the implication is that, as Christ's reflection, he should be prepared to do so. This question preoccupied thinkers for several centuries and, in 1446, Enea Silvio Piccolomini, later pope Pius II, dedicated *De ortu et auctoritate imperii Romani* to Frederick III, Habsburg emperor, which discussed a king's obligation to die *pro patria*. See Ernst Hartwig Kantorowicz, *The King's Two Bodies: A Study in Mediaeval Political Theology* (Princeton, NJ: Princeton University Press, 1957), pp. 30, 41, 260–61.

43. The graphicness of *La Christiada* needs to be considered in its literary and social context: while detailed and extensive — this is, after all, a lengthy epic poem — it is not extraordinary by early modern standards.

44. Although the text clearly mentions martyrs, not all those listed held such status or were even saints: 'Iñacio', presumably Ignatius Loyola, was beatified by Pope Paul V on 27 July 1609, and canonized by Pope Gregory XV on 12 March 1622. He died of natural causes and would not have been officially recognized as 'blessed' by the time Hojeda finished his poem.

45. Vicente Cristóbal notes a link between these 'tarjas' and Aeneas's elaborate shield; 'Virgilianismo y tradición clásica en *La Cristíada* de Fray Diego de Hojeda', *Cuadernos de Filología Clásica. Estudios Latinos*, 25.1 (2005), 49–78 (p. 66).

46. The eloquent collection of shields echoes the structure of triumphal arches, which included multiple illustrative scenes. These *octavas* also lend strength to Pierce's reading ('La Christiada') of Hojeda's text as a 'retablo' and remind us of the importance of visual aids in meditation, a practice already noted by Gregory the Great in the sixth century which found much favour amongst early Jesuits. Teresa of Ávila also encouraged her nuns to use images to facilitate dialogue with the Divinity. See David Freedberg, *The Power of Images: Studies in the History and Theory of Response* (Chicago, IL, and London: University of Chicago Press, 1989), pp. 161–91 and Teresa de Jesús, *Camino de perfección*, in *Obras completas*, ed. by Tomás Álvarez (Burgos: Monte Carmelo, 2001), pp. 415–612 (p. 533).

47. See footnote 324.

48. Hojeda also provides a catalogue of the seven deadly sins in Book 1 to warn the reader of his vulnerabilities (pp. 26–39). He lists numerous biblical and historical characters — from Adam to Henry VIII and Luther — alongside their better-known sins. His notes on gold-crowned Pride would have been timely reminders for Montesclaros as he arrived in Lima: 'en una silla de marfil preciosa | con ancha pompa de ambición sentada' [sitting in a costly ivory throne | with great

pomp and ambition] (p. 26); Greed is 'de oro cercada, llena de codicia' [surrounded by gold, full of cupidity] and 'que de sangre de pequeños se mantiene' [it lives on the blood of the weak] (p. 27). Three of the *octavas* devoted to Sloth voice direct criticism of specific sectors of the colonial elite: 'los holgazanes | de sangre noble, pero mal gastada, | que hijos son de bravos capitanes | y padres son de vida regalada' [lazy men | of noble but misspent blood | who are the children of brave captains | and fathers of idle living' (p. 36).

49. *La Christiada* foreshadows Quevedo's reminders to Philip IV in his *Política de Dios* that 'la corona' [the crown] (as cross) 'es peso molesto' [is a tiresome burden], that for the good prince the royal palace is but a 'patíbulo de una muerte viva' [scaffold for a living death]; Francisco de Quevedo, *Parte segunda póstuma de la política de Dios y gobierno de Cristo,* ed. by Rodrigo Cacho Casal, in *Obras completas en prosa,* 11 vols (Madrid: Castalia, 2012), v, 327–639 (p. 447).

50. Interestingly, *La Christiada* does not end with an account of the Resurrection but with Christ's burial.

51. The similarities between Philip II's agony as handover manual to his heir and the Hojeda's offering of Christ's Passion to Montesclaros add to the sense that the viceroy's appointment is the result of divine design rather than metropolitan politics.

52. Juan de Solórzano Pereira, *Política Indiana,* ed. by Miguel Angel Ochoa Brun, 5 vols (Madrid: Biblioteca de Autores Españoles, 1972); see, for example, II, 215.

53. Montesclaros was relieved from his post in 1614 and, as was required by royal directive, produced a detailed report on his governance for his successor, Francisco de Borja y Aragón, Prince of Esquilache.

54. Don Juan de Mendoza y Luna, *Luz de materias de Indias del Marqués de Montesclaros,* Copenhagen, Der Kongelige Bibliotek, MSS GkS 589 2°, fol. 1^v. See also Rolena Adorno, 'The account of Don Juan de Mendoza y Luna, the marquis of Montesclaros, viceroy of Peru, to his successor (GkS 589, 2°)', in <http://wayback-01.kb.dk/wayback/20101112075707/http://www2.kb.dk/elib/mss/mendoza/note-eng.htm>.

CHAPTER 7

'La soberana doctora de las escuelas divinas': Sor Juana's Mariology in her *villancicos* on the Feast of the Assumption (1676)

Alice Brooke

The *villancicos* for the Feast of the Assumption, 1676

The *villancicos*, or poetic medleys, written by Sor Juana Inés de la Cruz (1651–1695) for the Feast of the Assumption in 1676, to be set to music by the *maestro de capilla* of Mexico City Cathedral, José de Loaysa y Arguto, and to be performed there during the liturgy of Matins, were the first texts in Sor Juana's extensive corpus to be published as an independent work, although not bearing her name.[1] As public commissions for some of the most important liturgies of the cathedral's calendar, these early works were crucial to solidifying her reputation as a successful author of liturgical works, and as one of Mexico City's most renowned literary figures, a reputation that would later lead to her invitation to design the triumphal arch for the entrance of the viceroy, Don Tomás de la Cerda y Aragón, into Mexico City in 1680.[2]

For many years, given their status as 'arte menor' [minor works], Sor Juana's *villancicos* had been considered less worthy of scholarly consideration than her better-known writing.[3] In recent years, however, several scholars have focused their attention on these works of liturgical poetry. Specific emphasis has been placed on the *villancicos'* role in giving voice to marginalized sections of viceregal society, and to their engagement with early modern discourses of race and gender. In particular, several articles have highlighted the importance of the *villancico de negros* within the genre, and its subversive possibilities within a strictly racially ordered society.[4] A smaller, but nonetheless significant number of studies have focused on the *villancicos'* expression of female voices, and their portrayal of strong female characters.

Among these studies, several scholars have focused on the role of Mary in the *villancicos*, and on their relation to her representation in Sor Juana's works more broadly. Although earlier studies of Sor Juana's Mariology saw in her focus on the mother of Christ evidence for her religiosity, more recent analyses have found in her poetry an 'ardently pro-woman' portrayal of Mary whose purpose is to advocate for the equality of women with men.[5] Some have gone so far as to include Mary within the Trinity, elevating her status to that of a goddess, and connecting her with the female deities of indigenous American religious practices.[6] In contrast to earlier studies, which affirmed Sor Juana's 'active' depiction of Mary within the context of her own religious and devotional life, these more recent studies proceed from the assumption that any portrayal of Mary as a strong character must run counter to Catholic teaching, and therefore represents evidence of her 'pensamiento subversivo y combatiente' [subversive and rebellious thought], or of a '"dangerous" message' on Sor Juana's part.[7] With particular reference to Sor Juana's representation of Mary in roles traditionally prohibited to women, especially those in the academic and ecclesiastical worlds, these studies seek to answer how Sor Juana managed to '"pull-off" a performance of these "pro-woman" songs in the context of a seventeenth-century Catholic liturgy'.[8]

This study, in contrast, seeks to place Sor Juana's *villancicos* in the literary and theological context in which they were written, paying particular attention to their engagement with two significant fields of early modern Hispanic thought: the Baroque notion of 'ingenio' [wit] and the biblical hermeneutical practice of Catholic Mariology. In his 1648 treatise, *Agudeza y arte de ingenio* [Wit and the Art of Quick Thinking], Baltasar Gracián defines 'ingenio' as the faculty of mind that enables one to make connections between disparate objects, which he terms 'conceptos' [conceits], and to articulate these connections using a variety of rhetorical tropes.[9] While 'ingenio' expresses the ability to reconcile disparate things, its related concept 'agudeza' [quick thinking] values the speed with which these connections can be made. In both cases, the aesthetic ideal is the same: the greater the distance between the two objects being compared, and the greater the speed at which they can be brought together, the greater the intellectual talents required to reconcile them.

In the *villancicos*, Sor Juana develops a series of striking images for Mary — as a professor of theology, as a heavenly director of music, as a *caballera andante* [female knight errant], and as a teacher of rhetoric. By specifically choosing images that place Mary, a woman, within three early modern bastions of institutional, male-controlled knowledge and power — the Church, the military and the university — Sor Juana sparks this aesthetic discourse of *ingenio*. By studying each of the images she uses, I demonstrate how Sor Juana develops these unlikely comparisons and justifies their initial premise through recourse to scripture, in particular the Wisdom literature of the Old Testament, and to a centuries-old tradition of Marian iconography. By exploring how Sor Juana first posits, and then reconciles, these apparently incongruous images of Mary, I identify the ways in which these texts work within the bounds of traditional orthodoxy, at the same time as they innovate within and stretch them.

In their development of their chosen images of Mary, these *villancicos* achieve two purposes. First, in Sor Juana's presentation to her audience of new and ingenious ways of conceptualizing particular Marian doctrines, she demonstrates her own *ingenio* through her capacity to identify and to reconcile apparently disparate images. Second, by proposing Mary not only as a woman engaged in literary pursuits, but also as a figure of Wisdom, she incorporates her into a discourse of knowledge, thus subtly subverting traditional intellectual hierarchies and women's place within them. As many critics have explored, knowledge in the early modern world was the preserve of institutional structures to which women were denied access, a concern that is foregrounded in Sor Juana's works, in which she details her own exclusion from institutional learning because of her gender.[10] In particular, as we shall see, Sor Juana focuses in these *villancicos* on the Marian body as a site of creation of knowledge, and as the epitome of human poetic creativity. In doing so, she transposes the development of *ingenio* from a cerebral process to one that also incorporates the body, in this case a specifically female body, as figured in the person of Mary.[11]

Mary, Doctor of Divinity

The first particularly striking image of Mary is found in the third *villancico*, where Sor Juana posits her as a professor of theology, 'la soberana doctora de las escuelas divinas' [the heavenly teacher of the divine schools].[12] At the outset, the ambitious nature of the conceit is made clear by the unlikely nature of the scenario: with universities reserved for men, for a woman to occupy its highest rank would be impossible. However, Sor Juana reconciles the proposal by drawing a comparison between Mary's rise to heaven at the Assumption, and the rise through the professional ranks of the university to the most eminent position in the most important discipline, Theology. She further extends the metaphor by explaining how Mary achieved her knowledge through her own experience; she is particularly outstanding in the disciplines of Charity and Grace, given to her before her birth, and her own body becomes her textbook on the Incarnation, through which she becomes an expert on the Trinity. The angels become her students, and celebrate her victory:

> La soberana doctora
> de las Escuelas divinas,
> de que los Ángeles todos
> deprenden sabiduría
> por ser quien inteligencia
> mejor de Dios participa,
> a leer la suprema sube
> Cátedra de Teología.
> [...]
> Ninguno de *Charitate*
> estudió con más fatiga,
> y la materia de *Gratia*
> supo, aun antes de nacida.
> Después la de *Incarnatione*
> pudo estudiar en sí misma,
> con que en la de *Trinitate*
> alcanzó mayor noticia. (*OC*, II, 6)

[The heavenly teacher of the divine schools, from whom all the angels derive their wisdom, because she perfectly participates in God's knowledge, she rises to teach in the highest Chair of Theology. [...] No one studied Charity more tirelessly, and she knew the subject of Grace even before she was born. Later, she was able to study that of the Incarnation in herself, and by doing so she acquired the greatest understanding of the Trinity][13]

Beyond the most obvious justification for Sor Juana's conceit, grounded in the multiple possible interpretations of Mary's ascent, however, there lies a more biblically grounded foundation for her portrayal. Mary's epithet as 'doctora de las escuelas divinas' [teacher of the divine schools] also points to the connection made in traditional biblical interpretation between Mary and the Old Testament figure of Wisdom.[14] The Wisdom literature of the Old Testament, found in the books of Psalms, Proverbs, Job, Ecclesiasticus, and Baruch, presents Wisdom as a female personification, who can be read as a figure of Mary: she was created by God before the beginning of time (Proverbs 8. 22–26, Ecclesiasticus 24. 9, Wisdom 9. 9), she participates in His knowledge (Wisdom 8. 4), she dwelt on earth among humankind (Baruch 3. 37), and she now dwells in heaven (Baruch 3. 29; Wisdom 9. 4), from where she guides and helps humankind to follow the ways of God (Wisdom 9. 10–11).[15]

In the *villancicos*, Sor Juana draws on the description of Wisdom as both a teacher and a learned woman. In the Vulgate, Wisdom is described as 'doctrix' [learned woman], as she is schooled in God's knowledge, and a participant in his works: 'doctrix enim disciplinae Dei et electrix operum illius' [For she is an initiate in the knowledge of God, and an associate in his works] (Wisdom 8. 4). Sor Juana combines these attributes into her description of Mary as 'quien inteligencia mejor de Dios participa' [she who perfectly participates in God's knowledge]. Moreover, Wisdom does not only possess wisdom, but also teaches it to others: 'quaecumque sunt absconsa et inprovisa didici omnium enim artifex docuit me sapientia' [I learned both what is secret and what is manifest, for Wisdom, the fashioner of all things, taught me] (Wisdom 7. 21). When read figuratively with reference to Mary, it is her knowledge, and her closeness to God, that give her the privileged position of Doctor of Theology. Through recourse to these biblical sources, Sor Juana grounds her apparently unlikely conceit within an orthodox tradition of biblical interpretation. By doing so, therefore, she also posits a biblical basis for the subtly subversive situation the *villancico* presents — a woman not only as a participant within the institutional discourse of knowledge, but as sitting at the very head of its hierarchy.

In the subsequent verses, this parallel between Mary and Wisdom is taken further in the description of Mary's students, the angels, or spirits who live in heaven:

Los soberanos Cursantes
que las letras ejercitan
y de la Sagrada Ciencia
los secretos investigan,
con los Espíritus puros
que el eterno Solio habitan,

(e inteligencias sutiles
Ciencia de Dios se apellidan) (*OC*, ii, 6)

[The heavenly pupils who study the arts, and who investigate the secrets of holy science, along with the pure spirits, who surround the heavenly throne (intelligent and subtle spirits who are called the knowledge of God)]

While previous scholars have pointed to the connection between Sor Juana's presentation of Mary in these verses and the Wisdom literature of the Old Testament, those who have commented on this particular passage have ascribed it to Sor Juana's invention, and argue that Sor Juana's primary purpose here is to demonstrate the non-gendered nature of knowledge.[16] However, a close reading of the book of Wisdom shows that Sor Juana's development of her theme is drawn almost word for word from the Old Testament. In the *villancico*, the students study the secrets of theology, while in scripture Wisdom teaches what is both 'absconsa et improvisa' [secret and manifest]. In the following verse in the Book of Wisdom, the spirit of wisdom is described as a 'spiritus intellectus [...] qui capiat omnes spiritus intellegibiles mundos subtiles' [a spirit that is intelligent, [...] penetrating through all spirits that are intelligent, pure, and altogether subtle] (Wisdom 7. 22–23). In the *villancico*, closely mirroring this verse, the students achieve their knowledge through 'espíritus puros, que el eterno solio habitan, inteligencias sutiles' [pure spirits, who surround the heavenly throne, intelligent and subtle spirits].

By emphasizing the angelic pursuit of knowledge as engaged in the search for the 'secrets' of the hidden order within creation, Sor Juana shifts her focus from the person of Mary to her understanding of the cosmos as created according to a divine plan, as a harmonious and interconnected whole, in which all things display the mark of their creator. Her language is similar to that used in the *Respuesta*, where she seeks out 'secretos naturales' [secrets of nature] (*OC*, iv, 459) in the kitchen, and investigates the hidden causes of visible effects. The emphasis on secrets in the *villancicos* therefore connects Wisdom's ways of knowing in the Old Testament with Sor Juana's own epistemology. In the *Respuesta*, she writes:

> Nada veía sin refleja: nada oía sin consideración, aun en las cosas más menudas y materiales; porque como no hay criatura, por baja que sea, en que no se conozca el *me fecit Deus*, no hay alguna que no pasme el entendimiento, si se considera como se debe. (*OC*, iv, 458)

> [Nothing could I see without reflecting upon it, nothing could I hear without duly considering it, even to the most minute, material things. For there is no creature, however lowly, in which one cannot recognize the great '*God made me*'; there is not one that does not stagger the mind if it receives due consideration.][17]

Here, as in the *villancico*, knowledge of God is obtained by careful consideration of the hidden, or unseen, details of the universe. By grounding her portrayal both of Mary and of the angelic approach to knowledge, which closely reflects her own, in the scriptural tradition of the books of Wisdom, Sor Juana emphasizes their orthodox nature. What initially appeared as an unlikely comparison — Mary lecturing simultaneously on theology and natural philosophy — is revealed to be a biblically justified association, and one that provides her audience with a new way of conceptualizing one of Mary's most important attributes, her wisdom. Furthermore, by associating Mary's theological understanding to her corporal participation in the Incarnation, Sor Juana subtly integrates the female body into a traditionally male discourse of knowledge.

Mary, Divine Choirmistress

In the fourth *villancico*, Sor Juana further develops the connection she establishes above between Mary and the understanding of creation as filled with hidden harmonies. For Sor Juana and her contemporaries, the best disciplines through which to observe this hidden harmony were mathematics and music — for study of both of them revealed the hidden order and proportions that governed the universe. On their own, numbers and musical notes do not display harmony or order, but when viewed as a system, taking into account the proportional relationships between them, they create a harmonious whole. In turn, the proportional relationships found in mathematics and music could be mapped onto the order of the cosmos found in the distances between the planets — the Pythagorean harmony of the spheres.

This idea forms the basis of Sor Juana's fourth *villancico*, in which Mary appears as a divine choir mistress. Once again, Sor Juana draws on a long tradition of Marian imagery in the formation of her conceit. The identification of Mary, Jesus' mother, with Miriam, Moses' sister, has long been a theme of Christian typology. In Exodus, after the Israelites have been freed from Egypt, Miriam leads the people in praise of God for their liberation:

> sumpsit ergo Maria prophetis soror Aaron tympanum in manu egressaeque sunt omnes mulieres post eam cum tympanis et choris quibus praecinebat dicens cantemus Domino gloriose enim magnificatus est equum et ascensorem eius deiecit in mare. (Exodus 15. 20–21)

> [Then the prophet Miriam, Aaron's sister, took a tambourine in her hand; and all the women went out after her with tambourines and with dancing. And Miriam sang to them: 'Sing to the Lord, for he has triumphed gloriously, horse and rider he has thrown into the sea'.]

In his commentary on the Psalms, Augustine identified Mary with Miriam the tambourine player, as 'nostra tympanistria' [our tambourine player] because, like Miriam, she leads the people in praise of God through the words of the 'Magnificat'.[18]

However, in Sor Juana's elaboration of the identification between Miriam and Mary, and therefore of Mary as a music maker, she presents Mary not only as a musician, and director of a heavenly choir, but as the source of musical harmony itself. Here, the connection to the Assumption is made through the metaphor of the Pythagorean musical scale — from *ut*, the lowest note, or the lowliness of her status as 'ancilla' [handmaiden] at the Annunciation, Mary rises to *la*, the highest note on the scale. Throughout the *villancico*, Mary's role is to harmonize discordant notes — in the same way that she brought together the apparently irreconcilable heaven and earth. She is the most perfect counterpoint, not subject to the 'compasillo' [four-beat bar] of the world, but to the 'compás' [three-beat bar], and therefore the perfect proportions, of heaven. Through the Fall in the garden of Eden, human nature, and the cosmos, have become out of tune. Mary, however, can resolve this dissonance into harmony — by dividing the scale into proportional and harmonious tones, with no discordant notes (*OC*, ii, 7–8).

As Pamela Long has noted in her analysis of this *villancico*, these musical references are inseparable from Sor Juana's understanding of the cosmos.[19] According to the Pythagorean concept of the harmony of the spheres, the distances between harmonious notes on the musical scale mapped perfectly onto the distances between the planets as they move through the skies. Thus, the planets produce their own harmony — not audible to the human ear, but nonetheless present as it emanates through the cosmos. The connection between music and cosmology is made explicit throughout the *villancico*. In her ascent through the musical scale, and to heaven, Mary passes higher than *sol*, the middle note on the musical scale, but also 'el sol', the sun, which belongs to the movable spheres of the planets, sun and moon, and is below the firmament of the fixed stars and the heavens. In the *villancico*, Mary's own voice becomes this harmony of the spheres, accompanied by the heavenly choirs:

> Por los signos de los Astros,
> la voz entonada suena,
> y los Angélicos Coros
> el *contrabajo* le llevan. (*OC*, ii, 8)

[Through the heavenly signs, her tuneful voice rings out, and the angelic choirs raise to her voice the bass line.]

We should note here the complexity of the conceit — the '*signos* de los Astros' are both the signs of the Zodiac, and therefore the heavenly spheres, and the musical notes on the scale that correspond to the planets. Furthermore, by making reference to the star signs, which order both the celestial sphere and the calendar year, Sor Juana suggests that Mary's heavenly music extends throughout the cosmos in both space and time.

Once again, there is a close parallel between Sor Juana's Mary, the personification of Wisdom in the Old Testament, and, in this case, the doctrine of the Immaculate Conception — the belief that Mary was conceived without sin, free from the taint of original sin that has marked humankind since the Fall in the Garden of Eden. One of the most important connections between Wisdom literature and Mary, with particular relation to the doctrine of the Immaculate Conception, is its repeated claim that Wisdom, and therefore Mary, was created before time, before creation, and before the earth: 'Dominus possedit me initium viarum suarum antequam quicquam faceret a principio' [The Lord created me at the beginning of his work, the first of his acts of long ago] (Proverbs 8. 22–26), thus preserving her from the taint of original sin after the creation of the human race.[20] Furthermore, the books of Wisdom emphasize Wisdom's presence throughout *all* of creation. She is the cause of all things, 'quid sapientiae locupletius quae omnia operatur' [What is richer than wisdom, the active cause of all things?], and she knows the past, present, and future, 'et si multitudinem scientiae desiderat quis scit praeterira et de futuris aestimat', [and if anyone longs for wide experience, she knows the things of old, and infers the things to come] (Wisdom 8. 5–8). In Ecclesiasticus, she is poured out on God's works: 'ipse creavit illam spiritu sancto et vidit et dinumeravit et mensus est et effudit illam super omnia opera sua' [It is he who created her; he saw her and took her measure; he poured her out upon all his works] (Ecclesiasticus 1. 9).

In Sor Juana's fourth *villancico*, therefore, Mary becomes the harmony of the spheres. She is the order that holds the universe together. Through the connection between music and cosmology, Sor Juana's portrayal of Mary as the divine choirmistress dovetails with her presentation of her elsewhere as the one with perfect knowledge of creation. In her *Ejercicios devotos*, nine days of spiritual exercises in preparation for the Feast of the Immaculate Conception, Sor Juana relates Mary's wisdom specifically to her perfect knowledge of the workings of the cosmos. She writes:

> ¿Qué sería ver [...] la altísima sabiduría con que la gran Señora conoció todas las naturalezas y cualidades de todos aquellos luminares: sus influjos, giros, movimientos, retrogresiones, eclipses, conjunciones, menguantes, crecientes, y todos los efectos que pueden producir en los cuerpos sublunares, con perfectísima intuición? [...] ¡Sabiendo con clarísimo conocimiento todas las causas de estos admirables efectos que por tantos siglos han tenido suspensos y tan fatigados los entendimientos de los hombres en escrúpulos, sin llegar a tener perfecta ciencia de ellas! (*OC*, IV, 485)[21]

> [What would it have been like to see [...] the highest wisdom with which the great Lady understood with perfect intuition the retrogressions, eclipses, conjunctions, wanings and waxings, and all the effects they can produce in sublunar bodies? [...] She knew with very clear understanding all the causes of these marvellous effects that for so many centuries have held scrupulous men in suspense and so fatigued their understanding, without their ever achieving a science that perfectly explains such causes!][22]

Here, Mary's attribute of Wisdom shows her perfect knowledge to be superior to those of generations of men. Once again, Sor Juana's emphasis on Mary's knowledge of the causes of things 'las causas de estos admirables efectos' [the causes of these marvellous effects] relates her both to the figure of Wisdom, 'the active cause of all things', but also to Sor Juana's interest in natural philosophy, and the investigation of causes and effects.

Mary, *caballera andante*

It is, however, in the sixth and seventh *villancicos* that the full implications of Sor Juana's Mariology, in particular for her own poetic practice, become apparent. In the sixth *villancico*, Sor Juana represents Mary as a *caballera andante*, a female knight errant. She transposes the iconographical Marian attributes taken from the description of the woman in Revelation 12. 1–17, 'mulier amicta sole et luna sub pedibus eius et in capite eius corona stellarum duodecim' [a woman clothed with the sun, with the moon under her feet, and on her head a crown of twelve stars], into military attire. The sunrays become her armour, the stars her helmet, and the moon her spurs:

> Lleva de rayos del Sol
> resplandeciente armadura,
> de las Estrellas el yelmo,
> los botines de la Luna. (*OC*, II, 11)

[She wears shining armour of the sun's rays, and a helmet of stars, and spurs like the moon.]

She has become such a 'bizarra guerrera' [brave warrior] that earth can no longer contain her mighty power, and she has now been assumed to heaven in order to begin a new adventure, in which she will find the treasure of heaven for which so many search (*OC*, II, 10–12).

Sor Juana's representation of Mary as a source of military strength, with particular reference to the medieval practice of knight errantry, is drawn both from scripture and from Hispanic poetic tradition. The biblical basis for the connection between Mary and military might is first found in Genesis, where, after the Fall, God promises to place iniquity between the woman, Eve, and the serpent, who tempted her to sin: 'inimicitias ponam inter te et mulierem, et semen tuum et semen illius; ipsum conteret caput tuum, et tu conteres calcaneum eius' [I will put enmity between you and the woman, and between your seed and hers; he will strike your head, and you will strike his heel]. Although here, in Jerome's translation of the Vulgate, the neuter 'ipsum' [his], refers to the 'semen' [seed], it was later changed to the feminine 'ipsa' [her], and taken as a reference to the woman who would reverse the curse placed on Eve, and triumph over sin, that is Mary — a prophecy that is seen fulfilled in the passage of Revelation cited above. Following this interpretation, Mary then became the answer to the question of Proverbs 31. 10, 'mulierem fortem, quis inveniet?' [a wife of noble character, who can find?]. As Jaroslav Pelikan explains, it is Mary's fortitude that enables her to defeat the devil and thus become victorious in the battle in which Eve had been vanquished. As such, she could become the patron of victory.[23] Furthermore, in the Song of Songs, the attribute of fortitude can be seen to be applied particularly to warfare, where the beloved, one of whose allegorical interpretations in Christian tradition is Mary, is described as being 'terribilis ut castrorum acies ordinata' [terrible as an army with banners] (Song of Songs 6. 4). This reference is particularly pertinent in this context, given that it is one of the antiphons for the first nocturn at matins on the Feast of the Assumption, the liturgy for which Sor Juana's *villancicos* were composed, which also describes her glorious triumph, 'hodie gloriosa cum angelis triumphas' [today you triumph gloriously with the angels].[24]

As Amy Remensynder argues in her study of Marian martial imagery in the Hispanic world, this portrayal of Mary as a figure of military might found particular resonance in Hispanic literature of the medieval and early modern periods, where several texts present Mary as a figure of chivalric valour and military might.[25] In the fifteenth century, Gutierre Díez de Games wrote in *El Victorial* (1406–1448) of three orders of divine chivalry, in which each rank is captained by an immortal being — the Archangel Michael leads the charge of the angels, the martyrs are led by Christ, and the earthly kings, who defend the Church, are led by Mary: 'Otros cavalleros tiene nuestro señor Dios, que son los Buenos reyes de la tierra, justos, derechureros e temientes a Dios [...]. Desta cavallería de los Buenos defensores es caudillo e abogada la virgen Santa María' [Our Lord God has other knights, who are the good kings of the earth, who are righteous, just, and God-fearing [...]. The battle chief and advocate for this knighthood of good defenders is the blessed Virgin Mary].[26] In 1612, writing of a battle between Christians and *moriscos* in 1610 in *Liga deshecha por la expulsión de los moriscos*, Juan Méndez de Vasconcelos recounts how a vision of the Virgin Mary, fashioned as Santiago Matamoros, ensured a Christian victory:

> Una mujer de azul manto vestida,
> una espada en la mano ancha y desnuda
> en los rayos del sol toda encendida,
> dize el Moro que estuvo en nuestra ayuda;
> con un valor y fuerza no entendida.[27]

[A woman dressed in a blue cloak, a wide and naked sword in her hand, aflame with the rays of the sun, the Moor says that she came to our aid, with valour and astounding strength.]

In her portrayal of Mary as *caballera andante*, therefore, Sor Juana draws on a rich scriptural and literary tradition that is particularly associated with the Feast of the Assumption. However, she also introduces further particular details to her description that point to a subtler purpose of her choice of theme. At the beginning of the *villancico*, in her description of Mary's armaments, Sor Juana has her holding a shield, with the motto 'Tota pulchra' [altogether beautiful]: 'en un escudo luciente | con que al infierno deslumbra, | un mote con letras de oro | en que dice, *Tota pulchra*' [a shining shield, with which she dazzles hell, bears a motto in golden letters, which reads: *Altogether beautiful*] (*OC*, II, 11). The motto, a common topos of Marian iconography, refers to the description of the beloved in the Song of Songs, one of whose allegorical readings throughout Christian tradition is as referring to Mary, and her relationship with Christ: 'Tota pulchra es amica mea et macula non est in te' [You are altogether beautiful my love, and there is no blemish in you] (Song of Songs, 4. 7).

The allusion to Mary's complete beauty, as well as the lack of any flaw in her, constitutes a further reference to the Immaculate Conception, and thus another link between the two Marian doctrines. Furthermore, the term 'macula' [blemish] points back to the book of Wisdom, and the description there of the woman of Wisdom, the figure of Mary, and the source of the name of Mary as the 'speculum sine macula' [mirror without blemish]: 'candor est enim lucis aeternae et speculum sine macula Dei maiestatis et imago bonitatis illius' [For she is a reflection of eternal light, a spotless mirror of the working of God, and an image of his goodness] (Wisdom 7. 26). Following Catholic tradition, this reflection works in two ways: Mary acts as a perfect mirror of the divine to humankind on earth, thus enabling them to perceive more of the nature of God, while at the same time she acts as a mirror for humankind, in which they can perceive their own faults and sins. In both senses, her status as a perfect mirror also enables her to act as a 'speculum iustitiae' [mirror of justice or righteousness], a further title of Mary.[28] Her perfection puts in greater relief the sin of humankind and their need for redemption, and as a mirror of God, she reflects his perfect justice.

The understanding of Mary as 'speculum iustitiae' is clearly expressed in the *villancico*. Here, in a deviation from the poetic tradition explored above, Sor Juana's Mary does not fight specifically in the defence of Spain or of Christendom, but rather for the cause of justice:

> La que venga los agravios
> y anula leyes injustas,
> asilo de los pupilos,
> y amparo de las vïudas;
> la que libertó los presos
> de la Cárcel. (*OC*, ii, 11)

> [She who avenges wrongdoing, and overturns unjust laws, who is a refuge for orphans, and a shelter for widows, she who freed captives from imprisonment.]

In her emphasis on Mary's opposition to injustice, and her defence of the orphan and the widow, Sor Juana echoes the biblical injunction for righteousness given in Isaiah, 'discite benefacere quaerite iudicium subvenite oppresso iudicate pupillo defendite viduam' [learn to do good, seek justice, rescue the oppressed, defend the orphan, plead for the widow] (Isaiah 1. 17). By mirroring divine justice, Mary also reflects the compassion and charity demonstrated by Christ, who, according to the typological reading of the prophet Malachi, is the 'sol iustitiae' [sun of justice or righteousness]: 'Et orietur vobis timentibus nomen meum sol iustitiae et sanitas in pinnis eius' [But for you who revere my name the sun of righteousness shall rise, with healing in its wings] (Malachi 4. 2). In the *villancico*, it is Mary's shield that conquers hell by dazzling it with light, 'al infierno deslumbra' [she dazzles hell]; she does so by using her shield to reflect the sun's rays so powerfully that they are blinding, and therefore figuratively by reflecting Christ, the 'sun of righteousness' who conquers death and hell.

Furthermore, within the emblematic tradition of the seventeenth century, and in particular through its connection to an interest in the development of optical technology, with which Sor Juana elsewhere demonstrates her familiarity, Mary's status as a mirror of the 'sun of righteousness' is connected to her motherhood of Christ, and to her unique ability to carry God within her. In his treatise on emblematics, *Speculum imaginum veritatis*, the German Jesuit Jacob Masen describes an emblem that depicts Mary as the 'speculum divinitatis' [mirror of the divine], in which the sun is reflected in a flat mirror, with the motto 'in parvo totus' [everything in a small space].[29] As both Sor Juana and Masen were aware, a flat mirror gives a perfect reflection, as opposed to a convex or concave mirror, which reflect things as larger or smaller than they are. Just as a mirror can contain on its surface the whole sun, so could Mary contain God within herself, without resorting to distortion or illusion:

> Qui terras superat, speculari totus in orbe
> Cernitur immissis Phoebus ab axe rotis.
> O quam dissimilis speculo, similisque Maria est!
> Hoc totum orbe diem continet, illa Deum.
> (Masen, *Speculum*, pp. 616–17)

[Phoebus, who rises above the earth, may be seen in his entirety in the mirroring circle, the wheels having been thrown from his chariot. Oh, how dissimilar, yet similar, Mary is to that mirror! While it contains the whole day within its circle, she contains God.]

In the *villancico*, Sor Juana takes Masen's conceit one step further, by combining the two images. While it is Mary's shield that contains the sun's reflection and with it dazzles hell, it is her containing of Christ within herself in the Incarnation, as well as her mirroring of his righteousness as the 'mirror of justice', that spiritually defeats the powers of the devil. In her exploration of the image, and of the two terms of the 'speculum iustitiae', Sor Juana provides a further example of how her interest in scientific enquiry, here in the field of optics, can shed light on her understanding of the divine.

Furthermore, the connection to the notion of 'in parvo totus' points to a more explicit engagement with the notion of wit, particularly as it was explored in Masen's works. Masen's treatise was written in response to the Jesuit work of emblematics, *Imago primi saeculi*, which he argued employed well-worn images, and lacked the necessary originality to provoke 'admiratio' [admiration] in its readers. In his treatise, echoing other seventeenth-century treatises on poetics and rhetoric, he emphasizes the need to bring together unexpected images for best rhetorical effect, particularly in the service of theology, in such a way as to evoke the wonder due to the observation of the created world.[30] In her choice of unexpected images of Mary, which she nonetheless shows to be grounded in scripture and tradition, Sor Juana demonstrates the potential of his advice. However, it is in the following *villancico* that she brings the notion of 'in parvo totus' to full fruition, and demonstrates its implications not just for her Mariology, but indeed for her whole understanding of the poetic enterprise.

Mary, Teacher of Rhetoric

In the seventh *villancico*, Mary has gone from being Professor of Theology, through being the heavenly choir mistress, and is now a teacher of the 'new Rhetoric', her own 'arte de bien decir' [art of good speech] (*OC*, II, 12–14).[31] As she had done with music, Sor Juana weaves a series of conceits based on rhetorical terms to describe Mary. Here, the parallel created between Mary and rhetoric is based on her life story: the exordium is her Immaculate Conception, her life is the narration, her death the confirmation, and the epilogue is her Assumption. Once again, Sor Juana emphasizes the eternal nature of Mary's voice — because the subject of which she speaks is always God, she is addressing an eternal question. Her eloquence serves to advocate successfully in front of God, the eternal judge. Her perfection announces the proof of the 'silogismo galante' [gallant syllogism] (*OC*, II, 13), where the tripartite syllogism becomes a metaphor for the triune Godhead.

Once again, the source for Sor Juana's proposition of Mary as teacher of rhetoric is grounded in the Wisdom literature of the Old Testament. In Proverbs, Wisdom is presented as an orator, proclaiming that she will teach prudence and intelligence to those who lack it: 'iuxta portas civitatis in ipsis foribus loquitur dicens o viri ad vos clamito et vox mea ad filios hominum intellegite parvuli astutiam et insipientes animadvertite audite quoniam de rebus magnis locutura sum et aperientur labia mea ut recta praedicent' [beside the gates in front of the town, at the entrance of the portals she cries out: 'To you, O people, I call, and my cry is to all that live. O simple ones, learn prudence; acquire intelligence, you who lack it. Hear, for I will speak noble things, and from my lips will come what is right] (Proverbs 8. 3–6). Furthermore, in Wisdom, she is said to understand turns of speech and riddles: 'scit versutias sermonum et dissolutiones argumentorum' [she understands turns of speech and the solutions of riddles] (Wisdom 8. 8). More significantly, however, Wisdom is presented as an 'artifex' [craftswoman]: 'quis horum quae sunt magis quam illa est artifex' [who more than she is fashioner of what exists?] (Wisdom 8. 6). Her attributes, as described above in Wisdom 7. 22, are a spirit that is intelligent, subtle, and sharp: 'est enim in illa spiritus intellectus, [...] subtilis, [...] acutus' [there is in her a spirit that is intelligent, [...] keen, [...] and subtle]. Finally, to those who will follow her teachings, she gives quickness of mind: 'habebo propter hanc [...] acutus inveniar in iudicio' [Because of her, I shall be found keen in judgement] (Wisdom 8. 11).

In the scriptural emphasis on Wisdom's status as 'artifex', and on her attributes of mind, in particular the repeated emphasis on 'agudeza' [acuity], Sor Juana makes Wisdom, and therefore Mary, not only a model of female intelligence, but indeed a model for the aesthetics of Hispanic Baroque poetry. Her subtle mind and quick wittedness perfectly conform to the Baroque aesthetic ideals of speed and concision as expressed in Gracián's concept of *ingenio*, an aesthetic close in its emphasis to the one explored in Masen's treatise above. At its highest form, writes Gracián, *agudeza* is expressed in the aesthetic of 'multum in parvo' [a great deal in a small space] achieved by condensing as many meanings and attributes as possible into a single word, as Gracián describes the art of *apodos* or nicknames: 'unas *sutilezas* prontas, breves relámpagos del ingenio, que en una palabra encierran mucha alma de concepto' [quick subtleties, rapid flashes of the mind, that in one word encapsulate much of the spirit of the conceit] (*Agudeza*, II, p. 146).

In Mary, however, Sor Juana is able to take Gracián's aesthetic one step further, and to turn her into the epitome of the Baroque poet. For Mary, through her physical participation in the Incarnation, can go beyond even Gracián's aesthetic of 'multum in parvo' to achieve rhetorically, as well as physically, Masen's 'in parvo totus'. In the seventh *villancico*, Sor Juana demonstrates how in Mary, the most complex mystery in creation — the Incarnation — is expressed in one single world, the Logos, Christ:

> Tan *lacónica* introduce
> la persuasión, que acomoda
> cuando elegante más luce,
> que su *Retórica* toda
> a sólo un *Verbo* reduce. (*OC*, II, 14)

[She introduces her evidence so concisely, that she ensures, all the more brilliantly for its elegance, that her whole *Rhetoric* can be reduced to one *Word*.]

Following Gracián's aesthetic model, Sor Juana emphasizes how Mary's concision ('lacónica') is at the heart of the brilliance of her rhetorical elegance, yet that she supersedes even his highest aim — her whole rhetoric, indeed the whole of creation is reduced to one Word in her. In an image reminiscent of the poetic contests at which Sor Juana excelled, it is, at the end of the *villancico*, the singular brilliance of Mary's conceit that earns her the prize of her eternal place in heaven.

It is in this seventh *villancico* that we begin to see the full significance of Mary to Sor Juana's poetics, and the fulfilment of the purposes set out at the beginning of this study. Throughout these *villancicos*, Sor Juana repeatedly highlights Mary's achievement of unsurpassable knowledge, talent, and virtue. Here, in particular, by positing Mary as the epitome of *ingenio*, the one who can contain in one word the infinity of creation, Sor Juana emphasizes her traditional status as the most perfect of all human beings. At the same time, Sor Juana subtly challenges traditional hierarchies of gender within discourses of knowledge and literary creativity by connecting each of these attributes to Mary's specifically female embodiment. Throughout each *villancico*, Mary's ascent in each of the specialist fields of knowledge and skill is associated with her bodily assumption into heaven. As doctor of Theology, she acquires her supreme doctrinal knowledge through her own pregnant body: 'la de *Incarnatione*, pudo estudiar en sí misma' [she was able to study [the subject] of the Incarnation in herself]. In the sixth *villancico* it is her physical body, externally clothed for cosmic battle, and containing Christ within itself, that enables her to defeat the powers of darkness. Finally, in this seventh *villancico*, her rhetorical ingenuity found in her ultimate conceit of the Incarnation occurs simultaneously in her mind and in her womb. By emphasizing this close relationship between the embodied nature of the Marian doctrines of the Assumption and the Incarnation and Mary's access to divine knowledge, Sor Juana privileges the Marian body as a site of eternal knowledge and infinite creativity.

Furthermore, through her theologically orthodox development of an apparently incongruous connection between the female Marian body and Mary's participation in institutions of knowledge and power that were traditionally reserved for men, Sor Juana not only demonstrates her own *ingenio*, but also subtly legitimates her own place in both intellectual and poetic discourse as an imitation of Mary. While Mary's perfection of the Baroque art of wit, and its associated attributes of speed, concision, and dexterity present her as a model for all poets to imitate, her embodied presence in these poems also privileges a particular space for a specifically female-centred understanding of knowledge and creativity. In Sor Juana's development of her Marian images in a way that both demonstrates their orthodoxy and simultaneously stretches the bounds of traditional understandings of women's participation in discourses of knowledge, Sor Juana demonstrates that her own human ingenuity, if not on a par with Mary's cosmic wit, is nonetheless a worthy contender.

Notes to Chapter 7

1. *Villancicos a la Asunción* (Mexico City: Viuda de Bernardo Calderón, 1676). Sor Juana had previously published a laudatory sonnet in Diego de Ribera's *Poética descripción* (Mexico City: Francisco Rodríguez Lupercio, 1668). On Loaysa y Agurto's musical career at Mexico City Cathedral, see Robert Stevenson, 'Sor Juana's Mexico City Musical Coadjutors', *Inter-American Musical Review*, 15.1 (1996), 23–27.
2. On the entrance of the viceroy, and the triumphal arch by Carlos de Sigüenza y Góngora designed to be paired with Sor Juana's, see the chapter by Rolena Adorno in this volume.
3. See Sor Juana Inés de la Cruz, *The Answer/ La Respuesta*, ed. and trans. by Electa Arenal and Amanda Powell, 2nd edn (New York: Feminist Press at the City University of New York, 2009), p. 150.
4. See Georgina Sabat de Rivers 'Blanco, negro, rojo: semiosis racial en los villancicos de Sor Juana Inés de la Cruz', in *Crítica semiológica de textos literarios hispánicos*, ed. by Miguel Ángel Garrido Gallardo (Madrid: Consejo Superior de Investigaciones Científicas, 1986), pp. 247–55; Mabel Moraña, 'Poder, raza, y lengua: la construcción étnica del Otro en los villancicos de Sor Juana', *Revista Iberoamericana*, 63.181 (1997), 631–48; Nicholas Jones, 'Sor Juana's Black Atlantic: Colonial Blackness and the Poetic Subversions of *Habla de negros*', *Hispanic Review*, 86.3 (2018), 265–85.
5. On Mary as evidence for Sor Juana's religiosity, see Bénassy Berling, *Humanismo y religión en Sor Juana Inés de la Cruz* (Mexico City: Universidad Nacional Autónoma de México, 1983), p. 257. On 'pro-woman' analyses of the *villancicos*, see Oswaldo Estrada, 'Sor Juana y el ejercicio pedagógico en sus villancicos marianos', *Letras Femeninas*, 32.2 (2006), 81–100; Natalie Underberg, 'Sor Juana's Villancicos: Context, Gender, and Genre', *Western Folklore*, 60.4 (2001), 297–316 (p. 311); Cruz, *The Answer/ La Respuesta*, pp. 15–16.
6. Linda Egan, 'Donde Dios es todavía mujer: Sor Juana y la teología feminista', in *Y diversa de mí entre vuestras plumas ando*, ed. by Sara Poot Herrera (Mexico City: El Colegio de México, 1993), pp. 327–40. For a detailed refutation of Egan's claims with regard to the *villancicos*, see Lisa Amor Petrov, 'On the Divinity of Sor Juana's Virgin Mary: A Question of Feminist Heterodoxy or Intercultural Agency', *Calíope*, 13.2 (2007), 23–38.
7. Estrada, 'Sor Juana y el ejercicio pedagógico', p. 82; Underberg, 'Sor Juana's Villancicos', p. 298.
8. Underberg, 'Sor Juana's Villancicos', p. 298.
9. Baltasar Gracián, *Agudeza y arte de ingenio*, ed. by Evaristo Correa Calderón, 2 vols (Madrid: Castalia, 1969), I, 55.
10. See Stephanie Kirk, *Sor Juana Inés de la Cruz and the Gender Politics of Knowledge in Colonial Mexico* (Abingdon: Routledge, 2016), chapter 2. For Sor Juana's own exploration of her exclusion from institutional learning, see in particular Cruz, *The Answer/ La Respuesta*.
11. By emphasizing the significance of the Marian, and hence female, body within the *villancicos*, this study builds on recent analyses that have identified the importance of the functional body to Sor Juana's epistemology and poetics. See Tamara Harvey, *Figuring Modesty in Feminist Discourse across the Americas, 1633–1700* (Abingdon: Ashgate, 2008), chapter 2; Stephanie Kirk, 'Pain, Knowledge, and the Female Body in Sor Juana Inés de la Cruz', *Revista Hispánica Moderna*, 61.1 (2008), 37–53; Ruth Hill, *Sceptres and Sciences in the Spains: Four Humanists and the New Philosophy (ca.1680–1740)* (Liverpool: Liverpool University Press, 2000). These authors argue against earlier studies that interpreted Sor Juana's work as neutralizing the body by distancing the supposedly genderless soul from the female body, as outlined in Margo Glantz, 'Ciencia y experiencia en las querellas de las mujeres: Sor Juana', in *Nictímene... sacrílega: estudios coloniales en homenaje a Georgina Sabat de Rivers*, ed. by Mabel Moraña and Yolanda Martínez San-Miguel (Mexico City: Universidad del Claustro, 2003), pp. 173–86.

12. Sor Juana Inés de la Cruz, *Obras completas*, ed. by Alfonso Méndez Plancarte and Alberto G. Salceda, 4 vols (Mexico City: Fondo de Cultura Económica, 1951–57), II (1952), 6. All subsequent citations, unless noted, are taken from this edition (*OC*).

13. Unless otherwise indicated, all translations are my own. Translations of Biblical sources are taken from the New Revised Standard Version (Anglicized).

14. For further background on this connection, and its presence in medieval and Golden Age Spanish literature, see Lesley Twomey, *The Serpent and the Rose: The Immaculate Conception in Hispanic Poetry in the Late Medieval Period* (Leiden: Brill, 2008), pp. 175–216.

15. Ronald Murphy, 'Introduction to Wisdom Literature', in *The New Jerome Biblical Commentary*, ed. by Raymond Brown, Joseph Fitzmyer and Ronald Murphy (London: Chapman, 1990), pp. 447–52 (p. 450). I use the term 'figure' here in the sense of an Old Testament person or event that reveals the narrative of salvation of the New Testament. See Erich Auerbach, 'Figura', in *Scenes from the Drama of European Literature: Six Essays*, trans. by Ralph Manheim (Gloucester, MA: Peter Smith, 1973), pp. 11–76.

16. Martha Lilia Tenorio, *Los villancicos de Sor Juana* (Mexico City: El Colegio de México, 1999), pp. 96–97. Tenorio's interpretation follows a model of scholarship that emphasizes Sor Juana's appeal to the genderless mind as justification for her, and other women's, participation in intellectual discourse. In contrast, this study builds on more recent approaches that emphasize the specific place of the body, in particular the female body, in Sor Juana's self-incorporation into the systems of knowledge of the period. See Harvey, *Figuring Modesty*, Kirk, 'Pain, Knowledge', and Hill, *Sceptres and Sciences*. Note here that it is Mary's angelic students who are portrayed as the disembodied spirits, while Mary herself remains present in her corporeal reality.

17. Translation adapted from Cruz, *The Answer / La Respuesta*, p. 73.

18. Augustine, *Exposition on the Book of Psalms*, 6 vols (Oxford: John Henry Parker, 1847–57), III (1849), 67. 28.

19. Pamela Long, *Sor Juana / Música: How the Décima Musa Composed, Practiced, and Imagined Music* (New York: Peter Lang, 2009), pp. 88–91.

20. See also Sirach 24. 9.

21. Sor Juana's use of 'admirables' [marvellous] here is particularly significant in relation to the investigation of causes and effects. For Covarrubias, 'admirar' [to marvel] is, 'pasmarse, y espantarse de algun efecto que vee extraordinario, cuya causa ignora. Entre otras propiedades que se atribuyen al hombre, es ser admirativo: de aquí resulta el inquirir, escudriñar, y discurrir cerca de lo que se le ofrece, hasta quietarse con el conocimiento de la Verdad' [to be amazed, or stunned and shocked by the effect of something that seems extraordinary, the cause of which is unknown. Among the other characteristics that are attributed to mankind is to marvel: from here comes the impulse to inquire, to investigate, and to reflect on what he finds before himself, until he finds peace in the knowledge of the truth]; Sebastián de Covarrubias, *Tesoro de la lengua castellana o española*, ed. by Martín de Riquer (Barcelona: Alta Fulla, 1998). For Juan Eusebio Nieremberg, among other New Philosophers, 'admiratio' acts as a spur to inquiring into the causes of things, an idea which has its origin in Aristotle, *Metaphysics*, 982b. See Scott Hendrickson, *Jesuit Polymath of Madrid: The Literary Enterprise of Juan Eusebio Nieremberg* (Boston, MA, and Leiden: Brill, 2005), pp. 117–18.

22. Translation adapted from Grady Wray, *The Devotional Exercises / Los ejercicios devotos of Sor Juana Inés de la Cruz, Mexico's Prodigious Nun (1648/51–1695)* (Lewiston/Queenston/Lampeter: The Edwin Mellen Press, 2005), p. 153.

23. Jaroslav Pelikan, *Mary through the Centuries* (New Haven, CT: Yale University Press, 1997), p. 27.

24. Gregory the Great, *Liber responsalis sive antiphonarius S. Gregorii Magni*, in *Patrologiae cursus completus. Series latina*, ed. by Jacques-Paul Migne, vol. LXXVIII (Paris, 1844–55), p. 799.

25. Amy Remensnyder, *La Conquistadora: The Virgin Mary at War and Peace in the Old and New Worlds* (Oxford: Oxford University Press, 2014), pp. 92–118.

26. Gutierre Díez de Games, *El Victorial*, ed. by Alberto Miranda (Madrid: Cátedra, 1993), pp. 229–30.

27. Juan Méndez de Vasconcelos, *Liga deshecha por la expulsión de los moriscos* (Madrid: Alonso Martín, 1612), fol. 118^v.

28. Charles Renfrew, *The Litany of Loreto* (London: Catholic Truth Society, 2012), pp. 72–74.

29. Jacob Masen, *Speculum imaginum veritatis occultae* (Cologne: Joannis Antonii Kinchii, 1681). Evidence that Sor Juana knew and read Masen's text is found elsewhere in her work, notably as her source for *El divino Narciso*. Although little known among scholars today, the *Speculum imaginum* is cited elsewhere in the Spanish Golden Age, including Diego Suárez de Figueroa's commentary on José de Valdivielso's *Vida, excelencias y muerte del glorioso patriarca san Joseph... Coméntala el doctor don Diego Suárez de Figueroa*, 5 vols (Madrid: Francisco del Hierro, 1727–28), III, 26.

30. See Richard Dimler, 'Jakob Masen's *Imago figurata*: From Theory to Practice', *Emblematica*, 6.2 (1992), 286–90.

31. Sor Juana's connection between the art of music and the art of rhetoric here is reminiscent of the comparison made between the two arts in Pedro Cerone's *El melopeo y maestro* (Naples: Juan Bautista Gargano and Lucrecio Nucci, 1613), which Sor Juana read and annotated as part of her studies in musicology.

CHAPTER 8

The Harmonies of Conflict:
Poetry and the Musical Imaginary
between Spain and the New World

Lorena Uribe Bracho

Introduction

European and colonial poets of the sixteenth and seventeenth centuries often turned
to the cultural imaginary of music as a source of subject matter and metaphor for
their poems. Much has been said about the history of the ideas that shape that
imaginary — the music of the spheres, the principles of harmony, the evolution of
styles and modes.[1] Perhaps less has been said about how those ideas were adopted
by poetry, especially by poetry in Spanish, or, to go even further, by a tradition of
writing poetry that crossed the Atlantic at the beginning of the sixteenth century
and, without forgetting its origins, grew into a voice of its own, responding to
needs of its own.[2]

In this chapter I explore some of the different roles that musical imagery plays
in a selection of colonial poems. I will address music-related ideas inherited from
Renaissance and Baroque Europe that made their way across the Atlantic in
manuals, treatises and poems, to show how traditional musical imagery of harmony
was repeatedly invoked, although it never managed to erase conflict and dissonance
entirely. I will then explore some clashing opinions as to whether public music
leads to salvation or to perdition, and reflect on the role of musical allusion in
poetry that aims to persuade, a mechanism that is central to the colonial project of
evangelization. In this context, poets are constantly attracted by and aim to imitate
the persuasive powers of music, since music is often represented in early modern
times as able to exert a harmonizing force over those who listen. Specific kinds of
music were thought to elicit specific and similar reactions from the audience, who
could alternately be moved to joy, to sadness, to action, to a feeling of calm, etcetera.
In the much-recreated myth of Orpheus, for example, the most disparate entities —
entities that could otherwise be in conflict or belong to different categories, such
as wild animals, humans, trees, birds, the elements — are all brought together by a
similar feeling of awe at hearing Orpheus play.

Poems that engage with the subject of music in New Spain respond to the
strong presence that music had in the Spanish colonies. From the very beginning,

music played an important role in two parallel colonial projects: converting the indigenous people to Catholicism and providing the conditions that would enable Spaniards to settle in the new continent. In the first case music was used as a vehicle for Christian doctrine, and in the second as part of the ecclesiastical infrastructure around which a new 'criollo' community was built.[3] While the missionary friars used European-style music, in some cases with text in indigenous languages, as a key mechanism for imposing the Christian faith, accomplished musicians were imported from Spain to fill the role of the local cathedral's 'maestro de capilla', or chapelmaster, a job which involved taking charge of the music performed during religious services, as well as educating young musicians and musicians-to-be. Many important composers from the Spanish colonies — Hernando Franco, Gaspar Fernandes, Juan Gutiérrez de Padilla — came to the New World to fill this charge. But chapelmasters were, of course, not the only musicians who migrated to the Americas, nor were professional musicians, for that matter, the only ones making music and bringing European ideas about music into the New World. While chapelmasters added their own compositions to a canonical repertoire of Italian, French, German and Spanish polyphony, soldiers, sailors, craftsmen and settlers in general brought their own instruments and their own songs and dances with them.[4] There are many testimonies that boast of the skill and the enthusiasm with which the natives adopted this musical culture, among them the following passage in which the Franciscan missionary Fray Gerónimo de Mendieta speaks of how Indian craftsmen learned to construct European instruments with local woods:

> Los primeros instrumentos de música que hicieron y usaron, fueron flautas, luego chirimías, después orlos, y tras ellos vihuelas de arco, y ahora cornetas y bajones. Finalmente, no hay género de música en la iglesia de Dios, que los indios no la tengan y usen en todos los pueblos principales, y aun en muchos no principales, y ellos mismos lo labran todo, que ya no hay para qué traerlo de España como solían. Una cosa puedo afirmar con verdad, que en todos los reinos de la cristiandad (fuera de las Indias) no hay tanta copia de flautas, chirimías, sacabuches, orlos, trompetas y atabales, como en solo este reino de la Nueva España.[5]

> [The first musical instruments that they made and used were flutes, then shawms, then crumhorns, and after them bowed vihuelas, and now bugles and dulcians. Finally, there is no genre of music in the church of God that the Indians don't have and use in all the principal towns, and even in many that are not principal, and they themselves carve everything, and there is no longer need to bring them from Spain as they used to. One thing I can say with truth, that in all the realms of Christendom (outside of the Indies) there is no such abundance of flutes, shawms, sackbuts, crumhorns, trumpets and atabals, as in only this realm of New Spain.][6]

The position of power that the Spaniards held over the natives ensured that much of the music that was played was imported from Europe or composed according to European practice. The same is true of theoretical reflections on the subject of music, where ideas that were commonplace in the old continent quickly became commonplace amongst the inhabitants of the new, and also quickly filtered into the musical imaginary captured by poets. That said, music has shown to be a language more malleable to influence than poetry, and European musical practice, for all its hegemony, was slowly being transformed by both the indigenous population and the African population that had been brought to America as slaves.[7] Musical influence — furthered by the fact that a number of musicians who made the voyage to New Spain also made the voyage back — operated more evidently in one direction, and yet it also operated slowly but surely in the other.[8]

Making Harmony of Conflict

I would like to begin with the vision, in a few colonial poems, of the universe as a series of spaces that are *animated* by music. A vision where music acts as a vital force that travels down from the heavens, passes through the countryside stirring life into trees and fountains, and crosses down into the Underworld with Orpheus, who, in the words of Sor Juana, 'suspendió en canciones, furias, | desató en dulzuras, grillos' [suspended in songs furies, | untied in sweetness shackles].[9] This view derives from the pre-Copernican idea that celestial music relies on precise distances between a number of large concentric structures that were believed to produce sound when set in motion. Without the primordial harmony that determines the distances between one sphere and another — which according to Platonic texts is akin to *musical* harmony — the concord of the spheres would be impossible. 'The very universe', says Isidore of Seville in his *Etymologies*, 'is held together by a certain harmony of sounds, and the heavens themselves are made to revolve by the modulation of harmony'.[10]

Even though the music of the spheres is inaudible to the human ear, and was, for that reason, contested as a concept by later theorists — among them Fray Luis de León's friend and professor of music at the University of Salamanca Francisco Salinas[11] — or perhaps thanks to the possibilities opened to the imagination precisely *because* it is inaudible to the human ear, the movement of the celestial 'machine' and the idea of it being 'animated' by music is evoked time and again by poetry. The following panegyrical sonnet by Sancho de Rueda, published in Spain as part of the preliminary material to Martín de Tapia's musical theory treatise *Vergel de música spiritual speculativa y activa* [Orchard of Spiritual, Speculative and Active Music] is a characteristic example:[12]

> *Habla la música*
> En la mente divina colocado
> estuvo eternalmente mi concento;
> por mí el un cielo y otro y firmamento
> se mueven a compás tan acordado.
>   Yo doy vida al Zodiaco, y gobernado
> por él, Apolo sube tan contento;
> faltar jamás podrá solo un momento
> por mí siendo regido y alumbrado.
>   La tierra, el agua, el aire, con el fuego
> van haciendo entre sí dulce armonía,
> los brutos animales y las aves.

Del sueño el microcosmo vuelve luego,
contempla al sumo bien, y en él ponía
sus nobles conceptos, altos y suaves.[13]

[*Music speaks*
Within the mind divine my harmonizing
has held a place for all eternity;
by me the firmament, one sky, the other,
all move in time, and all to one accord.
I give life to the Zodiac, and ruled
by him, Apollo rises so content;
no single moment could he ever fail
while governed and illuminated by me.
The earth, the water and the air with fire
amongst themselves go making harmony,
and also the brute animals and birds.
From sleep the microcosm then comes back,
to contemplate the highest good, and set
its noble concepts in it, high and gentle.]

Rueda's poem, as is the case of most of the laudatory poems that precede musical treatises, is a collection of commonplace ideas on the subject, and for that reason it can be used to get a sense of which musical ideas were the most widespread: the 'compassed' movement of the heavens, the animation of the stars, and the relationship between macrocosm and microcosm, including the analogies with the four elements and the 'music' of beasts and birds.

The idea that music was able to bring opposing forces such as the four elements into harmony was soon adopted by religious poetry, often as a way to represent the mysteries and paradoxes that can operate as touchstones of Christian doctrine. Poems such as the following gloss dedicated to the Nativity of Christ by the Spanish-born poet and playwright Fernán González de Eslava who lived and wrote in New Spain, show how heaven and earth can come together encompassed by musical metaphors (*compás* is the musical 'bar', whereas *cifra* is a system of musical notation):

Al Nacimiento
Hoy dos estremos muy buenos,
cifrados en un compás:
que no puede dar Dios más
ni contentarnos con menos.
[...]
      Juntar lo mejor del cielo
con lo más vil de la tierra,
juntar la paz con la guerra
y hacer gloria del suelo;
a hacer bienes terrenos
que salgan de su compás:
Dios no pudo darnos más
ni contentarnos con menos.[14]

[*To the Nativity*
Today are two great extremes
encoded in a single bar:

that God could not give us more
nor content us with less.
[...]
        To join the best of the heavens
with the vilest of the earth,
to join peace with war
and of the ground make glory;
to make earthly goods
that surpass their measure:
God could not give us more
nor content us with less.]

Music, according to an idea recognized as Saint Augustine's, was placed in man by God at the intersection of the body and the soul. According to more than a few musical theorists, this creates in the soul a natural inclination for music, which in turn opens the possibility for music to serve as a vehicle for Christian spirituality.[15] The idea is explained in Andrés Lorente's 1672 *El porqué de la música* [Why Music], which according to Irving Leonard circulated in New Spain:[16]

> [...] de cosas distintas, que son el ánima y el cuerpo en el hombre nace esta música humana; y como Dios haya puesto en el hombre esta natural música, así el hombre tiene esta natural inclinación y amistad con ella: todo semejante apetece a su semejante y con él se goza.[17]

> [from two things as different as are the soul and the body in man, this human music is born; and as God has placed in man this natural music, so man has this natural inclination and friendship with it: everything is drawn to that which is similar, and takes pleasure in it.]

There was much effort on behalf of Spanish missionaries and chroniclers during the viceregal period, as there has been also on behalf of some critics in more recent times, to present the New World as a *locus amoenus* of sorts, where the native people's natural inclination to music sets the stage for their enjoyment of musical Christian rites, in easy harmony with the newly arrived Spaniards. Of course, proof that Spanish music was indeed adopted by the natives can be found in a vast array of sources, from the early and wide dissemination of stringed instruments, previously unknown in America, to — as Anna Jurek Nattan rightly points out — iconographical material such as the murals in the famous Baroque church in Tonantzintla, Puebla, where Indians and Europeans are shown making music together.

Fray Bernardino de Sahagún's early account of the success of teaching plainsong and polyphony to the Indians is full of optimism about the natives' docility and natural musical abilities.[18] Years later, however, Sahagún would change his view about the success of the Christian mission, while keeping music at the centre of the argument.[19] The author of the *Relación* complained that the Indians had tricked the Spanish friars into believing they had eradicated 'idolatry', while it later became evident that the natives had secretly continued with their practice of 'singing and dancing in honor of the old gods'.[20] As Gary Tomlinson points out, 'there are two modes of singing: one the blazon of the Indians' capacity to adopt European ways, the other the sorry measure of Indian deceit and missionary failure'.[21]

The Dangers and Benefits of Public Music

I have seen how music is used as a metaphor for social harmony, and now I will explore how its very material could be subject to doubt, and its social use a point of conflict. While there was indeed a school of Renaissance thought that praised human music as a reflection of universal harmony and therefore put it forward as an essential part of the education of body and mind, there was another, conflicting, school of thought that vehemently rejected music based on the opposite reasoning: music, because of how it appeals to the senses, can act against the health of the soul. Instead of leading to spiritual contemplation, music corrupts and draws away from divine truths.[22] The problem is addressed by St Augustine in the *Confessions*, where he hesitates as to whether to encourage or condemn the use of music:

> Yet when I recall the tears that I shed at the song of the Church in the first days of my recovered faith, and even now as I am moved not by the song but by the things which are sung — when chanted with fluent voice and completely appropriate melody — I acknowledge the great benefit of this practice. Thus I waver between the peril of pleasure and the benefit of my experience; but I am inclined, while not maintaining an irrevocable position, to endorse the custom of singing in church so that weaker souls might rise to a state of devotion by indulging their ears. Yet when it happens that I am moved more by the song than by what is sung, I confess to sinning grievously, and I would prefer not to hear the singer at such times. See now my condition![23]

Of course, as St Augustine's text already suggests when it mentions 'appropriate melody', the two opposite effects can be ascribed to the kind and the quality of the music being played, which is what some writers do instead of taking the rather more abstract philosophical or theological stance of either defending or discrediting music as a whole. According to Martín de Tapia, Plato used to say that one should take care not to alter anything in virtuous music, since there is no bigger stain to the republic than music's gradual loss of honesty.[24] Monteverdi, in his famous preface to his *Madrigali guerrieri et amorosi* [Madrigals of War and Love], quotes Boethius saying that 'music is related to us, and either ennobles or corrupts the character', while Richard Hooker, in a different context but as a response to the same argument, says in his *Lawes of Ecclesiastical Politie* that 'there is nothing more contagious and pestilent than some kinds of harmony; than some nothing more strong and potent unto good'.[25] This resonates with the following verses by Fernán González de Eslava, who speaks of the *style* of human music that he considers the most dignified:

> Con ser su canto el más digno
> que se vio en estilo humano,
> echó sobre el canto llano
> un contrapunto divino.
> Coge con obra y deseo
> fruto de divina planta,
> pues con los ángeles canta
> 'Gloria in excelsis Deo'.[26]

[Being his song the most worthy
that was seen in human style,
over the plainchant he built
a divine counterpoint.
With deed and desire he plucks
fruit from the divine plant,
since he sings with the angels
'Glory be to God on high'.]

The poem speaks of the first mass officiated by a young priest, and his words, either set to music or referred to metaphorically as music, are combined with the voices of the angels singing 'Glory be to God on high'. The refrain says that the priest sings *with* the angels, but the gloss develops the image in a way that is musically significant. 'Upon the *canto llano*' — the 'plainchant' — the verse says, he sang a 'divine counterpoint'. The juxtaposition of plainchant and counterpoint symbolically marks the synthesis of 'plain' human music and complex celestial music. It shows how from the baseline of human singing something can be constructed that is more akin to the celestial. Supporting this idea is a bit of music history: the invention of counterpoint, in the Middle Ages, came about — within liturgical music — with the development of new voices that acquired the freedom to rise and fall in harmony, elaborating upon the stable and linear *canto llano*.

On the opposite side of the spectrum are the examples of music that lures to evil, whether through the association of music with sorcery, as when Sor Juana says 'más que en estragos, Medea, | de sus músicos hechizos' [more than ravages Medea, | with her musical spells], or through the idea that there is such a thing as 'sinful' music.[27] The words of Gabriel Bocángel, for example, in Spain, echo the prohibition of certain songs and dances considered salacious both in Spain and the New World, not only because of their lyrics, but also because of the music itself: the dangerous rhythms that could awaken the desire for styles of dancing described by the Inquisition as obscene.[28] In the following lines, Bocángel describes the 'style' and the 'tricks' of a lascivious woman who sings and dances for an audience:

Cantabas [...]
    [...] por desnudar del más ministro
la modestia con tonos desenvueltos,
de tu lascivo amor primer registro.
    Si bailas, no miró miembros tan sueltos
en sus ninfas ribera gaditana,
ni pasos hacia Venus tan resueltos.[29]

[You sang [...]
    [...] to strip the most priestly
of modesty with forward tones,
first register of your lascivious love.
    If you dance, the riverbank of Cadiz
saw not in its nymphs such loosened limbs,
nor steps towards Venus so resolved.]

A famous example of 'miembros sueltos' and 'pasos hacia Venus' in New Spain is the passage quoted by Baudot and Méndez, taken from a 1766 inquisitorial process, in which an informant from Veracruz gives a hearsay report of the motions people went through when dancing the *Chuchumbé*:

> [...] me dicen que las coplas que remití se cantan mientras los otros bailan, o ya sea entre hombres y mujeres, o sea, bailando cuatro mujeres con cuatro hombres, y que el baile es con ademanes, meneos, zarandeos, contrarios todos a la honestidad y mal ejemplo de los que lo ven como asistentes, por mezclarse en él manoseos, de tramo en tramo, abrazos y dar barriga con barriga. Bien que también me informan, que esto se baila en casas ordinarias de mulatos y gente de color quebrado, no en gente seria, ni entre hombre circunspectos, y sí soldados, y marineros, y broza.[30]

> [they tell me that the verses I sent are sung while the others dance, either a man with a woman, or four women dancing with four men, and that the dancing is with gestures, swayings, shakings, all contrary to honesty and bad example to those who look on, since it is mixed up now and then with gropings, embraces, and the colliding of belly with belly. I am also informed that this is danced in ordinary homes of mulattos and people of broken colour, not amongst serious people, or amongst circumspect men, but instead amongst soldiers, and sailors, and low people.]

As in Bocángel's poem, a particular kind of music and dancing is being rejected for what it represents socially. But the object of rejection, between Spain and America, has changed. Whereas in the old world the 'looseness of the limbs' is used to make fun of the reprehensible gestures of a 'loose' woman whose social rank is not identified (she could as easily be a prostitute as she could be a member of the court), in the New World the equally 'obscene' dancing is used as a marker of class and of race. The ones who dance are now the soldiers and sailors that provide the manpower for the colonial scheme, as well as the people who belong to the complex hierarchic caste system based on different combinations of Spanish, Indigenous and African heritage, all of them subject to discrimination because of their 'broken' or mixed colour. It is no coincidence that many of the dances censored by the Inquisition — such as the *Chuchumbé*, described above, or the *Pan de Jarabe*[31] — were associated with Afrodescendant communities in the area of Veracruz, the point of entry for the slave trade.[32]

Music has always been a marker of social differentiation. Whereas a select minority would take private classes from musicians arrived from Spain and sponsor ostentatious musical events, the rest of society had their own musical practices.[33] As Urchueguía notes, the first songs that the Indians heard from the conquerors were not psalms and hymns but secular music, probably accompanied by plucked string instruments such as the *vihuela* or the lute.[34] Perhaps some of the songs they heard were of the sort that, according to the inquisitorial testimony about the *Chuchumbé*, belonged to the world of 'soldiers, and sailors, and low people'. If anything, the repeated prohibition of such singing and dancing shows how widespread the practice was, and how ingrained in popular culture.

Another social marker within the musical imaginary were the different kinds of instruments, with those considered easy to play — tambourines, castanets, drums, simple strings such as the *rabel* — used constantly by poets to represent 'rustic' merrymaking. A voice in a poem by the Mexican-born and reportedly son of a conqueror Juan Pérez Ramírez says 'Toca tu rabel, pastora, | que me fino de pracer', [Play your rebec, shepherdess, | for I die of pleasure], while another voice responds 'Yo daré mil castañetas | y saltos en derredor!' [I will sound a thousand castanets | and jump all around!].[35] The instruments in Pérez Ramírez's poem enliven the rhythm of music and, very importantly in this context, awaken the urge to dance. Unlike the melancholy lover who sings his pain in the solitude of a forest — a character who could easily be represented playing one of the *vihuelas* that Mendieta says were being constructed in New Spain — those who dance, at least in colonial and Golden Age poetry, do so in the company of others. Through dance, joy becomes contagious, and becomes collective. As in Fernán González de Eslava's famous 'Ensalada del tiánguez', in itself a celebration of the public place:

> — Vamos a tomar placer,
> señores, si a todos place,
> a un tiánguez que se hace,
> do veréis cosas de ver.
>
> — Vamos con grande alegría,
> cantando un cantar gracioso
> a manera de folía:
>
> Comadre y vecina mía,
> démonos un buen día.[36]
>
> [— Let us go take pleasure,
> gentlemen, if it pleases all,
> to a tiánguez that takes place,
> where you will see things worth seeing.
>
> — Let us go with great joy,
> singing a gracious song
> in the style of the folía:
>
> My friend and neighbour,
> let's give ourselves a good time.]

The poem, with the use of the word *tiánguez* [tianguis], Náhuatl for open-air market, mexicanizes the medieval allegory of the world as a marketplace where sins and virtues are on display.[37] The *tianguis* has the important role of providing a space where indigenous and European cultures can come together, a role that is also played by shared music and shared dance, such as the one alluded to in the gloss: the famous *folía*, which was adopted with great success in America. According to Covarrubias, the folía is a very loud dance that is performed by costumed and even cross-dressed characters with rattles and other instruments, who twirl, and dance, and play; and the noise is so much, he says, and the music so fast, that everyone seems to have gone mad. And that, Covarrubias ventures, is how the dance was named 'folía', from the Tuscan word *folle*, which means mindless and insane.[38] The *folía*, as José Rey explains, brought together dance, music, text and merriment; in folklore all of these elements coexisted, even though they later evolved separately and each kept the term 'folía' for itself. As a poetic form, the *folía* tended to be made up in its earliest stage of two-verse refrains, and later of four-verse refrains.[39] This is consistent with the fact that González de Eslava's two-verse *folía* from the sixteenth century was recorded in the early seventeenth century in a four-verse form by Gonzalo de Correas, who completes the first two verses with 'señor vecino y compadre, | con mañana y tarde' [my neighbour and friend, | with morning and evening].[40]

The Role of Music in the Poetry of Persuasion

Music's powers of persuasion were central at a time of conflict. Musicians and composers took the trouble to adapt catalogues of figures from ancient rhetoric — originally intended for verbal language — into the language of music, and wrote pieces in different 'modes' depending on how they wanted them to alter those who listened.[41] Juan de Espinosa's *Tractado de principios de música práctica e teórica sin dejar ninguna cosa atrás* [Treatise on the principles of practical and theoretical music without leaving anything out], that was published in Toledo around the same time as the conquest of Mexico was taking place, identifies eight musical modes — inherited from Boethius and Ptolemy — according to the different affects they awake in the listener. When the listener is moved, 'certain physical changes take place from which the term "affect" originates, in the sense of a physical effect'.[42] Thus, the first mode moves to joy, the second to tears, the third to wrath, the fourth appeases wrath, the fifth makes the sad rejoice, the sixth tempers those who are easily moved to sadness, the seventh is a pleasurable synthesis of sadness and joy, and the eighth resembles the seventh in pleasure and the first in natural cheer.[43] Music makes harmony of conflicting emotion, inasmuch as many musicians believed, at least in theory, that choosing to play in a specific mode would elicit a similar, unifying, emotional response in a previously emotionally disparate audience.[44]

These powers were very attractive to poets, who, just as musicians had turned to textual rhetoric, attempted to capture the way in which music was able to *move*. The possibility of moving one affect and stopping another — moving to joy and controlling wrath, for example — has its counterpart in poetry, where music is constantly either *moving* or *suspending* its surroundings, as in the following lines by Sor Juana's contemporary Diego de Ribera:

> Dulcemente sonora,
> no aquella que en diversos horizontes
> cítara ya canora
> las aguas enfrenó, movió los montes,
> y con dulce modelo
> fue quietud del abismo, es lustre al cielo;
>   sí la que, ingeniosa,
> a suspensión dichosa
> del alma propia los impulsos fía,
> siendo de tu concento
> racional cuerda cada entendimiento.[45]

[Sweetly sonorous,
not that which in diverse horizons
melodious zither
the waters bridled, moved the mountains,
and with sweet model
was stillness of the depths, is sheen to heaven;
    but that ingenious one
which yields the impulse of the soul
to glad suspension,
being to your harmony
rational string each understanding.]

As is common in early modern poetry, the reference to the pagan gods is maintained because of its role in poetic tradition, but at the same time transformed to serve religious Christian purposes: Ribera embraces the myth of Orpheus as part of the poetic paraphernalia needed to express musical effect, only to later reject the pagan setting by replacing Orpheus's cithara with one that is capable of suspending the *soul*, since it is inspired with religious, rather than mundane, feeling.[46] In any case, the choice of words falls in line with music's tendency within the poetic fiction to both 'move' and 'suspend': 'enfrenó', 'movió', 'quietud', 'suspensión', 'impulsos'.

In a context in which love is often represented as a force that lays siege to a vulnerable body which then goes on to develop the symptoms of a disease, it is common for poetic imagery to represent the penetration and the infection of bodies with musical weapons. In many cases the male poet — or the woman poet adopting male conventions — gives an account of the impression caused by a woman singing or playing as a sensuous combination of the visual and the aural.[47] The sound works together with the effects of sight to create an image of beauty in movement, or, as in the following lines from Sor Juana, beauty armed with 'vibration':

¿Quién podrá vivir seguro,
si su hermosura divina
con los ojos y las voces
duplicadas armas vibra?
        (*Lírica personal*, p. 44)

[Who could live safely,
if her divine beauty
with eyes and voices
vibrates twice the weapons?]

This could certainly be considered as one of the 'dangers of the senses' that drove certain ecclesiasts to speak ill of the effects of music. But as with most examples of musical imagery, its power can be turned in a different direction. The 'weapons' of music can be brandished, according to many examples of colonial poetry, in the name of Catholicism. Because, as violinist and scholar Judy Tarling points out, the weapons of music are the weapons of rhetoric.[48]

Just as Sor Juana's Narcisa can pierce the air with her voice and extract from its wounds her own echo — 'Hirió blandamente el aire | con su dulce voz Narcisa, | y él le repitió los ecos | por bocas de las heridas' [Soflty did Narcissa wound |

the air with her sweet voice, | and it gave back the echoes | from the gashes' open mouths] — the right kind of song can pierce the listener and move him to devotion (*Lírica personal*, p. 43). Amongst the various effects of music listed by Francisco de Montanos in his *Arte de música, teórica y prática* [Art of Theoretical and Practical Music], there is one that falls well into the imperial plan of religious expansion. Music, says Montanos, in line with St Augustine's words about the 'weaker souls' that might rise to devotion, awakens devotion and brings forth pious tears.[49] Spanish missionaries, from Pedro de Gante, who was the first music professor to come from Europe, to Bartolomé de las Casas and Bernardino de Sahagún, were quick to see how this Augustinian view of music could be of use.[50] Sahagún combined European music with texts in Nahuatl in a collection of psalms published in Mexico in 1583 entitled *Psalmodia Christiana*, while other surviving musical collections attest to the importance of music in missions across the Americas.[51]

The idea that music is key in the mechanism of moving someone to the Christian faith was used in many contexts; in the following quatrains by the Mexican-born María Estrada de Medinilla, this is employed to promote the rejection of Judaism. The poem appeared as part of the preliminaries to Francisco Corchero Carreño's *Desagravios de Christo en el triumpho de su Cruz contra el judaísmo* [Amends to Christ in the Triumph of his Cross over Judaism], published in Mexico City by Juan Ruiz in 1649:[52]

> Anfión de la fe que, en voz cadente,
> a los supremos coros diestro aspiras,
> tan docto campas, que a tu ingenio inspiras
> cuanto le admiran raro y elocuente.
> Sus ecos repitiendo dulcemente,
> clarín alado en tus acordes liras
> desencanto será de sus mentiras
> al vil contagio del inculto diente.[53]

> [Amphion of faith, that in melodious voice
> to the supreme choir dexterous you aspire,
> so learned you loom, that you inspire your wit
> when they admire it, high and eloquent.
> Its echoes sweetly reproducing,
> winged bugle in your tuneful song
> will disenchant them from their lies
> at vile infection of the ignorant tooth.]

Again a transformation *a lo divino* of a classical myth revolving around the idea of the power of music: Amphion, who built the wall of Thebes by animating the stones with his music and making them take their own place in the rampart, is morphed into an 'Amphion of faith', using the power of musical affect to pry away from the 'lies' of the 'serpent-like' Jews. A similar idea of affect operates in Carlos de Sigüenza y Góngora's *Primavera indiana*; when the Virgin of Guadalupe speaks to Juan Diego, her voice is 'la voz del *afectuoso ruego*' (which, according to common usage in Spanish syntax at the time, is 'a plea which *inspires* affect', as opposed to our modern syntactic reading of 'an affectionate plea'). Even though a 'voice' is, of course, not necessarily musical, it can be argued that Juan Diego's reaction lends a musical quality to the Virgin's words, since it is described with figures of speech almost identical to countless other cases in early modern poetry where there is an attempt to capture a reaction to music:[54]

> Mas que admirado, en dulces suspensiones
> Tiernamente robados los sentidos,
> Sin darle al gusto breves disgresiones,
> Vuela el Indio con pasos desmedidos.[55]

> [Beyond admired, in sweet suspensions
> tenderly the senses stolen,
> without allowing rest its brief digressions,
> the Indian flies with overreaching steps.]

When poetry represents persuasion, it easily falls into musical metaphor. Words that *move* are often imagined as musical; poetry that reflects upon its own ability to convince, to influence, to perform an action, more often than not describes itself as song. If early modern musical theory so often approached its subject in terms of the affect it was believed to produce, it is largely because both composition and interpretation were understood as rhetorical activities.

This idea, which already permeated poetic imagery of music in Spain, became even more important in the New World as a powerful way of thinking about and carrying out the vast project of evangelization. Music and poetry became even closer. Not only because they share the rise and fall of rhythm and rhyme, the melody of voice and intonation, but because they share the power of rhetoric: if they are dexterous enough with their instrument — 'monstruo de pluma es tu instrumento' [feathered/pen monster is your instrument],[56] says Sigüenza to Diego de Ribera — the musician and the poet can alter the course of discourse: can move, can suspend, can rejoice, can inflame, can elevate and can Christianize. Moreover, effective persuasion could create a certain degree of harmony amongst those whose affect, whose physical and emotional condition, was being altered. In a unified response to the persuasive powers of music, conflict could be glossed over.

Music is easily imagined as a discourse that conciliates opposites. Music and musical practice in the New World were intended to persuade, to minimize conflict, to harmonize the noisy dissonances of colonial society. Similarly, the inherent force of musical metaphor brings harmony to the forefront, downplaying clash and contention. But as much as it is harmony, music is also tension. The same music that was used as a forceful means to convert the Indians to the Christian faith — a weapon of persuasion — could also serve as a vehicle for the natives to assert their own cultural practice, as we have seen in the cases of Sahagún and the *chuchumbé*. Looking at the role musical imagery plays in colonial poetry, we can see voices coming together, and we can also discern the imbalance and the tension underlying relations of power. Music can operate as a source of metaphors for both harmony and tension: it can provide a lens through which to observe concord and conflict in the societies of the New World.

Notes to Chapter 8

1. See, for example, Germain Bazin, *The Baroque: Principles, Styles, Modes, Themes* (London: Thames and Hudson, 1968); Joscelyn Godwin, *Harmonies of Heaven and Earth: The Spiritual Dimensions of Music from Antiquity to the Avant-Garde* (Rochester, VT: Inner Traditions, 1987); Jacques Chailley, *L'imbroglio des modes* (Paris: A. Leduc, 1960).

2. More work has been done about the relationship that poetry has with music in the context of English literature, for example: James Anderson Winn, *Unsuspected Eloquence: A History of the Relations between Poetry and Music* (New Haven, CT: Yale University Press, 1981); John Hollander, *The Untuning of the Sky: Ideas of Music in English Poetry, 1500–1700* (New York: Norton, 1970); Marc Berley, *After the Heavenly Tune: English Poetry and the Aspiration to Song* (Pittsburgh, PA: Duquesne University Press, 2000).

3. See, for example, the collection of music taken from female institutions in New Spain — convents and schools for girls — edited by Josefina Muriel and Luis Lledías, *La música en las instituciones femeninas novohispanas* (Mexico City: Universidad Nacional Autónoma de México/ Claustro de Sor Juana, 2009).

4. According to Cristina Urchueguía, the process of exporting musical repertoire to America contributed, as a side effect, to the canonization in Spain of composers such as Cristóbal de Morales, Francisco Guerrero, Giovanni Pierluigi de Palestrina, Rodrigo de Ceballos and Tomás Luis de Victoria, since the musical material was subjected, prior to being sent to America, to a selection process that left out compositions considered too local or ephemeral. See 'La colonización musical de Hispanoamérica', in *Historia de la música en España e Hispanoamérica, II: De los Reyes Católicos a Felipe II*, ed. by Maricarmen Gómez (Madrid: Fondo de Cultura Económica, 2012), pp. 466–502 (p. 492).

5. Fray Gerónimo de Mendieta, *Historia eclesiástica indiana*, ed. by Joaquín García Icazbalceta (Mexico City: Antigua Librería, 1870), pp. 412–13.

6. All translations are my own, and I have modernized old spelling.

7. See, for example, José Manuel Pedrosa, 'La encrucijada española: cantos y músicas de Europa, África y América en los Siglos de Oro', *Edad de Oro*, 22 (2003), 221–45.

8. María Gembero Ustárroz warns against the limitations of traditional historiographical approaches, practised on both sides of the Atlantic, where a 'national' and sometimes 'isolationist' view downplays the exchanges between Spain and the New World in favour of singling out local peculiarities in musical practice. Her close study of the migration of musicians with a range of different hierarchies and social positions to America (and sometimes back to Europe) highlights the dissemination and mobility of instruments, repertoire, music books, styles and interpretative practices, and makes a strong case for the value of a transatlantic approach to music of the period. See 'Migraciones de músicos entre España y América (siglos XVI–XVIII): estudio preliminar', in *La música y el Atlántico. Relaciones musicales entre España y Latinoamérica*, ed. by María Gembero Ustárroz and Emilio Ros-Fábregas (Granada: Universidad de Granada, 2007), pp. 17–58.

9. Sor Juana Inés de la Cruz, *Obras completas de Sor Juana Inés de la Cruz, I. Lírica personal*, ed. by Antonio Alatorre (México: Fondo de Cultura Económica, 2012), p. 85. All translations are my own.

10. Isidore of Seville, *Etymologies*, book III, 17, in Oliver Strunk (ed.), *Source Readings in Music History*, rev. and ed. by Leo Treitler (New York and London: Norton, 1998), p. 150.

11. José Teruel says that Salinas is the first author to contest the theory of cosmic harmony, which for him is fundamentally a philosophical concept about the order and proportion of the different elements of the world. Even though Salinas recognizes a harmony in the celestial movements and the parts of the soul, he does not call it 'music', since it is not perceived by the ear; José Teruel, 'Contextos e implicaciones literarias en *De musica libri septem* de Francisco Salinas', *Edad de Oro*, 22 (2003), 79–93 (p. 86).)

12. According to Gabriela Villa Walls, Sor Juana could be speaking of Martín de Tapia (alongside Pietro Cerone) when she says in her famous 'Romance' to the Condesa de Paredes 'excusándose de enviar un libro de música' [excusing herself of not sending a book about music]: 'De don Martín y don Pedro | no podéis culpar de omisas | las diligencias, que juzgo | que aun

excedieron de activas' [Of don Martín and don Pedro | you cannot say that their diligences | are neglectful, for I even judge | that they are overactive] (Sor Juana, *Lírica personal*, p. 91). In any case, Sor Juana was familiar with Martín de Tapia's writings, which in fact were not his own, but a plagiarism of Juan Bermudo's 1549 *Libro primero de la declaración de instrumentos* [Book the First of the Declaration of Instruments]. Ironically, it was Tapia's book, and not Bermudo's, which was the most widely read during the seventeenth century, and thus it was Tapia who was profusely quoted by Cerone in his *Melopeo y maestro*, an important source for Sor Juana's knowledge of music. See Gabriela Villa Walls, 'El *melopeo y maestro*, "bisagra engarzadora" de la literatura y la música en Nueva España' (unpublished dissertation, Universidad Nacional Autónoma de México, 2011), p. 92.

13. Sancho de Rueda, 'maestresala del Ilustrísimo de Osma', in Martín de Tapia, *Vergel de música spiritual speculativa y activa, del cual muchas diversas y suaves flores se pueden coger* (Villa del Burgo de Osma: Diego Fernández de Córdoba, 1570), fol. 2.

14. Fernán González de Eslava, *Villancicos, romances, ensaladas y otras canciones devotas*, ed. by Margit Frenk (Mexico City: El Colegio de México, 1989), pp. 152–53.

15. Juan Bermudo, *Libro primero de la declaración de instrumentos* (Osuna: Juan de León, 1549), fol. 13; Tapia, *Vergel*, fol. 12.

16. Irving A. Leonard, 'On the Mexican Book Trade, 1683', *Hispanic American Historical Review*, 27.3 (1947), 403–35 (p. 416). Leonard mentions two musical treatises among the list of books that passed through Doña Paula Benavides' bookshop in 1683: Andrés Lorente, *El porqué de la música* (1672), and Francisco de Montanos, *Arte de canto llano* (1648).

17. Andrés Lorente, *El porqué de la música* (Alcalá de Henares: Nicolás de Xamares, 1672), p. 8.

18. In Fray Bernardino de Sahagún's excursus in the *Florentine Codex* entitled 'Relación del autor digna de ser notada' [Worthwile Account of the Author], quoted by Gary Tomlinson, *The Singing of the New World: Indigenous Voice in the Era of European Contact* (Cambridge: Cambridge University Press, 2007), pp. 178–80.

19. Sahagún's ambivalence contrasts with the view of some scholars. For Anna Jurek Nattan, 'Música novohispana de los siglos XVI y XVII: manifestación sincrética de lo europeo e indígena', *Antropología. Boletín oficial del Instituto Nacional de Antropología e Historia*, 91 (2011), 11–15 (pp. 13–14), music always confirms 'la armónica convivencia de ambas culturas en un evento religioso' [confirms the harmonious coexistence of both cultures in a religious event] and the 'plena aceptación de la música europea por parte de los nativos' [full acceptance of European music by the natives].

20. Tomlinson, *The Singing of the New World*, p. 179.

21. Idem.

22. For the tensions between these two conflicting schools of thought, see, for example, Hollander's chapter on 'Music Praised and Blamed', in *The Untuning*, pp. 104–22.

23. Saint Augustine, *Confessions*, in Strunk (ed.), *Source Readings*, p. 133.

24. Cf. Tapia, *Vergel de musica*, f. 35.

25. Claudio Monteverdi, *Madrigali guerrieri et amorosi*, in Strunk (ed.), *Source Readings*, p. 666; Richard Hooker, *Lawes of Ecclesiastical Politie* (1597), quoted in Robert Donnington, *The Interpretation of Early Music* (London: Norton, 1992), p. 111.

26. González de Eslava, *Villancicos*, p. 313.

27. Sor Juana, *Lírica personal*, p. 85.

28. See the section on 'Bailes, jarabes y sones' in Georges Baudot and María Águeda Méndez, *Amores prohibidos: la palabra condenada en el México de los virreyes* (Mexico City: Siglo XXI, 1997), pp. 25–79.

29. Gabriel Bocángel, *La lira de las musas*, ed. by Trevor J. Dadson (Madrid: Cátedra, 1985), p. 178.

30. Baudot and Méndez, *Amores prohibidos*, pp. 33–34.

31. For the history of the prohibition of both the *Chuchumbé* and the *Pan de Jarabe* (also known as *Jarabe gatuno*), see Elena Deanda Camacho, 'Maldito "Jarabe Gat|uno": poéticas de la censura inquisitorial en la Nueva España', *Vanderbilt e-journal of Luso-Hispanic Studies*, 10 (2014), 25–36, as well as the section on 'Bailes, jarabes y sones', in Baudot and Méndez, *Amores prohibidos*, pp. 25–79.

32. See Micaela Díaz-Sánchez and Alexandro D. Hernández, 'The *Son Jarocho* as Afro-Mexican Resistance Music', *The Journal of Pan African Studies*, 6.1 (2013), 187–209.

33. Miguel Molina Martínez, 'La ciudad colonial como escenario de la música en la América hispana', in *La música y el Atlántico: relaciones musicales entre España y Latinoamérica*, ed. by María Gembero Ustárroz and Emilio Ros-Fábregas (Granada: Universidad de Granada, 2007), pp. 183–97 (pp. 188–89).

34. Urchueguía, 'La colonización musical', p. 479.

35. Alfonso Méndez Plancarte (ed.), *Poetas novohispanos. Primer siglo (1521–1621)* (Mexico City: Universidad Nacional Autónoma de México, 1942), p. 12.

36. González de Eslava, *Villancicos*, p. 384.

37. See Margit Frenk's notes to the poem in her edition of *Villancicos*, p. 384.

38. Sebastián de Covarrubias Orozco, *Tesoro de la lengua castellana o española* (Madrid: Luis Sánchez, 1611), *s.v.* 'folía'.

39. See José Rey, *Danzas cantadas en el Renacimiento español* (Madrid: Sociedad Española de Musicología, 1978), pp. 52–69.

40. Gonzalo Correas, *Vocabulario de refranes y frases proverbiales y otras fórmulas comunes de la lengua castellana en que van todos los impresos antes y otra gran copia* (Madrid: Establecimiento Tipográfico de Jaime Rates, 1906), p. 357.

41. See, for example, Joachim Burmeister, *Musica poetica* (Rostock: Myliander, 1606).

42. Judy Tarling, *The Weapons of Rhetoric: A Guide for Musicians and Audiences* (St Albans, Herts: Corda Music, 2004), p. 71.

43. Juan de Espinosa, *Tractado de principios de música práctica [e] teórica sin dejar ninguna cosa atrás* (Toledo: Guillem de Brocar, 1520), chapter xxxviii.

44. It is interesting to note that, while some musical theorists, such as Athanasius Kircher, whose work circulated in New Spain, point out important differences in how the same piece of music may affect different people in different ways according to their temperament, in poetry the effects of music are almost always represented as unifying. Rarely is there a situation in an early modern Spanish or Colonial poem where someone is left in awe by a song and someone else is left impassive. Kircher explains, in his *Musurgia universalis*, that 'certain airs will have [...] great power over one person, and none over another. One person will be affected by this mode, another by that one, since all things depend on the different make up of the temperaments', in Strunk (ed.), *Source readings*, p. 711.

45. In Martha Lilia Tenorio (ed.), *Poesía novohispana. Antología*, 2 vols (Mexico City: El Colegio de México/Fundación Para las Letras Mexicanas, 2010), I, 568.

46. See Tenorio's note to these lines, where she explains that the stanza in question refers to the cithara plucked by the various 'wits' convened by the competition (the '*Certamen*'), each of which is a 'rational string', and that the cithara is superior to that of Orpheus, since it is motivated by a religious (Catholic) rather that a pagan/worldly inspiration; Tenorio (ed.), *Poesía novohispana*, I, 568.

47. For the figure of the singing woman in early modern poetry, see Linda Phyllis Austern, '"Sing Againe Syren": The Female Musician and Sexual Enchantment in Elizabethan Life and Literature', *Renaissance Quarterly*, 42.3 (1989), 420–48.

48. 'Whereas music and rhetoric were always recognized as having both physical and emotional affects, the analogy between the language and forms of music and those of rhetoric became closer than ever with the development of new expressive ideals of music from the sixteenth century onwards' (Tarling, *The Weapons of Rhetoric*, p. 1).

49. Francisco de Montanos, *Arte de música, teórica y prática* (Valladolid: Diego Fernández de Córdoba y Oviedo, 1592), fol. 4.

50. See Urchueguía, 'La colonización musical', pp. 484–97.

51. See, for example, music from the Jesuit missions, such as the opera 'San Ignacio de Loyola', which was preserved in the archives of Chiquitos and San Ignacio de Moxos in Bolivia.

52. See Tenorio's extensive notes to the poem; Tenorio (ed.), *Poesía novohispana*, I, 406.

53. María Estrada de Medinilla, in Tenorio (ed.), *Poesía novohispana*, I, 406.

54. Among the many possible examples are Sor Juana's line 'suspensión del sentido deseada'

[desired suspension of the senses], from the sonnet 'Alaba, con especial acierto, al de un músico primoroso' [Praises, with exceptional skill, that of an exquisite musician] (*Lírica personal*, p. 440).

55. Sigüenza y Góngora, *Obras* (Mexico City: Sociedad de Bibliófilos Mexicanos, 1928), p. 368 (*Primavera indiana*, stanza LI).

56. In Tenorio (ed.), *Poesía novohispana*, II, 695.

PART IV

Epic Poetry and the New Frontier

CHAPTER 9

A Poetics of *términos*:
Lexis and Moral Geography in
Ercilla's Expedition to the
Extreme South in *La Araucana*

Paul Firbas

Language, Body and War[1]

Ibero-American epic poetry of the sixteenth and seventeenth centuries symbolically connected the remote geography of the New World with the centre of the empires. The long epic poems were many-layered machines which worked both with the most prestigious models of Renaissance poetry and with a heterogeneous military and bureaucratic archive, in addition to the personal experiences of the eyewitness or soldier. In light of this, the thousands of lines that structured the poems are difficult to reconcile with an ideal monological imperial voice. The 'empire' included profound contradictions, with its militant Christianity and over-burdening legislation, its transatlantic praxis of power and the criticism of war and its interests by theologians and humanists. Epic poems were generally extraordinary artistic representations of those contradictions.

We might say that the great theme of Ibero-American epic was not directly war as such, but rather transgression, in spatial terms. In the *comedia* of the Golden Age, the catalyst for the dramatic action was also transgression, but social rather than spatial. In spite of this difference, epic and theatre shared a number of structuring principles, especially when the long speeches of the epic dramatized the narration, for example through numerous indigenous monologues, but also when the open spaces of epic were dramatized.[2]

Spatial transgression is what usually puts the epic narrative into motion. The poems progress because they are transgressing a space, creating territories and frontiers. This movement contributes to the construction of a particular map of the colonial world, a kind of 'moral geography' which takes shape in a process in which multiple discursive registers and concrete practices of occupation intervene.

Before entering in detail into the subject of this article — the analysis of how the poetic and lexical procedures of *La Araucana* connect the morality and decorum of the court with the imperial administration of space and the construction of its geography — it is worth pausing to consider a brief example which shows, within a single octave, the poetic operations by which Ercilla enriches the meanings of his text, in this case connecting language, body and war.

In the first part of *La Araucana*, recounting the battle on the hill of Andalicán, the poet introduces brief vignettes of the Spanish warriors: 'el viejo gran jinete Maldonado | voltea el caballo allí con mano diestra' [the grand old horseman Maldonado | airs his horse there with skilful hand] (5.38);[3] '[...] Pedro de Olmos de Aguilera | en todos los peligros se atraviesa' [Pedro de Olmos de Aguilera ventures into all the dangers]; 'Diego Cano a dos manos, sin escudo | no deja lanza enhiesta ni armadura' [Diego Cano with his two hands, without a shield, leaves not a lance erect nor armour intact]; and in this same octave, he introduces us to

> Peña, aunque de lengua tartamudo,
> se revuelve con tal desenvoltura
> cual Cesio entre las armas de Pompeo
> o en Troya el fiero hijo de Peleo. (5.40)

> [Peña, although with a stuttering tongue,
> dashes about with such ease
> as Cessius among the arms of Pompey
> or the fiery son of Peleus at Troy.]

The poem doesn't say anything more about Peña the soldier, of whom we do not even know his baptismal name. More than a historical character whose memory is thus preserved — although this could well be the case — the soldier is here an instrument for composing a vignette about poetry and war.[4] The lines about the stuttering Peña outline a particular relationship between language and war in the poetics of the epic, as if loosening the tongue and using the hand were intimately connected actions. We might remember that tongue and hand are the determining elements in the episode of Galvarino's punishment in the second part of *La Araucana* (cantos 22 and 23). In the case of the soldier Peña, in spite of his speech impediment, the poet says that with his weapons 'se revuelve con tal desenvoltura', inserting here, with this etymological repetition — 'revolver' [stir], 'desenvolver' [unwrap], a brief tongue twister in the scene of the body entering into battle. And we as readers enter into the hendecasyllable hoping not to get tripped up.

This way of connecting language with the body and war, drawing us in as readers, defines one of the modalities in which Ercilla and other epic poets intervene in the debates on politics and good government. Epic intervenes not only through the consecrated concepts of the political vocabulary, but because it puts them on the scene — it converts them into material for poetic mimesis — or because it finds another vocabulary, capable of establishing other connections, exploring the experience and testimony of colonial warfare. The poem constructs in this way new horizontal relations between deeds and words, as opposed to the verticality of traditions and genealogies, important as these are in the explicit apparatus of epic poetry. If we return to the passage about Peña the soldier, the first two hendecasyllables move on this horizontal plane of the experience on the battlefield, as opposed to references to the Latin and Greek world in the last two lines, which move and escape vertically, outlining genealogies and signalling the tradition.

In her study of the first canto of *La Araucana*, Sarah Dichy-Malherme interprets several octaves as cartographic poetry and indicates that these prefigure the martial encounters between Spaniards and Araucanians, as in the case of the famous lines about the two wide seas which 'pasando de sus términos' [overflowing their bounds] futilely aim to join together in the extreme South, battered and prevented by the rocks and waves (*La Araucana*, 1.8).[5] Ercilla conveys — or constructs — not only the physical geography of Chile, but also 'su geografía histórica, política e incluso hipotética' [its historical, political and even hypothetical geography], as Dichy-Malherme indicates. The cartographic discourse is thus 'perfectamente concorde con el registro épico' [in perfect accordance with the epic register] and shares its methods: cognitive and military dominion of space, including the uncertainties and desire for possession generated by the *terrae incognitae*.[6] In addition, the geography of Ercilla's poem, it should be noted, can acquire the characteristics of a dramatic persona, following the tradition of the classic figure of prosopopoeia.[7]

While geography is dramatized, participating in the blows of war, the poetics of the Spanish epic has affinities with the *comedia* of the Golden Age and its techniques, and with decorum, a central concept in the functioning of society and its symbols during the Renaissance and Baroque. And although the word 'decoro', or decorum, does not appear in any of the three parts of *La Araucana* — rightly so, since a war on the edge of the world was one of the most indecorous settings — I would argue that Ercilla's poem sets its limits and redefines decorum, adapting it to the register of the epic.

Decorum, Urbanity, *términos*

In his *Diálogo de la lengua* [Dialogue on Language] (*c.* 1536), Juan de Valdés explained that decorum was 'cuando queremos decir que uno se gobierna en su manera de vivir conforme al estado y condición que tiene [...]. Es propio este vocablo de los representadores de las comedias, los cuales estonces se decía que guardaban bien el decoro cuando guardaban lo que convenía a las personas que representaban' [when we wish to say that someone conducts himself in his manner of living in accordance with his station and condition [...]. This word is characteristic of those who perform comedias, of whom it was said that they maintained decorum well when they kept up what befitted the people they represented].[8] Maxime Chevalier has studied the meaning of the word in its transition from the sixteenth century to the beginning of the seventeenth, comparing Valdés's definition with that of Covarrubias in his dictionary the *Tesoro* (1611), for whom decorum was now 'respeto y mesura' [respect and moderation].[9] Chevalier demonstrates that for the authors of the Golden Age, like Lope de Vega or Miguel de Cervantes, the word signified 'respect owed to persons or things', and that this was the most common meaning, associated with an extension of the concept of court — one which surpassed the vision of Valdés, centred in the city of Toledo — until it became one of urbanity.[10] 'Decorum' is thus close to euphemistic speech in a city context. In Covarrubias there is no praise of the delights of rural life: the rural world is one of rusticity, barbarism and uncouth speech (*mal decir*, literally 'wrong saying'). Thus, the path of decorum towards urbanity places us within the confines of the city, far from the open fields of epic, but not far from the courtier Ercilla's place of enunciation.

Here, our interest in decorum is in its moral sense: on the one hand, 'morally appropriate' and virtuous conduct;[11] on the other, a collection of customs — as in the 'moral history' of the Jesuit José de Acosta (1590) — which correspond to a specific geographical nature. Moral history is indissociable from natural history; human practices or customs transpire in concrete geographical spaces which, to a certain extent, determine them.[12] Human beings must act with the 'respect and moderation', as Covarrubias would say, which the environment requires and which, in the case of the human practice par excellence, language, is expressed in speaking properly and in urbanity. These would be the ideal customs of the man of the city, a model of Christian politics.

How is this decorum transferred to the Araucanian battle ground? The answer lies, I would argue, in the enormous productivity and flexibility of the word 'término' [term, boundary, place], in phrases such as the 'término discreto' [discreet expression], or in 'consejo, término y cordura' [counsel, balance and good sense], but also in the 'distrito y término araucano' [Araucanian district and boundaries] and, particularly, in 'los términos lícitos pasando' [breaking the bounds of legitimacy], where the word reveals its double implication and symbolic power. As in the tongue of Peña the soldier, the *término* produces the necessary connections for the ideal functioning of the poetic machinery.

Poetic *términos*: Territorialized Decorum

It is not an easy task to define the word *término*. In the trilingual 1591 dictionary of Richard Percivale, *término* is defined as 'an end, a bound'. In Cristóbal de las Casas's dictionary of 1570 the entry reads: 'Término o linde' [término or boundary]. Covarrubias gives the same definition: 'linde o lindera' [boundary or bounds], that is, the boundaries of fields dedicated to agriculture, but he adds at least two meanings more: 'tomase por el fin de cualquier cosa' [it is understood as the end of anything] and 'hombre de buen término, el que procede con cordura' [a man of good término, he who proceeds with good sense]. The *Diccionario de Autoridades* [Dictionary of Authorities] (1739) enriches or complicates the scenario: it gives some twenty accepted meanings which we can summarize as: 'fin de alguna cosa, material o inmaterial' [the material or immaterial end of something]; 'mojón que se pone para distinguir los límites' [boundary stone which is placed to mark limits]; 'forma o modo de portarse u hablar en el trato común' [form or way of everyday behaviour or speech], which is illustrated by Cervantes's *Persiles*: 'me trataron los cosarios con mejor término que mis ciudadanos' [the corsairs treated me better than my citizens]; 'distrito o espacio de tierra' [district or space of land], exemplified with a quote from *La Florida* (Book 4.1) of the Inca Garcilaso: 'Por mostrar que no temen vuestras armas, pues las vienen a buscar fuera de sus términos' [to show that they do not fear your arms, since they come to seek them beyond their boundaries]; 'paraje señalado o meta fija para algún fin' [indicated spot or fixed goal for some end]; 'tiempo determinado [...] muy usado en lo forense' [determinate amount of time [...] very common in legal speech]; 'límite o confín de un lugar o provincia con otra' [limit or confine of one place or province with another]; 'en sentido moral, se toma por el objeto determinado de cualquier operación' [in a moral sense, it is understood as the determined object of any operation]; 'la voz o palabra propia de alguna facultad u oficio' [the proper word for some faculty or office]; 'estado o constitución de alguna cosa' [state or constitution of something] and its uses in metaphysics, logic, medicine etc.

The weight of the word 'término' is evident in some fundamental episodes in Ercilla's poem, even where the lines do not refer, at least directly, to terrain or geography, but to military and political restraint. Such is the case in the young García Hurtado de Mendoza's speech to prevent the excesses and cruelty of his soldiers (canto 21), or in the narrator's moral condemnation of Spanish violence after the punishment of the Indian Galvarino (canto 26):

> que pasando los términos la ira
> pierde fuerza el derecho ya violado,
> pues cuando la razón no frena y tira
> el ímpetu y furor demasiado
> el rigor excesivo en el castigo
> justifica la causa al enemigo. (21.56)

> [since when anger passes beyond its boundaries
> the rights of the injured party lose their force,
> since when reason does not rein in and restrain
> the undue force and fury
> excessive rigour in inflicting punishment
> justifies the enemy's cause.]

> como los nuestros hasta allí cristianos
> que los términos lícitos pasando
> con crueles armas y actos inhumanos
> iban la gran vitoria deslustrando. (26.7)

> [just as our men, Christians up to that point,
> passing the bounds of legitimacy
> with cruel arms and inhumane acts
> were tarnishing the great victory.]

A quantitative examination of the use of the word *término* allows us to corroborate that in the third part of *La Araucana* — when Ercilla explores the confines of the world and his poem — its frequency is greater than in Pedro de Oña's *Arauco domado* (1596), Juan de Miramontes Zuázola's *Armas antárticas* (c. 1608) or Luís de Camões's *Os Lusíadas* (1572).[13] Furthermore, one can note an increase in its use between the first and third parts of Ercilla's poem.

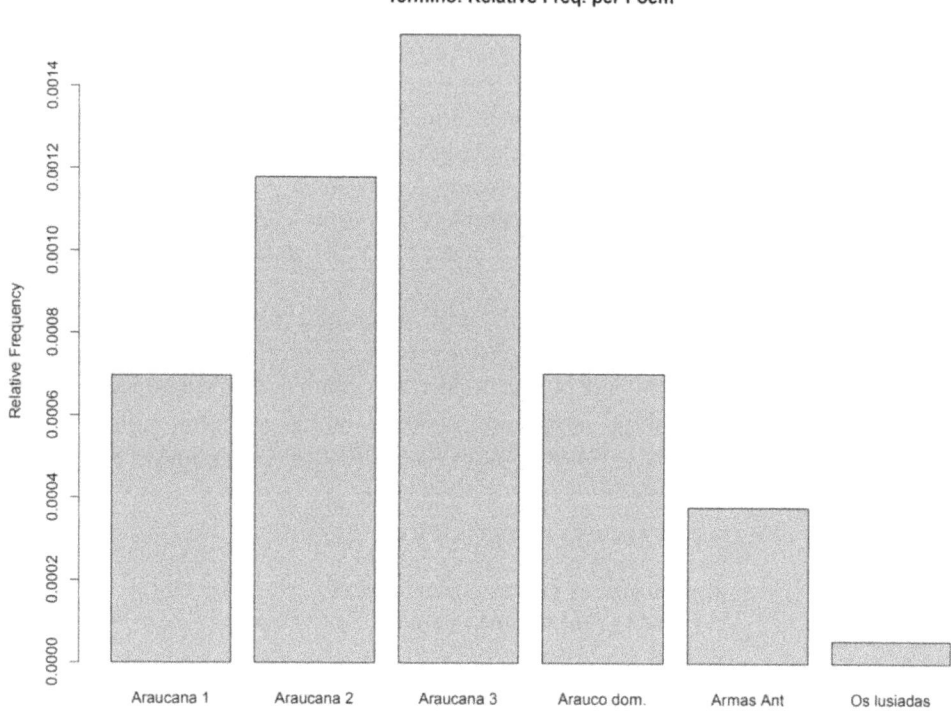

Término: Relative Freq. per Poem

Relative frequency of the use of the word *término* in four epic poems

Although I do not analyse Camões's poem here, it is worth observing the difference in usage of the words *término* and *termo* in the Portuguese in relation to Ercilla, despite sharing the same semantic field. In *Os Lusíadas*, the only four uses refer to cosmographical and naval transgressions, like the equator, the ends of the world or, in a moral sense, the limits of human deeds. One might conjecture that the absence of *términos* in a territorial sense in the Portuguese poem, so emphatic in *La Araucana*, reflects the fundamental difference in the Iberian colonial models during the sixteenth century: Portugal preferred coastal fortifications to penetrating inland.[14]

Some poetic uses of *término* might be exclusive to Ercilla, in that he intensifies the spatial-territorial sense of the word (the physical dimension) and connects it with its moral content, which is understood as an ideal of moderation. Ercilla himself links geography with the character of the Araucanians who, like the Spaniards, were 'amigos de domar estrañas gentes' [eager to subdue foreign peoples] (1.45). But, from the outset, the dominant meaning of 'término' refers to the indigenous territory or its geography. In the 1569 prologue, Ercilla indicates that the Araucanians only held 'veinte leguas de término' [twenty leagues of territory]; although, as he says in the poem, they held 'sujeto | lo más deste gran término' [subject most of this great region] (1.12). Still keeping the spatial sense, it is used to describe Araucanian strategies in war and how a squadron 'moverse de su término no puede' [cannot move from its formation] (1.24). Here the meaning now seems to confuse 'place' and 'condition'. And although the '[...] pena puesta | para aquel que del término saliese' [penalty imposed on anyone who strayed from their position] (4.96) refers to the prohibition imposed by Lautaro so that his men do not abandon their place on the battlefield, the transgression is not without a certain moral connotation. Likewise, when the conquistador Valdivia is captured by the Araucanians, the narrator describes Caupolicán's joy at seeing him 'en el estado y término presente' [in his present state and predicament] (3.64): the word brings together, not without productive overlaps, the condition, the place and the final outcome of the character.[15]

La Araucana shows other understandings of *término*, not related with the spatial-territorial dimension, where the breadth of semantic registers of this word can be noted: 'una cosa | que parece sin término notada' [something that might be noted which seems amiss] (2.37), which the narrator uses to draw the reader's attention to the Araucanian political system which lacked a 'cabeza señalada' [designated head]. The meaning here is close to 'mesura' [moderation], 'racionalidad' [rationality], as becomes clear in another line: 'sin término, sin causa y fundamento' [without término, without cause and foundation] (4.4). Such irrationality can also describe the climate and nature of the south, 'fuera de todo término y concierto' [beyond any bounds and order] (16.23). The 'desmesura' [excess] implicit in these examples adds a moral meaning to the territorial one and the word becomes loaded with reverberations in the poem. Thus, the 'término dudoso' [uncertain outcome], a phrase which is repeated four times in the first two parts, links the actual ending of a battle with the difficulty of its resolution: 'Renuévase el destrozo, reduciendo | a término dudoso el vencimiento' [The destruction is renewed, bringing | to an uncertain end the defeat] (26.18; see also 3.54).

The moral sense becomes clearer when it is closer to Covarrubias's *decoro*: as in the description of Lautaro, 'de gran consejo, término y cordura' [of great counsel, character and good sense] (3.87), or in the Araucanian senate: 'con término discreto' [proceeding wisely] (8.62). Its use in 'le fueron por sus términos narrando' [they were recalling him in their own way] (4.75) — when Valdivia's end is recounted among the Spaniards — refers to style and language and, in this way, also to *decoro*, as in the description of Colocolo's political ability, 'discurriendo por términos y modos | que redujo a su voto los de todos' [discoursing in such a way | that he brought everyone to vote his way] (21.21). The metapoetic octaves which open the eighteenth canto also reveal this link between *término* and *estilo*, or style. Ercilla apologizes for his ill judgement in daring too much: 'que salgo de los términos a tino' [I am fumbling around beyond my limits] (18.2).[16] If the thematic axis of the poem is the transgression of geographic and territorial *términos*, the transgression of poetic boundaries also gives a particular meta-narrative tension to the three parts of *La Araucana*.

Among the most clearly moral usages, that is, where the word *término* carries an adjective which qualifies the customs, behaviour, condition or state of characters or peoples, the following stand out: 'término alegre' [happy], 'alevoso' [treacherous], 'arrogante' [arrogant], 'discreto' [wise], 'desdeñoso' [disdainful], 'furioso' [furious], 'galante' [gallant], 'honesto' [honest], 'inhumano' [inhumane], 'insolente' [insolent], 'rabioso' [raging], 'sangriento' [bloody], 'sereno' [serene], 'terrible' [terrible]. For example, the poet describes the cacique of Ancud — as we shall see in due course — with curly black hair, a white face and 'grave término modesto' [solemn and modest bearing] (36.3).

In one of the most serious octaves in the whole poem, in canto 32, when it is demonstrated that the Spanish violence in Arauco has destroyed 'el esperado fruto de esta tierra' [the fruit hoped for from this land], the poet denounces — in almost Lascasian style — the way in which the Spanish conquests have, in their inhumanity, gone beyond 'las leyes y términos de guerra' [the laws and bounds of war] (32.4). This meaning, as with the *términos* of the metapoetic lines, also alludes to a collection of rules or ways of acting, to order and polity. We could, therefore, term this whole collection of lexical uses as a poetics of *términos*, defined by a basic tension between transgression and decorum.[17]

The ideal poetics of *términos* is, in practice, an exercise in transgressions, in the bounds of the battlefield, in moral restraint and in the norms of the genre. The poet and character Ercilla got too close to the human experience of war and, when he did so, he also transgressed the necessary distance and elevation of the heroic register.[18] In the epic, the demarcation of space, the production of territories which expand the imperial cartography, is fundamental. That process which symbolically defines the field of epic — the 'términos araucanos' [Araucanian bounds] of Ercilla or the 'américos linderos' [American borders] of Miramontes — can be termed *moral geography*.

The *términos* of the Expedition to Ancud

The expedition to the extreme south of the continent, 'al último confín' [to its furthest reach] (34.66), is probably one of the most poetically complex and elusive episodes of *La Araucana* (Fig. 9.1). It is central for the study and appreciation of Ercilla's many projects in his poem, and is something like the final outfall of the geographical and poetic *términos*.

The reader will remember that towards the end of the third part of *La Araucana*, immediately after the execution of Caupolicán, more than one hundred stanzas intervene (34.45 to 36.43) which narrate an expedition towards the Magellan Strait — deliberately imprecise in its coordinates — for the 'conquest' of another new world, once García Hurtado de Mendoza's men have arrived at the southern frontier of the State of Arauco: 'al término de Chile señalado' [to the allotted bound of Chile] (35.4), 'al término del orbe limitado' [to the ends of the known world] (35.5). From there, don García delivers a speech to inspire his soldiers, among them Ercilla, to take possession of 'nuevas provincias y regiones' [new provinces and regions] (35.8). This expedition will make the poet-soldier, for the first and only time, the protagonist and leader of the last advance. This therefore gives particularly intense scope for the construction of the poetic and historical 'yo' [I], within a poem which distinguishes itself precisely through its autobiographical character.

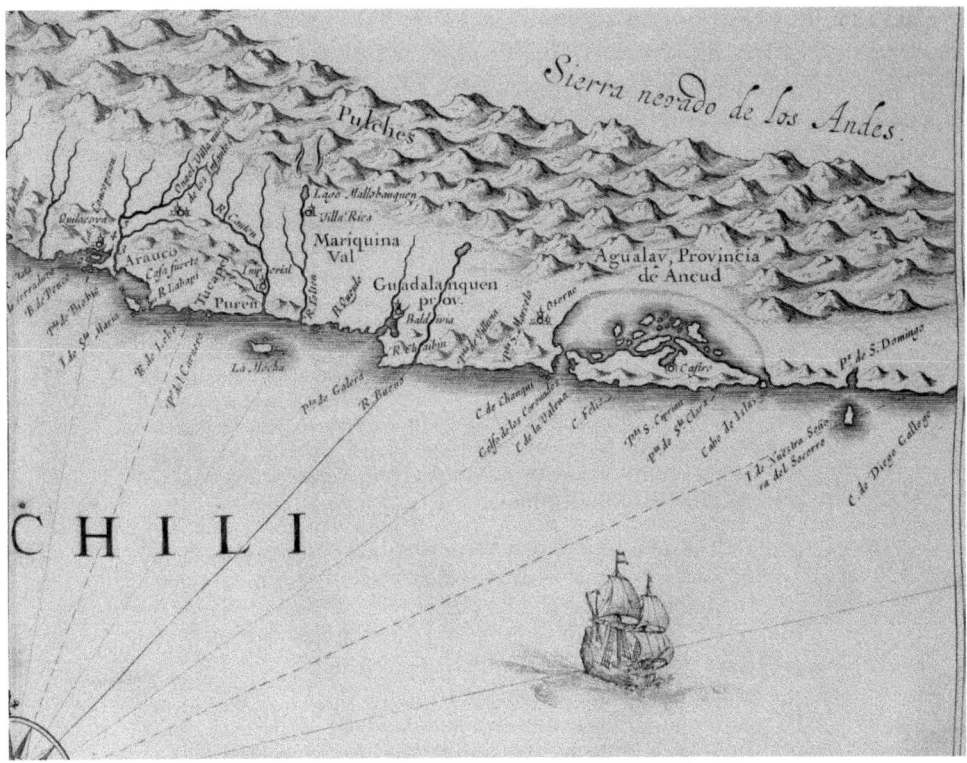

FIG. 9.1. Joan Blaeu, *America quae est Geographiae Blavianae pars quinta, liber unus, volumen undecimum* (Amsterdam: Joan Blaeu, 1662), map of Chili (detail). Courtesy of Special Collections and University Archives, Stony Brook University Libraries.

Critics have indicated that this long episode returns us to an original setting of conquest which recalls that of Columbus, with the bartering of glass beads and bells, and a narrative which has similarities to a *carta de relación*. Beatriz Pastor suggests that this episode condenses a whole century of representations of conquest from a position of 'crítica devastadora' [devastating critique] and shows 'una conciencia profundamente atormentada y dividida' [a profoundly tormented and divided conscience] in Ercilla.[19] The Magellan episode does indeed show the confrontation of the community values of a generous indigenous world and the destruction, evil and injustice of the war which the Spanish bring. The narrator assumes with the expression 'nosotros | destruyendo [...]' [we destroying] a moral tone and the blame for his modernity, expressed in the line 'plantó aquí la codicia su estandarte' [greed planted its standard here] (36.14). This entire episode, with its distance from the historical Araucanian frontier, allows Ercilla to unfold his poet–humanist vision and criticism of war, which might be confused with that of his indigenous characters. Thus, at the beginning of the expedition, the Indian Tunconabala refers to the Spaniards as 'barbudos crueles y terribles | del bien universal usurpadores' [cruel and terrible bearded men, usurpers of goods which are universal] (34.57) and later

on admonishes them to halt their advance and 'cudicia' [greed] (35.16). With his
direct speeches and his deceit — his theatrical display of poverty to dissuade the
Spanish — the Indian Tunconabala acquires something of the status of an author,
or stage director. This Indian, who reveals that he has been a soldier (35.18),
constructs for the Spanish a scene of human and geographical misery, presenting
himself with a company of Indians disguised as savages and an offering of wild fruits
and 'inmundas sabandijas' [filthy vermin] (35.20). The Spaniards remain, like us as
readers, astonished at this theatre:

> Admirónos la forma y la extrañeza
> de aquella gente bárbara notable,
> la gran selvatiquez y rustiqueza,
> el fiero aspecto y término intratable;
> la espesura de montes y aspereza
> y el fruto de aquel suelo miserable;
> tierra yerma, desierta y despoblada
> de trato y vecindad tan apartada. (35.21)

> [We were astonished at the form and strangeness
> of those remarkable barbarian people,
> their great savagery and rusticity,
> their fierce countenance and intractable condition;
> the thickness and ruggedness of the woods
> and the fruits of that impoverished soil;
> a barren, deserted and depopulated land
> so isolated from human contact and exchange.]

In the centre of this stanza is the 'término intratable' [intractable condition] which
describes the radically indecorous condition of the Indians. In the last line there is
an insistence on the 'trato y vecindad tan apartada' [isolation from human contact
and exchange] of this region which cannot be easily placed on the imperial map.
The stanza conveniently brings together moral and geographical terms, thus
participating in the politico-spatial order of early modernity. 'Trato' and 'término'
seem to become confused, as one can also read in one of the meanings quoted above
from the *Diccionario de Autoridades*, with the example of the *Persiles*. Both words fit
in the semantic field of customs or moral history. In the same sense, the Ancud or
Magellan episode expands the humanistic perspective that appears in other places
in the poem, but which here is presented explicitly as a truth which the poet finds
on 'el suelo' [the ground] (36.1) and which — as I understand it — refers to the
ethnographic register of 'ritos, ceremonias y costumbres' [rites, ceremonies and
customs] (36.20) and moral geography.

When the poet-soldier finally comes to know Ancud, 'el espacioso y fértil raso'
[the spacious and fertile plain] (35.40) which Tunconabala had taken pains to protect
from the Spanish advance, the inhabitants demonstrate a truth opposed to the
previous deceptive scene. A young and generous cacique offers them aid and lands.
The lines seem to present the reverse image to the previous scene. The inhabitants
of Ancud are notable for their size and bearing, their white colouring, their clothes
and their speech, as if they brought to the fore the concepts of *decoro* and *urbanidad*

which circulated in the cities of Iberia from the end of the sixteenth century. The young cacique also expresses himself with fluency and ease, demonstrating 'estilo' [style], with 'expedido término y lenguaje' [graceful *término* and language], like a court poet:

> Mucho agradó la suerte, el garbo, el traje
> del gallardo mancebo floreciente,
> el expedido término y lenguaje
> con que así nos habló bizarramente;
> el franco ofrecimiento y hospedaje,
> la buena traza y talle de su gente,
> blanca, dispuesta, en proporción fornida
> de manto y floja túnica vestida. (36.7)

> [The appearance, the garb, the dress
> of the handsome, blooming young man were all attractive,
> the ease of his language and expression
> with which he gallantly addressed us;
> the generous offering and hospitality,
> the good size and appearance of his people,
> white, well-proportioned, strongly built,
> dressed in a cloak and loose tunic.]

This complex Magellan episode of *La Araucana* connects, in its own terms, the epic register with the Utopian treatise, although this is not the place for that study. The main interest in these pages has been to analyse the *términos* of the poem. Ercilla's use of keywords within the epic genre can be considered an indicator — or a symptom — of some new socio-historical orders experienced by him as a courtier and veteran in Madrid. They express the poetic and political aspirations of Ercilla during some thirty years, from his experience in the Americas to the publication of the third part of his book. The expedition to Ancud is, among many other things, a journey of poetic experimentation and an examination of the limits of his work.[20]

José Toribio Medina studied Ercilla's journey to the Magellan region in a classic article of 1913. Medina — alongside almost the entire critical tradition to date — was certain that this episode had been published for the first time in the posthumous edition of 1597 (Ercilla died in 1594), overseen by Ercilla's widow and the editor Vares de Castro. At the time of Medina, the few copies of *La Araucana* published in 1589 and 1590 in which were 'interpolated' — according to some — the 115 stanzas that narrate the Magellan expedition were not known.[21] I have not yet been able to consult any of these four rare copies studied by Juan Alberto Méndez Herrera, Ángel Álvarez Vilela and Miguel Martínez. Recent works, based on the unpublished thesis of Méndez Herrera, demonstrate that the 115 stanzas were added to the 1589 and 1590 editions by the poet himself during the printing process in the workshop of Pedro Madrigal, in Madrid.[22] Although no scholar has questioned the authorship of these verses, José Durand considered them to be 'viejos borradores que Ercilla desechó hacia 1589' [old drafts which Ercilla discarded around 1589] and suggested that critical editions of the poem should restore the text to its original thirty-five cantos, closing the story with the death of Caupolicán.[23]

The complex problem of the editorial history of the third part of *La Araucana* is directly implicated in the questions about the *poetics of términos*. It is significant here that the cantos on the expedition to Ancud occupied an unstable position in the structure of the poem. Whether we consider them last-minute additions, old drafts discarded by the author or fragments of a fourth part, they appear to be a problem for the author himself. In a structural sense, the expedition to Ancud functions in a similar way to the episodes of Belona or Fitón (in the second part), that is, as flights from the dominant historiographical register. It is also a testimony to the limit of a field of experimentation in the poetics of the epic, where the exercise of both narrating and walking as a soldier had reached their end: geography and poetry were touching their boundaries.[24] In the aforementioned article of 1913, Medina writes that 'Ercilla hasta en sus últimos días veía trabajado su espíritu por los recuerdos de una expedición que marcaba el último límite a que alcanzó en su azarosa vida de aventuras de viaje' [Even in his final days, Ercilla's spirit was exercised by the memories of an expedition which marked the extreme limit his eventful life of travelling adventures reached].[25] That expedition and adventure were not only the office of a soldier, but also of a poet.

Furthermore, the disputed placement of these 115 stanzas in the editions of *La Araucana* (which increased the total number of cantos from 35 to 37) is interesting for the early reception of Ercilla's texts in the viceroyalty of Peru and the Kingdom of Chile, and for the extraordinary importance that the Magellan Strait acquired towards the end of the sixteenth century. Álvarez Vilela argues — without adducing any proof to this effect — that the augmented copies of the 1589 and 1590 editions were made for America.[26] If, as this author imagines, those lines circulated in Lima and their purpose was to undermine or silence the actions of García Hurtado de Mendoza and offer, instead, the protagonism of Ercilla in the Magellan expedition, it would be inexplicable for Pedro de Oña in his *Arauco domado* not to have taken up the episode again, to correct it, expand it and introduce Don García's actions, especially in the foundation of the city of Osorno, which took place precisely during that expedition. However, as Durand pertinently reminds us, Oña's vindication is made 'conociendo tan solo la versión en treintaicinco cantos' [familiar only with the version in thirty-five cantos].[27]

The expedition to Ancud — whether historical or fictional — throws up nothing but losses and achieves no productive result for the imperial machinery, but it is one of the best poetic episodes of the whole work, extremely rich in its possible contacts with other genres and autobiography, and with old humanistic topics actualized by the American experience. In that sense, it contributes to symbolically mapping out the region. However, since it did not register any direct benefits and situated the poet-soldier in the unofficial position of *adelantado* — carving on the bark of a tree, at the end of the world, a physical testimony of his location, which becomes one of the stanzas of the poem (36.29) — Ercilla must have doubted the pertinence of including this episode. In some ways, the account transgressed not only the territorial limits over which the poem ranged (the Araucanian state), but it also left behind its *poetic términos*. As well as doubts over the validity of this episode, we can imagine that Ercilla was confronting the problem of how to close an epic poem, and how to do so in relation to his autobiography. And if, indeed, as Méndez Herrera affirms, the stanzas on Ancud were added by the poet himself in the printer's workshop, it is necessary to ask ourselves about the motives of that act: were they reasons internal to the poem or historical forces that led Ercilla to insert more than a hundred extra stanzas?

Towards the end of the sixteenth century, the region around the Magellan Strait was acquiring greater centrality in European imperial circles. It was to remain, however, a territory which Spain could not claim with the legitimacy of occupation, especially after the tragic attempts of the governor Sarmiento de Gamboa to establish colonies on the Strait in the 1580s. It isn't difficult to imagine an encounter between Sarmiento and Ercilla in Madrid between 1590 and 1591 or that the author of *La Araucana* read some of Sarmiento's manuscript letters or *relaciones* around 1589, and that the decision to insert the episode of Ancud reflected, in that sense, the politics of the court and its forms.[28] In any case, the story of Ercilla's octaves, his poetics and politics continue to pose questions and stimulate our critical imagination. Ercilla's lines, his words and narratives, and his indirect reflection on the politics of the Catholic Monarchy, found in the remote world of the south a space to expand. The intense and varied uses of the word *término* in that context reveal the poetic operations of Ercilla, his connections with the ideals of courtly decorum and urbanity and his insertion into a network of practices, discourses and technologies of power in which his moral geography participates; but they also show us the limits and 'términos excesivos' (34.17) of that machinery, and the flight and loss of the 'yo' in the regions of poetry and in the uncertain *términos* where in 'cómoda estanza' (36.11) — the comfortable place of poetry itself — the soldiers rest.

Notes to Chapter 9

1. I am grateful to the participants of the conference 'Poets of the New World', held at the University of Cambridge in 2015, for their comments on the first version of this piece, to Javier Uriarte for his careful reading and suggestions, and to Imogen Choi for the translation, reviewed by the author.

2. The neo-Aristotelian poetics of the period noted three forms of imitation: when the poet used his own voice, when the characters spoke without the mediation of the poet, or when these two ways of imitating alternated. See Alonso López Pinciano, *Philosofía antigua poética*, ed. by José Rico Verdú (Madrid: Biblioteca Castro, 1998), pp. 139–40, 450. The first form corresponded to lyric poetry, the second to theatre, and the third to epic. The mixed character of the epic allowed long episodes, such as indigenous monologues, to function like theatrical scenes. On the relationship between genres and spaces, Thomas Greene has noted that the epic ideal is expansive and extends over spaces to dominate them; both tragedy and comedy, by contrast, operate in more restricted or closed spaces. See Thomas M. Greene, *The Descent from Heaven: A Study in Epic Continuity* (New Haven, CT: Yale University Press, 1970), pp. 10–17. In as much as epic poetry reproduces the imitative techniques of theatre (I refer here to the Golden Age comedia), the open spaces get, to some degree, reduced to dramatic scenes and the geography is transformed into scenography, which can facilitate the symbolic control of large territories.

3. Alonso de Ercilla, *La Araucana*, ed. by Marcos Morínigo and Isaías Lerner, 2 vols (Madrid: Castalia, 1979). I always quote from this edition, indicating the canto and octave number. Translations are Imogen Choi's.

4. In the second part of the poem, the surname Peña is mentioned twice, in two almost identical octaves which repeat two hendecasyllables, in cantos 22.25 and 26.26, where Ercilla gives a list of Spanish warriors. Although the name possibly has a historical referent (perhaps Francisco Peña de la Fuente, according to Morínigo and Lerner's index), it seems that the author also uses it out of poetic convenience. Lerner in his edition of the poem (Madrid: Cátedra, 1993) notes the etymologizing repetition of line 5.40e, p. 211.

5. Sarah Dichy-Malherme, 'El primer canto de *La Araucana*: una cartografía épica de Chile', *Criticón*, 115 (2012), 85–104.

6. Dichy-Malherme, 'El primer canto', p. 102. As we shall see, Ricardo Padrón also analyses La Araucana as a cartographic poem in *The Spacious Word, Cartography, Literature, and Empire in Early Modern Spain* (Chicago, IL, and London: University of Chicago Press, 2004), p. 44.

7. There is no doubt that the publication of Luís de Camões's *Os Lusíadas* in 1572 influenced the second and third parts of *La Araucana* (1578 and 1589). Camões personified in his poem the resistance of African nature — the promontory of the Cape of Good Hope — in the figure of the giant Adamastor. Although the poem of Ercilla didn't construct a similar figure, partly because his poetic always stayed closer to the historiographical register, the long scene of the poet's voyage to the extreme South — which we will comment on in due course — is an intense poetic exploration of geography.

8. Juan de Valdés, *Diálogo de la lengua*, ed. by José Enrique Laplana (Barcelona: Crítica, 2010), p. 224.

9. Maxime Chevalier, 'Decoro y decoros', *Revista de Filología Española*, 73.1/2 (1993), 5–24.

10. Chevalier, 'Decoro', p. 6.

11. David Mañero Lozano, 'Del concepto de decoro a la "teoría de los estilos"', *Bulletin Hispanique*, 111.2 (2009), 357–85 (p. 360). Mañero summarizes the different spheres of decorum: 1) moral; 2) literary, that is, 'la adecuación de las acciones, palabras, etc., a la caracterización de los personajes' [the adjustment of actions, words, etc., to characterization]; and 3) rhetorical, 'concordancia de elementos que conforman el discurso' [agreement between the elements which make up the discourse], p. 360. Lozano studies the evolution of the concept from Aristotle, for whom the distinct poetic genres were defined by the moral condition of the characters. In sixteenth-century modernity, the classic meaning of decorum did not exert a real pressure on the development of new 'polyphonic' genres like the Renaissance novel or minor theatre, p. 378. We might add that the Spanish literary epic, particularly that on American historical themes, although it affiliated itself with classical models, was in fact dominated by the successful formula of Ariosto.

12. See Nicolás Wey Gómez, *Tropics of Empire: Why Columbus Sailed South to the Indies* (Cambridge, MA: MIT Press, 2008), who studies geographical and climatological features associated with human customs and behaviour in the early texts of colonialism.

13. I have used online versions of the three parts of Ercilla's poem (Colección Averroes), Oña (Espapdf.com) and Camões (Instituto da Biblioteca Nacional); for Miramontes I have worked with my own transcription. The calculation is approximate; relative frequencies are rounded to five decimal places. In the first part of *La Araucana* the word 'término' is used 42 times (total word count = 60,277, relative frequency = 0.00070); 65 in the second (total word count = 55,165, relative frequency = 0.00118), and 50 in the third (total word count = 32,799, relative frequency = 0.00152). I include the 115 stanzas recounting the expedition to Ancud in the third part. In the whole poem it is used 157 times (total word count = 148,241, frequency of use = 0.00106, that is, a little over one in a thousand). In *Arauco domado* it is used 73 times (total word count = 104,064, relative frequency = 0.00070); in *Armas antárticas*, 33 times (total word count = 87,299, relative frequency = 0.00038). In *Os Lusíadas*, 'términos' is used three times and 'termos' once. I am grateful to Nicolás Firbas for his help with the calculations and diagram.

14. The four uses in *Os Lusíadas* are as follows: '[...] que foi buscar da roxa Aurora | os términos que eu vou buscando agora'[he left to seek the ends of the red Dawn which I am now seeking] (4.60); 'o término ardente ja passado' [the burning limit (of the equator) now passed] (5.13); 'os vedados términos quebrantas' [you are breaking forbidden boundaries] (5.41); 'que não passen o termo limitado' [let them not pass the appointed boundary] (6.27). I use the following edition:

Lusíadas, Comentadas por Manuel de Faria e Sousa [facsimile of Madrid, 1639], 2 vols (Lisbon: Imprensa Nacional — Casa da Moeda, 1972).

15. Compare with another two lines from *La Araucana*, referring to Flanders, in which the proximity between 'estado' [state], 'condición' [condition] and 'término' is made more explicit: 'trayendo a estado y condición las cosas | que durarán gran término dudosas' [bringing things to such a state and condition that for a long time they will be precarious] (18.47). Tegualda stresses her beloved Crepino's lineage and his 'condición y término loable' [laudable condition and conduct] (20.70).

16. The expression 'a tino' is equivalent to 'a tientas' [blindly], as Isaías Lerner notes in his edition of *La Araucana*, p. 518.

17. In Pedro de Oña's *Arauco domado* there are similar uses to those of Ercilla, both in the territorial meaning and in the moral: 'término cortés' [courteous bearing], 'término discreto' [wise conduct], etc. Oña also uses 'término' to mean 'style': 'mostrando estilo, término y lenguaje' [demonstrating style, conduct and language] (canto 17.65), or 'sin límite, sin término, sin modo' [without limit, without *término*, without method] (canto 11.99); and 'por tierno estilo y término amoroso' [in tender style and amorous vein] (canto 5.25), where it now belongs to the field of courtesy and urbanity. I use two editions of *Arauco domado*: the unpublished thesis of Victoria Pehl Smith (University of California, Berkeley, 1984); and the critical edition of Ornella Gianesin of the University of Pavia (Pavia: Ibis, 2014), from which I quote.

18. On the distance between the poet and his material, necessary for heroic elevation, see Paul Firbas, 'El sueño en la trama épica: la visión corográfica de San Quintín en *La Araucana* de Alonso de Ercilla', in *Los sueños en la cultura iberoamericana siglos XVI–XVIII*, ed. by Sonia Rose (Madrid: CSIC, 2011), pp. 385–407; and the introductory study to my edition of Juan de Miramontes Zuázola, *Armas antárticas* (Lima: Pontificia Universidad Católica del Perú, 2006), p. 74.

19. Beatriz Pastor, *Discurso narrativo de la conquista de América* (La Habana: Ediciones Casa de las Américas, 1983), pp. 540, 547. Pastor argues for an ideological rupture in Ercilla: 'ha dejado de poder identificarse plenamente con una concepción del mundo propia de la Europa del siglo XVI, sin poder, por ello, pasar a integrarse a una realidad histórica y cultural americana' [he has stopped being able to identify fully with a conception of the world which is that of sixteenth-century Europe, without being able to take the leap to be integrated in an American historical and cultural reality], reading in the poet the 'emergencia de una conciencia hispanoamerica' [emergence of a Hispano-American consciousness], pp. 547, 566. If we accept this argument, we would also have to accord a similar consciousness to Camões, bearing in mind the episode of the old man of Restelo in *Os Lusíadas*. The critique of greed, of Latin antecedents, could also reveal a conservative and elite ideological position; but, as Jaime Concha indicated, the reality of the American conquest gave a concrete socio-historical meaning to an old topic. In *La Araucana* greed becomes a structuring principle of the poem, according to Elizabeth B. Davis, *Myth and Identity in the Epic of Imperial Spain* (Columbia: University of Missouri Press, 2000), pp. 65–66. Ricardo Padrón has studied the Magellan episode as a parody of the genre of *cartas de relación*, with references to Lucian and Ariosto, and a form in which the poet pokes fun at his own identity as soldier and historian (*The Spacious Word*, p. 227).

20. Padrón has also studied *La Araucana* as cartographic literature. In his insightful interpretation of the cartographic strategies of the poem, he concentrates on the multiple meanings of 'estrecho' [narrow, tight; strait, channel] and 'estrecheza' [narrowness, confinement, predicament] to understand the articulation of masculine imperial desire, whose major trope is the unattainable penetration of the Magellan Strait (*The Spacious Word*, pp. 196–201). I believe that 'término' is another of those concepts, of broad register, which serve to encapsulate some of the central drives of the poetics of *La Araucana*. Indicating its proximity with 'decoro' also shows the ideals of the courtly culture of the author.

21. The doctoral thesis of Juan Alberto Méndez Herrera is still unpublished (Harvard University, 1976). I am familiar with it thanks to the study of Ángel Álvarez Vilela, 'La expedición a Ancud en *La Araucana* o la recuperación del mérito por parte de Ercilla', *Anales de Literatura Hispanoamericana*, 24 (1995), 77–89; and for the mention included in a note in José Durand's

article, 'La Araucana en sus 35 cantos originales', Anuario de Letras, 16 (1978), 291–94 (p. 293). According to Álvarez Vilela's summary of Méndez Herrera's thesis, the 'interpolated' or added stanzas have been identified in three copies of the Madrid octavo edition of 1590 and in one of the quarto editions of 1589 ('La expedición', p. 82). See also Miguel Martínez, 'Writing on the Edge: The Poet, the Printer, and the Colonial Frontier in Ercilla's La Araucana (1569–1590)', Colonial Latin American Review, 26.2 (2017), 132–53.

22. Martínez, 'Writing on the Edge', pp. 141–43

23. Durand, 'La Araucana en sus 35 cantos originales', pp. 293–94.

24. On the parallels between narrating and walking, see Cedomil Goiç, 'Poetización del espacio, espacios de la poesía', in La cultura literaria en la América virreinal: concurrencias y diferencias, ed. by José Pascual Buxó (Mexico City: Universidad Nacional Autónoma de México, 1996), pp. 13–25. In the hurried return journey from Ancud, for example, the poet says 'voy pasando por esto a toda prisa' [I am passing by all this with great haste] (36.31). It is possible that the remote southern expanse, being a poetic fiction, had some minimal historical basis.

25. José Toribio Medina, 'El viaje de Ercilla al Estrecho de Magallanes', Revista Chilena de Historia y Geografía, 6.10 (1913), 343–95 (p. 357).

26. This argument of Álvarez Vilela merited a note in James Nicolopulos's The Poetics of Empire in the Indies: Prophecy and Imitation in 'La Araucana' and 'Os Lusíadas' (University Park: Pennsylvania State University Press, 2000), p. 272: '[he] gives no indication of how he arrives at this conclusion'.

27. Durand, 'La Araucana en sus 35 cantos originales', p. 293. What edition or editions of La Araucana were read in America by Juan de Miramontes Zuázola or Diego Arias de Saavedra? How did Ercilla's poem influence the representation of the Magellan region in Armas antárticas or Purén indómito (c. 1603), respectively? Miramontes recounts that on entering the Strait, Sarmiento de Gamboa went on 'a ver la playa y términos postreros | de los nuevos américos linderos' [to see the beach and furthest limits of the new American borders] (octava 1519), lines which recall the 'término américo indiano' [American Indian limit] of La Araucana (34.3), printed in the standard 35-canto version from 1589. A study is necessary to document, as far as possible, which versions of Ercilla's poem were read by American poets at the end of the sixteenth and beginning of the seventeenth centuries.

28. After a storm blew him away from the Strait, where his hundreds of unfortunate colonists remained, Sarmiento de Gamboa was in Brazil, London and Paris, until he was taken prisoner by the Huguenots in France from the end of 1586 until 1590. From his pitiful confinement, Sarmiento sent letters to the Spanish court begging for his rescue and that of the colonists of the Strait, and imagining a new expedition to the south. He returned to Spain in 1590, and from the court continued to write on his plans to travel to the Magellan Strait. We know that at the end of 1591 he worked as the censor of the Elegías de varones ilustres de Indias [Elegies of Illustrious Men of the Indies], an epic poem by Juan de Castellanos, and published a sonnet in the preliminaries of the translations of Petrarch accomplished by the Portuguese Enrique Garcés, a long-term resident of Peru. Considering the American connection of both men and their work as literary censors, it would not be strange for Ercilla and Sarmiento to have met, but I do not know of any documentation which proves this. See José Miguel Barros Franco, 'Los últimos años de Sarmiento de Gamboa', Estudios de Historia Social y Económica de América, 3/4 (1988), 9–28; and Paul Firbas, 'Saberes hemisféricos: Sarmiento de Gamboa y sus textos sobre el estrecho de Magallanes', Anales de Literatura Chilena, 16 (2016), 41–57.

CHAPTER 10

Land and Sea in Juan de Castellanos

Luis Fernando Restrepo

Juan de Castellanos's monumental epic *Elegías de varones ilustres de Indias* [Elegies of Illustrious Men of the Indies] is a four-part text that tells the story of the conquest of the Caribbean and northern South America (present day Colombia and Venezuela).[1] Its broad geographical reach is paired with an equally ample historical framework, narrating events from Columbus's first voyage in 1492 to the 1590s urban disturbances in Tunja after the imposition of the royal sales tax [*alcabalas*]. Despite the formal symmetry of its more than one hundred thousand hendecasyllabic lines, composed for the most part in *octavas reales*, it is a highly heterogeneous text that incorporates multiple literary and non-literary genres in addition to the epic.[2] It also includes elegies, eulogies, ballads, pastoral, epigraphs, shipwreck narratives, stories of captivity, pilgrimage tales, maroon narratives, expedition accounts [*relaciones*], testimonies [*probanzas*], histories, chronicles, letters, chorographic descriptions, maps and illustrated plates.[3] Thematically, it describes the American landscape, its flora and fauna, as well as its ethnographic diversity. The major elements are the narratives of conquest and inter-ethnic warfare, and other historical events such as founding of cities, Aguirre's rebellion and Drake's attack on Cartagena. As a *probanza de méritos y servicios* [legal petition for royal favours for the services rendered], the *Elegías* highlights individual participation in the conquest of the Spaniards and identifies their heirs. The text is also rich in details of daily life. These heterogeneous elements make it a text that cannot be reduced to one genre. Here, the monumental blends with the everyday, the literary with the legal, the theological with the scientific, and *eros* with *tanatos*. The initial plan seemed to comprise a gallery of historical narratives dedicated to the lives of the great men in the conquest of America, drawing from the epic, the classical historical tradition as *magistra vitae* and Renaissance funeral elegy. In the first part, the text is organized into fourteen elegies, each divided into a variable number of cantos. After the first part, the text is composed of elegies, eulogies, *relaciones*, histories, catalogues and discourses, organized mostly geographically, narrating the history of the provinces in the jurisdiction of the *audiencia* [administrative centre] of Santa Fe de Bogotá.[4]

The complexity of this text is a living testimony to the effort to endow with meaning the Iberian interactions with unknown peoples and lands and to justify colonial violence. The crux of the matter is that the Atlantic expansion of imperial Iberia constituted a spatial revolution that tested the limits of the European conceptual frameworks for understanding the world. We can turn to literature to better understand the impact of this spatial revolution in the Hispanic worldview, where we can find concrete efforts to give form and meaning to the world in times of deep changes. With its tales of sea voyages and territorial conquests, the epic, in particular, provides us with valuable insights to better understand the transformations of Iberian culture throughout the ages.

In this chapter, I will concentrate on the representation of the land and the sea in *Elegías*. I contend that, despite its transoceanic reach, Castellanos's poem affirms a land-centred culture. Written in the Indies by a *baquiano* [veteran resident], the perspective of the *Elegías* is more regional than imperial, in contrast to Alonso de Ercillas's *La Araucana*.[5] The sea, nonetheless, has a significant presence in *Elegías*. It is an element with great poetic plasticity that allows the author to express the uncertainties of human life, where storms and other catastrophic events bring forth reflections regarding God's intervention in human affairs and the consequences of individual actions (free will). Thus, through a close look at its representations of the land and the sea, the *Elegías* offers valuable insights into the geographical imagination of the early modern colonial world. I will begin by examining two illustrations from the *Elegías* that highlight its heterogeneous texture and its geopolitical axis, the New Kingdom of Granada. Next, I will focus on the representations of the land and sea in the *Elegías*.

Colonial Territories, Satanic Epics and Holy Empires

In *Puritan Conquistadors*, historian Jorge Cañizares-Esguerra offers a pan-hemispheric perspective that documents the demonological and providential discourses that informed both Iberian and British colonialism, challenging the common perception that the British colonial enterprise was more modern and secular than the *Reconquista* mentality of Iberian colonialism.[6] The book thus debunks an important myth of American exceptionalism, demonstrating that 'the Puritan colonization of New England was as much an epic, crusading act of *reconquista* (against the devil) as was the Spanish conquest' (p. 31). In a chapter titled 'The Satanic Epic', Cañizares-Esguerra provides a sweeping overview of Iberian, English, American, Italian, Dutch and Flemish epics that operate with a common frame of mind, a siege mentality casting European colonialism as a holy war against the devil. The demonic discourse is adapted to fit specific political needs, targeting the obstacles to colonization, from a satanic landscape to the demonization of different peoples, including Amerindians, rival European forces and pirates. In this view, Cañizares-Esguerra (pp. 35–82) casts under the same 'satanic' matrix multiple epics, including Castellanos's *Elegías*, José de Anchieta's *De gestis Mendi de Saa* [The Deeds of Mendi de Saa], Alonso de Ercilla's *La Araucana*, Luís de Camões's *Os Lusíadas*, Torquato Tasso's *Gerusalemme liberata* [Jerusalem Liberated], John White's *The Planters' Plea*, and John Milton's *Paradise Lost*. Cañizares-Esguerra affirms:

> I could continue almost endlessly my analysis of the dozen of epic poems written
> about Iberian America in the late sixteenth and early seventeenth centuries,
> describing the historical adventures of liberating Christian conquistador heroes
> against Indians, Spaniards, *conversos*, pirates, and Nature. All of them, however,
> follow the same basic structure, with the conquest of the New World cast as a
> cosmic struggle pitting God against Satan. (p. 49)

This reading is true to some extent, but it is so schematic that the Latin American
historian changes his stance a few lines after this statement to address the complexity
of the New World epics, where beautiful Amerindian heroines mourn fallen
comrades and courageous natives demonstrate their prowess in battle (p. 49). With
this more reasonable approach that pays attention to the texts' complexities, we
can revisit the interpretation of the *Elegías* advanced by Cañizares-Esguerra, who
opens the chapter of the 'satanic epics' with a close and very erudite reading of the
frontispiece of the first edition (Fig. 10.1).

In this frontispiece the allegorical faithful maiden representing Spain ('Hispania
Virgo fidelis') is depicted slaying the dragon of the New World in a composition
that places Philip II, with his motto of *plus ultra*, as ruler of the world and defender
of the Church. The Holy Spirit and an angel descend upon the world. The
American landscape (palm, jaguar, turkey, monkey and parrot) is complemented
by the Old World landscape (a city, olive tree, peacock, bird). The illustration has
several biblical references written in Latin in the branches, the allegorical figure,
and emblems. Inscriptions such as 'Misericordia Dei plena est terra' [The world
is full of God's mercy] can be found in the plate. Glossing these inscriptions in
detail, Cañizares-Esguerra draws attention to the use of typology in the Spanish
colonization of the New World (p. 35). After analysing the image, Cañizares-
Esguerra concludes:

> This frontispiece makes explicit the biblical implication for the holy violence
> unleashed by the Spaniards on the natives. Colonization becomes a fulfillment
> of Biblical, apocalyptic prophecies, and act of liberation and wrathful divine
> punishment. *But there were more than biblical roots to the Spanish colonization, which
> was also mediated by classical texts.* (p. 37, my emphasis)

The biblical and imperial frameworks are certainly important elements of the
Elegías as Cañizares-Esguerra argues, but an analysis that goes beyond the initial
illustration and the encomiastic poems will find a heterogeneous text that, drawing
from multiple literary genres and other sources, seeks to make sense of the new
world and the colonization from the conquistadors' point of view. This regional
perspective, more humanist than providential, is evident when we take a closer look
at the first canto in the First Part and a map that was included in the third part:

> A cantos elegíacos levanto
> con débiles acentos voz anciana,
> bien como blanco cisne que con canto
> su muerte soleniza ya cercana.
>> (Castellanos, *Elegías*, p. 17)

Fig. 10.1. Juan de Castellanos, *Primera parte de las elegías de varones ilustres de Indias* (Madrid: En casa de la viuda de Alonso Gómez, 1589), frontispiece. Courtesy of the Hispanic Society of America (New York).

[In elegiac cantos I raise
in weakened notes my aged voice
as a white swan chants
its solemn death that nears]

The first elegy expresses the poet's concern for his own mortality. Seeking to make his death more honourable he sets out to tell the multiple stories of the great deeds of the conquistadors: 'Orbe de Indias es el que me llama | a sacar del sepulcro del olvido | a quien merece bien eterna fama' [The world of Indies calls me | to bring from the sepulchre of oblivion | those who well deserve eternal fame] (p. 17). The main humanist tenets are at work here: concern for life in this world, the cultivation of virtue and fame by deeds (conquistadors) and the arts (the poet). Looking at the whole poem, the monarch glorified in the frontispiece becomes a tacit reference in a text that yields the stage to the forgotten brave men that conquered the Indies, a nostalgic look at a glorious past that is also distant from the eschatological perspective of the frontispiece: 'Aquí se contarán casos terribles, | recuentos y proezas soberanas: | muertes, riesgos, trabajos invencibles [Here we will tell terrible events, | great tales and deeds: | deaths, danger, invincible undertakings] (p. 17). The timing of the poem is also important to note, as I argued in *Un nuevo reino imaginado* (pp. 75–120).

Briefly stated, Castellanos wrote the epic at the end of the sixteenth century, when the conquistadors and their heirs were losing the power and prestige that they enjoyed in the early decades after the conquest. Rewarded by the Crown for their services in the conquest with *encomiendas* and administrative posts, the first *encomenderos* [trustees of tribute] became a powerful group controlling land grants and Amerindian tribute and labour. By the end of the sixteenth century, a growing number of Crown officials and merchants had arrived in the Indies, gaining importance in colonial society. Seeking to affirm greater control of the affairs of the Indies and increase royal revenue, the Crown was placing a number of restrictions on the *encomienda* grants, which were also losing importance due to the drastic decline in the Amerindian population, reduced to one tenth in less than a century of Spanish occupation.[7] In this historical juncture, Castellanos appealed to the epic tradition to advocate for the respect and recognition that he considered that the first conquistadors and their descendants deserved. For this task, Castellanos drew on the recognition that the conquest of Chile had enjoyed with the publication of the first part of *La Araucana* in 1569. In the prologue of the fourth part, Castellanos admitted that he had imitated Ercilla to please his friends who were delighted by the sweet style of the poet of the conquest of Chile. However, Castellanos's imitation of Ercilla must be viewed critically, as Emiro Martínez Osorio argues: 'Critics who take the reference to Ercilla at face value overlook the fact that almost every time Castellanos borrows from or alludes to Ercilla, he does so through an iconoclastic impulse that calls for the immediate transformation of the model or its complete rejection'.[8] There is a marked ideological gap between both epic poets. Closer to the royal court than to the conquistadors and *encomenderos*, Ercilla defended the civilizing mission of Spanish colonialism and the legality of the conquest as a just war. Ercilla, nonetheless, is critical of the abuses of the conquistadors and their inability to defend colonial cities like Concepción, as canto VII of *La Araucana* suggests, when all the Spanish men abandon in panic the city besieged by Amerindians. Castellanos takes another direction. Instead of praising Ercilla, the poet of the New Kingdom of Granada is setting the record straight and restoring the honour of the conquistador group.

Another element of the *Elegías* where the text goes beyond the biblical frame of the frontispiece is in the map that Castellanos included in the third part of *Elegías* (Fig. 10.2). The map is titled *Traça chorographica de lo contenido en los tres braços que çerca de la [Equinoccial] haze la cordillera de las Sierras que se continuan desde el estrecho de [Magallanes]* [Describing the three branches of the Andean mountain range near the Equinoctial line which extends from the Magellan Strait].[9]

The *Traça* provides an overview of the territory of the central Andes in the New Kingdom of Granada. Informed by Renaissance cartographic practices, this is a very modern map that provides military and economic information about the region. Spanish cities, metonymically representing civilization, are highlighted through iconic, larger-than-scale depictions. What I want to stress here is that both the *Traça* and the *Elegías* offered a cosmographic perspective that complicates the eschatological perspective of the frontispiece. On the one hand, the Renaissance cosmographic imagination was a powerful empire building tool, allowing territories to be mapped and claimed without even setting foot on them. The representational grid, on the other hand, flattened and de-centred the world, conceiving the globe as a series of mathematically ordered geographical coordinates. In *Un nuevo reino imaginado* (pp. 186–97), I argued that through the *peregrinatio vitae* genre Castellanos's cosmographic perspective reinserted the decentred worldmap into the Christian telos by recasting the conquest as the biblical journey to the promised land. I will return to the use of this narrative genre below, when I discuss the land-centred perspective of the *Elegías*. In a recent paper examining the *Traça*, historian Andrés Vélez Posada follows this interpretation but provides a more nuanced view of the geographical imagination present in the map and the *Elegías*. Vélez Posada convincingly argues that *Elegías* and the map offer both a regional or chorographic perspective and a continental or cosmographic perspective. Although the map depicts only the northern Andes, Castellanos's text provides an overview of the continent from the tip of South America to North America, inscribing the region in the global imperial grid. The New Kingdom of Granada remains at the centre of the representation, while Tunja is on the centre right coordinate line. The corresponding passage is too long to cite it in its entirety here, but in the fragment below the poem starts panning upward from the southern tip of South America all the way to New Spain in North America:

> La cordillera de las altas sierras
> que salen de la parte del estrecho
> a quien dio Magallanes nombramiento,
> que es en cincuenta y dos grados y medio,
> do constituyen la templada zona
> del antártico polo los que miden

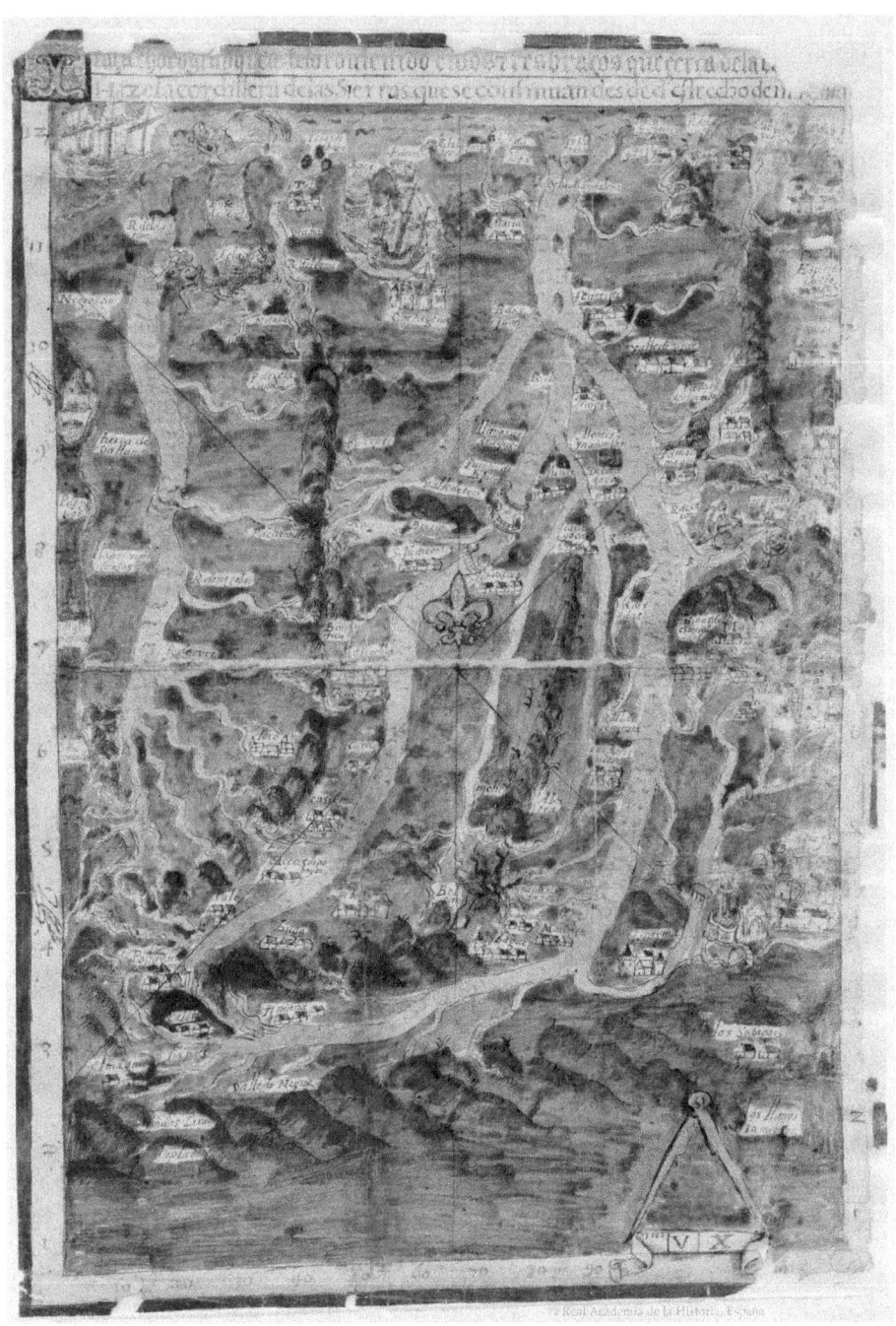

FIG. 10.2. *Traça chorographica de lo contenido en los tres braços que çerca de la [Equinoccial] haze la cordillera de las Sierras que se continuan desde el estrecho de [Magallanes].* Real Academia de la Historia, Colección Juan Bautista Muñoz, Volumen 71, Folio 170, document 1.576, Ink over paper (30.5 x 42.5 cm). Courtesy of the Real Academia de la Historia (Madrid).

latitud y longura de lugares,
al norueste viene declinando,
con grandes brazos della dependientes
a diferentes vías estendidos
incluyendo las sierras de los Andes.
Pues al sur le demoran las grandezas
de Chile, Pirú, Quito; y a la parte
del norte lo del río de la Plata,
Brasil y Marañón, y las provincias
a las árticas ondas adyacentes;
y en la continuación de su corriente
se viene por la tórrida metiendo
y la equinoccial atravesando. (p. 967)

[The high sierras of the mountain range
That emerge from the strait
That Magellan named
At fifty and two and a half degrees
Where the temperate zone is
From the Antarctic pole for those who measure
The latitude and longitude of places
To the northeast tilts its course
With great branches attached
In different directions extending
Including the sierras of the Andes.
To the South it tarries at the greatness
Of Chile, Peru, Quito, and to the
North at the River Plate,
Brazil and Marañón, and the provinces
Adjacent to the artic waves
And continuing its course
Comes entering into the torrid [zone]
And crossing the equinoctial line.]

Castellanos's sweeping view of the continent passes over the Río de la Plata, Brazil, Chile, Peru, Quito, the New Kingdom of Granada, Panama, Central America and New Spain. Tunja, Bogotá, Popayan, Cartagena and Antioquia are drawn on the cardinal lines of the map. At the centre of the map and text is the New Kingdom of Granada where the sacred and the modern geographical discourses are intertwined, supporting the military, economic and religious colonization of the Indies. However, this does not necessarily rule out the presence of the cosmic and imperial perspectives that Cañizares-Esguerra highlights in his analysis of the *Elegías*'s frontispiece and other early modern epics. More than a contradiction, the frontispiece can be read as a strategic appeal to a distracted monarch, caught up in European conflicts. It gives equal importance to the Indies and Europe, as the symmetrical presentation of both worlds suggests. Furthermore, the frontispiece may even seem to tilt the balance towards the Indies, where the real battle against the dragon was won. It is a dragon whose tail encircled the whole world, as Castellanos's epigraphic poem accompanying the frontispiece suggests: 'Hic serpens ingens orben circundat utrimque' [The great serpent encircles the whole world]. With the serpent defeated by Hispania, the warrior maiden, Phillip II now reigns over the whole world.[10] Therefore, the frontispiece can be viewed as a strategic interpellation of the sovereign: the exaltation of Philip II is ultimately a plea for recognition of the conquistadors for riding the world of the demon (serpent). The flattering image and epigraphic poem come with a hefty supplement, in excess of one hundred thousand verses — the *Elegías*. The long poem seems to state: 'Look at us King, see what we have done for you'. Thus the poem's main thrust is the conquest of the land and the sea journeys that made it possible, as discussed in the next section.

Land and Sea in the Hispanic World and the *Elegías*

In *Land and Sea*, an essay originally published in 1942, political philosopher and jurist Carl Schmitt invites us to consider how territorial expansions lead to spatial revolutions that alter significantly how societies see themselves and their place in the world. Schmitt's essay leads us to examine how land and sea have shaped the geographical imagination of Spain, especially in the age of its Atlantic expansion.

In the Hispanic tradition, land conquests are central to the medieval epic poems *Poema de Mio Cid* and the *Poema de Fernán González*. The territorial quest is evident in the Cid's campaign in Valencia:

> En tierra de moros prendiendo e ganando
> E durmiendo los dias e las noches tranochando,
> en ganar aquellas villas Mio Çid duro .iii. años.[11]

> [In the land of the Moors taking and winning
> Sleeping by day and marching by night
> Mio Cid spent three years winning those towns.]

In the opening stanzas of *Fernán González* there is also a reiterated preoccupation with the land. The poet narrates 'commo cobros' la tierra toda de mar a mar' [how the land was gained from sea to sea].[12] With the transatlantic experience, new complex visions of the land and sea emerged in the epic genre. The horizon broadens considerably with *La Araucana* by Alonso de Ercilla, where the narrative encompasses the conquest of Chile, the battle of Saint Quentin, the suppression of the Alpujarra rebellion and the Mediterranean battle of Lepanto, in addition to the story of the rise of Carthage under Dido's rule. The transoceanic experiences begin to shape the experience of the land. In a key essay on Gaspar Pérez de Villagrá's epic poem *Historia de la conquista de la Nueva México* [History of the Conquest of New Mexico] (1610), Elizabeth Davis examines the myriad of sea images, words and metaphors used by the colonial writer to tell the story of a land conquest.[13] These two examples suggest that the transatlantic experience transformed the Iberian epic.

As I mentioned above, Castellanos endows the American landscape with meaning through the *peregrinatio vitae* [pilgrimage] narrative, where the hardships endured by the conquistadors as they go through plague-infested and infernal tropical forests — up the Magdalena river into the central Andes — leads them to a 'tierra de promisión', a promised land: 'tierra buena, tierra buena, | tierra que pone fin a nuestra pena' [Good land, good land, | Land that ends our hardships] (p. 593). These are some of the most celebrated lines of Castellanos. They are above all an affirmation of the violent appropriation of the land. The appropriation of the Andes highlands to found the New Kingdom of Granada is already foreshadowed in the First Canto of the *Elegías*. The first elegy, dedicated to Columbus, begins by alluding to Gonzalo Jiménez de Quesada's expedition into the central Andes. The narrative telos is not the mastery of the sea, but conquest of the land:

> Veréis romper caminos no sabidos
> montañas bravas y nublosas cumbres [...]
> Veréis ganarse grandes potentados
> impugnables peñas, altos riscos. (p. 18)

> [You will see unknown paths opened
> rough mountains, cloudy hilltops [...]
> You will see great polities conquered
> Difficult climbs, high cliffs.]

Castellanos envisions the world as one land separated by a body of water since the Flood and reunited by Columbus, who placed it under the Spanish Crown by divine will: 'Levantó Dios un hombre, que lo diese | a rey que lo tenía merecido' [God created a man who would give it | to a king who deserved it] (pp. 18–19). He describes the Indies focusing mainly on its land wealth:

> Hay infinitas islas y abundancia
> de lagos dulces, campos espaciosos,
> sierras de prolijísima distancia,
> verdes florestas, prados deleitosos
> de cristalinas aguas dulces fuentes
> diversidad de frutos excelentes. (p. 18)

> [There are infinite islands and abundance
> of sweet lakes, ample fields
> mountain ranges of vast distance,
> green forests, pleasing pastures
> Of crystal-clear waters, sweet springs
> varieties of excellent fruits.]

Water, springs, lakes, and rivers, are an integral part of this land-centred world. They are an attribute of the land. There is a very poetic description of the ocean in the first elegy to which I will return later, when we will examine the sea in Castellanos's geographical imagination. One part of the *Elegías* that places the land at the cornerstone of Hispanic culture is the *Discurso del Capitan Francisco Draque*, describing the siege of the Caribbean port city of Cartagena.[14]

As I have discussed in *Un nuevo reino imaginado*, one of the narrative traditions that Castellanos draws from is the elegiac narratives of the fall of cities, present in the classical and biblical traditions, such as the psalms, the book of Job and the Book of Lamentations.[15] According to Lise Segas, Castellanos's description of Cartagena recalls the history of the fall of Mediterranean cities like Carthage and others described in the classical epic tradition.[16] Its roots are the Judeo-Christian sense of sin and corruption in which the cities are punished for their disobedience by a vengeful God, as Paul Ricoeur discusses in *Symbolism of Evil*.[17] There is a sense of guilt that confuses suffering and punishment: 'If you suffer, if you are ill, if you fail, if you die, it is because you have sinned'.[18] In my earlier work I suggested that Castellanos viewed the fall of Cartagena as divine punishment, expressed through a soldier's voice: 'Digo pues que ninguno desespere | sino que todos vivan confiados | de la vitoria cuando sucediere | y si, señores, otra cosas fuere | creamos ser castigo de pecados' [Let no one worry, | but rather let everyone believe and trust | that victory will occur | and, sirs, if this is not the case | let us believe it is a punishment for our sins] (p. 1121). However, expressed through the point of view of a common, nameless soldier, Castellanos seems to take distance from the interpretation of the attack as divine punishment. Men's arrogance and vengeance seems to be the cause of the fall. This is more coherent with the overall plan of the *Elegías*, which underscores human actions by a heroic group. Left at the mercy of merchants and bureaucrats, not men of arms, New World cities are vulnerable to pirate attacks.[19] Castellanos draws from the pagan classical tradition to express that Drake's attack is not divine punishment but an assault by men driven by human greed and arrogance. Drake and his crew are described as arrogant men inspired by the vengeful Furies: 'estimulados del furor rabioso | de Alceto, Thesiphones y Megera' [incited by the angry fury | of Alceto, Thesipone and Megera] (p. 1125).

A centrepiece of the *Discurso* is the letter-poem that Castellanos sends to the president of the Audiencia of Santafé de Bogotá, Dr Guillén Chaparro. In this letter, Castellanos outlines a plan of defence of New Granada, a well-equipped and trained army paying attention to the vulnerable points for an attack or invasion (from the sea). Castellanos is looking from the hinterland to the outside. The narrative axis of the *Elegías* is the interior of New Granada, Tunja and Bogotá, as reflected in the *Traça* discussed above (Fig. 10.2). In the *Discurso*, this is also in evidence in the attention given to the troops that the interior cities put together for the defence of Cartagena: 'No merecieron menos alabanzas, los nobles moradores de Pamplona | prestos con arcabuces y con lanzas | para servir a la Real Corona' [Deserving no less accolades | the noble Pamplona residents | ready with spears and harquebuses | to serve the Royal Crown] (p. 1113). This discourse is concerned with land and the land-owning class, a martial aristocracy of *beneméritos* (meritorious men) who, according to Castellanos's poem, deserve a privileged place in colonial society, as we discussed above. The poem is a response to the diminishing power of the first conquistadors and *encomenderos* to the new bureaucracy of the Crown and merchants. Bureaucrats and merchants are associated with luxury and lack the character and integrity of the conquistador class. This is particularly noticeable in cities such as Lima, where they lead a comfortable life sleeping without any worries, whereas the opposite is true for those warriors whose only adornment are their weapons and who keep watch rather than sleeping, as the well-known romance 'Mis arreos son las armas' [my possessions are my weapons] proclaims:

> Pocos que sepan militar oficio
> por carescer del uso y ejercicio,
> todos los usos son de mercaderes
> letrados, scribanos, negociantes,
> combites y lascivias de mujeres,
> ejercicios de lánguidos amantes
> y para los presentes menesteres
> diferentes de los que fueron antes. (p. 1084)

> [Few are familiar with military arts,
> they have no practice, no training,
> they only know the merchant's trade,
> Writers, scribes, and businessmen
> festivities and lusting after women,
> the care of languid lovers,
> and for the present matters
> different from those who came before.]

The lack of honour of its residents contributes to the city's downfall. Castellanos makes this case not only for Lima but also for Santo Domingo and Cartagena. The pirate attack represents much more than a material loss, it is a defilement of sacred spaces, as the Protestant invaders ransack churches and perform ritual violence on religious images. From a Hispanic viewpoint, it is also shameful to see women and nuns out in the streets, unprotected, running for their lives.[20] Men's inability to protect the women under their jurisdiction is a great dishonour: 'Huyen por las montañas las profesas | monjas de los sagrados monesterios, | sin velo, descubiertas las gargantas | y por espinas duras, blandas plantas' [Nuns fleeing to the mountains | from the sacred monasteries | without veil, uncovered necks | over hard thorns, soft feet] (p. 1096).

The poetics investing the land with meaning that we have found in Castellanos is, so far, linked to its fertility: a promised land, gained through human suffering and sacrifice. It is also a moral landscape, needed to be defended with honour and subject to defilement. The authorities and men from Cartagena and other Spanish ports like Lima and Santo Domingo lack the honour and integrity required to defend the city and its population, especially the women and nuns. The fate of the Indies does not depend on the interventions of a vengeful God. These are human failures and vices that bring down the besieged cities. This analysis of the representation of the land in the *Elegías* also seems to indicate that the land-centred mentality was not significantly altered by the transatlantic experience. The *Elegías* is a text where the poet affirms his place and that of his fellow conquistadors in the conquered land. The sea, nonetheless, is present in this epic.

The Sea and the Iberian Transatlantic Experience

Although the land occupies a central place in the *Elegías*, the transatlantic experience of early modern Iberia has a deep impact on the poet's vision of the sea. Castellanos's text is witness to the deep transformation of the Mediterranean societies that rose from a collection of kingdoms and city states to the first modern colonial empire, through advances in navigation, warfare and capitalism, as described by Ferdinand Braudel.[21]

As documented by the collection of essays *Mare Nostrum? Navigating Mediterranean Crosscurrents in Spanish Poetry* published in the journal *Calíope* (2014), there is an ample corpus of literary texts related to the Spanish sea experience and its imperial aspirations, most notably in relation to the battle of Lepanto. For example, the defeat of the Ottoman naval fleet in 1571 is recast by Ercilla and Juan Rufo as the classical literary rendition of the battle of Actium by Virgil revealing the *translatio imperii* aspirations of sixteenth-century Spain, as Quint and Davis have argued.[22]

Vicente Cristóbal and James Nicolopulos have traced the representations of the sea storm in epic poets, including Homer, Virgil, Lucan, Ovid, Ariosto, Ercilla and other authors.[23] We need to add Castellanos to the list, as we shall see below. Davis questions why literary and cultural critics have not paid enough attention to the perils of transoceanic travels and its textual representations, although transoceanic voyages had a deep impact on the European imagination.[24] In Golden Age poetry, epic and lyric, there is an ambivalent view of seafaring. On the one hand, there is a negative perspective to the experience of the sea, associated with its perils. On the other hand, facing storms and rough seas is a heroic deed. However, the epic narrator often uses open sea storms to moralize on the motives for travel, mainly greed.[25]

In the representations of the sea in the *Elegías* we also find a rich poetics and moral landscape. The sea has a significant presence in Castellanos's text. As Manuel Alvar has highlighted, there is an ample variety of navigation terms in the *Elegías*.[26] However, for Castellanos, the sea is a treacherous place. From the First Canto, sea travel is described as a dangerous and insecure livelihood, 'vivienda de peligros mal segura' (p. 19). In the Second Canto, Columbus and his crew are presented as fearless Argonauts: 'ni temen del dragón ardiente cola' [they do not fear the dragon's burning tail] (p. 23). However, as they sail into the open sea, they falter: 'del largo caminar los marineros | y cada día ver mares mayores | no iban en sus fuerzas tan enteros | ni faltos totalmente de temores' [From the long journey the sailors | seeing wider seas every day | were not with all their strength | and not entirely free from fear] (p. 23). In the Third Canto, during the first voyage, they encounter a powerful storm in which the sea becomes an allegorical figure of life's hardships and reversals of fortune: 'hecho su blando gozo duro | por un tempestuoso torbellín | incitador de lloros y de espantos | [...] | ninguna cosa por las ondas suena | que de pavor mortal no venga llena' [the joyful ride turned sour | by a sweeping tempest | inciting cries and fears | [...] | no sound is heard from the waves | that is not full of fear for mortals] (p. 28). The desperate cries of the soldiers are similar to the 'clamorque virum' [crying men] of Virgil, Ovid and Ercilla.[27] Another *topos* of the classical description of the storm that features in the poem is the waves as mountains of water, found in Virgil (Canto I), Camões (Canto VI), and Ercilla (Canto XV).[28] The ships in the *Elegías* are rocked by immense waves, reaching incredible heights after plummeting into the abyss:

Las naves al profundo sumergidas
a veces a las nubes encumbradas
por uno y otro bordo combatidas
y del oleaje cuasi zozobradas
desconfiaban todos de las vidas
las manos a los cielos levantadas
y de los sobresaltos y temblores
nacían grandes gritos y clamores. (p. 28)

[The ships falling into the deep abysm
and then risen to high clouds
from one and the other side assailed
almost sinking from the waves
everyone fearing for their lives
hands raised to the skies
and from the frights and tremors
loud cries and supplications.]

The sailors pray Hail Mary and other prayers, invoking 'san Telmo' and 'san Erasmo', two patron saints of sailors. As Davis has shown in her seminal essay on the sea in early modern Spanish poetry, the votive offering theme is frequent in shipwreck stories, with multiple allegorical meanings, such as the perils of love.[29] In Castellanos's poem, the sailors lament leaving a safe pastoral life at home for an uncertain future in the sea, 'Quien por inquietud de marineros, | dejó la quietud de su cabaña, | quien olvidó cabritos y corderos | por ver aquesta loba que se ensaña' [Who for sailors' toil | left the his peaceful cabin | who forgot goats and sheep | to see this furious wolf] (p. 29). Castellanos's moralism does not undermine completely the courage of the Spanish Argonauts. After all, he is laying the heroic foundations of the Spanish colonial settlements. Thus, although the storm has shaken the sailors' confidence, the heroic voyage continues with Vicente Yáñez, a seasoned sailor, who inspires the men to press on, despite the hardships. As a result, in Castellanos's narrative, overcoming the described storm builds the heroic character of the Spaniards. A humanist rather than a providential view of life is implicit here.

In the 'History of Cartagena', the Fourth Part of the *Elegías*, there is a noteworthy sea tragedy that precedes Drake's attack. It is the drowning of Don Pedro de Heredia, the first governor of Cartagena, narrated in Canto Nine. Two ships collide in the middle of the storm:

Todo cuanto tenía la cubierta
al mar tempestuoso se convierte;
a las saladas aguas abrió puerta
para trance mortal infausta suerte.
Pues allí si se vía cosa cierta
era la certidumbre de la muerte:
óyense grandes gritos y alaridos
de los que de las aguas son sorbidos. (p. 820)

[Everything on the ship's deck
fell to the stormy sea,
unfortunate luck opened the door

> to the mortal blow of sea waters.
> For one thing was clear,
> the certainty of death:
> one could hear the cries and screams
> of those swallowed by the waters.]

This is one of the most poetic and articulate funeral elegies in the text, with a beautiful planctus by the Governor's niece lamenting the death of Heredia (p. 823). This is an undeserved death for a beloved parental figure: 'No merecía ser vuestro desvío | fatal entre furores de agua y viento' [you did not deserve | that fatal turn in water and wind] cries doña Constanza. There is, however, another side to this narrative, since the other passengers that drown with the Governor are shown to deserve such a death. These are the bureaucrats: 'notarios escribanos y malsines' [notaries, scribes, informants] (p. 821). They are the usual suspects condemned by Castellanos, who favours the first conquistadors and despises the newcomers: 'hambrientos lobos que todo lo quieren', who 'robando viven y robando mueren' [Hungry wolves that want it all, who live stealing and stealing die] (p. 821). For Castellanos, Heredia did not deserve such death, 'indigno de morir tan mala muerte' [undeserving to die such awful death] (p. 823). It is regrettable that his body was not found in order to give him a proper burial. Mortal remains unburied and scattered are a recurrent preoccupation in epic texts. Here the demand for a proper land burial is an affirmation of a land-centred human experience.

To conclude, in the *Elegías* a regional perspective is highlighted in a text that inscribes the conquest of the Indies in the imperial and Christian realms. But more than a cosmic battle of a 'satanic epic', this is a text about human deeds. The conquest is seen nostalgically as a heroic deed more than an apocalyptic event. Nonetheless, the biblical discourse coexists with early modern cartographic knowledge. Both discourses jointly articulate a military, economic and spiritual colonization of the Indies. The poem affirms a land-centred culture and, as such, the sea is seen, as in the epic tradition, as a perilous space where the role of fate and the consequences of human actions are somehow uncertain. In contrast, in regards to the land and the fate of cities, the poet seems to understand human misfortunes, such as the fall of Cartagena, Santo Domingo and Lima, more as consequences of human failings (the lack of a military elite ready to defend the Spanish American ports) than the direct interventions of divine justice. The epic narrative helps to justify the conquest and give meaning to the contingencies of the transatlantic experience, in a narrative whose heroic impetus inspires daring sea voyages but comes to rest with the possession of the land.

Notes to Chapter 10

1. Only the first part of the *Elegías* was published in 1589 during Castellanos's times, although the other three had been granted approval for publication. The original manuscript of the first part is lost but the *princeps* edition survived; manuscripts of parts two and three are held at the Real Academia de la Historia, in Madrid (Mss. 70 and 71) and were published in 1847 in the Biblioteca de Autores Españoles collection edited by Rivadeneyra. The manuscript of the fourth part, the *Historia del Nuevo Reino de Granada* [History of the New Kingdom of Granada], is held at the

Biblioteca Nacional de España in Madrid (Ms. 3022). It was first published by Antonio Paz y Melia in 1886. The first complete edition of the *Elegías* was published in 1955 in Colombia by the Editorial ABC. The most reliable and accessible edition is the one published by Gerardo Rivas Moreno in 1997. All citations and page references in this essay correspond to this last edition. All English translations are mine.

2. The first three parts of the *Elegías* are composed in *octavas reales*, the fourth part in free hendecasyllabic verses. In the third part, there is a letter written in *tercetos* (three-line stanzas), related to Drake's attack to Cartagena. The manuscript copy of *Discurso del capitán Francisco Draque* [Discourse of Captain Francis Drake] is at the Instituto Valencia de Don Juan, in Madrid. There were at least three manuscript copies of the *Discurso*. The first one was written right after the attack, between 1586 and 1587, described in a letter dated 1 April 1587 and addressed by Castellanos to Melchor Pérez de Arteaga, the abbot of Burgo Hondo, in Ávila, Spain. The second manuscript copy, now untraced, was removed from the *Historia de Cartagena* [History of Cartagena] in 1591 by the censor Pedro Sarmiento de Gamboa. Castellanos also mentions another manuscript copy of *Discurso* that he had sent to Spain. It was first published in 1921 by Ángel González Palencia.

3. For a review of scholarship on Castellanos, see Isaac Pardo, *Juan de Castellanos: estudio de las 'Elegías de varones ilustres de Indias'* (Caracas: Academia Nacional de la Historia, 1991), pp. 83–123; Héctor Orjuela, *Historia crítica de la literatura colombiana. Literatura colonial*, 3 vols (Bogotá: Editorial Kelly, 1992), I, 232–67; and Luis Fernando Restrepo, *Un nuevo reino imaginado: las 'Elegías de varones ilustres de Indias' de Juan de Castellanos* (Bogotá: Instituto Colombiano de Cultural Hispánica, 1999). More recently, see Emiro Martínez-Osorio, *Authority, Piracy, and Captivity in Colonial Spanish American Writing: Juan de Castellanos's 'Elegies of Illustrious Men of the Indies'* (Lewisburg, PA: Bucknell University Press, 2016).

4. The first part narrates the life and voyages of Columbus and the conquest of various Caribbean islands (Puerto Rico, Cuba, Jamaica, Trinidad, Margarita). The second part recounts the conquest of Venezuela, the Goajira Peninsula, and the province of Santa Marta. The third part describes the history of Cartagena and Popayán. The fourth part concentrates on the Nuevo Reino de Granada, which in the sixteenth century included mostly the highland Andean regions surrounding Santa Fe de Bogotá and Tunja.

5. For an overview of Castellanos's life, see Ulises Rojas, *El beneficiado Juan de Castellanos: cronista de Colombia y Venezuela* (Bogotá: Gerardo Rivas, 1997).

6. Jorge Cañizares-Esguerra, *Puritan Conquistadors: Iberianizing the Atlantic, 1550–1700* (Stanford, CA: Stanford University Press, 2006).

7. Michael Francis, 'Población, enfermedad y cambio demográfico, 1537–1636. Demografía histórica de Tunja: una mirada crítica', *Fronteras de la Historia*, 7 (2002), 15–95.

8. Martínez Osorio, *Authority, Piracy, and Captivity*, p. 22.

9. Real Academia de la Historia, Colección Juan Bautista Muñoz, Volumen 71, Folio 170, document 1.576, Ink over paper (30.5 x 42.5 cm). At some point, the *Traça* was removed from the manuscript of the third part. Although previous scholarship had identified it as the one described in the *Elegías*, Andrés Vélez Posada is the first rigorously to confirm that this is the map commissioned by Castellanos by matching the correspondence of the geographical coordinates and the coincidences in the language used in the map's title and the poem. See Andrés Vélez Posada, 'Andean Valleys and Cosmographical Scales: The *Carta corografica* in J. de Castellanos' Chronicle -16C'. Paper delivered at the 27th *International Conference on the History of Cartography*, Thursday 13 July 2017, Belo Horizonte, Brazil. Copy provided by the author.

10. In the interpretation of the epigraphic poem, Cañizares-Esguerra explains that it is up to Phillip II to defeat the dragon. In my view, the dragon has already been defeated by Hispania and the Spanish monarch now rules over the whole world. See Cañizares-Esguerra, *Puritan Conquistadors*, p. 39.

11. *Poema de Mio Cid*, ed. by Colin Smith (Madrid: Cátedra, 1993), lines 1167–69.

12. *Poema de Fernán González*, ed. by Juan Victorio (Madrid: Cátedra, 1990), 2d. The land conquest is reiterated a few verses below: 'ir vos he yo contando | commo fueron la tierra perdiendo e cobrando' (5a–b) [I will tell you how they lost and regained the land].

13. Elizabeth Davis, 'De mares y ríos: conciencia transatlántica e imaginería acuática en la *Historia de la Nueva México* de Gaspar Pérez de Villagrá (1610)', in *Épica y colonia: ensayos sobre el género épico en Iberoamérica (siglos XVI y XVII)*, ed. by Paul Firbas (Lima: Universidad Nacional Mayor de San Marcos, 2008), pp. 263–86.

14. Emiro Martínez-Osorio examines the emerging proto-nationalist identity articulated in the *Discurso*, where Castellanos emphasizes an American locus of enunciation, from the Indies, not an imperial one, as suggested by Jorge Cañizares-Esguerra; Martínez-Osorio, '"En éste, nuestro rezental aprisco": Piracy, Epic and Identity in Cantos I–II of *Discurso del Capitán Francisco Draque* by Juan de Castellanos', *Calíope*, 17.2 (2011), 5–34.

15. For the fall of cities narrative tradition, see Margaret Alexious, *The Ritual Lament in Greek Tradition* (Cambridge: Cambridge University Press, 1974).

16. Lise Segas, 'Cartagena de Indias en la obra de Juan de Castellanos: de la fundación a la destrucción de la ciudad', *Aguaita*, 24 (2012), 28–47.

17. Paul Ricoeur, *The Symbolism of Evil*, trans. by Emerson Buchanan (New York: Harper and Rowe, 1967).

18. Ricoeur, *The Symbolism of Evil*, pp. 31–32.

19. Besides Drake's raids, Castellanos includes raids by other pirates such as the French Jacques de Sores in a narrative that stresses the need of a well-trained defence force to properly defend the Crown's possessions. See Raúl Marrero-Fente, *Poesía épica colonial del siglo XVI* (Madrid and Frankfurt: Iberoamericana/Vervuert, 2017), p. 190.

20. This is also present in the fall of Concepción in *La Araucana*, where unprotected women run seeking safety and there is a sick woman who scorns the men for their lack of courage; Ercilla, *La Araucana*, ed. by Isaías Lerner (Madrid: Cátedra, 1993), Canto VII, p. 239.

21. Braudel, *The Mediterranean and the Mediterranean World in the Age of Phillip II*, 2 vols (Berkeley: University of California Press, 1995), II, 659.

22. David Quint, *Epic and Empire* (Princeton, NJ: Princeton University Press, 1993), p. 49, and Elizabeth B. Davis, *Myth and Identity in the Epic of Imperial Spain* (Columbia: University of Missouri Press, 2000), p. 77.

23. Vicente Cristóbal, 'Tempestades épicas', *Cuadernos de Investigación Filológica*, 14 (1988), 125–48; James Nicolopulos, *The Poetics of Empire in the Indies: Prophecy and Imitation in 'La Araucana' and 'Os Lusíadas'* (University Park: Pennsylvania State University Press, 2000); Elizabeth B. Davis, 'Travesías peligrosas: escritos marítimos en España durante la época imperial, 1492–1650', in *Edad de Oro Cantabrigense: Actas del VII Congreso de la Asociación Internacional del Siglo de Oro (AISO)*, ed. by Anthony Close (Madrid and Frankfurt: Iberoamericana/Vervuert, 2006), pp. 31–41. See also Davis, 'De mares y ríos', and, more recently, 'From the Mare Nostrum to the Mar Océano and Back: Oceanic Studies, Mediterranean Studies, and the Place of Poetry', *Calíope*, 19.1 (2014), 196–216.

24. Davis, 'Travesías', p. 31.

25. Davis 'Travesías', p. 33. Davis also notes that the shipwreck theme is used in various ways by Golden Age poetry, as a metaphor for love, uncertainties of court politics, earthly pleasures, etc. 'Travesías', p. 34. A recent study on the shipwreck theme in early modern Hispanic texts, including Fernando González de Oviedo's natural history of the New World, is Sarissa Carneiro's *Retórica del infortunio: persuasión, deleite y ejemplaridad en el siglo XVI* (Madrid and Frankfurt: Iberoamericana/Vervuert, 2015).

26. Manuel Alvar, *Juan de Castellanos: tradición española y realidad americana* (Bogotá: Caro y Cuervo, 1972), pp. 48–52.

27. Cristóbal, 'Tempestades épicas', p. 136.

28. Vicente Cristóbal, 'De *La Eneida* a *La Araucana*', *Cuadernos de Filología Clásica: Estudios Latinos*, 9 (1995), 68–101 (p. 82).

29. Davis, 'Travesías', p. 5.

CHAPTER 11

Os Lusíadas and Armas antárticas: Eros and Eris at the Frontiers of Empire

Imogen Choi

Juan de Miramontes Zuázola's *Armas antárticas* [Antarctic Arms] (*c.* 1608–09), an epic poem composed in Lima by a veteran of the city's coastal defence fleet, or *Armada del Mar del Sur*, is full of 'aventuras de amor y de guerra confundidas' [mingled adventures of love and war].[1] Its overarching theme of armed conflict in the viceroyalty of Peru, the 'Antarctic' region of the title, from the fall of the Inca empire to the seaborne incursions of English and Dutch corsairs to Pedro Sarmiento de Gamboa's abortive settlement of the Magellan Strait in the 1580s, is a loose one. The large geographical and temporal scope excludes the possibility of any single hero; there are several narrative leaps and one very extensive digression, and in contrast to *La Araucana*, in which the testimonial voice of the poet provides a unifying thread, here the narrative persona is minimal and muted. Instead, a number of love stories, intertwined with the ongoing strife and echoing each other in their language and structure, provide a means of connecting and comparing the otherwise disparate theatres of conflict.

   All of these stories feature a love triangle, in which a reciprocal union of love between equals is disrupted by the violent, if ignorant, intervention of a more powerful male figure. In the first, the English corsair John Oxenham sets out for the Pacific in the company (anachronistically) of Francis Drake, with the aim of dominating between them the Spanish Pacific. While Drake heads south for the Magellan Strait, Oxenham strikes up an alliance with the community of African fugitive slaves or *cimarrones* in hiding in the jungle of Ballano near the Isthmus of Panama. No sooner has he entered Spanish waters, however, than he is entranced by the fair Estefanía, a *criolla* who is sailing to a first meeting with her betrothed, and kidnaps her in exchange for the liberty of the vessel. Shortly afterwards, Oxenham's lieutenant, Briano, finds his eye caught by the *cimarrona* Marta, and when wooing fails, unceremoniously abducts her from the bed of her beloved *cimarrón* Biafara. Both of these forced unions backfire for the besotted Englishmen: Oxenham, Briano, and the English and African settlements are eventually betrayed to the Spanish by Estefanía and Biafara. As the victorious Spaniards triumphantly return to Lima, a veteran soldier whiles away a calm voyage by recounting a story from the distant pre-Hispanic past. In this interpolated tale, which occupies a full seven cantos of the total twenty, two noble Inca lovers, Chalcuchima and Curicoyllor, are separated when the younger brother of the Inca of Cuzco, Chuquiaquilla of Vilcabamba, forcefully takes Curicoyllor to be his bride. Like Oxenham and Briano, Chuquiaquilla cannot enjoy his prize for long, since the two former lovers escape; he soon succeeds in having Chalcuchima killed, but Curicoyllor then commits suicide. All of these episodes begin with echoes of the novella or Byzantine or Moorish romance, but end abruptly in violence. They are insistently reflected throughout the work by echoes of similarly possessive passions, whether it be the lust of Henry VIII triggering a schism with Rome and enmity with Spain, the Amerindian interpreter Felipillo betraying the last Inca, Atahualpa, in his lust for his king's wife, or the *cimarrón* Jalonga's account of Apollo's thwarted pursuit of Daphne.

Amatory material, of course, is no stranger to epic. Renaissance poets needed look no further than the *Iliad* or *Aeneid* for illustrious precedents of the interweaving of erotic and military conflict. Virgil invokes Erato, the muse of love poetry, instead of the patrons of history or tragedy, to open the second half of his poem, foreshadowing the rivalry over the hand of Lavinia which will eventually prove the crucible for a lasting union between the Trojan and Italian peoples. The gesture is imitated by Miramontes in a second epic proem in his third canto.[2] In his influential *Discorsi del poema eroico* [Discourses on the Heroic Poem] (1594), Torquato Tasso asserted that the beauty of love naturally befits the beauty of epic, and in another dialogue went as far as to propose an etymological link between heroism and love, *eros* and *heros*.[3] Recent criticism has illuminated the ways in which epic and love lyric interpenetrate and question each other in complex ways in the early modern period. Building on Roland Greene's suggestive coinage of the 'unrequited conquests' of imperial lyric, where the unattained possession of the beloved object is equated to the unrealizable sating of colonial desire, much criticism of Garcilaso in particular notes the breakdown of imperial epic motifs into lyric subjectivity.[4] As Isabel Torres puts it, 'Petrarchan "norms" were subject to a continuous process of reformulation before, and during, their encounter with transatlantic "otherness"', while love is an apt 'master metaphor' for confronting many fraught interactions of subjectivity and identity in imperial Spain.[5] Scholars such as Cyrus Moore and Felipe Valencia have argued that a similar process might be at work in epic poems such as *La Araucana*, in which the intrusion of feminine voices introduces a note of lyric melancholy whose 'alteridad lingüística' [linguistic alterity] acts as an expression of 'subjetividad frente a discursos hegemónicos y heteronormativos' [subjectivity in the face of hegemonic and heteronormative discourses].[6]

This chapter also argues for the interconnectedness of a problematic discourse of erotic desire and a questioning of imperial expansion in Miramontes's poem, but from a different source, with different intent and from a standpoint which is emphatically not that of the desiring subject. There is no doubt that the lettered community of the viceroyalty in this period was a grouping very much under the spell of Renaissance Petrarchism and Neoplatonism, in which Italian might be heard in cultivated circles and a Portuguese resident, Enrique Garcés, would publish a translation of Petrarch's *Canzoniere* in 1591.[7] Miramontes's introduction of different varieties of love into his epic — the Petrarchan affections of Estefanía and her betrothed, the Neoplatonic union of Chalcuchima and Curicoyllor, and Biafara and Marta's unaffected celebration of sensuality — and the dramatization of traditional Petrarchan conceits of captivity, love and death, would not be lost on his local readers. Equally significant, however, is an epic intertext: Luís de Camões's *Os Lusíadas* [The Lusiads] (1572). This epic rendition of Vasco da Gama's voyage to India has its own peculiar overlay of erotic and colonial desire, which Miramontes distorts for his own purposes in the love intrigues of the poem. The influence of Camões on the Iberian Peninsula has long been acknowledged, to which one might add that it left an equally significant mark on the literary culture of the viceroyalty;[8] Enrique Garcés published the third Castilian translation of *Os Lusíadas* in the same year as his *Canzoniere*. The conceptual and lexical parallels between the opening stanzas of the two epics would be hard to miss, especially when compared with Garcés's version:

> Las armas y proezas militares
> de españoles católicos valientes
> que por ignotos y soberbios mares
> fueron a dominar remotas gentes,
> poniendo al Verbo eterno en los altares
> que otro tiempo, con voces insolentes,
> de oráculos gentílicos espanto
> eran del indio (agora mudas), canto. (*AA*, I. 1)

> [The arms and military prowess
> of valiant Catholic Spaniards
> who by unknown and proud seas
> went to subdue distant peoples,
> placing the eternal Word on the altars
> which in past times, with insolent voices,
> of gentilic oracles (now mute), were
> the terror of the Indian, I sing.]

> Las armas y varones señalados
> de l'occidental playa lusitana,
> que por los mares nunca navegados
> pasaron más allá de Taprobana:
> en peligros y guerras esforzados
> más que prometer puede fuerza humana,
> determino esparcir en toda parte
> si a tanto me ayudare ingenio y arte.

> Y a vueltas las memorias gloriosas
> de aquellos reyes que iban dilatando
> imperio y fe, y las tierras populosas
> de l'África y de l'Asia devastando:
> y aquellos que por obras valerosas
> se van de olvido eterno libertando,

y entre remotas gentes conquistaron
insignes reinos que los sublimaron.[9]

[The illustrious arms and men
of the western Lusitanian beach,
who by ne'er-navigated seas
passed beyond Taprobana:
more zealous in perils and wars
than human might could promise,
I resolve to spread everywhere
if talent and art so assist me.

And also the glorious memories
of those kings who expanded
empire and faith, and devastated
the teeming lands of Africa and Asia:
and those who by their valiant deeds
and conquered among distant peoples
prestigious kingdoms which exalted them.]

While both poets sing of the maritime conquests of distant peoples, however, and
the spreading of 'imperio y fe', for Camões, the emphasis falls on the former. His
version of heroism is fundamentally predicated on the devastation of the native
inhabitants of Africa and Asia, and the expansion of territory, whereas Miramontes
underplays this element in order to stress the evangelical enterprise.

As Miguel Martínez has shown, Camões proved susceptible to remaking in the
image of whichever early modern realm currently directed its attention eastwards,
making the translation of his epic a 'profitable imperial cultural practice', and after
Philip II's annexation of Portugal in 1580 there was a concerted effort to make of
him the bard of a united Iberian empire.[10] The distance that Miramontes's proem
takes from the imperial dimension of the work is therefore a significant gesture,
and a similar independence is shown with regard to the intertwining of *eros* and
eris, love and strife, in the narrative. To borrow the classic terminology of Thomas
M. Greene or George W. Pigman, there is much that is 'emulative' or 'eristic' in
this dialogue with Camões, and — as Torres explores in the case of the Iberian
lyric — this eristic imitative impulse often has a strongly erotic colouring.[11] In
this case, though, the imitation is an eclectic one, which also peers backwards
over the shoulder of Camões to the classical tradition and sideways to engage with
contemporary polemics.[12] The illustrious intertext is, in contrast to the classicizing
vision of Greene and Pigman, a recent one, and the challenge to it is not so much
a struggle for humanist self-definition in the wake of an overwhelming past than
a reflection of a decided stance of scepticism towards contemporary imperial
practices. Miramontes had a personal investment in these debates; his precarious
career as a soldier in Lima's coastal defence fleet had depended on the favour of
successive viceroys who might at any time (and often did) choose to invest military
resources in more adventurous imperial exploits in the southern or eastern Pacific
or pour them into fortifying and expanding the threatened frontiers of Spanish
hegemony in Chile and the River Plate.

Taking the emulation of Camões as a starting point, therefore, I first establish that erotic love is generally a positive and natural force in *Os Lusíadas*, but transformed into a frustrated and tragic one in *Armas antárticas*. Secondly, I discuss how the desire for erotic possession and the urge to territorial conquest and domination are symbolically and literally intertwined in the latter. Finally, I relate this overarching discourse to contemporary polemics in Lima and the viceroyalty over the potential for future expansion, and the dilemma of the region's restive frontiers.

'Considera | que hay pocos Scipïones Africanos' [Consider | that Scipio Africanuses are few] (X. 928): The Punishments and Rewards of Love

To the Spanish or Hispano-American reader of the sixteenth and seventeenth centuries, *Os Lusíadas* was a poem of many attractions. At the cusp of the union of the Spanish and Portuguese monarchies, it sang of the glories of the Portuguese overseas acquisitions in Africa and Asia. At a time of intense experimentation in the Spanish poetic tradition, it provided a rich and sonorous store of poetic resources, neologisms and formulae for the budding literary circles of the turn of the century. With its panoramic scope, encompassing both the Greco-Roman heavens and the ocean depths, the marvellous exotica of the Indies and the breadth of Portuguese history, it exercised an encyclopaedic fascination over the imagination. With its deliberate emulation of Virgil and the Virgilian acclamation of imperial Rome, it furnished an Iberian epic weighty enough to rival both ancients and moderns. Little wonder, then, that it created a sensation in courts, universities and military circles, eliciting three erudite translations and a host of imitations from the 1580s.

Another of its allures must have been the humour, liberty and frankness with which Camões handled the subject of romantic love. While, as we have seen, amatory material has a long history in epic, *Os Lusíadas* takes the more unprecedented step of incorporating the sensuality and lightness of touch with which the *romanzo* treats affairs of the heart within the higher moral and political pretensions of a classicizing epic framework. The two approaches mingle from the outset in the protagonism of the patron goddess of the Portuguese, Venus. On the one hand, Camões's Venus unmistakably emulates Virgil's, the chief advocate of her Trojan and Caesarian descendants pre-destined to lordship, and hence the grand Virgilian vision of imperialism. On the other, there is a wink to the reader that the Lusitanians possess other qualities to attract the deity's favour too: 'me hão-de venerar e ter em preço' [they will venerate me and hold me in esteem], as she confides to her son Cupid towards the end of the work.[13]

One of the most iconic episodes in which this ambivalent Venus intervenes takes place in the final two cantos. On their triumphant return voyage from India, Da Gama and his men are rewarded with a respite on the *Ilha dos Amores*, or Island of Love, a tropical paradise thoughtfully conjured up by Venus and populated by amorous nymphs precisely for that purpose. The episode, in which the seafarers enjoy uninhibited lovemaking and feasting, while a magical globe displays the world they have begun to open up and a prophecy describes the governor-captains of India who will follow them, was among the most imitated of Camões's poem. As Mercedes Blanco puts it, without its inspiration, 'era difícil pensar en una fusión tan completa de la *libido sciendi*, a la que se da expresión y satisfacción en el despliegue cartográfico del globo presentado por Tetis, de la *libido dominandi*, que tiene por resultado la apertura del camino hacia las riquezas de las Indias, y de la *libido fruendi*, que el poeta portugués simboliza en el paraíso erótico de la isla de Venus' [it would be difficult to imagine such a complete fusion of the lust for knowledge, given expression and satisfaction in the cartographic unfolding of the globe presented by Tethys, of the lust for power, which results in the opening of the route to the riches of the Indies, and of the lust for pleasure, which the Portuguese poet symbolizes in the erotic paradise of the island of Venus] (pp. 379–80). While Camões attempts to cast the delicate veil of allegory over his narration, clarifying that the island 'outra cousa não è que as deleitosas | honras que a vida fazem sublimada' [is nothing else but the delightful | honours which make life sublime] (IX. 89), by this point the physical coupling has been described in quite some detail. At the outset, the poet vituperates those who prefer worldly ambitions to the delights of Venus, and later on anticipates his moralist critics in jocular tone: 'milhor é exprimentá-lo que julgá-lo, | mas julgue-o quem não pode exprimentá-lo' [better to experience it than to judge it, | but let him judge it who cannot experience it] (IX. 83).

Erotic love in Camões, then, in contrast to much of the epic tradition, is neither tragic nor perverse, but perfectly natural and compatible with heroism. Where Virgil uses erotic union as a symbol for the birth of an empire which comes at great human cost, the Island of Love shows both colonial and heteronormative desire fully and unproblematically sated. Elsewhere, male weaknesses of the flesh are treated with similar indulgence, and it is on the contrary an undue severity which attracts the harshest criticism. In the catalogue of viceroys which features as a prophecy in the tenth canto, one governor is censured for having executed one of his men for raping a female slave; 'a fraca humanidade e amor desculpa' [frail humanity and love excuses him] (X. 46), pleads the poet, furnishing a series of classical exempla of similarly tempted heroes in his defence. The excursus also has the effect of clarifying for the reader under exactly what circumstances such conduct should be condoned: not in the case of the violation of a virgin, relative or 'pure' married woman, but admissible in that of a slave, captive, or — as we implicitly glimpse, I believe, on the *Ilha dos Amores* — an indigenous woman.

In *Armas antárticas*, the results of similar escapades are very different. Oxenham's infatuation with Estefanía steadily brings about the decline of his ambitions. Motivated not by clemency but by lust, as the fury of cruelty gives way to the 'amoroso | fuego' [amorous flame] of his passion (IV. 300), the captain releases the ship whose crew will betray his presence to the authorities in exchange for the beautiful passenger. 'Amor me disculpa, amor la ofrece | mi vida, si ella quiere; si no, justo | me es como vencedor hacer mi gusto' [Love excuses me, love offers her my life, if she wants; if not, it is just for me as the winner to do what I like] (IV. 302), he pleads, the convoluted syntax of the stanza reflecting the twisted logic by which he attempts to persuade himself of the legitimacy of his action. Soon, the smitten corsair forsakes his aspirations for further plunder in order to stay near Estefanía in his fort, making him an easier target for the party setting out in his pursuit. Meanwhile, in bed with Marta and heedless of her injured lover Biafara, his lieutenant Briano awakens to discover the latter burying a mace in his head, having facilitated a night-time ambush of the maroon *palenque* by the Spanish troops. Anticipating a bloody final siege, Oxenham eventually orders Estefanía along with other civilians to be released from the English fort for their protection and greater strategic effectiveness.

Unlike the compliant or silent love objects of Camões, however, after several cantos of tearful acquiescence Oxenham's captive now takes an unexpectedly vocal part in defending her honour. Her betrayal of her captor to the Spanish and donning of arms to avenge herself is an act of revenge which highlights the discrepancy between his Petrarchist pretensions and the effective lack of respect his actions have shown her: 'me importa | ver si de aqueste inglés la valentía | corta en mis carnes, como en mi honor corta' [I need to see if this Englishman is as bold in piercing my flesh as he pierces my honour] (X. 925) she insinuates to her rescuers in a scornfully alliterative outburst. When Oxenham eventually surrenders to her, his excuse precisely echoes the defence of the frail but forgivable lovers of *Os Lusíadas* who commit similar violations against women in their power:

> Si siendo mi divina prisionera
> por rendirme a tus ojos soberanos
> no pude contenerme, considera
> que hay pocos Scipïones Africanos. (*AA*, X. 928)

> [If, when you were my divine prisoner
> and I surrendered to your sovereign eyes
> I could not contain myself, consider
> that Scipio Africanuses are few.]

This time, though, the example chosen — of the Roman republican hero who famously relinquished his claim to a beautiful Spanish captive already betrothed to a Celtiberian chieftain — works against the out-manoeuvred general. The reader's laughter is directed at the would-be lover himself, rather than, as in *Os Lusíadas*, at his critics.

The love triangle which transpires in the interpolated story of Chalcuchima and Curicoyllor develops the association between the forced possession of a woman and moral, political and military decline much more extensively. The framing of the story, as a tale recounted to beguile a calm voyage, recalls a similar tale in *Os Lusíadas* of the 'Twelve of England', a legendary demonstration of Portuguese chivalry towards the fairer sex, and thus draws especial attention to the themes of honour and possession which, here, are given a very different twist. Like Oxenham, Chuquiaquilla's semi-idolatrous rendering of homage to the 'divine' beauty he beholds is swiftly undermined by his impetuous decision to 'roballa, | que lo que al poderoso se le niega | es donde su violencia más se entrega' [abduct her, for what is denied to the powerful man is where his violence is most unrestrained] (XII. 1093). Like Oxenham, his abject surrender to his passion is 'excused' again in a double-edged exemplum, in this case a series of biblical kings and judges similarly corrupted by lust (XII. 1095–98). The disenchanted courtier-turned-shepherd Oparo, as often with such figures a vehicle for critique of the court and its corruption, is quick to highlight how ill-befitting such behaviour is to the Infante. On realizing the circumstances surrounding the prince's consummation of his passion, which took place in his humble hut, he feigns to doubt the truth of his eyes: 'pues no cabe en razón que tal se diga | de Chuquiaquilla, Infante en virtud raro, | a quien su sangre y calidad obliga | que sea de mujeres firme amparo' [for it cannot be right that such a thing is said of Chuquiaquilla, a prince of rare virtue, whose blood and nobility oblige him to be the firm defender of women] (XIV. 1233). From this point on, the reign of the virtuous Infante becomes a steady spiral of decadence, as he abandons his scouts to be eaten by cannibals, falls into a drunken stupor, treacherously sends assassins to kill Chalcuchima in his brother's capital when the separated lovers seize the opportunity to escape, and then attempts to mount an unjust war on Cuzco before beating an ignominious retreat.

In one scene in particular, the lines between erotic conquest and political decline are drawn very sharply indeed, and with a striking analogy to contemporary Hispanic political discourse. When the Infante re-enters Vilcabamba in triumph with his prize wife on a ceremonial litter, the celebrations which take place explicitly mimic those staged on the entrance of a new viceroy in the Spanish American city. Anachronistically, the procession is accompanied by European festive dress; colourful display of banners and tapestries; 'danzas, regocijos, invenciones | de máscaras, libreas, galas, juegos, | hogueras, luminarias, hachas, fuegos' [dances, celebrations, the devising of new masks, liveries, finery, games, bonfires, festival lights, candles, fireworks] (XII. 1121); music of 'dulzainas, sacabuches, chirimías' [dulzainas, sackbuts, shawms] (XIII. 1122); ephemeral triumphal arches (1125) and popular chants, all of which recall such civic festivities.

Most striking of all, however, is the imposing façade of the palace, decorated with scenes from classical mythology which are described in detail. The ekphrasis evokes the similarly decorated façade of the palace of Calcutta in *Os Lusíadas* (VII. 50–66), especially since it is followed, as in Camões, by a rival ekphrasis recounting the history of the future conquerors of the territory (the Portuguese heroes of the reconquest, and the Spanish conquerors and viceroys of Peru). Within the overall context, though, the reader could hardly fail to think of the exemplary classical mythology which almost invariably adorned the ephemeral arches through which the incoming viceroy (and his wife) passed in this period, in a ritual modelled on the ceremonial royal entries of Europe.[14] The mention of triumphal arches which shortly precedes the description is noteworthy in this light; the Jesuit José de Acosta's popular history of the Indies (1590) made a point of noting that among all the impressive monuments of the Incas, they lacked these constructs.[15] Their significance in terms of Hispanic political thought, on the other hand, would escape no one: Alejandro Cañeque argues that the arches 'were essentially visual treatises on good government as understood in the seventeenth-century Hispanic world; they were visual "mirrors for princes", or, more exactly, "mirrors for viceroys"', allegorical representations of particular political virtues.[16] The reader could, then, hardly fail to appreciate the irony of the vignettes which now mirror the 'virtues' of Chuquiaquilla: Jupiter's rape of Europa, of Danae, of Calisto, 'adonde el primo artífice declara | cuán lacivo, cuidoso andaba y listo | Júpiter en robar vírgenes bellas, | aunque inmortal, muriéndose por ellas' [in which the expert craftsman reveals how lascivious, insistent and cunning Jupiter was in abducting beautiful maidens, for all his immortality, dying for them] (XIII. 1132). The point is reinforced by the fact that the pictures are glimpsed through the eyes of the violated Curicoyllor, who is in such distress that she can barely take them in.

In all of these cases then, the hollowness of the violent usurping of erotic possession is emphasized. Despite their lack of active defiance, the reluctant captives of these sequences, however exalted their new station and devoted their smitten lovers, never cease to pine for their first beloved. All retain their inward independence and a capacity for resistance despite the appearance of surrender. This is clearest in the case of Curicoyllor, whose virginity is violated 'dejando inmaculada la alma entera | si el cuerpo padeció la fuerza injusta' [leaving her soul immaculate and whole while her body suffered the unjust rape/force] (XII. 1116). Protecting her sentiments with evasiveness and courtly double-entendre until she can create the opportunity for her escape with Chalcuchima, she eventually declares to the latter that 'No he sido coya yo, sino cautiva | tuya [...] que yo coya no quiero | ser si no es Inga aquel mi amor primero' [I have not been a *coya* (Inca queen), no, but your captive, for I do not want to be the *coya* of anyone unless my first love is the Inca] (XVI. 1430). Yet even the least developed of these characters, Marta, who never utters a word and to all appearances remains a sensuous object to her admirers, is shown to be capable of an interior resistance towards 'quien por fuerza la gozaba' [he who enjoyed her by force] (IX. 801). Her true sentiments remain a mystery even to Biafara, 'pues no es posible | escudriñar el hombre el pensamiento | de ajeno corazón incomprensible' [for it is not possible for man to scrutinize the thoughts of the incomprehensible heart of another] (IX. 775).

Overall, therefore, while the enjoyment of the fruits of love is closely bound up with a heteronormative vision of heroism in Os Lusíadas, in which the will to power and conquest is symbolically rewarded with the complete gratification of concupiscence, and any infringements on the part of the colonizers are looked upon with good-humoured indulgence, Miramontes repeatedly alludes to his epic predecessor only to turn the dynamic on its head. Even if silent at first, his love objects are never fully compliant. The misdirected rhetoric of their violators repeatedly reveals the hollowness of their professions of devotion, and the physical possession of the captives proves to be transient, illusory and eventually tragic in its consequences for the political community of which the lover is the head. As a direct result of the love intrigues in which the captain, lieutenant and Infante become involved, the English explorers are all killed or captured; the *cimarrones* are slaughtered and enslaved, and the beginnings of Inca decadence symbolically lead to the passing of Peru to their more worthy viceregal successors. Is this studied recasting of Camões simply a return to a more orthodox moralizing interpretation, one which, perhaps, reflects the gradual hardening of attitudes towards the didactic function of epic in the wake of Tasso? I believe that there is more at stake here. For the desire for possession of the beloved closely overlaps within the plot with the desire for territorial possession; both are mutually implicated in the failure and decline of the lovers. The poem, in fact, pervasively explores the dynamics of expansion, desire, and conquest through the language of *eros*, and I turn now to its implications for other kinds of colonial interaction in the work.

'La gente deseosa | de hollar la tierra' [The people longing to tread the land] (III. 236): Expansive Desires and Poisoned Arrows

In the third canto of *Armas antárticas*, Drake outlines to Queen Elizabeth and the assembled parliament his plan to circumnavigate the globe by way of recalling the only navigator to have accomplished this feat before him, Ferdinand Magellan. His account is, for the most part, a summary overview of the Lusitanian's voyage, but one episode develops into a much more elaborate narration: that of Magellan's death on the island of Cybú (Cebu) in the Philippines. The landing at Cybú bodes well at the outset: having successfully weathered the hostile climate of the Strait and the vast expanse of the Pacific, the 'valle deleitoso' [delightful valley] which appears on the horizon as a rosy dawn awakens appears to beckon the weary crew to 'tomar algún reposo' [take some rest] (III. 235). It is, in fact, painted with an unmistakeable resemblance to another celebrated resting point on a heroic return voyage of discovery, an allusion all the more transparent for the emphasis placed in Drake's account on Magellan's Portuguese nationality: the 'vale ameno' [pleasant valley] of the *Ilha dos Amores* we have already encountered. The landings in both poems are infused with a desire in which the colonial lust for pleasure, for power and for knowledge are intertwined, and they begin in very similar fashion. After a first glimpse of the beach, leafy springs and hills, the longing of the mariners for land is stressed ('la gente deseosa | de hollar la tierra salta en la ribera', *AA* III. 236 [the people longing to tread the land leap onto the shore]; 'os fortes mançebos que na praia | ponham os pés, de terra cobiçosos' [the brave youths set foot on the beach, longing for land], *OL* IX. 66), and their gleeful activities on landing described, as they run along the beach, bathe in the pools, and hunt wild animals.

From this point on, though, their arrivals in paradise take a very different turn. While Vasco da Gama's men plunge into the forest 'para ferir os cervos' [to wound the deer] (*OL* IX. 67) only to find the water nymphs, already wounded by Cupid's arrow, fall meekly into their nets, Magellan's, diving naked into the water 'como el ciervo herido' [like the wounded deer] (*AA* III. 237) are unaware that the roles have been reversed. Having unwittingly crossed a forbidden line, a 'raya' drawn in the sand (III. 245), they themselves are shortly to become the prey of the watching Indians. While Da Gama finds himself led to the bed of the love-struck queen of the sea nymphs, Tethys, his compatriot, leaping past the driftwood behind which his men have put to flight the barbarians to pursue the survivors, is himself struck by an unhappy arrow (III. 261), this one steeped in a very literal poison.

This version of Magellan's death, one apparently unique to Miramontes, has a number of significant emphases. The imagery of an arcane transgression, of an unnamed foreboding, crossing an unseen 'raya', refusing an unknown tribute, and finally eating the 'fresca, deseada y dulce fruta' [fresh, desired and sweet fruit] (III. 255) which proves the mortality of the newcomers to the dubious natives and bears within it the figurative poison of their captain's demise, is highly symbolic. It seems to speak in archetypal language of prohibited desire and its punishment — except that the immediate sin is not clear. In Magellan's only, brief, soliloquy, he dismisses such omens, affirming that his quest for 'la fragante especería' [fragrant spices] (III. 241) is contained within the will of God and the legitimate allotment to the Spanish emperor of the Spice Islands by the papal disposition of Tordesillas. As Jason McCloskey points out, Magellan's overall presentation in this canto is far more eulogistic than in many of the poet's sources: Drake (admittedly a somewhat ambivalent mouthpiece) repeatedly acclaims him as a hero; the historical mutinies and complaints of his men are silenced (III. 262–66), and the role played by Sebastián de Elcano in bringing the spice-laden ship safely back to Spain is here attributed solely to faith and fortune rather than the clueless crew. McCloskey nonetheless argues that Drake's imitation of Magellan demonstrates the 'destabilizing effects of mimesis', raising the question of who is the original pirate, and traces a correspondence between the forbidden 'raya', Caesar's crossing of the Rubicon, and the elusive antemeridian supposedly demarcating Spanish and Portuguese territories in the Indo-Pacific, whose coordinates remained contested. Magellan's ventures thus attract castigation because they recall 'the continued violation of the boundary hammered out in the Treaty of Zaragoza by the presence of Spain in the Philippines'.[17]

In asserting Magellan's overall innocence in his tragic demise, however, McCloskey neglects one significant detail: Magellan is shot when, 'más presto | de lo que en aquel caso era importante' [more swiftly than was needful in that situation] (III. 260), he leaps beyond the defensive trench to pursue an enemy who is already fleeing. The reader might recall a parallel scene in Os Lusíadas, when the reckless Fernão Veloso ventures among the savages of St Helena Bay. The soldier is ignominiously chased back to ship, with the hapless natives receiving 'red caps' for their pains (V. 24–36), in a humorously dismissive and somewhat grotesque prelude to the ambiguous curse of the giant Adamastor (37–60). Here, of course, the outcome is reversed, and for tragic rather than comic effect. At this moment, what has heretofore been a licit, defensive, successful and perhaps even providential engagement overflows into a more aggressive action, of questionable ethical and pragmatic grounding. It is at this point that the surviving men realize the impossibility (at least in the short term) of exacting vengeance, however 'justa', and conquering the coveted island, across which 'ya el caribe fiero | por la áspera montaña huyó ligero' [the fierce Carib had already fled over the rugged mountain] (III. 266). The islanders of Cebu are, for all their bellicosity, easily controlled in a purely defensive war, but apparently unamenable to total conquest by force. In a peculiar exception to their overall barbarism, they are, however, scrupulously compliant with *ius gentium*, the unwritten law between peoples elaborated by sixteenth-century scholastics, in their policy regarding the seafarers who arrive on their shore. They afford a free landing, basic supplies and provisions for further commerce provided that a nominal tribute is paid and there is no trespass beyond where the law permits. While this addition opens up the possibility of an alternative, non-possessive, form of interaction and exchange, the initial promise of discovery, conquest and possession, with its echoes of Camões and his imitators, proves wholly, and paradigmatically, fruitless.

The canto after we see Magellan succumb to the sweet fruits of Cebu and the poisoned arrow which follows them, Oxenham, too, is struck by 'en lugar de flechas, rayo ardiente' [instead of arrows, a burning ray] (IV. 298) of longing for the beautiful Estefanía — in both cases, after the navigators overcome an initial tremor of foreboding. Where a strictly colonial desire is, in the account of Magellan's death, rendered through the language of *eros*, in the downfall of Oxenham something of the reverse is true: his erotic desire overlaps with a desire for territorial possession. As we have seen, Miramontes draws a deliberate parallel between the two English corsairs, Drake and Oxenham, who set out on a united mission to dominate the Pacific, but whose fortunes take very different trajectories. While Drake suffers initial losses on the Strait, he returns victoriously to England, loaded with stolen riches, whereas Oxenham meets with early success, but is subsequently pursued and trapped by two Spanish expeditions, losing his ship, his allies, his fort and eventually his liberty. Of course, the latter's delusional attempt to win the heart of his prisoner Estefanía is very much implicated in his downfall. So too, however, is his delusional ambition to possess the fertile lands of the Spanish Indies. While Drake remains at sea, a mobile target attacking other vessels and ports before moving swiftly on, his companion ventures further onto land, establishing a base in Panama and engaging the Spanish in direct combat. Inciting the Africans to 'levantar el vuelo | a la conquista del indiano suelo' [raise their aspirations | to the conquest of the land of the Indies] (V. 387), he appears to model himself on Cortés (V. 409–10), or Pedro Arias Dávila (V. 442). As he boldly sinks his ships in the Atlantic and proceeds by land with his new-found allies and a handful of soldiers to subjugate the Mar del Sur, he is no longer explorer, but conquistador, and in an ironic reversal of the Black Legend, accrues most of the negative stereotypes associated with this part.

Complicating matters further, a similar parallel is drawn between Briano's abduction of Marta and the whole sequence of the English alliance with the maroons. In this case, the diplomatic wooing of the Africans by the newcomers is itself framed in terms of courtship and conquest. The ambassadors Bruno and Guillermo who are sent to seek the fugitive Africans on the Englishmen's landing in the Arcadian landscape of Panama resemble two wandering knights of *romanzo*. As they pause 'Al pie de un fresco mirto' [at the foot of a fresh myrtle] (IV. 312, the plant of Venus) and recline during the siesta in a *locus amoenus* by a spring, the reader's expectations are laid for an erotic encounter. All the more so when the topos of hunting is added — another staple of the romance tradition — as a moribund boar collapses at their feet. Rather than a sprightly nymph or damsel in distress, however, the boar is shortly followed by its muscular Ethiopian hunter, Jalonga. Nonetheless, after a brief struggle (in a missing folio) the sinewy *cimarrón* renders himself the willing captive of the stranger who 'pudiera fácilmente hacerme fuerza' [could easily force himself upon me] (IV. 323) and meekly accompanies the two men back to the ship, 'quieto y reconciliado por amigo' [quietly and reconciled in friendship] (325) like the playful nymphs of Camões.

The communal feasts which celebrate the alliance, on Oxenham's ship and later in the 'ameno valle deleitoso' [pleasant and delightful valley] of the maroon settlement of Ronconcholo (V. 425), continue the symbolic seduction with their resemblance to a wedding banquet. As the two leaders share their cares 'con ya reconciliados corazones' [now with reconciled hearts] (408) and the English leer at the dancing girls, the African 'diestros músicos gentiles' [skilled gentile musicians] (403) transfix their listeners. Their song, which expounds the secrets of seasons, weather and celestial bodies, is a paraphrase of that of Iopas, the Carthaginian singer who regales the banquet with which Virgil's Dido welcomes Aeneas to Carthage, another notorious epic sequence of alliance and seduction in an African setting. Of course, the English romance with both the Ethiopians and, via Estefanía, the allures of Spanish Peru, are equally doomed to fail. The 'wedding' of the former is portrayed as false and monstrous, especially given the contemporary anxieties about miscegenation in the viceroyalty on which it plays. An 'amistad fingida' [feigned friendship] (III. 276), it is sterile, based on deception on both sides, and fuelled above all by greed:

> Monstruosa bestia hidrópica sedienta,
> torpe, viciosa, hinchada, detestable,
> que cuanto más el pasto se te aumenta
> tanto despiertas la hambre insacïable:
> ¿quién si no tú, codicia fraudulenta,
> pudo trabar en liga inseparable
> dos diferentes géneros de gentes
> remotamente en todo diferentes? (V. 408)

> [Monstrous dropsical thirsty beast,
> graceless, depraved, swollen, despicable,
> who, however much your feed is increased
> awaken ever more your insatiable hunger:
> who except you, fraudulent greed,
> could tie together in an inseparable bond
> two different kinds of peoples
> utterly different in every way?]

While the English find the Ethiopians unreliable partners as the danger mounts, the Ethiopians, their settlement destroyed and people killed or captured, come to realize the sham of the pirates' promises. As the rueful Biafara puts it, their captivity effectively persists in their subjection to their allies' desires (IX. 767, 771).

From Magellan's 'valle deleitoso', then, to the English flirtation with an Ethiopian kingdom, to the mirroring rapes of Estefanía, Marta and Curicoyllor, an erotic impulse indulged without true consent and a territorial fantasy based on illusion and deception are mutually reflective and equally destructive passions. The concept of 'fuerza' is repeatedly applied both to sexual violation and violent territorial aggression, and capable of achieving only an ephemeral and costly victory. We have already seen that Miramontes, like Virgil, invokes the muse Erato in a second epic proem which precedes these amorous intrigues. Whereas Virgil's invocation marks the transition from the long navigation of the Trojans to the territorial conquest of Italy and first origins of Rome, however, Miramontes's marks a transition from the territorial conquest of Peru and foundation of Lima, 'otra sumptuosa Roma' [another sumptuous Rome] (I. 75), to the seaborne peregrinations around the Antarctic world which will comprise most of the remaining epic. The contrast indicates that the new maritime conflicts will themselves be a series of attempted conquests, except that in Antarctic Peru, in contrast to Trojan Latium, there are no felicitous unions, no projected offspring, and, as a consequence, no satisfying closure to the tales of love and conquest which alternate within the plot. What begins in the poem with the need to magnify the threat of piratical attack ends up feeding into a broader scepticism concerning the possibility of conquest and expansion, of any variety, within this new world.

Defensive Wars and New Worlds

It only remains to demonstrate briefly that such scepticism towards imperialist conquest has a very concrete basis in contemporary debates in the viceroyalty of Peru, and particularly in Lima. Two of these debates in particular place Miramontes in a starkly different world from the empire envisaged by Camões. First is the lengthy polemic sparked in Lima in the wake of the 1598–1604 Curalaba Rebellion, a massive Mapuche uprising in the province of Chile which threatened to destroy the Spanish hold over the region. The suggestion was raised in some quarters that Mapuche intransigence (and that of other resistant peoples in the border regions of Spanish control) might be the direct result of the injustices perpetrated by the colonists, most notably the imposition of forced labour by *encomenderos*. In 1603, a junta in Lima formulated a plan to phase out such unjust practices and extend a general pardon with the offer of peace to the rebels under the rubric of *guerra defensiva*, or defensive warfare. The reforms were to be set on a lasting basis by establishing a fortified frontier — a *raya* — along the river Biobío, across which the only parties to pass would be the peaceful envoys of Church and commerce. The *guerra defensiva* in Chile formed part of a broader shift in overseas policy during the government of Philip III and Lerma (and Lerma's protégés, such as the Marquis of Montesclaros, the incoming viceroy and dedicatee of *Armas antárticas*). This policy of entrenchment had earlier origins in the Americas, where costly conflicts on the frontiers of New Spain and in present-day Bolivia, Argentina and Paraguay gave way at the turn of the century to concerted efforts to defuse tensions.[18] Although officially endorsed by the viceroy and Crown in the early seventeenth centuries, such initiatives were stoutly and vocally resisted by many of those directly implicated in their implementation on the ground, who clamoured that a continuing, expansive war was the only way of keeping Amerindian aggression at bay.

Secondly, the polemic over the perceived alternatives of reconquest or truce at the frontiers of Spanish Peru coincided with what can only be described as a new appetite for exploration and expansion beyond them. In the Indo-Pacific, the turn of the century saw increased investment in augmenting and consolidating territory in the Philippines and Moluccas in response to Dutch expansion, culminating in a speedy (if short-lived) 'reconquest' of Ternate and Tidore in 1606 by a fleet dispatched under Montesclaros from Mexico. To the south, the vast hypothetical Terra Australis which continued to appear on maps became a renewed object of interest. A number of expeditions were sent to the Solomon Islands from Callao to claim the new continent: in 1567 and 1595 under Álvaro de Mendaña with Pedro Fernandes de Queirós as pilot, and in 1605 under Queirós. The latter explored Vanuatu and other Pacific islands, returning to Madrid in 1607 to publicize his findings and agitate for a new era of discovery and colonization, while his rival Luís Vaz de Torres sailed the Torres Strait between Australia and New Guinea on his return to Manila. These initiatives, too, had more than a circumstantial impact in Lima: in addition to the three official missions organized and embarked from the city, further projected voyages constantly disrupted the small naval community during the 1580s and 90s. Here, their advocates competed for attention and resources with those involved, like Miramontes, in the defence of the coastline against piracy, with the primary role in adjudicating between them assumed by the viceroy.

Both polemics shed some light on the underlying structure of the navigations and attempted conquests of which the poem is composed. While Miramontes studiously avoids direct engagement with contemporary disagreements over the *guerra defensiva*, his rhetoric allows little attraction, and less feasibility, to the alternative vision of conquest, of any variety. Arguably, when Magellan crosses the *raya* drawn on the beach of a tropical island and embarks on a thwarted attempt to win it, the reader immersed in the local context of Lima would be more likely to think of the *raya* polemically proposed as the sine qua non of the *guerra defensiva* in Chile, or of contemporary plans to begin a new era of discovery in the Indo-Pacific (it is also used in this sense in *La Araucana*), than of the historical disputes over the Treaty of Zaragoza. The language of *eris* and *eros*, of frustrated passion and incomplete conquests, is therefore a symbolic vehicle for a dialogue both intertextual and political. The poem's diachronic engagement with the problematic theme of love and war through the epic tradition and most immediately in Camões thus also reflects synchronically a local, colonial viewpoint, one from which the question of conquest and expansion seemed far from buried.

Armas antárticas has conventionally been said to uphold an orthodox ethos of militaristic heroism in the realms of Peru. While this may hold true as far as the coastal defence initiatives in which the poet was directly involved are concerned, the overall picture is more complex. The war which is consistently upheld as just and heroic is, in the poem's own terms, a defensive one — the preventative measures and reprisals taken against English and Dutch privateers who are in turn figured as explorers, discoverers and conquistadors. By contrast, the urge towards conquest and expansion, one framed in terms of desire and a frustrated will to dominate and possess, is symbolically bound up with an erotic passion which almost invariably proves futile and tragic for both ruler and community. The elaborate layers of textual imitation and emulation of *Os Lusíadas* in the poem, as Camões's easy, and alluring, equation between heroic conquest and gratified desire is made problematic, illustrates one way in which intensely controversial and immediate political questions could be formulated and addressed imaginatively in the indirect language of epic.

Notes to Chapter 11

1. 'Una lectura: los héroes en el mapa colonial', in *Armas antárticas*, ed. by Paul Firbas (Lima: Pontificia Universidad Católica del Perú, 2006), pp. 69–115 (p. 95). Quotations from the poem are taken from this critical edition based on the autograph manuscript, and designated by canto and stanza number. All translations are my own unless otherwise indicated; elsewhere I abbreviate the title to *AA*.

2. The choice is not entirely atypical: in the *Suplemento* to his Castilian dictionary, Sebastián de Covarrubias affirms that Erato '[p]reside a los que cantan las hazañas de los héroes e invictos varones' [presides over those who sing the deeds of heroes and unconquered men] as well as amatory poets: *Tesoro de la lengua castellana o española*, ed. by Ignacio Arellano and Rafael Zafra (Madrid and Frankfurt: Iberoamericana/Vervuert, 2006), p. 800.

3. Torquato Tasso, *Discourses on the Heroic Poem*, trans. by Mariella Cavalchini, and Irene Samuel (Oxford: Clarendon Press, 1973), pp. 44–49; 'Il messaggiero', in *Prose*, ed. by Ettore Mazzali (Milan and Naples: R. Ricciardi, 1959), pp. 3–73 (p. 55).

4. Roland Greene, *Unrequited Conquests: Love and Empire in the Colonial Americas* (Chicago, IL: University of Chicago Press, 1999).

5. Isabel Torres, *Love Poetry in the Spanish Golden Age: Eros, Eris and Empire* (Woodbridge: Tamesis, 2013), pp. x–xi.

6. Felipe Valencia, 'Las "muchas (aunque bárbaras)" voces líricas de *La Araucana* y la índole poética de una "historia verdadera"', *Revista de Estudios Hispánicos*, 49.1 (2015), 141–71 (pp. 164, 153); Cyrus Moore, *Love, War, and Classical Tradition in the Early Modern Transatlantic World: Alonso de Ercilla and Edmund Spenser* (Tempe: Arizona Center for Medieval and Renaissance Studies, 2014).

7. See Alicia de Colombí-Monguió, *Petrarquismo peruano: Diego Dávalos y Figueroa y la poesía de la 'Miscelánea Austral'* (London: Tamesis, 1985).

8. Eugenio Asensio established the intense interest in the poem on both sides of the Peninsula, adding that, alongside the court and universities, the naval 'escuadras luso-hispanas' [Luso-Hispanic squadrons] seem to have particularly cultivated its reading and imitation: 'La fortuna de *Os Lusíadas*', in *Estudios portugueses* (Paris: Fundação Calouste Gulbenkian, Centro Cultural Português, 1974), pp. 303–24 (p. 314). His conclusions have recently been expanded upon by a number of scholars, notably in Mercedes Blanco, *Góngora heroico: 'Las Soledades' y la tradición épica* (Madrid: Centro de Estudios Europa Hispánica, 2012), and James Nicolopulos, *The Poetics of Empire in the Indies: Prophecy and Imitation in 'La Araucana' and 'Os Lusíadas'* (University Park: Pennsylvania State University, 2000).

9. *Los Lusíadas de Luis de Camoes*, trans. by Enrique Garcés (Madrid: Guillermo Drouy, 1591), sig. A1.

10. Miguel Martínez, 'A Poet of Our Own: The Struggle for *Os Lusíadas* in the Afterlife of Camões', *Journal for Early Modern Cultural Studies*, 10.1 (2010), 71–94 (p. 76).

11. Thomas M. Greene, *The Light in Troy: Imitation and Discovery in Renaissance Poetry* (New Haven, CT: Yale University Press, 1982), p. 45; George W. Pigman, 'Versions of Imitation in the Renaissance', *Renaissance Quarterly*, 33.1 (1980), 1–32.

12. As Jesús Ponce Cárdenas demonstrates, eclectic imitation or *imitación compuesta* was in fact the dominant model during the Spanish Golden Age, in *La imitación áurea (Cervantes, Quevedo, Góngora)* (Paris: Éditions Hispaniques, 2016).

13. *Os Lusíadas*, ed. by Maria Letícia Dionísio (Sintra: Publicações Europa-América, 2007), IX. 38. Quotations from the poem are taken from this edition and designated by canto and stanza number; elsewhere I abbreviate to *OL*.

14. Víctor Mínguez, 'La fiesta política virreinal: propaganda y aculturación en el México del siglo XVII', in *La formación de la cultura virreinal*, ed. by Karl Kohut and Sonia Rose, 3 vols (Madrid and Frankfurt: Iberoamericana/Vervuert, 2000–06), II, 359–74.

15. José de Acosta, *Historia natural y moral de las Indias*, ed. by Edmundo O'Gorman (Mexico City: Fondo de Cultura Económica, 1962), p. 298.

16. Alejandro Cañeque, 'Imaging the Spanish Empire: The Visual Construction of Imperial Authority in Habsburg New Spain', *Colonial Latin American Review*, 19.1 (2010), 29–68 (p. 48).

17. Jason McCloskey, 'Crossing the Line in the Sand: Francis Drake Imitating Ferdinand Magellan in Juan de Miramontes's *Armas antárticas*', *Hispanic Review*, 81.4 (2013), 393–415 (pp. 401, 403, 409).

18. Horacio Zapater, *La búsqueda de la paz en la guerra de Arauco: Padre Luis de Valdivia* (Santiago de Chile: Editorial Andrés Bello, 1992), pp. 50–57.

CHAPTER 12

Classical *Epyllion* and Tropical Cornucopia in Silvestre de Balboa's *Espejo de paciencia*

Raúl Marrero-Fente

Espejo de paciencia [Mirror of Patience] is a poem written by Silvestre de Balboa (Gran Canaria, 1563–Cuba, *c.* 1649) in 1608 to commemorate the kidnapping and freeing of the Bishop of Cuba, Juan de las Cabezas Altamirano, on 29 April 1604 near the town of Bayamo in Cuba.[1] The poem has two cantos. The first narrates the kidnapping and captivity of Bishop Cabezas by French pirates. This first canto ends with the liberation of the bishop, after the payment of an enormous ransom. The second recounts the combat between the creoles and the French pirates, which ends with the victory of the creoles.

The final section of canto I of *Espejo de paciencia* narrates a scene with mythological beings and the offering of a tropical cornucopia to Bishop Cabezas Altamirano. The bucolic genre is the frame of the episode, expressed formally in the verse form of *octavas*. Unlike its literary models Garcilaso de la Vega, Alonso de Ercilla, Gabriel Lobo Lasso and Pedro de Oña, there are no elements typical of amatory lyric because the principal character is a religious authority, but it maintains the conventional format of the description of nature. The scene begins with a *locus amoenus* through the motif of the 'verdes yerbas y esmaltadas flores' [Green grass and adorning flowers] going back to Garcilaso;[2] the woodland inhabited by various species of mythological beings; the entry of the fauns, satyrs and woodland deities who make the first offering of the tropical cornucopia: the soursops, jijiras and star apples; then the woodland nymphs appear and make their mixed offering of animals, plants, flowers, fruits and vegetables: parrots, coffee flowers, maize, tobacco, mammees, pineapples, prickly pears, avocados, bananas, Spanish lime and tomatoes. The hamadryads appear with four dryads who present an offering of fruits, plants, flowers and trees: luffas, *macaguas*, dragon fruits, black berries, and jaguas; followed by the nayads, and their offerings of seafood: crevalle jack, mountain mullet, mullet, shrimps, cichlid, and twospot lebiasana; then come the epimeliads; and the leimakids who give the turtles of Masabo; then the acclamation of the centaurs and sagittari; and finally, the orads offer iguanas, ducks and hutias. The section finishes with a scene of musical parade, another of the topics of the bucolic genre.

Although Balboa follows the conventions of the *locus amoenus*, there is no list of trees, as in the poems of Lobo Lasso and Oña; in their place he mentions the divinities associated with trees, springs, pools, mountains, forests and woods, offering a novel interpretation of the motif of the *silva amoena*.[3] For Lola González, Balboa's poem distinguishes itself from the epic tradition of the New World because, unlike other models, especially Ercilla's *La Araucana*, it shows an interest in American nature.[4] Following the tradition of Virgilian bucolic, poets generally favoured the description of nature dictated by the classical canons and revived in the Renaissance. Lola González also emphasizes Balboa's peculiarity in representing nature through pastoral bucolic, although he follows the 'canon descriptivo de la época' [descriptive canon of the period].[5] Among the allusions to nature González emphasizes those of a thematic character, and points out the well-known influences of Garcilaso, Luis Barahona de Soto and Bartolomé Cairasco de Figueroa. But she clarifies that despite following the conventions of the topos, Balboa introduces a realist note into his descriptions of nature. In this way González refutes the thesis of José María Chacón y Calvo, who established for literary historiography the image of a poem which says little about the nature of the island. For González, Balboa's treatment of nature might be seen as the creation of a 'nueva selva mixta' [new mixed forest], in the style of those assembled by medieval rhetoric, which brings an extraordinary novelty to colonial epic, and constitutes the greatest originality of Balboa's poem.[6]

The image of the countryside in *Espejo de paciencia* appeals to various senses: visual (the colours of flowers and fruits), olfactory (the smells of flowers and fruits) and auditory (the song of the nymphs and music of the fauns). The description of nature constitutes a renewal of the topic in colonial epic poetry. Unlike Ercilla, Lobo Lasso and Oña, the countryside described by Balboa includes flowers, plants, fruits, trees and animals which are part of the nature of the island. It is a realistic landscape because of its description of nature, and at the same time it is a marvellous landscape because of the presence of mythological beings. This mixed landscape is a novelty of Balboa's absent in Juan de Castellanos's *Primera parte de las elegías de varones ilustres de Indias* [First Part of the Elegies of Illustrious Men of the Indies] (Madrid, 1589), because the latter separates into two different cantos the tropical cornucopia and mythological beings.[7] On the other hand, it is a *locus amoenus incultus*, because this is a savage nature which has not been transformed by agriculture and which represents the topos of the riches of the tropics, through the symbol of the horn of plenty.

Unlike canto XVII of *La Araucana* which introduces a marvellous scene through the poet's dream, in Balboa's work the bishop appears as himself, without the aid of any supernatural resource. Balboa uses the adjective before the noun: 'las verdes yerbas y esmaltadas flores' [the green grass and adorning flowers], alluding to the lines of *La Araucana* and to the familiar phrases of Garcilaso's eclogues and Petrarchan bucolic.[8] The arrival of the bishop is similar to that of Hernán Cortés in canto XI of Lobo Lasso de la Vega's *Mexicana* which also employs the technique of resuming the action interrupted at the end of the previous canto: 'el ancho prado, verde y florecido, | de diversos matices esmaltado, | con apacible Céfiro enviaba, |

que suave a toda parte respiraba' [the wide meadow, green and blooming, painted with many hues, blown by a pleasant Zephyr, which breathed sweetly everywhere].[9] It is also present in Pedro de Oña's *Arauco domado*: 'En todo tiempo el rico y fértil prado | está de yerva y flores guarnescido, | las cuales muestran siempre su vestido' [In every season the rich and fertile meadow is adorned with grass and flowers, which always don their garments] (p. 191). As Avalle-Arce highlights,

> la naturaleza descrita no corresponde a la circunstancia real del poeta, a su Chile natal, sino que viene directamente de la tradición literaria. En el *Arauco domado* los cánones poéticos desplazan la realidad física [...]. Los prados que transitan araucanos y españoles son de neto garcilasismo, poetizados de espaldas a la realidad física, con la tradición literaria obsesivamente ante los ojos.[10]

> [the nature described does not correspond to the real circumstances of the poet, to his native Chile, but comes directly from the literary tradition. In *Arauco domado* the poetic canons displace the physical reality [...]. The meadows which Araucanians and Spaniards traverse are pure Garcilasism, poeticized with backs turned to the physical reality, with the literary tradition obsessively before one's eyes.]

Balboa's stanza alludes to the 'propiedades mágicas que tienen determinados elementos de la naturaleza' [magic properties which certain elements of nature have], and to the therapeutic properties of the pleasant spot.[11] The animism which Rafael Lapesa analyses is present in Balboa, who uses an 'enumerative style' to imbue local flora and fauna with a new poetic protagonism, something similar to the poetry of Barahona de Soto, where 'la cornucopia enmarcada en un bodegón poético de frutas y animales' [the cornucopia set within a poetic still life of fruits and animals] organizes a 'cortejo frutal' [cortege of fruits].[12] At the head of this cortege are semi-goats, satyrs, fauns and woodland deities. The mythological beings in Balboa recall the fourth canto of the first elegy of Juan de Castellanos's *Primera parte de las elegías de varones ilustres de Indias*, when the Spaniards describe the first indigenous Americans on the Lucayan islands. Castellanos compares the inhabitants of the Americas with beings from classical mythology; Balboa does not mention the indigenous population, and only speaks of mythological beings as the inhabitants of the Cuban land.

The bucolic scene in Balboa is not ornamental, since the bishop forms part of it, he is integrated with it, and the mythological characters approach him to offer the bounty of the land. In this case too we can say that 'los términos enumerados perfilan las dimensiones reales del paisaje y aluden a una geografía, si no real, coherente con el juego entre ficción y mundo' [the terms enumerated sketch out the real dimensions of the landscape and they allude to a geography which is, if not real, coherent with the play between fiction and world].[13] The landscape has antecedents in Ercilla: 'cantaban dulces letras amorosas, | con cítaras y liras en las manos | diestros sátiros, faunos y silvanos' [there sang sweet amorous songs, with lyres and zithers in their hands, skilful satyrs, fauns and sylvans], who in turn alludes to Garcilaso in Elegía I, vv. 169: 'Sátiros, faunos, ninfas, cuya vida | sin enojos se pasa' [satyrs, fauns, nymphs, whose life is spent without trouble]; and Égloga 2, vv.

1157: 'sátiros y silvanos soltá todos' [release all the satyrs and sylvans].[14] It is a motif imitated too by Juan de Castellanos: 'Si son sátiros estos, o silvanos, | y ellas aquellas ninfas de Aristeo: | o son faunos lascivos y lozanos' [whether these are satyrs, or sylvans, and those the nymphs of Aristaeus: or are they lascivious and strapping fauns]; repeated in Lobo Lasso: 'Sátiros, Faunos, Ninfas campesinas' [satyrs, fauns, country nymphs]; and in Pedro de Oña: 'de sátiros y faunos perseguidas' [pursued by satyrs and fauns], but in these examples there is no interaction between the main character and the mythological characters.[15] In Balboa's poem the scene can be seen as an allegory of the subordination of pagan symbols to Christianity and as an example of Christian bucolic. The scene alludes to the classical model of the *Metamorphoses*, 1. 193–94: 'I have my demigods, my fauns and satyrs, my nymphs and rustic sprites of wold and wood'.[16] Balboa also includes the sylvans, who in classical mythology were deities of the fields and woods, protectors of the crops (Horace, *Epodes* 2.22). The satyrs and nymphs are the so-called lesser gods and they were mortals, unlike the Olympian gods who were immortal.[17] As Vicente Cristóbal indicates, the woodland deities were patrons of the bucolic genre. Balboa's poem belongs to the pastoral genre, but the number of nymphs and their order in the poem is different.[18] Although there are several poetic texts which Balboa could have imitated, we cannot prove his knowledge of them, with the exception of that of Juan de Castellanos, with which there are clear textual correspondences.

The scene of the bishop's welcome combines two passages of Castellanos's poem: the reference to mythological beings in the second elegy and the enumeration of tropical fruits in the fourteenth. Castellanos modifies the classical locus of the pleasant spot with the incorporation of American nature, through the episode of the tropical cornucopia which presents a list of the flora and fauna of Margarita Island:

> Hay muchos higos, uvas, y melones
> dignísimos de ver mesas de reyes;
> pitahayas, guanábanas, anones,
> guayabas y guaraes y mameyes;
> hay chica, cotuprises y mamones,
> piñas, curibijuris, caracueyes
> con otros muchos más que se desechan
> e indios naturales aprovechan.
>   (Castellanos, *Elegías*, p. 294)

> [There are many figs, grapes, and melons
> most worthy to see the tables of kings;
> dragon fruits, soursops, annonas,
> guavas and guaranas and mammees,
> there is chica, cotoperis and Spanish lime,
> pineapples, piñuelas, canistel
> with many more which are discarded
> and the native Indians make use of them.]

The first line begins with a reference to three fruits (figs, grapes, melons) in accordance with the classical prescriptions for the model of an idyllic landscape in bucolic poetry. This trope is rapidly replaced by a dozen American fruits (dragon fruits, soursops, annonas, guavas, guaranas, mammees, chica, cotoperis, Spanish lime, pineapples, piñuelas, canistel) in the form of a catalogue or sample of the wealth of the region. The influence of the Latin classics in Balboa is mediated by *contaminatio* with the models of Garcilaso, Barahona, Sannazaro and Castellanos, among others. This debt is expressed through some bucolic topoi which structure the episode of the bishop and the mythological beings, 'enmarcado en una presentación del paisaje, realzado hasta constituir un *locus amoenus*' [framed in a presentation of the landscape, exalted to the point of being a *locus amoenus*], situated 'en un escenario familiar al poeta' [in a setting familiar to the poet].[19] Balboa also follows Barahona's innovation in 'presentarnos a ninfas cantando y no a pastores' [presenting us with singing nymphs and not shepherds], in imitation of Garcilaso's third eclogue, and presents some centaurs who 'de dos en dos cantan a solas' [sing among themselves in pairs].[20] In this way Balboa introduces 'el motivo del mágico poder de la música sobre la naturaleza' [the motif of the magic power of music over nature], taken from Virgil's Eclogue 8.1–5 and Garcilaso's Égloga 1.4–6.[21]

Balboa, like Garcilaso, links the landscape with the classical tradition and mythology, but gives a new dimension to the description of nature when he adds the flora and fauna of the tropics. In this way the meeting of the bishop and the mythological beings attains a new significance through the conjunction of the richness of elements of the classical tradition with the physical American referent. Balboa creates a new repertory based on the motif of the cornucopia, incorporating a new array of vegetable species, together with fruits and animals, each one of them related to sensory characteristics (colour, smell, taste, touch), reworking the classical topos. We are presented with an arboreal catalogue of plants, vegetables and animals endemic to America. Balboa describes nature through mythological ornamentation and verbal exuberance, situating his description in a 'rincón' 'reducido' [small corner] of the countryside close to Yara.[22] In Balboa there is also 'una poética de la intensificación' [a poetic of intensification], with the objective of achieving the 'recreación de una naturaleza pródiga y sensorial' [recreation of a prodigal and sensory nature] expressed as an 'enumeración acumulativa' [accumulative enumeration] in which the bucolic tradition with its variety of trees, plants and fruits is joined with the mythological sphere which the characters of nymphs and fauns symbolize.[23] In Balboa the insistence on the physical characteristics of nature predominates, by means of 'matices visuales' [visual shades] of the cornucopia with a descriptive and pictorial function.[24]

The 'instrumentalización de la naturaleza' [instrumentalization of nature] is the central axis of the composition of Balboa, because the natural elements serve as a basis for the *argumentatio* of the tropical offerings given by the mythological beings. In this way, Balboa focalizes the attention of the passage on the display of fruits, displacing the importance of the mythological beings, who remain silent. It is necessary to clarify that the offering of the cornucopia acts as a reparative allegory for the transgressions of the inhabitants of the island, responsible for the capture of the bishop by the French corsairs. Beyond this key political interpretation, Balboa also modifies the topos, because he includes descriptive local elements alongside those taken from classical mythology. In this way he creates a new aetiology based on American nature, renewing the original symbolism of classical mythology. The new aetiology does not come from mythology or the symbolism of classical plants, because the range of trees and tropical plants that appears in *Espejo de paciencia* does not exist in Europe.

The keys to interpreting the American natural world do not appear in classical mythology, but rather in the chroniclers of the Indies, the founders of the discourse on the marvels of America. The connection between Balboa's poem and the chronicles of the Indies is suggested by Lola González, especially the connection with the *Sumario de la Natural historia de las Indias* [Summary of the Natural History of the Indies] by Gonzalo Fernández de Oviedo.[25] In the texts of the chronicles of the Indies, especially in Pedro de Anglería, Bartolomé de las Casas, Fernández de Oviedo and Francisco López de Gómara, we find the accounts of a new American mythology. The imitation of Garcilaso, the foundation of the general structure of the passage, is contaminated by the poem's imitation of Juan de Castellanos, the immediate epic model for Balboa, which elevates American nature to the category of a universal myth similar to the classical models. Among the novel features of Balboa is the incorporation of the nymphs and fauns into the tropical cornucopia and their representation (which implies subordination and labour), and the flora and fauna with their sensory variety. These descriptive segments impose a realist vision of the landscape expressed through locative elements with a concrete identification, displacing in this way the conventionality of the bucolic landscape of the Virgilian and Garcilasian models.

As Juan Montero points out, the publication of profane and religious eclogues increases between 1560 and 1580, 'ya que el tratamiento religioso del género gana considerable terreno en esos años y hasta final del siglo' [since the religious treatment of the genre gains considerable ground in those years and towards the end of the century].[26] The description of nature in Balboa's poem also forms part of this religious tendency of the bucolic genre, emphasized by Antonio Prieto, in which the 'paisaje bucólico en cuanto fondo o marco se acrecienta [...] hasta funda-mentar su novedad [...] con una percepción sensorial de la naturaleza que enfatiza sus dones en la misma sonoridad del vocablo que los designa' [bucolic landscape as a background or frame expands to the point of founding its novelty on a sensory perception of nature which emphasizes its gifts in the very sonority of the syllables that designate them].[27] This landscape is the most famous in the poem on account of the richness of the descriptions and the mixture of the classical and island world, which demonstrates the novelty of American culture. The representation of American nature recalls the technique of the *epyllion* in classical poetry, that is, a 'short epic'.[28] This passage, which develops an epic motif in a concentrated way, functions like an intercalated eclogue because the bishop appears like a shepherd or pastor, in a double poetic and religious sense. It is necessary to clarify, however, that, unlike the eclogue, the bishop is a silent shepherd in the poem and his pains are not those of love, but the consequences of his captivity among the French pirates. The complexity of the noted models should not be understood as a series of superficial connections, but as a result of the inclusive tendency of the epic, which seeks to represent an encyclopaedic vision of the culture which produces it.[29] This trait of inclusion appears through the use of various resources of the European literary tradition, which coexist with the local culture, expressed through a heterogeneous mythology and nature. It is this tendency which permits epic poetry to establish connections between different cultures, and thus in the poem of Balboa cultural heterogeneity is one of the modes of exchange between European and local culture.

The first line begins with the mention of three fruits: soursops, jijiras and star apples, imitating the classical prescriptions on the landscape of bucolic poetry:

> Sálenlo a recibir con regocijo
> de aquellos montes por allí cercanos,
> todos los semicapros del cortijo,
> los sátiros, los faunos y silvanos.
> Unos le llaman padre, y otros hijo;
> y alegres, de rodillas, con sus manos
> le ofrecen frutas con graciosos ritos,
> guanábanas, gegiras y caimitos.
>
> Vinieron de los pastos las napeas,
> y al hombro trae cada una un pisitaco,
> y entre cada tres de ellas dos bateas
> de flores olorosas de navaco.
> De los prados que acercan las aldeas
> vienen cargadas de mehí y tabaco,
> mameyes, piñas, tunas y aguacates,
> plátanos y mamones y tomates.
>
> Bajaron de los árboles en naguas
> las bellas amadríades hermosas,
> con frutas de siguapas y macaguas
> y muchas pitajayas olorosas.
> De virijí cargadas y de jaguas
> salieron de los bosques cuatro diosas,
> Dríades de valor y fundamento,
> que dieron al Pastor grande contento.
>
> De arroyos y de ríos a gran prisa
> salen náyades puras, cristalinas,
> con mucho jaguará, dajao y lisa,
> camarones, biajacas y guabinas;
> y mostrando al pastor con gozo y risa
> de las aguas mil cosas peregrinas,
> de le ofrecieron y con gran prudencia
> le hizo cada cual la reverencia.
>
> Luego sin detenerse un punto apenas
> vienen efedríades de las fuentes;
> y con mil diferencias de verbenas,
> coronadas las sienes y las frentes,
> esparcen por el aire las melenas,
> más que el oro de Arabia relucientes;

y con plática dulce y regalada
le dan el parabién de su llegada.

Luego de los estanques del contorno
vienen las lumníades tan hermosas,
que casi en el donaire y rico adorno
quisieron parecer celestes diosas;
y por regaladísimo soborno
le traen al buen obispo, entre otras cosas,
de aquellas hicoteas de Masabo
que no las tengo y siempre las alabo.

[...]

Las hermosas oréades dejando
el gobierno de selvas y montañas,
a Yara van alegres, y cazando
como suelen diversas alimañas.
Y viendo al santo príncipe, humillando
su condición y abiertas sus entrañas,
le ofrecieron con muchas cortesías
muchas iguanas, patos y jutías. (pp. 110–13)

[There go out to meet him with joy
from the neighbouring woods,
all the country Pans,
the satyrs, fauns and sylvans.
Some call him father, and others son;
and joyfully, on their knees, with their hands
they offer him fruit with gracious rites,
soursops, jijiras and star apples.

The napaeae come to meet him from the fields,
and each one carries a *pisitaco* on her shoulder,
and each third one carries two trays
of fragrant *navaco* flowers.
From the meadows which surround the villages
they come loaded with *mehí* and tobacco,
mammees, pineapples, prickly pears and avocados,
bananas and Spanish lime and tomatoes.

There came down from the trees in petticoats
the beautiful, fair hamadryads
with fruits of luffas and *macaguas*
and many scented dragon fruits.
Loaded with black berries and jaguas
four goddesses came from the wood,
true and valorous dryads,
who made the pastor very content.

There hasten from springs and rivers
pure, crystalline nayads,
with crevalle jack, mountain mullet, mullet,
shrimps, cichlid and twospot lebiasana;

And showing the pastor with pleasure and laughter
a thousand strange things from the water
they offered them to him with great prudence
and each one made a curtsey.

Then, hardly waiting an instant
there come ephedryads from the springs;
and with a thousand kinds of verbenas,
crowing their temples and foreheads
they scatter their tresses to the breeze,
shining more than the gold of Arabia;
and with sweet and pleasant voices
they congratulate him on his arrival.

Then from the pools around
the lumniads come, so beautiful,
that in their grace and rich adornment
they almost appeared celestial goddesses;
and as a pleasurable enticement
they bring to the good bishop, among other things
some of those turtles of Masabwhich I don't have and always praise.

[...]

The beautiful oreads leaving
their rule of forests and mountains
go happily to Yara, hunting,
as they are wont to do, different vermin.
And seeing the holy prince, humbling
their condition and with open hearts,
they offered him with many courtesies
many iguanas, ducks and hutias.]

The novelty in this case is that these are American flowers and fruits, incorporated as a catalogue or sample of the richness of the region. The natural world of the Americas irrupts into the poem, through the topos of the tropical cornucopia. This motif was modified by Balboa based on his experience of living in Cuba. The result is a scene which imitates the classical and Renaissance models with the differentiating frame of a double register: on the one hand there is an erudite reading which privileges the sonorous sound of the line above its signifying value, following the tradition of classical epic.[30] This preference for a 'sonorous exoticism' combines an indigenous and Castilian lexis. On the other, there is a sensory reading, that of a reader who recognizes the American reality described in the poem.[31] In this universe of readers, Balboa positions himself as a privileged observer and translator, capable of using European cultural codes and synthesizing them with American reality. This singular experience of a Spaniard who lives in America is transmitted in the lines which describe the tropical cornucopia, motifs embedded in the pastoral convention which frames the bucolic scenes of the bishop's encounter with the mythological beings.

In accordance with the models of poetic imitation, Balboa uses indigenous terms for the flora and fauna of the island to describe the abundance of the American natural world. The presence of the island's flora and fauna in the poem follows a model tradition which seeks to renew the description of the ideal landscape which comes from the genre of the classical bucolic eclogue of Theocritus and Virgil, transformed by the Renaissance eclogue of Garcilaso. Among the more significant changes are the use of an American lexis and accumulative descriptions, which, through their reiteration, insist on the abundance and richness of the lands of the Americas. Balboa thus creates an image of a different landscape, modelled on the norms of the genre of the classical and Renaissance bucolic, where the tropical fauna, flora and fruits have an almost corporeal visualization. The locative elements of the landscape in Balboa's poem are organized through an indigenous lexis contextualized through the models of imitation of classical and Renaissance epic, and they give way to an aetiology, that is, a foundation myth. This American aetiology, modelled on the motif of the tropical cornucopia based on the imitation of Ovid's *Metamorphoses* and the poetry of Garcilaso, has the function of constructing a foundational tale of prominent geographical places, of the trees, flowers and fruits of the Americas. This explains the relationship between the aetiologies and the description of the landscape, and in a special way, poses the question of how to interpret this landscape.[32] The transformation of the rhetorical conventions concerning the description of the landscape in the lines we are commenting on is Balboa's principal innovation. The author seeks to present the reader with a different landscape to that of the European literary tradition, a task which he fulfils especially with the use of an indigenous lexis to name the fruits.

According to Michael Woods, the motif of the cornucopia insists on the preciosity and penchant for detail in the description, through three techniques.[33] Firstly, through the idea that the poet is really interested in the theme. Secondly, the necessity for making amplificatory enumerations to demonstrate the abundance and richness of nature determines the accumulative descriptions. This is why Balboa includes the strophes on the cornucopia with a sample of fruits, vegetables and animals of delicious gastronomical connotations. This catalogue, together with the inventory of the trees and plants of the island, modelled on the Ovidian tradition, produces a feeling towards the land, because they are associated with the American world since in the poem they appear as representations of the endemic products of the geographical area described. This sentiment towards the land demonstrates the close relationship of the poet with American nature, and it is an important marker of difference among Balboa's descriptions of landscape. Thirdly, the preciosity of the descriptions allows attention to be concentrated in their details, and their capacity to inspire marvel. This is the most important achievement of the reworking of the classical motif of the tropical cornucopia in the poem. Balboa demonstrates a new poetic sensibility towards American landscape and nature in which, in spite of the conventions of the models of poetic imitation (Theocritus, Ovid, Virgil, Garcilaso, Camões, Ercilla, Castellanos), the author privileges the use of an indigenous lexis as a technique for stressing the difference between American and European locative elements. Balboa describes the landscape poetically, the flowers, fauna, fruits and other aspects of the American natural world, as a new reality, represented in literary terms as a marvel because it has no equivalent in European reality. In this sense Balboa's work belongs to the tradition of the chronicles of the conquest of America which present the New World as a marvel.

When following the models of poetic imitation, Balboa prefers to use local terms for flora and fauna to distinguish himself from his European models, and find a new poetic space from which the poetic voice manages to differentiate itself from its predecessors. On a first reading this imitation might seem like a continuation of the poetic tradition of the bucolic genre, but a careful reading allows us to see that beyond this there is a search to differentiate its poetic subjectivity. In other words, the presence of the fauna and flora of Cuba in the poem follows a tradition which seeks to rework the description of the ideal bucolic landscape based on the inclusion of elements of American nature. In this sense, Balboa follows the tradition of European bucolic which has a strong symbolic value. It is necessary to nuance this with the fact that the symbolism of Balboa's poem cannot be entirely understood from the European perspective of the period, since there is no sphere of reference in the tradition of epic models which would include these new American settings and the necessary vocabulary to define them. Among the most significant changes can be noted, among others, the presence of accumulative descriptions of tropical fruits: 'De los prados que acercan las aldeas | vienen cargadas de mehí y tabaco, | mameyes, piñas, tunas y aguacates, | plátanos y mamones y tomates' [From the meadows which surround the villages they come loaded with *mehí* and tobacco, mammees, pineapples, prickly pears and avocados, bananas and Spanish lime and tomatoes] (p. 111).

Therefore, in spite of the exoticism and defamiliarization of his description, Balboa manages to present a vision of a poetic landscape in accordance with the norms of the genre of the eclogue, where the fauna, flora and tropical fruits achieve an almost corporeal visualization. The locative elements of the landscape in Balboa's poem are organized around the countryside of Yara, but in the passage of the offering to Bishop Cabezas we also find allusions to other regions of the island. The most significant aspect of Balboa's modification is that the plane of the reality described surpasses, in its richness, the schemes of European literary models. It is necessary to insist that one of the functions of aetiologies in epic poems is to recount the origin of prominent geographical places, of trees, flowers and fruits. In this sense, Susanne Wofford points out that aetiologies are connected with the description of the landscape in the poem, and pose the question of how to interpret this landscape.[34] In Balboa's poem, the American natural world appears as a predominant element above the literary elements. This innovation is achieved through the mention of tropical flora and fauna, which appear as a heterogeneous nature in two senses. Firstly, through their own autochthonous condition; secondly, through the language which names this flora and fauna, also formed by American terms.

This extensive enumeration of the fruits and animals also fulfils the function of emphasizing the authenticity of the feats narrated in the poem. This topos was a typical technique in the poetry of the period and achieves its greatest development in the seventeenth century. As Michael Woods notes, the motif of the cornucopia is characterized by its preciosity and detailed description, based on two moments.[35] Firstly, by giving the impression that the poet is captivated by his theme: this explains Balboa's emphasis on emotion, personified in the welcome which the satyrs, nymphs, fauns and sylvans offer to the bishop. Balboa presents these mythological beings as intimate with Bishop Cabezas Altamirano, which oscillates between the sentiments of Christian devotion and a pagan atmosphere, with scenes of adorations which include the offering of autochthonous products of the fauna and flora of the island. Secondly, the necessity to make more extensive lists to demonstrate the richness of nature determines the accumulative descriptions. Thus, we see the scene of cornucopia in Balboa's poem which shows in rapid succession a list of fruits, vegetables and animals of delicious gastronomic connotations: soursops, star apples, mammees, pineapples, avocados, bananas, Spanish lime, tomatoes, crevalle jack, mountain mullet, mullet, shrimps, cichlid, and twospot lebiasana, turtles, iguanas, ducks and hutias. The preciosity of the descriptions allows the attention to concentrate on details and their capacity to inspire marvel. The greatest value of the episode of the cornucopia in Balboa is its capacity to represent the new by means of the familiar, in a mix which necessarily implies a consciousness of the difference between European and American nature, seen from the perspective of America. This position of the poetic voice demonstrates a sensibility towards the landscape and the nature of Cuba in which, despite the conventions of the models of poetic imitation, Balboa maintains the separation of European and American elements, which appear together but without becoming confused. The scene of the hamadryads in petticoats particularly stands out here, where the poetic image is created by a superposition of two opposed realities, and in which the presence of the indigenous vocabulary serves as a sign of difference between the American and the Peninsular. This superposition is achieved through the simile of the hamadryads which aims to stress the differentiating elements between the two realities: on the one hand, the hamadryads recall the European poetic tradition; while the American flora and fauna, named through an indigenous vocabulary, represent the American reality:

> Bajaron de los árboles en naguas
> las bellas amadríades hermosas,
> con frutas de siguapas y macaguas
> y muchas pitajayas olorosas.

> [There came down from the trees in petticoats
> the beautiful, fair hamadryads
> with fruits of luffas and *macaguas*
> and many scented dragon fruits.]

This reworking of the theme of the landscape in Balboa also appears in the imitation of the motif of the Garden of Eden, one with a long tradition from the classical Arcadia, a poetic transposition of an earthly paradise as a place of happiness and serenity. The description of the nature of the island as a Garden of Eden follows the conventions of a source of rest and satisfaction.[36] Unlike the gardens of the classical literary tradition (Virgil, *Aeneid* VI; *Bucolics* III) and the Renaissance

(Ariosto, *Orlando furioso*, X; Camões, *Os Lusíadas*, IX), Balboa introduces an important innovation, because 'vestir a las ninfas con "naguas", aparte de privilegiar lo americano al colocarlo como signo junto a lo culto y a lo clásico, "cubaniza" a las ninfas, las hace tangibles y las coloca del lado americano' [dressing the nymphs with 'petticoats', apart from privileging the American, putting it as a sign on a level with the erudite and classical, 'cubanizes' the nymphs, it makes them tangible and places them on the American side].[37] In Balboa's imitation the garden is emblematic of an ethical valuation following the Horatian precept of the admonitions and precepts of the Christian epic of Tasso. The inclusion of the mythological figures in the American setting is a technique adopted by Balboa to comply with the norms of the genre, but it demonstrates the conflict caused by the appropriation of the mythological machinery, following Tasso's precepts of subordinating the pagan mythological machinery to the necessities of Christian epic.

Notes to Chapter 12

1. On Silvestre de Balboa's poem see the studies of Enrique Saínz, *Silvestre de Balboa y la literatura cubana* (La Habana: Letras Cubanas, 1982); Juana Goergen, *Literatura fundacional americana: 'El Espejo de paciencia'* (Madrid: Pliegos, 1993); Raúl Marrero-Fente, *Epic, Empire and Community in the Atlantic World: Silvestre de Balboa's 'Espejo de paciencia'* (Lewisburg, PA: Bucknell University Press, 2008); and Graciella Cruz-Taura, *'Espejo de paciencia' y Silvestre de Balboa en la historia de Cuba* (Madrid and Frankfurt: Iberoamericana/Vervuert, 2009).

2. Silvestre de Balboa, *Espejo de paciencia*, ed. by Raúl Marrero-Fente (Madrid: Cátedra, 2010), p. 110. All translations are Imogen Choi's unless otherwise stated.

3. See Rafael Osuna, 'Un caso de continuidad literaria: la silva *amoena*', *Thesaurus*, 24 (1969), 377–407; and Pedro de Oña, *Arauco domado*, ed. by Ornella Gianesin (Pavia: Ibis, 2014), p. 187.

4. Lola González, 'La naturaleza en el *Espejo de paciencia* de Silvestre de Balboa', *Arrabal*, 1 (1998), 13–22 (p. 13).

5. González, 'La naturaleza', p. 16.

6. González, 'La naturaleza', p. 19.

7. Castellano's *Elegías* have four parts and more than 113,000 lines, although only the first part appeared in the author's lifetime. The rest of the work was published in fragments from 1847 (the first three parts), and the fourth in 1886.

8. Alonso de Ercilla, *La Araucana*, ed. by Isaías Lerner (Madrid: Cátedra, 1993), p. 510. See Isaías Lerner, 'Garcilaso en Ercilla', *Lexis*, 2 (1978), 201–21 (p. 206).

9. Gabriel Lobo Lasso de la Vega, *De Cortés valeroso y Mexicana*, ed. by Nidia Pullés-Linares (Madrid and Frankfurt: Iberoamericana/Vervuert, 2005), p. 313.

10. Juan Bautista de Avalle-Arce, *La épica colonial* (Pamplona: EUNSA, 2000), p. 73.

11. Garcilaso de la Vega, *Obra poética y textos en prosa*, ed. by Bienvenido Morros (Barcelona: Crítica, 1995), p. 473.

12. José Lara Garrido, *La poesía de Luis Barahona de Soto (Lírica y épica del Manierismo)* (Málaga: Servicio de Publicaciones, Diputación Provincial de Málaga, 1994), pp. 246, 251, 258.

13. Joaquín Roses, 'Retórica y naturaleza en la Égloga cuarta de Barahona de Soto', in *De saber poético y verso peregrino: la invención manierista en Luis Barahona de Soto*, ed. by José Lara Garrido (Málaga: Universidad de Málaga, 2002), pp. 279–95 (p. 286).

14. Ercilla, *La Araucana*, p. 510; Garcilaso de la Vega, *Obra poética*, pp. 100, 194.

15. Juan de Castellanos, *Elegías de varones ilustres de Indias*, ed. by Gerardo Rivas Moreno (Bogotá: Gerardo Rivas, 1997), p. 34; Lobo Lasso, *De Cortés valeroso*, p. 312; Oña, *Arauco domado*, p. 192.

16. Ovid, *Metamorphoses*, trans. by A. D. Melville (Oxford: Oxford University Press, 1986), p. 6.

17. Antonio Ruiz de Elvira, *Mitología clásica* (Madrid: Gredos, 1995), p. 94.

18. Vicente Cristóbal, 'La tradición clásica en la poesía de Luis Barahona de Soto', in *De saber poético*

y verso peregrino: la invención manierista en Luis Barahona de Soto, ed. by José Lara Garrido (Málaga: Universidad de Málaga, 2002), pp. 87–104.

19. Cristóbal, 'La tradición clásica', p. 96.
20. Cristóbal, 'La tradición clásica', p. 96; Balboa, *Espejo*, p. 113.
21. Cristóbal, 'La tradición clásica', p. 97.
22. José Fernández Dougnac, 'Naturaleza, topografía y mito en la poesía de Barahona de Soto', in *De saber poético y verso peregrino: la invención manierista en Luis Barahona de Soto*, ed. by José Lara Garrido (Málaga: Universidad de Málaga, 2002), pp. 229–56 (p. 231).
23. Fernández Dougnac, 'Naturaleza', p. 231.
24. Fernández Dougnac, 'Naturaleza', p. 235.
25. González, 'La naturaleza', p. 19.
26. Juan Montero, 'La égloga en la poesía española del siglo XVI: panorama de un género (desde 1543)', in *La égloga*, ed. by Begoña López Bueno (Seville: Universidad de Sevilla, 2002), pp. 183–206 (p. 201).
27. Antonio Prieto, *La poesía española del siglo XVI, II. Aquel valor que respetó el olvido* (Madrid: Cátedra, 1998), p. 699.
28. On the genre of the epyllion see the works which appear in Manuel Baumbach and Silvio Bär (eds), *Brill's Companion to Greek and Latin Epyllion and Its Reception* (Leiden and Boston: Brill, 2012). See also Sofie Kluge, 'Mirror of Myth: The Baroque Epyllion', in *Diglossia: The Early Modern Reinvention of Mythological Discourse* (Kassel: Edition Reichenberger, 2014), pp. 139–55; and 'Espejo del mito: algunas consideraciones sobre el epilio barroco', *Criticón*, 115 (2012), 159–74.
29. Margaret Beissinger, Jane Tylus and Susanne Wofford (eds), *Epic Traditions in the Contemporary World: The Poetics of Community* (Berkeley: University of California Press, 1999), p. 2.
30. Lara Garrido, *La poesía de Luis Barahona de Soto*, p. 247.
31. Lara Garrido, *La poesía de Luis Barahona de Soto*, p. 249.
32. Susanne Wofford, 'Epic and the Politics of the Origin Tale: Virgil, Ovid, Spenser, and Native American Aetiology', in Beissinger, Tylus and Wofford (eds), *Epic Traditions*, pp. 239–69 (p. 242).
33. Michael J. Woods, *The Poet and the Natural World in the Age of Góngora* (Oxford: Oxford University Press, 1978), pp. 99–102.
34. Wofford, 'Epic', p. 242.
35. Woods, *The Poet and the Natural World*, p. 100.
36. A. B. Giamatti, *The Earthly Paradise and the Renaissance Epic* (Princeton, NJ: Princeton University Press, 1966), p. 179.
37. Goergen, *Literatura fundacional*, p. 78.

BIBLIOGRAPHY

Academia burlesca que se hizo en Buen Retiro a la majestad de Filipo cuarto el Grande, ed. by María Teresa Julio (Madrid and Frankfurt: Universidad de Navarra/Iberoamericana/Vervuert, 2007)

ACOSTA, JOSÉ DE, *Historia natural y moral de las Indias*, ed. by Edmundo O'Gorman (Mexico City: Fondo de Cultura Económica, 1962)

ACOSTA, LEONARDO, 'El Barroco de Indias y la ideología colonialista', in *Ensayos escogidos* (La Habana: Editorial Letras Cubanas, 2009), pp. 219–69

ADORNO, ROLENA, 'Reconsidering Colonial Discourse for Sixteenth- and Seventeenth-Century Spanish America', *Latin American Review*, 28.3 (1993), 135–45

——*Guaman Poma: Writing and Resistance in Colonial Peru* (Austin: University of Texas Press, 2000)

——'The account of Don Juan de Mendoza y Luna, the marquis of Montesclaros, viceroy of Peru, to his successor (GkS 589, 2°)' [2001] in http://wayback-01.kb.dk/wayback/20101112075707/http://www2.kb.dk/elib/mss/mendoza/note-eng.htm

——*The Polemics of Possession in Spanish American Narrative* (New Haven, CT, and London: Yale University Press, 2007)

——*Colonial Latin American Literature: A Very Short Introduction* (Oxford and New York: Oxford University Press, 2011)

——'Carlos de Sigüenza y Góngora (1645–1700): "el amante más fino de nuestra patria"', *Hispanófila*, 171 (2014), 11–27

——'El México antiguo en el Barroco de Indias: don Carlos de Sigüenza y Góngora', *Anales de Estudios Latinoamericanos*, 35 (2015), 1–42

AGUIRRE ZAMORANO, PILAR, 'Poder ordinario del virrey del Pirú sacadas de las cédulas que se han despachado en el Real Consejo de las Indias', *Historiografía y Bibliografía Americanistas*, 29.2 (1985), 15–97

ALATORRE, ANTONIO, 'Avatares barrocos del romance', in *Cuatro ensayos sobre arte poética* (Mexico City: El Colegio de México, 2007), pp. 55–85

ALCINA ROVIRA, JUAN F., 'Cristóbal Cabrera en Nueva España y sus *Meditatiunculae ad principem Philippum*', *Nova Tellus*, 2 (1984), 131–63

ALEXIOUS, MARGARET, *The Ritual Lament in Greek Tradition* (Cambridge: Cambridge University Press, 1974)

ALLEN, MICHAEL, *Icastes: Marsilio Ficino's Interpretation of Plato's Sophist* (Berkeley and Los Angeles: University of California, 1989)

ALVAR, MANUEL, *Juan de Castellanos: tradición española y realidad americana* (Bogotá: Caro y Cuervo, 1972)

ÁLVAREZ VILELA, ÁNGEL, 'La expedición a Ancud en *La Araucana* o la recuperación del mérito por parte de Ercilla', *Anales de Literatura Hispanoamericana*, 24 (1995), 77–89

AMOR PETROV, LISA, 'On the Divinity of Sor Juana's Virgin Mary: A Question of Feminist Heterodoxy or Intercultural Agency', *Calíope*, 13.2 (2007), 23–38

ANDRADE, VICENTE DE P., *Ensayo bibliográfico mexicano del siglo XVII* (Mexico City: Imprenta del Museo Nacional, 1899)

ANTONIO, NICOLÁS, *Biblioteca Hispana Nova*, 2 vols (Madrid: Joaquín de Ibarra, 1783)

ARELLANO, IGNACIO, *El ingenio de Lope de Vega: escolios a las Rimas Humanas y divinas del Licenciado Tomé de Burguillos* (New York: Idea, 2012)

ARES QUEIJA, BERTA, 'Las danzas de los indios: un camino para la evangelización en el virreinato del Perú', *Revista de Indias*, 44.174 (1984), 445–63

Archivo Digital del Romancero, <http://fundacionramonmenendezpidal.org/archivodigital/collections/show/22>

ASENSIO, EUGENIO, 'La fortuna de *Os Lusíadas*', in *Estudios portugueses* (Paris: Fundação Calouste Gulbenkian, Centro Cultural Português, 1974), pp. 303–24

AUERBACH, ERICH, 'Figura', in *Scenes from the Drama of European Literature: Six Essays*, trans. by Ralph Manheim (Gloucester, MA: Peter Smith, 1973), pp. 11–76

AUGUSTINE, *Exposition on the Book of Psalms*, 6 vols (Oxford: John Henry Parker, 1847–57)

AUSTERN, LINDA PHYLLIS, '"Sing Againe Syren": The Female Musician and Sexual Enchantment in Elizabethan Life and Literature', *Renaissance Quarterly*, 42.3 (1989), 420–48

AVALLE-ARCE, JUAN BAUTISTA DE, *La épica colonial* (Pamplona: EUNSA, 2000)

AVELLANEDA, JOSÉ IGNACIO, *The Conquerors of the New Kingdom of Granada* (Albuquerque: University of New Mexico Press, 1995)

BAÉZ RUBÍ, LINDA, *Mnemosine novohispánica* (Mexico City: Universidad Nacional Autónoma de México, 2005)

BAKHTIN, MIKHAIL, *Rabelais and his World*, trans. by Helen Iswolsky (Bloomington: Indiana University Press, 1984)

BALBOA, SILVESTRE DE, *Espejo de paciencia*, ed. by Raúl Marrero-Fente (Madrid: Cátedra, 2010)

BALBUENA, BERNARDO DE, *Grandeza mexicana*, ed. by Asima F. X. Saad Maura (Madrid: Cátedra, 2011)

BARLOW, R. H., 'Some Remarks on the Term "Aztec Empire"', *The Americas*, 1.3 (1945), 345–49

BARROS FRANCO, JOSÉ MIGUEL, 'Los 'últimos años de Sarmiento de Gamboa', *Estudios de Historia Social y Económica de América*, 3–4 (1988), 9–28

BARTELINK, G. J. M., 'Hieronymus und Ovid', *Greek, Roman and Byzantine Studies*, 4 (1975), 13–19

BATAILLON, MARCEL, *Erasmo y España: estudios sobre la historia espiritual del siglo XVI*, trans. by A. Alatorre (Mexico City: FCE, 2007)

BAUDOT, GEORGES, *Utopia and History in Mexico* (Niwot: University of Colorado Press, 1995)

—— AND MARÍA ÁGUEDA MÉNDEZ, *Amores prohibidos: la palabra condenada en el México de los virreyes* (Mexico City: Siglo XXI, 1997)

BAUMBACH, MANUEL, and SILVIO BÄR (eds), *Brill's Companion to Greek and Latin Epyllion and Its Reception* (Leiden and Boston, MA: Brill, 2012)

BAZIN, GERMAIN, *The Baroque: Principles, Styles, Modes, Themes* (London: Thames and Hudson, 1968)

BEARD, MARY, *Laughter in Ancient Rome: On Joking, Tickling and Cracking up* (Berkeley: University of California, 2014)

BEISSINGER, MARGARET, JANE TYLUS and SUSANNE WOFFORD (eds), *Epic Traditions in the Contemporary World: The Poetics of Community* (Berkeley: University of California Press, 1999)

BENÍTEZ LABORDE, EDNA MARGARITA, 'La poesía de Agustín de Salazar y Torres' (unpublished PhD dissertation, SUNY, Albany, 1998)

BENVENISTE, ÉMILE, *Problems in General Linguistics*, trans. by Mary Elizabeth Meek (Coral Gables, FL: University of Miami, 1971)

BERCÉ, YVES-MARIE, *History of Peasant Revolts* (Ithaca, NC: Cornell University Press, 1990)

BERISTÁIN DE SOUZA, JOSÉ MARIANO, *Biblioteca hispano-americana septentrional*, 3 vols (Mexico City: Oficina de don Alejandro Valdés, 1816–21)

BERLEY, MARC, *After the Heavenly Tune: English Poetry and the Aspiration to Song* (Pittsburgh, PA: Duquesne University Press, 2000)

BERLING, BÉNASSY, *Humanismo y religión en Sor Juana Inés de la Cruz* (Mexico City: Universidad Nacional Autónoma de México, 1983)

BERMUDO, JUAN, *Libro primero de la declaración de instrumentos* (Osuna: Juan de León, 1549)

BEUTLER, GISELA, *Estudios sobre el romancero español en Colombia en su tradición escrita y oral desde la época de la Conquista hasta la actualidad* (Bogotá: Instituto Caro y Cuervo, 1977)

BEYERSDORFF, MARGOT, 'Rito y verbo en la poesía de fray Luis Jerónimo de Oré', in *Mito y simbolismo en los Andes: la figura y la palabra*, ed. by Henrique Urbano (Cuzco: Centro de Estudios Regionales Andinos 'Bartolomé de las Casas', 1993), pp. 215–37

——'Luis Jerónimo de Oré', in *Guide to Documentary Sources for Andean Studies, 1530–1900*, ed. by Joanne Pillsbury, 3 vols (Norman: University of Oklahoma Press, 2008), III, 472–75

BLANCO, MERCEDES, *Góngora heroico: 'Las Soledades' y la tradición épica* (Madrid: Centro de Estudios Europa Hispánica, 2012)

BOCÁNGEL, GABRIEL, *La lira de las musas*, ed. by Trevor J. Dadson (Madrid: Cátedra, 1985)

BOONE, ELIZABETH H., *Incarnations of the Aztec Supernatural: The Image of Huitzilopochtli in Mexico and Europe* (Philadelphia: Transactions of the American Philosophical Society, 1989)

BOUZA, FERNANDO, *Corre manuscrito: una historia cultural del Siglo de Oro* (Madrid: Marcial Pons, 2001)

BRADING, D. A., *The First America: The Spanish Monarchy, Creole Patriots and the Liberal State, 1492–1867* (Cambridge: Cambridge University Press, 1991)

BRAUDEL, FERDINAND, *The Mediterranean and the Mediterranean World in the Age of Philip II*, 2 vols (Berkeley: University of California Press, 1995)

BROWN, KENNETH, *Anastasio Pantaleón de Ribera (1600–1629): ingenioso miembro de la República literaria española* (Madrid: Studia Humanitatis/José Porrúa Turanzas, 1980)

BURMEISTER, JOACHIM, *Musica poetica* (Rostock: Myliander, 1606)

BURKE, PETER, *Popular Culture in Early Modern Europe* (Burlington, VT: Ashgate, 2009)

BURRUS, E. J., 'Cristóbal Cabrera (c. 1515–98), First American Author: A Checklist of his Writings in the Vatican Library', *Manuscripta*, 4 (1960), 67–89

——'Cristóbal Cabrera on the Missionary Methods of Vasco de Quiroga', *Manuscripta*, 5 (1961), 17–27

CABELLO VALBOA, MIGUEL, *Miscelánea Antártica*, ed. by Isaías Lerner (Seville: Fundación José Manuel Lara, 2011)

CABRERA, ALONSO DE, *Sermón que predicó el maestro fray Alonso de Cabrera, predicador de su Majestad del Orden de predicadores. A las honras de nuestro Señor el serenísimo y católico Rey Filippo Segundo, que esté en el Cielo: que hizo la Villa de Madrid en S. Domingo el Real último de octubre 1598* (Roma: Luis Zaneti, 1599)

CABRERA, FRAY CRISTÓBAL, *Meditatiunculae ad Serenissimum Hispaniarum Principem Philippum* (Pinciae [Valladolid]: Franciscus Ferdinandez Cordubensis, 1548)

CACHO CASAL, RODRIGO, 'Zanahorias y otras picardías: Hurtado de Mendoza ante la tradición bernesca', *Calíope*, 12.2 (2006), 13–32

CAMÕES, LUÍS DE, *Los Lusíadas de Luis de Camoes*, trans. by Enrique Garcés (Madrid: Guillermo Drouy, 1591)

——*Lusíadas, Comentadas por Manuel de Faria e Sousa* [facsimile of Madrid, 1639], 2 vols (Lisboa: Imprensa Nacional, Casa da Moeda, 1972)

——*Os Lusíadas*, ed. by Maria Letícia Dionísio (Sintra: Publicações Europa-América, 2007)

CAMPOS, LEOPOLDO, 'Métodos misionales y rasgos biográficos de don Vasco de Quiroga según Cristóbal Cabrera, Pbro.', in *Don Vasco de Quiroga y el Arzobispado de Morelia*, ed. by Manuel Ponce (Mexico City: Jus, 1965), pp. 107–58

CÁNCER, JERÓNIMO DE, *Obras varias* (Lisbon: Henrique Valente de Oliveira, 1657)

CANO GUTIÉRREZ, DIEGO, *Relación de las fiestas triunfales que la insigne Universidad de Lima hizo a la Inmaculada Concepción de nuestra Señora* (Lima: Francisco Lasso, 1619)

CAÑEQUE, ALEJANDRO, *The King's Living Image: The Culture and Politics of Viceregal Power in Colonial Mexico* (New York and London: Routledge, 2004)

——'Imaging the Spanish Empire: The Visual Construction of Imperial Authority in Habsburg New Spain', *Colonial Latin American Review*, 19.1 (2010), 29–68

CAÑIZARES-ESGUERRA, JORGE, *Puritan Conquistadors: Iberianizing the Atlantic, 1550–1700* (Stanford: Stanford University Press, 2006)

CARAMUEL, JUAN, *Primer Cálamo. Rítmica*, ed. by Isabel Paraíso (Valladolid: Universidad de Valladolid, 2007)

CARNEIRO, SARISSA, *Retórica del infortunio: persuasión, deleite y ejemplaridad en el siglo XVI* (Madrid and Frankfurt: Iberoamericana/Vervuert, 2015)

CARVAJAL Y ROBLES, RODRIGO DE, *Fiestas que celebró la Ciudad de los Reyes del Pirú al nacimiento del serenísimo príncipe don Baltasar Carlos de Austria nuestro señor* (Lima: Gerónimo de Contreras, 1632)

CASAS, BARTOLOMÉ DE LAS, *Brevísima relación de la destruición de las Indias*, ed. by José Miguel Martínez-Torrejón (Barcelona: Círculo de Lectores, 2009)

CASTAÑEDA DE LA PAZ, MARÍA, *Pintura de la peregrinación de los culhuaque-mexitin (Mapa de Sigüenza): análisis de un documento de origen tenochca* (Zinacantépec, Estado de México: El Colegio Mexiquense, AC, and Conaculta: Instituto Nacional de Antropología e Historia, 2006)

CASTELLANOS, JUAN DE, *Historia del Reino de Nueva Granada*, ed. by Antonio Paz y Meliá, 2 vols (Madrid: Pérez Dubrull, 1886)

——*Elegías de varones ilustres de Indias*, ed. by Gerardo Rivas Medrano (Bogotá: Gerardo Rivas, 1997)

CASTILLO GÓMEZ, ANTONIO, *Entre la pluma y la pared: una historia social de la escritura en los Siglos de Oro* (Madrid: Akal, 2006)

CASTRO-IBASETA, JAVIER, 'Monarquía Satírica. Poética de la caída del Conde Duque de Olivares' (unpublished PhD dissertation, Universidad Autónoma de Madrid, 2008)

——*Beware the Poetry: Political Satire and the Emergence of the Spanish Public Sphere (1600–1645)*, forthcoming.

CEPEDA, FERNANDO DE, and FERNANDO ALFONSO CARRILLO, *Relación universal legítima y verdadera del sitio en que está fundada la muy noble, insigne y muy leal Ciudad de México* (Mexico City: Francisco Salvago, 1637)

CERONE, PEDRO, *El melopeo y maestro* (Naples: Juan Bautista Gargano and Lucrecio Nucci, 1613)

Certamen poético (Mexico City: Viuda de Bernardo Calderón, 1654)

CERVANTES, MIGUEL DE, *La Galatea*, ed. by Francisco López Estrada and María Teresa García-Berdoy (Madrid: Cátedra, 1999)

CERVERA DE LA TORRE, ANTONIO, *Testimonio auténtico, y verdadero de las cosas notables que pasaron en la dichosa muerte del Rey nuestro Señor Don Phelipe segundo* (Valencia: Pedro Patricio Mey, 1599)

CHAILLEY, JACQUES, *L'imbroglio des modes* (Paris: A. Leduc, 1960)

CHANG-RODRÍGUEZ, RAQUEL (ed.), *Venid, ninfas del sur, venid ligeras: voces poéticas virreinales* (Madrid and Frankfurt: Iberoamericana/Vervuert, 2008)

——'Felipe Huaman Poma de Ayala y Luis Jerónimo de Oré, dos ingenios andinos', *Libros & Artes* (Revista de Cultura de la Biblioteca Nacional del Perú), 13.78–79 (2016), 11–14

CHARTIER, ROGER, *The Cultural Origins of the French Revolution*, trans. by Lydia Cochrane (Durham, NC: 1991)

CHEVALIER, MAXIME, 'La Fortune du romancero ancien (fin du XVe-début du XVIIe siècle)', *Bulletin Hispanique*, 90.1 (1988), pp. 187–95

——'Decoro y decoros', *Revista de Filología Española*, 73.1–2 (1993), 5–24

CHOI, IMOGEN, 'Conflict Ethics and Political Community in Early Peruvian Epic' (unpublished PhD dissertation, University of Cambridge, 2016)

CLOSA FARRÉS, JOSEP, 'Notas sobre el primer texto latino publicado en América', *Universitas Tarraconensis*, 1 (1976), 143–54

COELLO, ÓSCAR, *Los inicios de la poesía castellana en el Perú* (Lima: Pontificia Universidad Católica, 1999)

COHEN SUÁREZ, ANANDA, *Heaven, Hell and Everything in Between: Murals of the Colonial Andes* (Austin: University of Texas Press, 2016)

COLOMBÍ-MONGUIÓ, ALICIA DE, *Petrarquismo peruano: Diego Dávalos y Figueroa y la poesía de la 'Miscelánea Austral'* (London: Tamesis, 1985)

CONTI, NATALE, *Mythologiae*, trans. by John Mulryan and Steven Brown, 2 vols (Tempe, AZ: Arizona Center for Medieval and Renaissance Studies, 2006)

COOK, NOBLE DAVID, 'Luis Jerónimo de Oré: una aproximación', in *Symbolo Catholico Indiano*, ed. by Antonine Tibesar (Lima: Australis, 1992), pp. 35–63

COOKE, JOHN DANIEL, 'Euhemerism: A Medieval Interpretation of Classical Paganism', *Speculum*, 2.4 (1927), 396–410

CORNEJO POLAR, ANTONIO, *Escribir en el aire: ensayo sobre la heterogeneidad socio-cultural en las literaturas andinas* (Lima: Centro de Estudios Literarios 'Antonio Cornejo Polar'/ Latinoamericana Editores, 2003)

CORREAS, GONZALO, *Vocabulario de refranes y frases proverbiales y otras fórmulas comunes de la lengua castellana en que van todos los impresos antes y otra gran copia* (Madrid: Establecimiento Tipográfico de Jaime Rates, 1906)

COVARRUBIAS, SEBASTIÁN DE, *Tesoro de la lengua castellana o española*, ed. by Martín de Riquer (Barcelona: Alta Fulla, 1998)

—— *Tesoro de la lengua castellana o española*, ed. by Ignacio Arellano and Rafael Zafra (Madrid and Frankfurt: Iberoamericana/Vervuert, 2006)

CRISTÓBAL, VICENTE, 'Tempestades épicas', *Cuadernos de Investigación Filológica*, 14 (1988), 125–48

——'De *La Eneida* a *La Araucana*', *Cuadernos de Filología Clásica: Estudios Latinos*, 9 (1995), 68–101

——'La tradición clásica en la poesía de Luis Barahona de Soto,' in *De saber poético y verso peregrino: la invención manierista en Luis Barahona de Soto*, ed. by José Lara Garrido (Málaga: Universidad de Málaga, 2002), pp. 87–104

——'Virgilianismo y tradición clásica en *La Cristíada* de Fray Diego de Hojeda', *Cuadernos de Filología Clásica. Estudios Latinos*, 25.1 (2005), 49–78

CRUZ, SOR JUANA INÉS DE LA, *Villancicos a la Asunción* (Mexico City: Viuda de Bernardo Calderón, 1676)

——*Obras completas*, ed. by Alfonso Méndez Plancarte and Alberto G. Salceda, 4 vols (Mexico City: Fondo de Cultura Económica, 1951–57)

——*Neptuno alegórico*, in *Inundación castálida*, ed. by Georgina Sabat de Rivers (Madrid: Castalia, 1982), pp. 365–447

——*La Respuesta / The Answer*, ed. and trans. by Amanda Powell and Electa Arenal (New York: City University of New York, 1994)

——— *Obras completas de Sor Juana Inés de la Cruz, I. Lírica personal*, ed. by Antonio Alatorre (Mexico City: Fondo de Cultura Económica, 2012)

CRUZ-TAURA, GRACIELLA, *'Espejo de paciencia' y Silvestre de Balboa en la historia de Cuba* (Madrid and Frankfurt: Iberoamericana/Vervuert, 2009)

CUADRIELLO, JAIME, 'Los jeroglíficos de la Nueva España', in *Juegos de ingenio y agudeza: la pintura emblemática de la Nueva España* (Mexico City: Patronato del Museo Nacional de Arte, AC, 1994), pp. 84–113

CUEVAS, MARIANO, *Historia de la Iglesia en México*, 5 vols (Mexico City: Ediciones Cervantes, 1942)

DANDELET, THOMAS JAMES, *Spanish Rome* (New Haven, CT, and London: Yale University Press, 2001)

DÁVALOS Y FIGUEROA, DIEGO, *Miscelánea austral* (Lima: Antonio Ricardo, 1602)

DAVIS, ELIZABETH B., 'The Politics of Effacement: Diego de Hojeda's Humble Poetics', *Bulletin of Hispanic Studies*, 71.3 (1994), 339–57

——— *Myth and Identity in the Epic of Imperial Spain* (Columbia: University of Missouri Press, 2000)

——— 'Travesías peligrosas: escritos marítimos en España durante la época imperial, 1492–1650', in *Edad de Oro Cantabrigense: Actas del VII Congreso de la Asociación Internacional del Siglo de Oro (AISO)*, ed. by Anthony Close (Madrid and Frankfurt: Iberoàmericana/Vervuert, 2006), pp. 31–41

——— 'De mares y ríos: conciencia transatlántica e imaginería acuática en la *Historia de la Nueva México* de Gaspar Pérez de Villagrá (1610)', in *Épica y colonia: ensayos sobre el género épico en Iberoamérica (siglos XVI y XVII)*, ed. by Paul Firbas (Lima: Universidad Nacional Mayor de San Marcos, 2008), pp. 263–86

——— 'From the Mare Nostrum to the Mar Océano and Back: Oceanic Studies, Mediterranean Studies, and the Place of Poetry', *Calíope*, 19.1 (2014), 196–216

DEALY, ROSS, *Vasco de Quiroga's Thought on War: Its Erasmian and Utopian Roots* (Bloomington: Indiana University Press, 1975)

DEANDA CAMACHO, ELENA, 'Maldito "Jarabe Gat|uno": poéticas de la censura inquisitorial en la Nueva España', *Vanderbilt e-journal of Luso-Hispanic Studies*, 10 (2014), 25–36

DI STEFANO, GIUSEPPE (ed.), *Romancero* (Madrid: Castalia, 2013)

DÍAZ DEL CASTILLO, BERNAL, *The Conquest of New Spain*, trans. by Alfred Maudslay, 5 vols (Nendeln: Kraus Reprint, 1967)

——— *Historia de la verdadera conquista de Nueva España*, ed. by Joaquín Ramírez Cabañas (México: Porrúa, 1994)

DÍAZ ROIG, MERCEDES, *Romancero tradicional de América* (Mexico City: El Colegio de México, 1990)

——— *Del romancero hispánico* (Mexico City: El Colegio de México, 2008)

DÍAZ-SÁNCHEZ, MICAELA, and ALEXANDRO D. HERNÁNDEZ, 'The Son Jarocho as Afro-Mexican Resistance Music', *The Journal of Pan African Studies*, 6.1 (2013), 187–209

DICHY-MALHERME, SARAH, 'El primer canto de La Araucana: una cartografía épica de Chile', *Criticón*, 115 (2012), 85–104

DÍEZ DE GAMES, GUTIERRE, *El Victorial*, ed. by Alberto Miranda (Madrid: Cátedra, 1993)

DIMLER, RICHARD, 'Jakob Masen's *Imago figurata*: From Theory to Practice', *Emblematica*, 6.2 (1992), 286–90

DONNINGTON, ROBERT, *The Interpretation of Early Music* (London: Norton, 1992)

DURAND, JOSÉ, 'La Araucana en sus 35 cantos originales', *Anuario de Letras*, 16 (1978), 291–94

DURSTON, ALAN, *Pastoral Quechua. The History of Christian Translation in Colonial Peru, 1550–1650* (Notre Dame, IN: University of Notre Dame, 2007)

EGAN, LINDA, 'Donde Dios es todavía mujer: Sor Juana y la teología feminista', in *Y diversa de mí entre vuestras plumas ando*, ed. by Sara Poot Herrera (Mexico City: El Colegio de México, 1993), pp. 327–40

EGIDO, AURORA, 'Góngora y la batalla de las musas', in *Góngora hoy*, ed. by Joaquín Roses (Córdoba: Diputación de Córdoba, 2002), pp. 95–126

EIRE, CARLOS M. N., *From Madrid to Purgatory: The Art and Craft of Dying in Sixteenth-Century Spain* (Cambridge: Cambridge University Press, 1995)

ERASMUS, DESIDERIUS, *Opus Epistolarum*, ed. by P. S. Allen, 12 vols (Oxford: Clarendon Press, 1906–58)

——*Evripidis Hecvba et Iphigenia Latinae facta Erasmo interprete*, in *Opera Omnia*: I. 1, ed. by J. H. Waszink (Amsterdam: North-Holland, 1969), pp. 193–359

——*Colloquia*, in *Opera Omnia*: I.3, ed. by L.-E. Halkin, F. Bierlaire and R. Hoven (Amsterdam: North-Holland, 1972)

——*Institutio Principis Christiani*, in *Opera Omnia*: IV.1, ed. by O. Herding (Amsterdam: North-Holland, 1974), pp. 95–219

——*Moriae encomium id est Stultitiae Laus*, in *Opera Omnia*: IV.3 ed. by Clarence H. Miller (Amsterdam and Oxford: North-Holland, 1979)

——*Adagiorum chilias secunda*, in *Opera Omnia*: II.3, ed. by M. Szymański (Amsterdam: Elsevier Science, 2005)

ERCILLA, ALONSO DE, *La Araucana*, ed. by Marcos Morínigo and Isaías Lerner, 2 vols (Madrid: Castalia, 1979)

——*La Araucana*, ed. by Isaías Lerner (Madrid: Cátedra, 1993)

ESCOBAR CHICO, ÁNGEL, 'La pervivencia del corpus teológico ciceroniano en España', *Revista Española de Filosofía Medieval*, 4 (1997), 189–202

ESPINOSA, JUAN DE, *Tractado de principios de música práctica [e] teórica sin dejar ninguna cosa atrás* (Toledo: Guillem de Brocar, 1520)

ESPINOZA SORIA, MIGUEL ÁNGEL, *La catequesis en fray Luis Jerónimo de Oré, OFM. Un aporte a la nueva evangelización* (Lima: Provincia Misionera de San Francisco Solano del Perú, 2012)

ESTENSSORO FUCHS, JUAN CARLOS, *Del paganismo a la santidad: la incorporación de los indios del Perú al catolicismo, 1532–1750*, trans. by Gabriela Ramos (Lima: Instituto Francés de Estudios Andinos and Fondo Editorial, PUCP, 2003)

ESTÉVEZ MOLINERO, ÁNGEL, 'Señas de identidad de la poesía hispanoamericana en el siglo XVII', in *Tras el canon: la poesía del Barroco tardío*, ed. by Ignacio García Aguilar (Vigo: Academia del Hispanismo, 2009), pp. 127–42

ESTRADA, OSWALDO, 'Sor Juana y el ejercicio pedagógico en sus villancicos marianos', *Letras Femeninas*, 32.2 (2006), 81–100

FARRELL, ALLAN P., SJ (trans. and ed.), *The Jesuit 'Ratio Studiorum' of 1599* (Washington, DC: Conference of Major Superiors of Jesuits, 1970)

FASQUEL, SAMUEL, *Quevedo et la poétique du burlesque au XVIIe siècle* (Madrid: Casa de Velázquez, 2011)

FERNÁNDEZ DE OVIEDO, GONZALO, *Historia general y natural de las Indias*, 4 vols (Madrid: Real Academia de la Historia, 1851–55)

FERNÁNDEZ DOUGNAC, JOSÉ, 'Naturaleza, topografía y mito en la poesía de Barahona de Soto,' in *De saber poético y verso peregrino. La invención manierista en Luis Barahona de Soto*, ed. by José Lara Garrido (Málaga: Universidad de Málaga, 2002), pp. 229–56

FIRBAS, PAUL, 'Una lectura: los héroes en el mapa colonial', in *Armas antárticas*, ed. by Paul Firbas (Lima: Pontificia Universidad Católica del Perú, 2006), pp. 69–115

——(ed.), *Épica y colonia: ensayos sobre el género épico en Iberoamérica (siglos XVI y XVII)* (Lima: Universidad Nacional Mayor de San Marcos, 2008)

——'El sueño en la trama épica: la visión corográfica de San Quintín en *La Araucana* de Alonso de Ercilla', in *Los sueños en la cultura iberoamericana siglos XVI–XVIII*, ed. by Sonia Rose (Madrid: CSIC, 2011), pp. 385–407

——'Saberes hemisféricos: Sarmiento de Gamboa y sus textos sobre el estrecho de Magallanes', *Anales de Literatura Chilena*, 16 (2016), 41–57

FRANCIS, MICHAEL, 'Población, enfermedad y cambio demográfico, 1537–1636. Demografía histórica de Tunja: una mirada crítica', *Fronteras de la Historia*, 7 (2002), 15–95

FREEDBERG, DAVID, *The Power of Images: Studies in the History and Theory of Response* (Chicago, IL, and London: University of Chicago Press, 1989)

FRENK, MARGIT (ed.), *Cancionero folklórico de México*, 5 vols (Mexico City: El Colegio de México, 1975–85)

——'Un siglo de especulaciones', in *Las jarchas mozárabes y los comienzos de la lírica románica* (Mexico City: El Colegio de México, 1985), pp. 3–43

——*Nuevo corpus de la antigua lírica popular hispánica*, 2 vols (Mexico City: UNAM/El Colegio de México/Fondo de Cultura Económica, 2003)

——*Entre la voz y el silencio: la lectura en tiempos de Cervantes* (Mexico City: FCE, 2005)

——*Poesía popular hispánica: 44 estudios* (Mexico City: FCE, 2006)

GALLARDO, BARTOLOMÉ JOSÉ, *Ensayo de una biblioteca española de libros raros y curiosos*, 4 vols (Madrid: M. Rivadeneyra, M. Tello, 1863–89)

GALLEGO MORELL, ANTONIO, *Garcilaso de la Vega y sus comentaristas* (Madrid: Gredos, 1972)

GARCÍA CANCLINI, NÉSTOR, *Culturas híbridas: estrategias para entrar y salir de la modernidad* (Mexico City: Grijalbo, 1990)

GARCÍA DE ENTERRÍA, MARÍA CRUZ, 'Romancero: ¿cantado, recitado, leído?', *Edad de Oro*, 7 (1988), pp. 89–104

GARCÍA ICAZBALCETA, JOAQUÍN, *Don Fray Juan de Zumárraga, primer obispo y arzobispo de México*, 4 vols (Mexico City: Porrúa, 1947)

——*Bibliografía mexicana del siglo XVI* (Mexico City: FCE, 1981)

GARCILASO DE LA VEGA, *Obra poética y textos en prosa*, ed. by Bienvenido Morros (Barcelona: Crítica, 1995)

GARCILASO DE LA VEGA, EL INCA, *Historia general del Perú*, ed. by Ángel Rosenblat and José de la Riva Agüero, 3 vols (Buenos Aires: Emecé, 1944)

——*Comentarios reales de los incas*, ed. by Ángel Rosenblat (Buenos Aires: Emecé, 1945)

GAYLORD, MARY, 'The Grammar of Femininity in the Traditional Spanish Lyric', *Revista Interamericana*, 12.1 (1982), 115–24

GEMBERO USTÁRROZ, MARÍA, 'Migraciones de músicos entre España y América (siglos XVI–XVIII): estudio preliminar', in *La música y el Atlántico. Relaciones musicales entre España y Latinoamérica*, ed. by María Gembero Ustárroz and Emilio Ros-Fábregas (Granada: Universidad de Granada, 2007), pp. 17–58

GIAMATTI, A. B., *The Earthly Paradise and the Renaissance Epic* (Princeton, NJ: Princeton University Press, 1966)

GLANTZ, MARGO, 'Ciencia y experiencia en las querellas de las mujeres: Sor Juana', in *Nictímene... sacrílega: estudios coloniales en homenaje a Georgina Sabat de Rivers*, ed. by Mabel Moraña and Yolanda Martínez San-Miguel (Mexico City: Universidad del Claustro, 2003), pp. 173–86

GODWIN, JOSCELYN, *Harmonies of Heaven and Earth: The Spiritual Dimensions of Music from Antiquity to the Avant-Garde* (Rochester, VT: Inner Traditions, 1987)

GOERGEN, JUANA, *Literatura fundacional americana: 'El Espejo de paciencia'* (Madrid: Pliegos, 1993)

GOIÇ, CEDOMIL, 'Poetización del espacio, espacios de la poesía', in *La cultura literaria en la América virreinal: concurrencias y diferencias*, ed. by José Pascual Buxó (Mexico City, Universidad Nacional Autónoma de México, 1996), pp. 13–25

GÓNGORA, LUIS DE, *Obras completas*, ed. by Juan Millé y Giménez and Isabel Millé y Giménez (Madrid: Aguilar, 1961)

GÓNGORA, MARIO, *Los grupos de conquistadores en Tierra Firme (1509–1532)* (Santiago de Chile: Editorial Universitaria, 1962)

GONZÁLEZ, LOLA, 'La naturaleza en el *Espejo de paciencia* de Silvestre de Balboa,' *Arrabal*, 1 (1998), 13–22

GONZÁLEZ, MIRTA A., 'Primeras parodias del español hablado por indios y africanos en la Nueva España', in *Actas del XXIX Congreso del Instituto Internacional de Literatura Iberoamericana*, ed. by Joaquín Marco, 3 vols (Barcelona: PPU, 1994), I, 381–87

GONZÁLEZ DE ESLAVA, FERNÁN, *Villancicos, romances, ensaladas y otras canciones devotas*, ed. by Margit Frenk (Mexico City: El Colegio de México, 1989)

GONZÁLEZ ESTÉVEZ, ESCARDIEL, 'De fervor regio a piedad virreinal: culto e iconografía de los siete arcángeles', *Sémata*, 24 (2012), 111–32

GONZÁLEZ PÉREZ, AURELIO, *El romancero en América* (Madrid: Síntesis, 2003)

—— 'El romance: transmisión oral y transmisión escrita', *Acta Poética*, 26 (2005), 221–37

—— (ed.), *La copla en México* (Mexico City: El Colegio de México, 2007)

GONZÁLEZ SÁNCHEZ, CARLOS ALBERTO, *Los mundos del libro. Medios de difusión de la cultura occidental en las Indias de los siglos XVI y XVII* (Seville: Universidad de Sevilla, 1999)

GRABES, HERBERT, *The Mutable Glass: Mirror-Imagery in Titles and Texts of the Middle Ages and English Renaissance*, trans. by G. Collier (Cambridge: Cambridge University Press, 1982)

GRACIÁN, BALTASAR, *Agudeza y arte de ingenio*, ed. by Evaristo Correa Calderón, 2 vols (Madrid: Castalia, 1969)

GRANADA, FRAY LUIS DE, *Introducción del Símbolo de la Fe*, ed. by José María Balcells (Madrid: Cátedra, 1989)

GREENE, ROLAND, *Unrequited Conquests: Love and Empire in the Colonial Americas* (Chicago, IL: University of Chicago Press, 1999)

GREENE, THOMAS M., *The Descent from Heaven: A Study in Epic Continuity* (New Haven, CT: Yale University Press, 1970)

—— *The Light in Troy: Imitation and Discovery in Renaissance Poetry* (New Haven, CT: Yale University Press, 1982)

GREGORY THE GREAT, *Liber responsalis sive antiphonarius S. Gregorii Magni*, in *Patrologiae cursus completus. Series latina*, ed. by Jacques-Paul Migne, vol. LXXVIII (Paris, 1844–55)

GRIFFIN, CLIVE, *The Crombergers of Seville: The History of a Printing Dynasty* (Oxford: Clarendon Press, 1988)

GRIFFIN, NIGEL, 'Enigmas, Riddles, and Emblems in Early Jesuit Colleges', in *Mosaics of Meaning: Studies in Portuguese Emblematics*, ed. by Luís Gomes (Glasgow: Glasgow University Press, 2009), pp. 21–39

GRUZINSKI, SERGE, *La Colonisation de l'imaginaire: sociétés indigènes et occidentalisation dans le Mexique espagnol, XVIe–XVIIe siècle* (Paris: Gallimard, 1988)

—— *La Pensée métisse* (Paris: Fayard, 1999)

HAMPE MARTÍNEZ, TEODORO, 'La biblioteca del arzobispo Hernando Arias de Ugarte', *Thesaurus*, 42.2 (1987), 337–51

HARVEY, TAMARA, *Figuring Modesty in Feminist Discourse across the Americas, 1633–1700* (Abingdon: Ashgate, 2008)

HENDRICKSON, SCOTT, *Jesuit Polymath of Madrid: The Literary Enterprise of Juan Eusebio Nieremberg* (Boston, MA, and Leiden: Brill, 2005)

HENRÍQUEZ UREÑA, PEDRO, 'Barroco de América', in *Ensayos*, ed. by José Luis Abellán and Ana María Barrenechea (Madrid: ALLCA XX/Universidad de Costa Rica, 1998), pp. 353–57

HERRERA Y TORDESILLAS, ANTONIO DE, *Historia general de los hechos de los castellanos en las Islas y Tierra Firme del mar Océano que llaman Indias Occidentales* (Antwerp: Juan Bautista Verdussen, 1728)

HESSUS, HELIUS EOBANUS, *Medicinae Laus* (Paris: apud Simonem Colinaeum, 1533)

HILL, RUTH, *Sceptres and Sciences in the Spains: Four Humanists and the New Philosophy (ca.1680–1740)* (Liverpool: Liverpool University Press, 2000)

HOBERMAN, LOUISA, 'Bureaucracy and Disaster: Mexico City and the Flood of 1629', *Journal of Latin American Studies*, 6.2 (1974), 211–30

HOJEDA, DIEGO DE, *La Christiada* (Seville: Diego Pérez, 1611)

——*La Christiada*, ed. by Mary Helen Patricia Corcoran (Washington, DC: Catholic University of America, 1935)

——*La Cristiada*, ed. by Frank Pierce (Salamanca: Anaya, 1971)

HOLLANDER, JOHN, *The Untuning of the Sky: Ideas of Music in English Poetry, 1500–1700* (New York: Norton, 1970)

ÍÑIGO SILVA, ANDRÉS, 'Los sonetos derivados de las predicaciones que en 1618 acompañaron la fiesta de la Inmaculada Concepción y sus respuestas: propuesta de edición crítica' (Tesis de Licenciatura, Universidad Nacional Autónoma de México, 2012)

JESÚS, TERESA DE, *Camino de perfección*, in *Obras completas*, ed. by Tomás Álvarez (Burgos: Monte Carmelo, 2001), pp. 415–612

JUREK NATTAN, ANNA, 'Música novohispana de los siglos XVI y XVII: manifestación sincrética de lo europeo e indígena', *Antropología. Boletín oficial del Instituto Nacional de Antropología e Historia*, 91 (2011), 11–15

KAGAN, RICHARD, *Students and Society in Early Modern Spain* (Baltimore, MD: Johns Hopkins University Press, 1974)

KAJANTO, IIRO, *Classical and Christian Studies in the Latin Epitaphs of Medieval and Renaissance Rome* (Helsinki: Suomalainen Tiedeakatemia, 1980)

KANTOROWICZ, ERNST HARTWIG, *The King's Two Bodies: A Study in Mediaeval Political Theology* (Princeton, NJ: Princeton University Press, 1957)

KIRK, STEPHANIE, 'Pain, Knowledge, and the Female Body in Sor Juana Inés de la Cruz', *Revista Hispánica Moderna*, 61.1 (2008), 37–53

——*Sor Juana Inés de la Cruz and the Gender Politics of Knowledge in Colonial Mexico* (Abingdon: Routledge, 2016)

KLOR DE ALVA, J. JORGE, 'Colonialism and Postcolonialism as (Latin) American Mirages', *Colonial Latin American Review*, 1.1–2 (1992), 3–23

KLUGE, SOFIE, 'Espejo del mito: algunas consideraciones sobre el epilio barroco', *Criticón*, 115 (2012), 159–74

——'Mirror of Myth: The Baroque Epyllion', in *Diglossia: The Early Modern Reinvention of Mythological Discourse* (Kassel: Edition Reichenberger, 2014), pp. 139–55

KÜGELEN, HELGA VON, 'Carlos de Sigüenza y Góngora, su *Theatro de Virtudes Políticas que constituyen a un príncipe* y la estructuración emblemática de unos tableros en el Arco de Triunfo', in *Juegos de ingenio y agudeza: la pintura emblemática de la Nueva España* (Mexico City: Patronato del Museo Nacional de Arte, AC, 1994), pp. 151–61

LAIRD, ANDREW, 'Migration und Ovids Exildichtung in der lateinischen Kultur Kolonialmexicos', in *2000 Jahre Wiederkehr der Verbannung des Ovid: Exil und Literatur*, ed. by Veronika Coroleu and Gerhard Petersmann (Horn and Salzburg: Berger, 2011), pp. 101–18

——'Franciscan Humanism in Post-Conquest Mexico: Fray Cristóbal Cabrera's Epigrams on Classical and Renaissance Authors (*Vat Lat* 1165)', *Studi Umanistici Piceni*, 33 (2013), 195–216

——'Classical Letters and Millenarian Madness in Post-Conquest Mexico: The *Ecstasis* of Fray Cristóbal Cabrera (1548)', *International Journal of the Classical Tradition*, 24.1 (2017), 78–108

LARA, JAIME, 'Roman Catholics in Hispanic America', in *Oxford History of Christian*

Worship ed. by Geoffrey Wainwright and Karen B. Westerfield Tucker (Oxford: Oxford University Press, 2006), pp. 633–50

LARA GARRIDO, JOSÉ, *La poesía de Luis Barahona de Soto (Lírica y épica del Manierismo)* (Málaga: Servicio de Publicaciones, Diputación Provincial de Málaga, 1994)

LATASA VASSALLO, PILAR, *Administración virreinal en el Perú: Gobierno del Marqués de Montesclaros (1607–1615)* (Madrid: Centro de Estudios Ramón Areces, 1997)

LATTIMORE, RICHMOND, *Themes in Greek and Latin Epitaphs* (Urbana: University of Illinois, 1942)

LAVRIN, ASUNCIÓN, 'Sexuality in Colonial Mexico: A Church Dilemma', in *Sexuality and Marriage in Colonial Latin America*, ed. by Asunción Lavrin (Lincoln: University of Nebraska, 1989), pp. 47–95

LECERCLE, FRANÇOIS, *La Chimère de Zeuxis: portrait poétique et portrait peint en France et en Italie à la Renaissance* (Tübingen: Narr, 1987)

LEONARD, IRVING A., 'On the Mexican Book Trade, 1683', *Hispanic American Historical Review*, 27.3 (1947), 403–35

——*Don Carlos de Sigüenza y Góngora: un sabio mexicano del siglo XVII*, trans. by Juan José Utrilla (Mexico City: Fondo de Cultura Económica, 1984)

——*Books of the Brave: Being an Account of Books and of Men in the Spanish Conquest and Settlement of the Sixteenth-Century New World* (Berkeley and Los Angeles: University of California Press, 1992)

LERNER, ISAÍAS, 'Garcilaso en Ercilla', *Lexis*, 2 (1978), 201–21

LEZAMA LIMA, JOSÉ, *La expresión americana* (La Habana: Instituto Nacional de Cultura, 1957)

LOBO LASSO DE LA VEGA, GABRIEL, *De Cortés valeroso y Mexicana*, ed. by Nidia Pullés-Linares (Madrid and Frankfurt: Iberoamericana/Vervuert, 2005)

LOCKHART, JAMES, *The Men of Cajamarca: A Social and Biographical Study of the First Conquerors of Peru* (Austin: University of Texas Press, 1972)

——*Nahuatl as Written* (Stanford, CA: Stanford University Press, 2001)

——AND STUART B. SCHWARTZ, *Early Latin America: A History of Colonial Spanish America and Brazil* (Cambridge: Cambridge University Press, 1983)

LOHMANN VILLENA, GUILLERMO, 'Romances, coplas y cantares de la conquista del Perú', *Mar del Sur*, 9 (1950), 18–40

LONG, PAMELA, *Sor Juana / Música: How the Décima Musa Composed, Practiced, and Imagined Music* (New York: Peter Lang, 2009)

LONGHI, SILVIA, *Lusus: il capitolo burlesco nel Cinquecento* (Padova: Antenore, 1983)

LÓPEZ DE GÓMARA, FRANCISCO, *Historia general de las Indias*, in *Historiadores primitivos de Indias I*, Biblioteca de Autores Españoles 22 (Madrid: Rivadeneyra, 1852), pp. 155–294

LÓPEZ PINCIANO, ALONSO, *Philosofía antigua poética*, ed. by José Rico Verdú (Madrid: Biblioteca Castro, 1998)

LORENTE, ANDRÉS, *El porqué de la música* (Alcalá de Henares: Nicolás de Xamares, 1672)

MAÑERO LOZANO, DAVID, 'Del concepto de decoro a la "teoría de los estilos"', *Bulletin Hispanique*, 111.2 (2009), 357–85

MANSFIELD, ELIZABETH, *Too Beautiful to Picture: Zeuxis, Myth, and Mimesis* (Minneapolis: University of Minnesota Press, 2007)

MARINO, GIAMBATTISTA, *Dicerie sacre* (Venice: Nicolò Pezzana, 1674)

MARRERO-FENTE, RAÚL, *Epic, Empire and Community in the Atlantic World: Silvestre de Balboa's 'Espejo de paciencia'* (Lewisburg, PA: Bucknell University Press, 2008)

——*Poesía épica colonial del siglo XVI: historia, teoría y práctica* (Madrid and Frankfurt: Iberoamericana/Vervuert, 2017)

MARTÍNEZ, JESÚS P., *Historia de España, I: Edades antigua y media* (Madrid: EPESA, 1963)

MARTÍNEZ, MIGUEL, 'A Poet of Our Own: The Struggle for *Os Lusíadas* in the Afterlife of Camões', *Journal for Early Modern Cultural Studies*, 10.1 (2010), 71–94

——*Front Lines: Soldiers' Writing in the Early Modern Hispanic World* (Philadelphia: University of Pennsylvania Press, 2016)

——'Writing on the Edge: The Poet, the Printer, and the Colonial Frontier in Ercilla's *La Araucana* (1569–1590)', *Colonial Latin American Review*, 26.2 (2017), 132–53

MARTÍNEZ-OSORIO, EMIRO, ' "En éste, nuestro rezental aprisco": Piracy, Epic and Identity in Cantos I–II of *Discurso del Capitán Francisco Draque* by Juan de Castellanos', *Calíope*, 17.2 (2011), 5–34

——*Authority, Piracy, and Captivity in Colonial Spanish American Writing: Juan de Castellanos's 'Elegies of Illustrious Men of the Indies'* (Lewisburg, PA: Bucknell University Press, 2016)

MARTIRIUS ANGLERINUS, PETRUS, *De orbe novo, Decades I–III* (Basel, Ioannem Bebelium: 1533)

MASEN, JACOB, *Speculum imaginum veritatis occultae* (Cologne: Joannis Antonii Kinchii, 1681)

MAURA Y GAMAZO, GABRIEL, DUQUE DE MAURA, *Vida y reinado de Carlos II*, 2 vols (Madrid: Espasa-Calpe, 1954)

MAZA, FRANCISCO DE LA, 'Sor Juana y don Carlos: explicación de dos sonetos hasta ahora confusos', *Cuadernos Americanos*, 145.2 (1966), 190–204

MAZZOCCO, ANGELO, *Linguistic Theories in Dante and the Humanists: Studies of Language and Intellectual History in Late Medieval and Early Renaissance Italy* (Leiden: Brill, 1993)

McCLOSKEY, JASON, 'Crossing the Line in the Sand: Francis Drake Imitating Ferdinand Magellan in Juan de Miramontes's *Armas antárticas*', *Hispanic Review*, 81.4 (2013), 393–415

MEDINA, JOSÉ TORIBIO, *La imprenta en México (1539–1821)*, 8 vols (Santiago de Chile: Impreso en casa del autor, 1907–12)

——'El viaje de Ercilla al Estrecho de Magallanes', *Revista Chilena de Historia y Geografía*, 6.10 (1913), 343–95

——*Vida de Ercilla* (Santiago: Imprenta Elzeviriana, 1917)

——*Los romances basados en La Araucana* (Santiago: Imprenta Elzeviriana, 1918)

MELE, EUGENIO, 'Una oda inédita de Garcilaso de la Vega y tres poesías a él dedicadas por Cosimo Anisio', *Revista Crítica de Historia y Literatura Españolas, Portuguesas e Hispanoamericanas*, 3 (1898), 362–68

MÉNDEZ DE VASCONCELOS, JUAN, *Liga deshecha por la expulsión de los moriscos* (Madrid: Alonso Martín, 1612)

MÉNDEZ PLANCARTE, ALFONSO (ed.), *Poetas novohispanos: primer siglo (1521–1621)* (Mexico City: Universidad Nacional Autónoma de México, 1942)

——(ed.), *Poetas novohispanos: segundo siglo (1621–1721)*, 2 vols (Mexico City: Universidad Nacional Autónoma de México, 1944–45)

——'Notas', in *Obras completas de Sor Juana Inés de la Cruz, I Lírica personal*, ed. by Alfonso Méndez Plancarte (Mexico City: Fondo de Cultura Económica, 1976), pp. 361–617

MENDIETA, FRAY GERÓNIMO DE, *Historia eclesiástica indiana*, ed. by Joaquín García Icazbalceta (Mexico City: Antigua Librería, 1870)

MENDOZA Y LUNA, JUAN DE, *Luz de materias de Indias del Marqués de Montesclaros*, Copenhagen, Der Kongelige Bibliotek, MSS GkS 589 2°

MENÉNDEZ PIDAL, RAMÓN, *Los romances de América y otros estudios* (Buenos Aires: Espasa-Calpe, 1939)

——*Romancero hispánico (hispano-portugués, americano y sefardí): historia y teoría*, 2 vols (Madrid: Espasa-Calpe, 1968)

MENÉNDEZ Y PELAYO, MARCELINO, *Historia de la poesía hispanoamericana*, 2 vols (Madrid: V. Suárez, 1911–13)

MERRIM, STEPHANIE, *The Spectacular City, Mexico, and Colonial Hispanic Literary Culture* (Austin: University of Texas Press, 2010)

MESA, JOSÉ DE, and TERESA GISBERT, *Historia de la pintura cuzqueña*, 2 vols (Lima: Fundación Banco A. N. Wiese, 1982)

MÍNGUEZ, VÍCTOR, 'La fiesta política virreinal: propaganda y aculturación en el México del siglo XVII', in *La formación de la cultura virreinal*, ed. by Karl Kohut and Sonia Rose, 3 vols (Madrid and Frankfurt: Iberoamericana/Vervuert, 2000–06), II, 359–74.

———, INMACULADA RODRÍGUEZ MOYA, PABLO GONZÁLEZ TORNEL and JUAN CHIVA BELTRÁN (eds), *La fiesta barroca. Los virreinatos americanos (1560–1808)* (Castellón de la Plana: Universitat Jaume I and Universidad de las Palmas de Gran Canaria, 2012)

MIRANDA, LUIS DE, *Romance*, ed. by Silvia Tieffemberg (Madrid and Frankfurt: Iberoamericana/Vervuert, 2014)

MIRAMONTES ZUÁZOLA, JUAN DE, *Armas antárticas*, ed. by Paul Firbas (Lima: Pontificia Universidad Católica del Perú, 2006)

MIRÓ QUESADA, AURELIO, *El primer poeta-virrey en América* (Madrid: Gredos, 1962)

MOLINA MARTÍNEZ, MIGUEL, 'La ciudad colonial como escenario de la música en la América hispana', in *La música y el Atlántico: relaciones musicales entre España y Latinoamérica*, ed. by María Gembero Ustárroz and Emilio Ros-Fábregas (Granada: Universidad de Granada, 2007), pp. 183–97

MOLL, JAIME, 'Los surtidos de romances, coplas, historias y otros papeles', in *Actas del Congreso Romancero-Cancionero. UCLA (1984)*, ed. by Enrique Rodríguez Cepeda, 2 vols (Madrid: José Porrúa Turanzas, 1990), I, 205–16

MONTANOS, FRANCISCO DE, *Arte de música, teórica y prática* (Valladolid: Diego Fernández de Córdoba y Oviedo, 1592)

MONTERO, JUAN, 'La égloga en la poesía española del siglo XVI: panorama de un género (desde 1543)', in *La égloga*, ed. by Begoña López Bueno (Seville: Universidad de Sevilla, 2002), pp. 183–206

MOORE, CYRUS, *Love, War, and Classical Tradition in the Early Modern Transatlantic World: Alonso de Ercilla and Edmund Spenser* (Tempe: Arizona Center for Medieval and Renaissance Studies, 2014)

MORAÑA, MABEL, 'Poder, raza, y lengua: la construcción étnica del Otro en los villancicos de Sor Juana', *Revista Iberoamericana*, 63.181 (1997), 631–48

—— *Viaje al silencio: exploraciones del discurso barroco* (Mexico City: Universidad Nacional Autónoma de México, 1998)

MORE, THOMAS, *The Latin Epigrams of Thomas More*, ed. by Leicester Bradner and Charles Arthur Lynch (Chicago, IL: Chicago University Press, 1953)

MORNER, MAGNUS, 'Spanish Migration to the New World Prior to 1800: A Report on the State of Research', in *First Images of America: The Impact of the New World on the Old*, ed. by Fredi Chiappelli, 2 vols (Berkeley and Los Angeles: University of California, 1976), II, 737–82

MURIEL, JOSEFINA, *Cultura femenina novohispana* (Mexico City: Universidad Nacional Autónoma de México, 1994)

—— AND LUIS LLEDÍAS, *La música en las instituciones femeninas novohispanas* (Mexico City: Universidad Nacional Autónoma de México/Claustro de Sor Juana, 2009)

MURPHY, RONALD, 'Introduction to Wisdom Literature', in *The New Jerome Biblical Commentary*, ed. by Raymond Brown, Joseph Fitzmyer and Ronald Murphy (London: Chapman, 1990), pp. 447–52

NICOLOPULOS, JAMES, *The Poetics of Empire in the Indies: Prophecy and Imitation in 'La Araucana' and 'Os Lusíadas'* (University Park, PA: Pennsylvania State University Press, 2000)

NIEDEREHE, HANS-J., 'La *Gramática de la lengua castellana* (1492) de Antonio de Nebrija', *Boletín de la Sociedad Española de Historiografía Lingüística*, 4 (2004), 31–42

NOLAN, EDWARD P., *Now through a Glass Darkly: Specular Images of Being and Knowing from Virgil to Chaucer* (Ann Arbor: University of Michigan Press, 1991)

OCAÑA, DIEGO DE, *Memoria viva de una tierra de olvido: relación del viaje al Nuevo Mundo de 1599 a 1607*, ed., introduction and notes by Beatriz Carolina Peña (Barcelona: CECAL/ Paso de Barca, 2013)

O'CONNOR, THOMAS, 'Antecedentes inmediatos de la "Aprobación" del padre Guerra: el "Discurso de la vida y escritos de don Agustín de Salazar y Torres" de Vera Tassis', in *El escritor y la escena VII: estudios sobre teatro español y novohispano de los Siglos de oro: Dramaturgia e Ideología*, ed. by Ysla Campbell (Ciudad Juárez: Universidad Autónoma de Ciudad Juárez, 1999), pp. 159–67

O'DONNELL, JAMES J., *Cassiodorus* (Berkeley and Los Angeles: University of California Press, 1979)

OLIVARI, MICHELE, *Avisos, pasquines y rumores: los comienzos de la opinión pública en la España del siglo XVII* (Madrid: Cátedra, 2014)

OÑA, PEDRO DE, *Arauco domado*, ed. by J. T. Medina (Santiago de Chile: Imprenta Universitaria, 1917)

——*Arauco domado*, ed. by Victoria Pehl Smith (unpublished PhD dissertation, University of California, Berkeley, 1984)

——*Arauco domado*, ed. by Ornella Gianesin (Pavia: Ibis, 2014)

ORÉ, LUIS JERÓNIMO DE, *Rituale, seu Manuale Peruanum, et Forma Brevis administrandi apud Indos Sacrosancta Baptismi poenitentiae, Eucharistiae, Matrimonij & Extremae unctionis Sacramenta* (Naples: Iacobus Caarlinum & Conftantinum Vitalem, 1607)

——*Symbolo Catholico Indiano*, edited by Antonine Tibesar, with studies by Luis Enrique Tord and Noble David Cook, Facsimile edition (Lima: Australis, 1992)

——*Relación de la vida y milagros de San Francisco Solano*, edited by Noble David Cook (Lima: Fondo Editorial de la PUCP, 1998)

——*Account of the Martyrs in the Provinces of La Florida*. Ed. and translated by Raquel Chang-Rodríguez and Nancy Vogeley (New Mexico: University of New Mexico Press, 2017)

ORJUELA, HÉCTOR, *Historia crítica de la literatura colombiana. Literatura colonial*, 3 vols (Bogotá: Editorial Kelly, 1992)

ORTEGA, SERGIO, 'Teología novohispana sobre el matrimonio y comportamientos sexuales, 1519–1570', in *De la santidad a la perversión, o por qué no se cumplía la Ley de Dios en la sociedad novohispana*, ed. by Sergio Ortega (Mexico City: Grijalbo, 1986), pp. 19–48

OSORIO, ALEJANDRA, 'La entrada del virrey y el ejercicio del poder en la Lima del siglo XVII', *Historia Mexicana*, 55.3 (2006), 767–831

OSORIO ROMERO, IGNACIO, *La enseñanza del latín a los indios* (Mexico City: Universidad Nacional Autónoma de México, 1990)

OSUNA, RAFAEL, 'Un caso de continuidad literaria: la silva *amoena*', *Thesaurus*, 24 (1969), 377–407

OVID, *Metamorphoses*, trans. by A. D. Melville (Oxford: Oxford University Press, 1986)

——*Metamorphoses*, trans. by David Raeburn and Denis Feeney (London: Penguin Classics, 2004)

Oxford Dictionary of the Christian Church, ed. by F. L. Cross and E. A. Livingstone (Oxford: Oxford University Press, 1997)

PADRÓN, RICARDO, *The Spacious Word: Cartography, Literature, and Empire in Early Modern Spain* (Chicago, IL, and London: University of Chicago Press, 2004)

PARDO, ISAAC, *Juan de Castellanos: Estudio de las 'Elegías de varones ilustres de Indias'* (Caracas: Academia Nacional de la Historia, 1991)

PASTOR, BEATRIZ, *Discurso narrativo de la conquista de América* (La Habana: Ediciones Casa de las Américas, 1983)

——— *The Armature of the Conquest: Spanish Accounts of the Discovery of America, 1492–1589*, trans. by Lydia Longstreth Hunt (Stanford, CA: Stanford University Press, 1992)

———AND SERGIO CALLAU (ed.), *Lope de Aguirre y la rebelión de los marañones* (Madrid: Castalia, 2011)

PAZ, OCTAVIO, *Sor Juana o las trampas de la fe* (Mexico City: Fondo de Cultura Económica, 1997)

PEDROSA, JOSÉ MANUEL, 'La encrucijada española: cantos y músicas de Europa, África y América en los Siglos de Oro', *Edad de Oro*, 22 (2003), 221–45

PELIKAN, JAROSLAV, *Mary through the Centuries* (New Haven, CT: Yale University Press, 1997)

PEÑA, MARGARITA (ed.), *Flores de baria poesía: cancionero novohispano del siglo XVI* (Mexico City: Fondo de Cultura Económica, 2003)

PHELAN, JOHN LEDDY, *The Millenial Kingdom of the Franciscans in the New World* (Berkeley: University of California, 1970)

PICÓN-SALAS, MARIANO, *A Cultural History of Spanish America: From Conquest to Independence*, trans. by Irving A. Leonard (Berkeley and Los Angeles: University of California Press, 1962)

———*De la conquista a la independencia: tres siglos de historia cultural hispanoamericana* (Mexico City: Fondo de Cultura Económica, 1985)

PIERCE, FRANK, '*La Christiada* of Diego de Hojeda: A Poem of the Literary Baroque', *Bulletin of Spanish Studies*, 17 (1940), 203–18

——— 'Some Aspects of the Spanish "Religious Epic" of the Golden Age', *Hispanic Review*, 12.1 (1944), 1–10

PIGMAN, GEORGE W., 'Versions of Imitation in the Renaissance', *Renaissance Quarterly*, 33.1 (1980), 1–32

PITA ANDRADE, JOSÉ MANUEL, 'Pinturas y pintores de Isabel la Católica', in *Isabel la Católica y el arte*, ed. by Gonzalo Anés and Alvarez de Castrillón (Madrid: Real Academia de la Historia, 2006), pp. 13–72

Poema de Fernán González, ed. by Juan Victorio (Madrid: Cátedra, 1990)

Poema de Mio Cid, ed. by Colin Smith (Madrid: Cátedra, 1993)

PONCE CÁRDENAS, JESÚS, 'El oro del otoño: glosas a la poesía de Agustín de Salazar y Torres', *Criticón*, 103–04 (2008), 131–52

———*La imitación áurea (Cervantes, Quevedo, Góngora)* (Paris: Éditions Hispaniques, 2016)

POLITZER, ROBERT L., 'Synonymic Repetition in Late Latin and Romance', *Language*, 37.4 (1961), 484–87

PORRAS BARRENECHEA, RAÚL, 'Prólogo', in Diego González de Holguín, *Vocabulario de la lengua general de todo el Perú llamada lengua qquichua o del Inca* (Lima: Instituto de Historia, Universidad Nacional Mayor de San Marcos, 1952), pp. v–xliv

PRIETO, ANTONIO, *La poesía española del siglo XVI, II. Aquel valor que respetó el olvido* (Madrid: Cátedra, 1998)

QUEVEDO, FRANCISCO DE, *Parte segunda póstuma de la política de Dios y gobierno de Cristo*, ed. by Rodrigo Cacho Casal, in *Obras completas en prosa*, 11 vols (Madrid: Castalia, 2012), V, 327–639

QUINT, DAVID, *Epic and Empire* (Princeton, NJ: Princeton University Press, 1993)

QUIÑONES MELGOZA, JOAQUÍN, *Poesía neolatina en México en el siglo XVI* (Mexico City: Universidad Nacional Autónoma de Méixco, 1991)

———(ed.), *Hispana seges nova* (Mexico City: Universidad Nacional Autónoma de México, 2012)

QUIROGA, GASPAR DE, *Index et catalogus librorum prohibitorum mandato Illustriss. Inquisitoris D. D. Gasparis a Quiroga Cardinalis Archiepiscopi Toletani, ac in regnis Hispaniarum Generalis Inquisitoris, denuo editus* (Madrid: Alphonsus Gomezius, 1583)

RAMA, ÁNGEL, *La ciudad letrada* (Hanover: Ediciones del Norte, 1984)

RAPPAPORT, JOANNE, and TOM CUMMINS, *Beyond the Lettered City: Indigenous Literacies in the Andes* (Durham, NC, and London: Duke University Press, 2012)

Recopilación de leyes de los reinos de las Indias, 4 vols (Madrid: Julián de Paredes, 1681)

REMENSNYDER, AMY, *La Conquistadora: The Virgin Mary at War and Peace in the Old and New Worlds* (Oxford: Oxford University Press, 2014)

RENFREW, CHARLES, *The Litany of Loreto* (London: Catholic Truth Society, 2012)

RESTALL, MATTHEW, and FELIPE FERNÁNDEZ-ARMESTO, *The Conquistadors: A Very Short Introduction* (Oxford: Oxford University Press, 2012)

RESTREPO, LUIS FERNANDO, *Un nuevo reino imaginado: las 'Elegías de varones ilustres de Indias' de Juan de Castellanos* (Bogotá: Instituto Colombiano de Cultural Hispánica, 1999)

——'Somatografía épica colonial: las *Elegías de varones ilustres de Indias* de Juan de Castellanos', *MLN*, 115.2 (2000), pp. 248–67

REY, JOSÉ, *Danzas cantadas en el Renacimiento español* (Madrid: Sociedad Española de Musicología, 1978)

REYES, ALFONSO, 'Rosas de Oquendo en América', in *Capítulos de literatura española (Primera serie)* (Mexico City: La Casa de España en México, 1939), pp. 21–71

REYNOLDS, WINSTON A., *Romancero de Hernán Cortés: estudio y textos de los siglos XVI y XVII* (Madrid: Ediciones Alcalá, 1967)

——*Hernán Cortés en la literatura del Siglo de Oro* (Madrid: Editora Nacional, 1979)

RIBADENEYRA, PEDRO DE, *Tratado de la religión y virtudes que debe tener el príncipe cristiano para gobernar y conservar sus estados: contra lo que Nicolás Machiavelo y los políticos deste tiempo enseñan* (Madrid: P. Madrigal, a costa de Juan de Montoya, 1595)

RIBERA, DIEGO DE, *Poética descripción* (Mexico City: Francisco Rodríguez Lupercio, 1668)

RICOEUR, PAUL, *The Symbolism of Evil*, trans. by Emerson Buchanan (New York: Harper and Rowe, 1967)

RICHTER, FEDERICO, 'Primera parte: Fray Luis Jerónimo de Oré (biografía) 1554–1630. Segunda parte: Información de oficio en la Real Audiencia de La Plata del Perú, de los méritos del biografiado (tres piezas)', in *Anales de la Provincia Franciscana de los Doce Apóstoles de Lima* (Huamanga: Imprenta de la Universidad de San Cristóbal de Huamanga, 1986), pp. 1–41

RODRÍGUEZ, PEDRO, *El Catecismo Romano ante Felipe II y la Inquisición española* (Madrid: Rialp, 1998)

RODRÍGUEZ MOÑINO, ANTONIO (ed.), *Silva de varios romances (Valencia: 1561)* (Valencia: Castalia, 1953)

——*Pliegos poéticos de la Biblioteca Colombina* (Berkeley: University of California Press, 1974)

RODRÍGUEZ MOSQUERA, MARÍA JOSÉ, *'Flores de baria poesía* (México, 1577): estudio y análisis del manuscrito' (unpublished PhD dissertation, Universitat de Barcelona, 2013)

ROJAS, ULISES, *El beneficiado Juan de Castellanos: cronista de Colombia y Venezuela* (Bogotá: Gerardo Rivas, 1997)

ROMERO, EMILIA, *El romance tradicional en el Perú* (Mexico City: El Colegio de México, 1952)

Rosarium Beatae Benedictæq[ue]; & Almæ Virginis Dei genitricis Mariæ... Meditatione Trilingui meditatum (Rome: Vincentius Accoltus, 1584)

ROSES, JOAQUÍN, 'Retórica y naturaleza en la Égloga cuarta de Barahona de Soto,' in *De saber poético y verso peregrino. la invención manierista en Luis Barahona de Soto*, ed. by José Lara Garrido (Málaga: Universidad de Málaga, 2002), pp. 279–95

——'Góngora en la poesía hispanoamericana del siglo XVII', in *Parnaso de dos mundos: de literatura española e hispanoamericana en el Siglo de Oro*, ed. by José María Ferri and

Juan Carlos Rovira (Madrid and Frankfurt am Main: Universidad de Navarra/ Iberoamericana/Vervuert, 2012), pp. 161–88

RUBIO MAÑÉ, JOSÉ IGNACIO, *Introducción al estudio de los virreyes en Nueva España 1535–1746*, 4 vols (Mexico City: Universidad Nacional Autónoma de México, 1955–63)

RUEDA RAMÍREZ, PEDRO, *Negocio e intercambio cultural. El comercio de libros con América en la carrera de Indias (siglo XVII)* (Seville: Universidad de Sevilla/CSIC, 2005)

RUIZ, ELISA, 'Cristóbal Cabrera, apóstol grafómano', *Cuadernos de Filología Clásica*, 12 (1977), 59–147

RUIZ DE ELVIRA, ANTONIO, *Mitología clásica* (Madrid: Gredos, 1995)

SABAT DE RIVERS, GEORGINA, 'Blanco, negro, rojo: semiosis racial en los villancicos de Sor Juana Inés de la Cruz', in *Crítica semiológica de textos literarios hispánicos*, ed. by Miguel Ángel Garrido Gallardo (Madrid: Consejo Superior de Investigaciones Científicas, 1986), pp. 247–55

——*Estudios de literatura hispanoamericana: sor Juana Inés de la Cruz y otros poetas barrocos de la colonia* (Barcelona: PPU, 1992)

SAHAGÚN, BERNARDINO DE, *Florentine Codex: Introductions and Indices*, trans. by Arthur J. O. Anderson and Charles Dibble (Salt Lake City: University of Utah, 1982)

SAÍNZ, ENRIQUE, *Silvestre de Balboa y la literatura cubana* (La Habana: Letras Cubanas, 1982)

SALAZAR Y TORRES, AGUSTÍN DE, *Cítara de Apolo, varias poesías divinas y humanas, que escribió Don Agustín de Salazar y Torres; y saca a luz D. Juan de Vera Tasis y Villarroel, su mayor amigo [...]. Primera parte* (Madrid: Antonio González de Reyes, 1694)

SALOMON, H. P., and I. S. D. SASSOON, 'Introduction to the English Edition', in António Jose Saraiva, *The Marrano Factory: The Portuguese Inquisition and its New Christians 1536–1765*, trans. by H. P. Salomon and I. S. D. Sassoon (Leiden: Brill, 2001), pp. ix–xiv

SÁNCHEZ-ALBORNOZ, NICOLÁS, 'The Population of Colonial Spanish America', in *The Cambridge History of Latin America. Volume II: Colonial Latin America* ed. by Leslie Bethell (Cambridge: Cambridge University Press, 1984), pp. 3–35

SANTILLANA, MARQUÉS DE, *Obras completas*, ed. by Ángel Gómez Moreno and Maxim P. A. M. Kerkhof (Barcelona: Planeta, 1988)

SAXONY, LUDOLPHUS OF, *Vita Christi cartujano romanzado por fray Ambrosio* (Alcalá de Henares: Estanislao Polono, 1502–03)

SCREECH, M. A., 'Good Madness in Christendom', in *The Anatomy of Madness: Essays in the History of Psychiatry, I: People and Ideas*, ed. by W. F. Bynum, Roy Porter and Michael Shepherd (London: Routledge, 2004), pp. 25–39

SCHONS, DOROTHY, 'The Influence of Góngora on Mexican literature during the Seventeenth Century', *Hispanic Review*, 7 (1939), 22–34

SCHROEDER, H. J., OP (trans. and introduction), *Canons and Decrees of the Council of Trent* (Rockford, Ill: Tan Books, 1941)

SCHWALLER, JOHN F., and HELEN NADER, *The First Letter from New Spain: The Lost Petition of Cortés and His Company, June 20, 1519* (Austin: University of Texas Press, 2014)

SEGAS, LISE, 'Cartagena de Indias en la obra de Juan de Castellanos: de la fundación a la destrucción de la ciudad', *Aguaita*, 24 (2012), 28–47

SEED, PATRICIA, *To Love, Honor, and Obey in Colonial Mexico, 1574–1821* (Stanford, CA: Stanford University Press, 1988)

SIGÜENZA Y GÓNGORA, CARLOS DE, *Teatro de virtudes políticas, que constituyen a un príncipe advertidas en los monarcas antiguos del mexicano imperio, con cuyas efigies se hermoseó el arco triunfal que la muy noble, muy Leal, imperial Ciudad de México erigió para el digno recibimiento en ella del excelentísimo señor virrey Conde de Paredes, Marqués de La Laguna* (México: viuda de Bernardo Calderón, 1680)

——*Obras* (Mexico City: Sociedad de Bibliófilos Mexicanos, 1928)

——*Teatro de virtudes políticas*, in Carlos Sigüenza y Góngora, *Obras históricas*, ed. by José Rojas Garcidueñas (Mexico City: Editorial Porrúa, 1983), pp. 225–361

——*Teatro de virtudes políticas que constituyen a un príncipe* (Mexico City: Coordinación de Humanidades UNAM/Miguel Ángel Porrúa, 1986)

——*'Dulce canoro cisne mexicano': la poesía completa de Carlos de Sigüenza y Góngora*, ed. by Daniel Torres (Barcelona: CECAL, 2012)

SILVA PRADA, NATALIA, *La política de una rebelión: los indígenas frente al tumulto de 1692 en la Ciudad de México* (Mexico City: El Colegio de México, 2007)

——'Cultura política tradicional y opinión crítica: los rumores y pasquines iberoamericanos de los siglos XVI al XVIII', in *Tradición y modernidad en la historia de la cultura política. España e Hispanoamérica, siglos XVI y XVII*, ed. by Riccardo Forte and Natalia Silva Prada (Mexico City: Universidad Autónoma Metropolitana, 2009), pp. 89–141

——'Pasquines contra visitadores reales: opinión pública en las ciudades hispanoamericanas de los siglos XVI, XVII y XVIII', in *Cultura escrita y espacio público en la ciudad hispánica del Siglo de Oro* (Gijón: Trea, 2010), pp. 373–98

SKINNER, QUENTIN, *The Foundation of Modern Political Thought*, 2 vols (Cambridge: Cambridge University Press, 1978)

——*Visions of Politics, I: Regarding Method* (Cambridge: Cambridge University Press, 2002)

SOLÓRZANO PEREIRA, JUAN DE, *Política Indiana*, ed. by Miguel Angel Ochoa Brun, 5 vols (Madrid: Biblioteca de Autores Españoles, 1972)

STEVENS, WALLACE, *Collected Poetry and Prose* (New York: Library of America, 1997)

STEVENSON, ROBERT, 'Sor Juana's Mexico City Musical Coadjutors', *Inter-American Musical Review*, 15.1 (1996), 23–27

STRONG, ROY, *Art and Power in Renaissance Festivals, 1450–1650* (Woodbridge: Boydell and Brewer, 1986)

STRUNK, OLIVER (ed.), *Source Readings in Music History*, revised and ed. by Leo Treitler (New York and London: Norton, 1998)

TAPIA, MARTÍN DE, *Vergel de música spiritual speculativa y activa, del cual muchas diversas y suaves flores se pueden coger* (Villa del Burgo de Osma: Diego Fernández de Córdoba, 1570)

TARLING, JUDY, *The Weapons of Rhetoric: A Guide for Musicians and Audiences* (St Albans: Corda Music, 2004)

TASSO, TORQUATO, *Discourses on the Heroic Poem*, trans. by Mariella Cavalchini, and Irene Samuel (Oxford: Clarendon Press, 1973)

——'Il messaggiero', in *Prose*, ed. by Ettore Mazzali (Milan and Naples: R. Ricciardi, 1959), pp. 3–73

TAYLOR, GERALD, *El sol, la luna y las estrellas no son Dios...: la evangelización en quechua (siglo XVI)* (Lima: Instituto Francés de Estudios Andinos/Fondo Editorial, PUCP, 2003)

TENORIO, MARTHA LILIA, *Los villancicos de Sor Juana* (Mexico City: El Colegio de México, 1999)

——'Agustín de Salazar y Torres: discípulo de Góngora, maestro de sor Juana', *Nueva Revista de Filología Hispánica*, 57 (2010), 157–89

——(ed.) *Poesía novohispana. Antología*, 2 vols (Mexico City: El Colegio de México/ Fundación para las Letras Mexicanas, 2010)

——*El gongorismo en Nueva España: ensayo de restitución* (Mexico City: El Colegio de México, 2013)

TERUEL, JOSÉ, 'Contextos e implicaciones literarias en *De musica libri septem* de Francisco Salinas', *Edad de Oro*, 22 (2003), 79–93

THAYER OJEDA, TOMÁS, and CARLOS LARRAÍN, *Valdivia y sus compañeros* (Santiago: Imprenta Universitaria, 1951)

TOMLINSON, GARY, *The Singing of the New World: Indigenous Voice in the Era of European Contact* (Cambridge: Cambridge University Press, 2007)

TORD, LUIS ENRIQUE, 'Luis Jerónimo de Oré y el *Symbolo catholico indiano*', in *Symbolo Catholico Indiano*, ed. by Antonine Tibesar (Lima: Australis, 1992), pp. 22–24

TORRE VILAR, ERNESTO DE LA, *Fray Pedro de Gante, maestro y civilizador de América* (Mexico City: Seminario de Cultura Mexicana, 1973)

TORRES, DANIEL, *El palimpsesto del calco aparente: una poética del Barroco de Indias* (New York: Peter Lang, 1993)

TORRES, ISABEL, *Love Poetry in the Spanish Golden Age: Eros, Eris and Empire* (Woodbridge: Tamesis, 2013)

TWOMEY, LESLEY, *The Serpent and the Rose: The Immaculate Conception in Hispanic Poetry in the Late Medieval Period* (Leiden: Brill, 2008)

UNDERBERG, NATALIE, 'Sor Juana's Villancicos: Context, Gender, and Genre', *Western Folklore*, 60.4 (2001), 297–316

URCHUEGUÍA, CRISTINA, 'La colonización musical de Hispanoamérica', in *Historia de la música en España e Hispanoamérica, II: De los Reyes Católicos a Felipe II*, ed. by Maricarmen Gómez (Madrid: Fondo de Cultura Económica, 2012), pp. 466–502

URTEAGA, HORACIO, 'Los copleros de la conquista', *Mercurio Peruano*, año IV, 6.32 (1921), 120–41

VALDÉS, JUAN DE, *Diálogo de la lengua*, ed. by José Enrique Laplana (Barcelona: Crítica, 2010)

VALDIVIELSO, JOSÉ DE, *Vida, excelencias y muerte del glorioso patriarca san Joseph... Coméntala el doctor don Diego Suárez de Figueroa*, 5 vols (Madrid: Francisco del Hierro, 1727–28)

VALENCIA, FELIPE, 'Las "muchas (aunque bárbaras)" voces líricas de *La Araucana* y la índole poética de una "historia verdadera"', *Revista de Estudios Hispánicos*, 49.1 (2015), 141–71

VARGAS MACHUCA, BERNARDO DE, *Milicia y descripción de las Indias* (Madrid: Pedro Madrigal, 1599)

——— *The Indian Militia and Description of the Indies*, ed. by Kris Lane, trans. by Timothy Johnson (Durham, NC: Duke University Press, 2008)

VARGAS UGARTE, RUBÉN, *Concilios Limenses (1551–1772)*, 3 vols (Lima: Talleres Gráficos de la Tipografía Peruana, 1951)

VEGA, LOPE DE, *Rimas humanas y divinas del licenciado Tomé de Burguillos*, ed. by Macarena Cuiñas Gómez (Madrid: Cátedra, 2008)

VÉLEZ MARQUINA, ELIO, 'Posicionamiento discursivo del narrador épico colonial de *La Christiada*, de Diego de Hojeda', in *Eros divino. Estudios sobre la poesía religiosa iberoamericana del siglo XVII*, ed. by Julián Olivares (Zaragoza: Universidad de Zaragoza, 2010), pp. 421–33

VILLA WALLS, GABRIELA, '*El melopeo y maestro*, "bisagra engarzadora" de la literatura y la música en Nueva España' (unpublished PhD dissertation, Universidad Nacional Autónoma de México, 2011)

WALTER, HANS, *Initia carminum ac versuum Medii Aevi posterioris Latinorum* (Göttingen: Vandenhoeck and Ruprecht, 1959)

WARDLE, D., *Suetonius' Life of Caligula. A Commentary* (Brussels: Collection Latomus, 1994)

WEY GÓMEZ, NICOLÁS, *Tropics of Empire: Why Columbus Sailed South to the Indies* (Cambridge, MA: MIT Press, 2008)

WHINNOM, KEITH, 'The Problem of the Best-Seller in Spanish Golden Age Literature', *Bulletin of Hispanic Studies*, 57 (1980), 189–98

WILSON-LEE, EDWARD, *The Catalogue of Shipwrecked Books: Young Columbus and the Quest for a Universal Library* (London: William Collins, 2018)

WINN, JAMES ANDERSON, *Unsuspected Eloquence: A History of the Relations between Poetry and Music* (New Haven, CT: Yale University Press, 1981)

WOFFORD, SUSANNE, 'Epic and the Politics of the Origin Tale: Virgil, Ovid, Spenser, and Native American Aetiology', in Margaret Beissinger, Jane Tylus and Susanne Wofford (eds), *Epic Traditions in the Contemporary World: The Poetics of Community* (Berkeley: University of California Press, 1999), pp. 239–69

WOODS, MICHAEL J., *The Poet and the Natural World in the Age of Góngora* (Oxford: Oxford University Press, 1978)

WRAY, GRADY, *The Devotional Exercises / Los ejercicios devotos of Sor Juana Inés de la Cruz, Mexico's Prodigious Nun (1648/51–1695)* (Lewiston/Queenston/Lampeter: The Edwin Mellen Press, 2005)

ZAPATER, HORACIO, *La búsqueda de la paz en la guerra de Arauco: Padre Luis de Valdivia* (Santiago de Chile: Editorial Andrés Bello, 1992)

ZULAÍCA GÁRATE, ROMÁN, *Los franciscanos y la imprenta en México en el siglo XVI* (Mexico City: Pedro Robredo, 1939)

INDEX